Knowledge Management Systems: Value Shop Creation

Petter Gottschalk
Norwegian School of Management BI, Norway

IDEA GROUP PUBLISHING
Hershey • London • Melbourne • Singapore

Acquisition Editor: Michelle Potter
Senior Managing Editor: Jennifer Neidig
Managing Editor: Sara Reed
Development Editor: Kristin Roth
Copy Editor: Michael Goldberg
Typesetter: Jessie Weik
Cover Design: Lisa Tosheff
Printed at: Integrated Book Technology

Published in the United States of America by
Idea Group Publishing (an imprint of Idea Group Inc.)
701 E. Chocolate Avenue
Hershey PA 17033
Tel: 717-533-8845
Fax: 717-533-8661
E-mail: cust@idea-group.com
Web site: http://www.idea-group.com

and in the United Kingdom by
Idea Group Publishing (an imprint of Idea Group Inc.)
3 Henrietta Street
Covent Garden
London WC2E 8LU
Tel: 44 20 7240 0856
Fax: 44 20 7379 3313
Web site: http://www.eurospan.co.uk

Library of Congress Cataloging-in-Publication Data

Gottschalk, Petter, 1950-
Knowledge management systems : value shop creation / Petter Gottschalk.
p. cm.
Summary: "This book combines knowledge management with other subject areas within the management information systems field. Its scholarly value can be found in insights generated from the contingent approach to linking knowledge management to other IT management topics and their uses"--Provided by publisher.
ISBN 1-59904-060-3 (hardcover) -- ISBN 1-59904-061-1 (softcover) -- ISBN 1-59904-062-X (ebook)
1. Knowledge management. 2. Management information systems. I. Title.
HD30.2.G675 2007
658.4'038011--dc22
2006019126

British Cataloguing in Publication Data

A Cataloguing in Publication record for this book is available from the British Library.

All work contributed to this book is new, previously-unpublished material. The views expressed in this book are those of the authors, but not necessarily of the publisher.

Knowledge Management Systems: Value Shop Creation

Table of Contents

Foreword

This is a blockbuster of a book that Professor Petter Gottschalk has produced. A blockbuster in the sense of breaking new ground. Textbooks abound in the area of knowledge management as they do in e-business and, to a lesser extent, on outsourcing. But what is missing in the literature is a book that connects the dots.

What this current book by Gottschalk does is not only conceptually link up these three, till now, relativley separate areas of study — KM, e-business, and outsourcing — into a holistic picture, but also theoretically point the way through a series of research propositions to how these disparate areas can actually be aligned in a meaningful way to achieve the creation, transfer and application of knowledge.

This, of course, is what knowledge management is all about — how to support the creation, transfer and application of knowledge. And this book delivers "big" on that "know-how" in the twin domains of electronic business and IT outsourcing relationships. The book not only informs the reader wanting to see the links and get the know-how, but also entertains with practical case studies and intriguing insights.

The journey that Gottschalk takes the reader on begins with a macro-lens view of e-business in Chapter I. The same lens is then applied to outsourcing in Chapter II. The focus of Chapter III switches the interest to IT Insourcing to provide a contrasting perspective on outsourcing, which helps to illuminate the differences. The focus really begins to zoom in with Chapter IV, devoted to a run-through of a forest of theories about IT outsourcing that provides a wealth of information on the critical factors necessarily involved in successful IT outsourcing relationships. The next two Chapters, V and VI, complete the outsourcing picture with a clear exposition of the role of leadership in managing outsourcing projects (Chapter V) while Chapter VI wraps it all up with a strong emphasis on the need for a goverance model for IT.

The last three chapters of the book present a thought provoking look at the application of knowledge management, firstly in relation to two relatively new areas of endeavour, at least in relation to being written about with schorarly authority. These emerging areas are the fields of policing (Chapter VII) and law (Chapter VIII). The last Chapter, IX, provides a view of the current knowledge management systems with an eye also to the future and how KM systems are likely to evolve over the ensuing decade.

I will take the opportunity to offer a view from my own area of expertise in the fields of policing and law. I have for many years taught police investigators and lawyers and often wondered how the knowledge they use and acquire in and on the job could be better managed. The "law firm," as you will discover in Chapter VIII, has readily embraced the knowledge management wave. Lawyers, unlike police, are quick to see and seize any competitive advantage that can make them an extra dollar!

Police organisations, on the other hand, have by and large come to knowledge management late in the day. This situation is not improving, for even in 2004 one finds comments in the scholarly literature like "the concept of knowledge management is an emerging field of study in both the business and educational realms. In the rank of policing, knowledge management is still relatively unexplored."[1] However, at last someone with well-honed experience in the field of knowledge management is doing some exploring. Petter Gottschalk writes lucidly about KM and Policing and, in particular, that of police investigations. Chapter VII provides a good start in remedying this oversight in the scholarly literature for those readers interested in this specific area of knowledge management application.

I wholeheartedly recommend this book to student and practitioner alike, for each will find a wealth of knowledge within its pages to suit their needs and interests.

Dr. Geoff Dean

Senior Lecturer, School of Justice Studies, Queensland University of Technology

Reference

Colaprete, F. (2004). Knowledge management. *Law and Order*, *52*(10), 82.

Geoff Dean is a senior lecturer on the Justice Studies staff in the Faculty of Law at Queensland University of Technology. His doctoral research was on the experience of investigation for detectives. Major publications include refereed journal articles on family therapy, child abuse, police education and training; domestic violence; policing by consent and reforming operational policing practices, investigative thinking, criminal profiling and terrorism, in particular suicide bombers. Dean is registered as an international expert with EUROPOL in the Knowledge Management Centre, The Hague.

Preface

For a long time, we thought the only possible value configuration for organizations was the value chain developed by Porter (1985). Insights emerged, however, that many organizations have no inbound or outbound logistics of importance, they don't produce goods in a sequential way and they don't make money only at the end of their value creation. Therefore, two alternative value configurations have been identified: labeled value shop and value network, respectively (Afuah & Tucci, 2003; Gottschalk, 2005; Stabell & Fjeldstad; 1998).

As we move into the knowledge society, more and more organizations make their living from knowledge creation and knowledge application. The typical value configuration where we find such knowledge work is the value shop. The value shop is a value configuration creating value by applying knowledge to customer problems. A hospital applies medical knowledge to patients' problems, a law firm applies legal knowledge to clients' problems and police detectives apply law enforcement knowledge to criminal investigations.

Even where the main value configuration of an organization is the value chain, we find more and more examples of value shop activities within the organization. For example, successful electronic business is dependent on knowledge management organized as problem solving in the value shop. In IT outsourcing relationships, the vendor is a value shop when solving client problems. In IT insourcing, similar knowledge management challenges emerge. In IT governance, knowledge management has to support decision-making through knowledge-based value shop activities to be successful.

This book is titled *Knowledge Management Systems: Value Shop Creation* to present knowledge management systems in the context of organizations as value shops based on knowledge work. A number of topics are introduced and discussed in the book. These topics are of two kinds. The first category of examples is from the information technology management field itself, where we look at knowledge management systems in the important IT management areas of e-business, outsourcing, insourcing and governance. The second category of examples is from organizations that have the dominating value configuration of the value shop, such as police investigation units and law firms.

The main objective of knowledge management is to support the creation, transfer and application of knowledge. Researchers and practitioners have emphasized the important role of knowledge management in electronic business and IT outsourcing relationships. By linking IT topics such as knowledge management and e-business, knowledge management becomes a tool and critical success factor for e-business. Similarly, by linking knowledge management to IT outsourcing, knowledge management becomes a tool and critical success factor in outsourcing relationships.

In areas such as knowledge management, e-business and outsourcing, many textbooks can be found. However, it remains for me to discover a book covering links between these areas. The market challenge for this new book will be the extent of awareness of and interest in knowledge management as a tool and critical success factor in other fields, rather than only its own.

Knowledge management success is dependent on appropriate applications. For example, it has been argued that knowledge management is the most important critical success factor in the second e-business wave (El Sawy, 2001; Fahey et al., 2001; Holsapple & Singh, 2000; Malhotra, 2000, 2002; Plessis & Boon, 2004; Singh et al., 2004; Tsai et al., 2005). However, there is a lack of conceptual work to guide knowledge management applications in e-business. In this book, we fill this conceptual gap by discussing knowledge management in e-business models, e-business process redesign, value configurations and stages of knowledge management technology.

Similarly, it has been argued that knowledge management is the most important critical success factor in IT outsourcing relationships. Again, there is a lack of conceptual work to guide knowledge management applications in such client-vendor relationships. In this book, we fill this conceptual gap by discussing strategic intent for IT outsourcing, resource-based theory and knowledge strategy. When two organizations enter a long-term relationship as vendor and customer for IT services, the outsourcing relationship develops over time and can either improve or deteriorate. By exchanging knowledge and establishing mutual systems for knowledge management, the likelihood of a prosperous relationship increases and the likelihood of a deteriorating relationship decreases.

In addition, this book presents research studies of knowledge management in police investigation units and in law firms. Both represent knowledge businesses, one from the public sector and the other from the private sector. Furthermore, they both deal with legal issues. While detectives in police investigation units work on collecting information and knowledge work to identify a pattern of actions so that a criminal can be brought to justice, lawyers work on collecting information for knowledge work to make it unlikely that their client is a criminal.This book is designed as compulsory literature for courses in management information systems at colleges and universities. It can be considered supplementary literature in marketing courses and organizational behavior courses. In addition, practitioners in business and public organizations as well as the IT industry itself will benefit from insights in this book. This book is based on the premise that it is difficult, if not impossible, to manage an organization without at least some understanding of knowledge management and knowledge management systems.

This book combines knowledge management with other subject areas within the management information systems field. The subject of knowledge management is no longer a separate topic, as research and practice have moved into linking knowledge management to its uses. The scholarly value of this proposed book can be found in insights generated from the contingent approach to linking knowledge management to other IT management topics and its uses. Each chapter in this book is organized in terms of research propositions. The idea is that topics covered are presented and structured in terms of research propositions, enabling readers to think about and discuss whether they believe in the suggested relationship and what it might be dependent upon. Each chapter in this book has a conclusion which presents a causal loop diagram of some of the important concepts discussed in the chapter. The diagram is based on Vensim (www.vensim.com), which is a visual modeling tool to conceptualize, document, simulate, analyze and optimize models of dynamic systems. Causal loop diagrams are called that because each link has a causal interpretation. An arrow going from A to B indicates that A causes B. Causal loop diagrams can be very helpful in conceptualizing and communicating structures and causal relationships for knowledge management in e-business, outsourcing and other application areas.

Introduction to Chapters

Knowledge Management Systems: Value Shop Creation tries to have a balance between the theoretical and the practical. A literature review concerning the topic of the chapter is followed by cases illustrating or validating the models presented in the theoretical part. By providing a thorough literature review and applying theories and models to the topics discussed in each chapter, this book should clearly illustrate the issues, problems and trends described. By providing a number of research studies and case studies, this book can be used in case study discussions for instructional purposes.

The book discusses theoretical propositions and then uses case studies and research results to substantiate important points. The extension of the value configuration model of value shop across the chapters helps the reader understand the role of knowledge management systems in knowledge-intensive activities, such as e-business and outsourcing, and in knowledge-intensive organizations, such as police departments and law firms.

Research propositions are presented in each chapter for instructional purposes. The research propositions are not conclusions. Rather, they are for discussion and empirical testing.

The book consists of three sections. The first section (Chapters I-IV) covers introductory material and background topics that are used in the rest of the book. The second section (Chapters V-VIII) is concerned with *knowledge-intensive value shop activities*, while the third and final section (Chapters IX-X) covers two examples of *knowledge-intensive value shop organizations*.

Chapter I introduces the important notion of the value shop that is a knowledge-intensive and problem-solving value configuration. Value shops have primary and secondary activities that can be supported by knowledge management systems. Chapter II covers general topics on knowledge management, such as characteristics of knowledge, knowledge value levels, identification of knowledge needs and classification of knowledge categories. For those readers unfamiliar with the topic of knowledge management, this chapter provides important background material.

Similarly, Chapter III provides important background material on the role of information technology in knowledge management. IT in knowledge management is presented in terms of knowledge management processes and knowledge management systems. Knowledge management systems are exemplified by advanced technologies included in expert systems.

Knowledge management technology is simply defined as technology that supports knowledge work in organizations. According to the distinction between information and knowledge, computers handle information while people handle knowledge. Knowledge management technology is technology that supports knowledge workers both at the individual and organizational levels. An important implication of this understanding of knowledge management technology is that word-processing tools, for example, are as much knowledge management technology as case-based reasoning systems. This book focuses on technology that can improve efficiency and effectiveness of knowledge work's knowledge-intensive activities and knowledge-intensive organizations.

There are several benefits from applying the four-stage model for knowledge management technology. First, it can explain the evolution of knowledge management technology in knowledge intensive organizations. Next, it can predict the direction for future knowledge management projects. Third, it can guide the accumulation of technologies and techniques as well as infrastructures and architectures to support more sophisticated applications of information technology over time.

The stages of growth model consisting of four stages is introduced in Chapter IV. The stages are applied in this book mainly as an organizing framework for systems classification, as it is too early to tell whether stages two, three and four are truly observed in activities and organizations. Furthermore, what will happen after stage four is not clear — maybe a more cyclical behavior will occur involving some or all of the stages.

The first stage in the growth model, person-to-technology, is concerned with information technology tools available to knowledge workers. The second stage, person-to-person, is concerned with communication between knowledge workers enabled and supported by information and communication technology. The third stage, person-to-information, is concerned with the electronic storage and retrieval of information that is useful to knowledge workers. The fourth, and final, stage in the growth model, person-to-application, is concerned with the applications of artificial intelligence to knowledge work to support knowledge workers in their problem solving.

The extended discussion on knowledge management systems and stages of growth model are included in this book to provide sufficient background for identifying applications. Specifically, the stages of growth model provides a framework for understanding how different and accumulated information technologies can support knowledge work.

Chapter IV is about the stages of growth model for knowledge management technology, and concludes the first part of the book concerned with introductory and background material about value shops and knowledge management systems.

The second part of the book is concerned with knowledge management systems in information technology management. Chapter V is about knowledge management in electronic business, while chapter VI is about knowledge management in IT outsourcing relationships.

Chapter V develops a contingent approach to knowledge management in e-business. Depending on the e-business model, value configuration and other contingent factors, effective approaches to knowledge management will vary. In this chapter, the stages of growth model for knowledge management is applied in this and the following chapters. Similarly, the value configuration of "value shop" is applied in this chapter and reapplied in following chapters.

Chapter VI presents and discusses knowledge transfer in outsourcing relationships, strategic intent in IT outsourcing and intangible assets. The vendor value proposition is discussed in terms of knowledge exchange.

Chapter VII presents the reversal of Chapter VI that some organizations are undertaking: They move from outsourcing to insourcing. It is interesting to see how outsourcing theories and frameworks can be mirrored to discuss the termination strategy of insourcing.

So far, this book focuses on the link between the information technology management topics of knowledge management systems and the topics of e-business and outsourcing. Another interesting link is to the topic of IT governance, which is presented in Chapter VIII. As examples of knowledge-intensive value-shop organizations from the research of the author, police departments and law firms are presented in Chapters IX and X, respectively.

Knowledge work in police investigations is based on a variety of information sources, such as incident reports, crime scene investigator reports, witness statements, suspect statements, tip lines, crime scene photographs and drawings, fingerprints, DNA, physical evidence (ballistics, tool marks and blood spatters), informants and property tracking.

In larger departments, a division or bureau is responsible for follow-up investigations; the chief of police assigns special investigations. Additionally, this function also covers the recovery of stolen property, the gathering of criminal intelligence and the preparation of cases for trial. Organizationally, this division may be titled Detective, Central Investigation or Criminal Investigation.

The role of the investigator is probably the most glamorous one in the police department. This modern Sherlock Holmes is portrayed in movies, television and novels as a meticulous and tireless gatherer of evidence that miraculously leads to the arrest and conviction of criminals. As shown on several television series, this super police officer is a bit unorthodox, normally at odds with his superiors, and willing to bend the rules, especially if this involves a deliberate violation of departmental directives. Embedded in a web of unsavory informers, the heroic investigator maintains integrity in his unrelenting pursuit of crime and the master criminal.

Law enforcement is of concern to both police departments and law firms. A law firm can be understood as a social community specializing in the expeditious and efficientcreation and transfer of legal knowledge. The client is a customer of the firm, rather than a particular lawyer.

Petter Gottschalk

Norwegian School of Management BI, Oslo, Norway

February 2006

List of References

Afuah, A., & Tucci, C. L. (2003). *Internet business models and strategies* (2nd ed.). Boston: McGraw-Hill.

El Sawy, O. A. (2001). *Redesigning enterprise processes for e-business*. Boston: McGraw-Hill.

Fahey, L., Srrivastava, R., Sharon, J. S., & Smith, D. E. (2001). Linking e-business and operating processes: The role of knowledge management. *IBM Systems Journal, 40*(4), 889-907.

Gottschalk, P. (2005). *Strategic knowledge management technology*. Hershey, PA: Idea Group Publishing.

Holsapple, C. W., & Singh, M. (2000). Electronic commerce: From a definitional taxonomy toward a knowledge-management view. *Journal of Organizational Computing and Electronic Commerce, 10*(3), 149-170.

Malhotra, Y. (2000, Summer). Knowledge management for e-business performance: Advancing information strategy to 'Internet time'. *Information Strategy: The Executive's Journal*, 5-16.

Malhotra, Y. (2002, Spring). Enabling knowledge exchanges for e-business communities. *Information Strategy: The Executive's Journal*, 26-31.

Plessis, M., & Boon, J. A. (2004). Knowledge management in eBusiness and customer relationship management: South African case study findings. *International Journal of Information Management*, 24, 73-86.

Porter, M. L. (1985). *Competitive strategy*. New York: The Free Press.

Singh, R., Iyer, L., & Salam, A. F. (2004). Web service for knowledge management in e-marketplaces. *e-Service Journal*, 32-52.

Stabell, C. B., & Fjeldstand, Ø. D. (1998). Configuring value for competitive advantage: On chains, shops, and networks. *Strategic Management Journal, 19,* 413-437.

Tsai, M. T., Yu, M. C., & Lee, K. W. (2005, March). Developing e-business systems based on KM process perspective: A case study of Seven-Eleven Japan. *The Journal of American Academy of Business*, 285-289.

Section I: Introduction and Background

The first section of this book covers introductory material and background topics that are used throughout the remainder of the text.

Chapter I introduces the important notion of the "value shop" that is a knowledge-intensive and problem-solving value configuration. A value configuration is a model of an organization in terms of its primary and secondary activities. The most famous value configuration is still the traditional value chain, which belonged to the manufacturing age. More recently, the dominating value configuration is the value shop, which solves problems for its clients.

Chapter II covers general topics on knowledge management. Chapters I and II are strongly interlinked, as knowledge often is the most important resource in the value shop. In Chapter II, characteristics of knowledge, knowledge value levels, identification of knowledge needs and classification of knowledge categories are presented.

Of special interest to knowledge firms are strategic knowledge resources. Such resources enable a firm to be innovative and leading in its industry. To be classified as such, a strategic resource has to be rare, valuable, nontransferable, non-substitutable, nonreplaceable and combinable. Organizations having such knowledge will typically experience satisfied clients that remain loyal to the firm.

Chapter III provides important background material on the role of information technology (IT) in knowledge management (KM). Based on the assumption that computers handle information while human brains handle knowledge, the challenge of IT in KM is the interaction between computers and brains. One challenge is making information in computers available to knowledge workers. Another challenge is making knowledge in human brains available to computers in terms of information. The second challenge seems mostly overlooked, as most people still spend a lot of time using three to five fingers typing information which represents their knowledge. The typical example is e-mail.

How information technology can support knowledge work is structured in Chapter IV in terms of the stages of growth model. At the first stage, knowledge workers, like everyone else in the organization, get access to end-user tools. At the following stages, knowledge workers find support in more sophisticated information systems.

This first section of the book should give the reader important insights into knowledge work in value shops supported by information technology.

Chapter I

Value Shop Configuration

Introduction

To comprehend the value that information technology provides to organizations, we must first understand the way a particular organization conducts business and how information systems affect the performance of various component activities within the organization. Understanding how firms differ is a central challenge for both theory and practice of management. For a long time, Porter's (1985) value chain was the only value configuration known to managers. Stabell and Fjeldstad (1998) have identified two alternative value configurations. A value shop schedules activities and applies resources in a fashion that is dimensioned and appropriate to the needs of the client's problem, while a value chain performs a fixed set of activities that enables it to produce a standard product in large numbers. Examples of value shops are professional service firms, as found in medicine, law, architecture and engineering. A value network links clients or customers who are, or wish to be, interdependent. Examples of value networks are telephone companies, retail banks and insurance companies.

A value configuration describes how value is created in a company for its customers. A value configuration shows how the most important business processes function to create value for customers and represents the way a particular organization conducts business.

Figure 1.1. Examples of IS/IT in the value chain

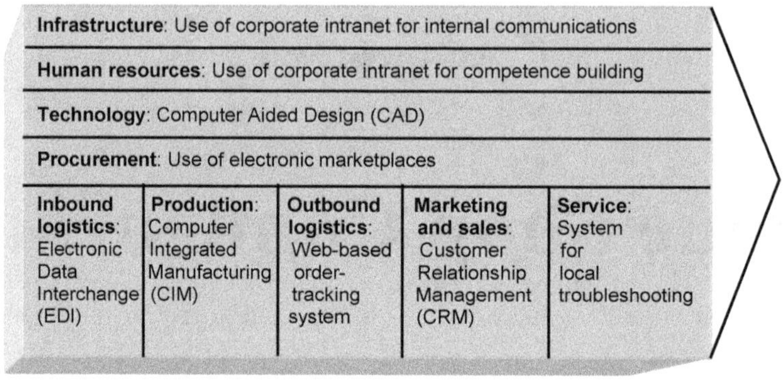

The Organization as Value Chain

The best-known value configuration is the value chain. In the value chain, value is created through efficient production of goods and services based on a variety of resources. The company is perceived as a series or chain of activities. Primary activities in the value chain include inbound logistics, production, outbound logistics, marketing and sales and service. Support activities include infrastructure, human resources, technology development and procurement. Attention is focused on performing these activities in the chain in efficient and effective ways. In Figure 1.1, examples of IS/IT are assigned to primary and support activities. This figure can be used to describe the current IS/IT situation in the organization as it illustrates the extent of coverage of IS/IT for each activity.

The knowledge intensity of systems in the different activities can be illustrated by different shading, where dark shading indicates higher knowledge intensity. In this example, it is assumed that the most knowledge intensive activities are located in computer aided design and customer relationship management.

The Organization as Value Shop

Value cannot only be created in value chains. Value can also be created in two alternative value configurations: value shop and value network (Stabell & Fjeldstad,

1998). In the value shop, activities are scheduled and resources are applied in a fashion that is dimensioned and appropriate to the needs of the client's problem, while a value chain performs a fixed set of activities that enables it to produce a standard product in large numbers. The value shop is a company that creates value by solving unique problems for customers and clients. Knowledge is the most important resource, and reputation is critical to firm success.

While typical examples of value chains are manufacturing industries such as paper and car production, typical examples of value shops are law firms and medical hospitals. Often, such companies are called professional service firms or knowledge-intensive service firms. Like the medical hospital as a way to practice medicine, the law firm provides a standard format for delivering complex legal services. Many features of its style — specialization, teamwork, continuous monitoring on behalf of clients (patients) and representation in many forums — have been emulated in other vehicles for delivering professional services (Galanter & Palay, 1991).

Knowledge-intensive service firms are typical value shops. Sheehan (2002) defines knowledge-intensive service firms as entities that sell problem-solving services, where the solution chosen by the expert is based on real-time feedback from the client. Clients retain knowledge-intensive service firms to reduce their uncertainty Clients hire knowledge-intensive service firms precisely because the client believes the firm knows something that the client does not and believes is necessary to solve their problems.

While expertise plays a role in all firms, its role is distinctive in knowledge-intensive service firms. Expert, often professional, knowledge is at the core of the service provided by the type of firm. Knowledge-intensive service firms not only sell a problem-solving service, but equally a problem-finding, problem-defining, solution-execution and monitoring service. Problem finding is often a key for acquiring new clients. Once the client is acquired and their problem is defined, not all problems will be solved by the firm. Rather, the firm may only clarify that there is no problem (i.e., the patient does not have a heart condition) or that the problem should be referred to another specialist (i.e., the patient needs a heart specialist). If a problem is treated within the firm, then the firm needs to follow up the implementation to assure that the problem in fact has been solved (i.e., is the patient's heart now working properly?). This follows from the fact that there is often uncertainty in both problem diagnosis and problem resolution.

Sheehan (2002) has created a typology of knowledge-intensive service firms consisting of the following three types: First, knowledge-intensive search firms search for opportunities. The amount of value they create depends on the size of the finding or discovery, where size is measured by quality rather than quantity. Examples of search firms include petroleum and mineral exploration, drug discovery in the pharmaceutical industry and research in the biotechnology industry. Second, knowledge-intensive diagnosis firms create value by clarifying problems. Once the problem has been identified, the suggested remedy usually follows directly. Examples of diagnosis firms include doctors, surgeons, psychotherapists, veterinarians, lawyers, auditors and tax accountants and software support. Finally, knowledge-intensive design firms create value by conceiving new ways of constructing material or immaterial artifacts. Examples of design firms include architecture, advertising, research and development, engineering design and strategy consulting.

Knowledge-intensive service firms create value through problem acquisition and definition, alternative generation and selection, implementation of an alternative and follow-up to see if the solution selected resolves the problem. To reflect this process, Stabell and Fjeldstad (1998) have outlined the value configuration of a value shop.

A value shop is characterized by five primary activities: problem finding and acquisition, problem solving, choice, execution and control and evaluation, as illustrated in Figure 1.2. Problem finding and acquisition involves working with the customer to determine the exact nature of the problem or need. It involves deciding on the overall plan of approaching the problem. Problem-solving is the actual generation of ideas and action (or treatment) plans.

Choice represents the decision of choosing between alternatives. While the least important primary activity of the value shop in terms of time and effort, choice is also the most important in terms of customer value. Execution represents communicating, organizing and implementing the decision, or performing the treatment.

Figure 1.2. Examples of IS/IT in the value shop

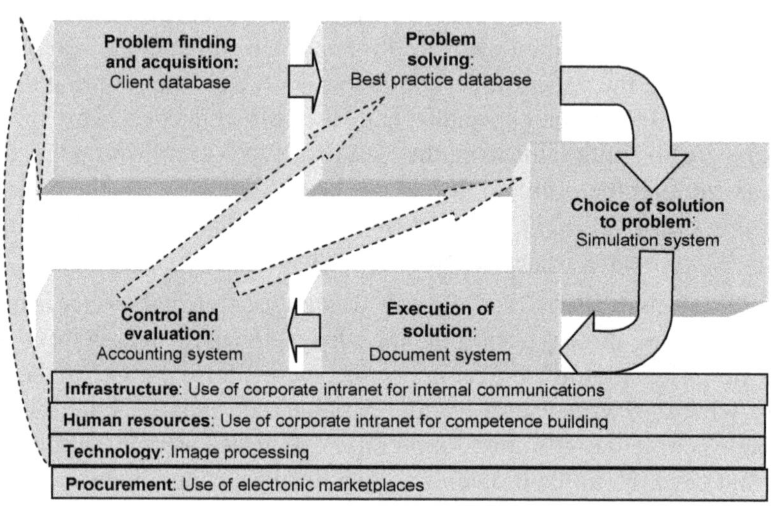

Control and evaluation activities involve monitoring and measuring how well the solution solved the original problem or met the original need.

This may feed back into the first activity, problem finding and acquisition, for two reasons. First, if the proposed solution is inadequate or did not work, it feeds back into learning why it was inadequate and begins the problem-solving phase anew. Second, if the problem solution was successful, the firm might enlarge the scope of the problem-solving process to solve a bigger problem related to, or dependent upon, the first problem being solved.

Figure 1.2 can be used to identify current IS/IT in the organization. We let a law firm serve as an example in Figure 1.3. Within each of the five activities, there are many tasks in a law firm. For each task, there may be IS/IT support. For example, problem solving may consist of the two tasks of case analysis and reference search. Lawyers will be eager to discuss the case and to search for more information on similar cases. A system for case-based reasoning may be installed, where the current case can be compared to similar cases handled by the law firm. Also, intelligent search engines with thesaurus capability may be available in the law firm to find relevant information on the Internet and in legal databases.

Knowledge-intensive service firms are typical value shops, and such firms depend on reputation for success, as reputation is a key driver of firm value creation. Reputation is a relational concept, in the sense that firms are judged by their stakeholders relative to their competitors. Reputation is what is generally said or believed about an entity by someone; it is the net perception of a firm held by stakeholders judged relative to other firms. According to Sheehan (2002), there are four conditions which must be present for reputation to work. First, rents earned from maintaining a good reputation must be greater than not. Second, there must be a minimum of contact

Figure 1.3. Examples of IS/IT in the value shop

Activities	Tasks	IS/IT
Problem finding and acquisition	Register client information Register case information	Financial system Case database
Problem solving	Do case analysis Do reference search	Case-based reasoning Library search engine
Choice	Evaluate alternatives Make recommendation to client	Case-based reasoning Office systems
Execution	Participate at meetings Revise recommendation	Office systems Office systems
Control and evaluation	Register recommendation Check client satisfaction	Case database Financial system

among stakeholders to allow for the changes in reputation to be communicated. Third, there needs to be a possibility of repeat business. And last, there must be some uncertainty regarding the firm's type and/or behavior.

Reputation is related to the asymmetry of information, which is a typical feature of knowledge-intensive service firms. Asymmetry is present when clients believe the firm knows something that the clients do not and believe is necessary to know to solve their problems.Reputation can be classified as a strategic resource in knowledge-intensive firms. To be a strategic resource, it has to be valuable, rare and costly to imitate, and possible to organize. Reputation is valuable as it increases the value received by the client. Reputation is rare, as by definition only a few firms can be considered best in the industry. Reputation is costly to imitate as it is difficult to build a reputation in the short run. Reputation is possible to organize in the general sense of controllability, which implies that a firm can be organized to take advantage of reputation as a resource.

The Organization as Value Network

The third and final value configuration is the value network. A value network is a company that creates value by connecting clients and customers that are, or want to be, dependent on each other. These companies distribute information, money, products and services. While activities in both value chains and value shops are done sequentially, activities in value networks occur in parallel. The number and combination of customers and access points in the network are important value drivers in the value network. More customers and more connections create higher value to customers.

Stabell and Fjeldstad (1998) suggest that managing a value network can be compared to managing a club. The mediating firm admits members that complement each other, and in some cases exclude those that don't. The firm establishes, monitors and terminates direct or indirect relationships among members. Supplier-customer relationships may exist between the members of the club, but to the mediating firm they are all customers. Examples of value networks include telecommunication companies, financial institutions such as banks and insurance companies and stockbrokers. Value networks perform three activities (see Figure 1.4):

- Development of a customer network through marketing and recruiting of new customers, to enable increased value for both existing and new customers;
- Development of new services and improvement in existing services; and

Figure 1.4. Examples of IS/IT in the value network

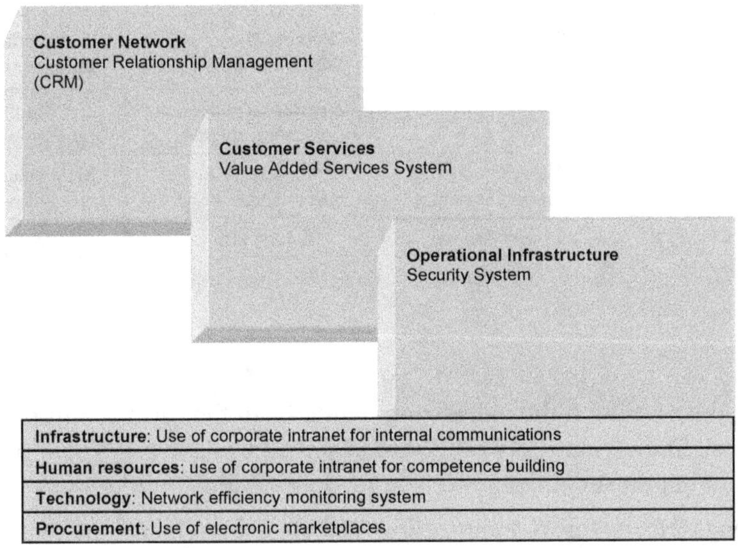

- Development of infrastructure so that customer services can be provided more efficiently and effectively.

The current IS/IT situation in a value network will mainly be described through the infrastructure that typically consists of information technology. In addition, many of the new services may be information systems that will be used by customers in their communication and business transactions with other customers. The knowledge component will mainly be found in the services of a value network, as information systems are made available to customers to exchange relevant information.

Comparison of Value Configurations

Value chain, value shop and value network are alternative value configurations that impact the use of information technology in the company as illustrated in Figure 1.5. While the role of IT is to make production more efficient in a value chain, IT

Figure 1.5. Characteristics of value configurations

Characteristics	Value Chain	Value Shop	Value Network
Value creation	Transformation of input to output	Solving clients and customers' problems	Connecting clients and customers to each other
Work form	Sequential production	Integrated and cyclical problem solving	Monitored and simultaneous connections
Information systems	Making production more efficient	Adding value to the knowledge work	Main value by use of IT infrastructure
Example	Paper factory	Law firm	Telecom company

creates added value in the value shop, while IT in the form of infrastructure is the main value in the value network. Some companies have more than one value configuration, but most companies have one dominating configuration.

In the long term, business organizations can choose to change their value configurations. A bank, for example, can be a value shop when it focuses on converting inputs to outputs. The value resides in the output, and once you have the output, you can remove the production organization. This removal does not impact the value of the output. The value shop is a solution provider. It's somebody that solves problems. The input is a problem. The output is a solution to the problem. A bank that does this would view itself as a financial service operator, a financial advisor that also has the ability to provide the money as part of the solution. But what it would do is identify client problems, address those problems, select a solution together with the client and help to implement it. It would have stringent quality controls (Chatzkel, 2002). Or, the bank can be a value network, which is basically the logic of the marketplace. The bank would define its role as a conduit between people that do not have money and those people that do. What the bank does is to arrange the flow of cash between them. The bank will attract people with money to make deposits and investments. The bank will also attract people without money to make loans. As a value network, the bank will connect people with opposite financial needs. The network consists of people with different financial needs (Chatzkel, 2002)

One of the interesting studies of information technology in the value shop was carried out by Huang et al. (2002). Their research analyzed relationships between the attitudes of CEOs toward IT and benefits from IT investments via the value shop configuration. Among the firms with IT adoption and investment, the benefits for business activities in the value shop model — problem finding and acquisition, problem solving, choice, execution and control and evaluation — were obvious.

The typical value shop is a knowledge firm, since it creates value by solving unique problems for customers. Mobilizing resources—essentially, relevant knowledge—in order to solve particular problems, creates value (Fjeldstad & Haanæs, 2001). Since the typical value shop is a knowledge firm, and since knowledge is the important resource, this book uses value configuration and resource-based theory as the framework for discussing knowledge management systems in value shop creation.

Questions for Discussion

1. Identify some business and public organizations and discuss the main value configuration for each of them.
2. What is the role of knowledge sharing in each value configuration?
3. How does iterative knowledge-work take place in the value shop?

List of References

Chatzkel, J. (2002). A conversation with Göran Roos. *Journal of Intellectual Capital,* 3(2), 96-117.

Fjeldstad, Ø. D., & Haanæs, K. (2001). Strategy tradeoffs in the knowledge and network economy. *Business Strategy Review*, 12(1), 1-10.

Galanter, M., & Palay, T. (1991). *Tournament of lawyers, the transformation of the big law firms*. Chicago: The University of Chicago Press.

Huang, S. M., Ku, C. Y., Chu, Y. T, & Hsueh, H. Y. (2002). A study of value factors for adopting information technology in professional service industry: A demonstrative case of accounting firms in Taiwan. *Review of Pacific Basin Financial Markets and Policies*, *5*(4), 509-519.

Porter, M. E. (1985). *Competitive strategy*. New York: The Free Press.

Sheehan, N. T. (2002). *Reputation as a driver in knowledge-intensive service firms*. Series of Dissertations 4/2002, Norwegian School of Management, Sandvika, Norway.

Stabell, C. B., & Fjeldstad, Ø. D. (1998). Configuring value for competitive advantage: On chains, shops, and networks. *Strategic Management Journal*, *19*, 413-437.

Chapter II

Knowledge Management

Introduction

Knowledge is an important organizational resource. Unlike other inert organizational resources, the application of existing knowledge has the potential to generate new knowledge. Not only can knowledge be replenished in use, it can also be combined and recombined to generate new knowledge. Once created, knowledge can be articulated, shared, stored and recontextualized to yield options for the future. For all of these reasons, knowledge has the potential to be applied across time and space to yield increasing returns (Garud & Kumaraswamy, 2005).

The strategic management of organizational knowledge is a key factor that can help organizations to sustain competitive advantage in volatile environments. Organizations are turning to knowledge management initiatives and technologies to leverage their knowledge resources. Knowledge management can be defined as a systemic and organizationally specified process for acquiring, organizing and communicating knowledge of employees so that other employees may make use of it to be more effective and productive in their work (Kankanhalli et al., 2005).

Knowledge management is also important in inter-organizational relationships. Inter-organizational relationships have been recognized to provide two distinct potential benefits: short-term operational efficiency and longer-term new knowledge creation. For example, the need for continual value innovation is driving supply chains to evolve from a pure transactional focus to leveraging inter-organizational partnerships for sharing information and, ultimately, market knowledge creation. Supply chain partners are engaging in interlinked processes that enable rich (broad-ranging, high quality and privileged) information sharing, and building information technology infrastructures that allow them to process information obtained from their partners to create new knowledge (Malhotra et al., 2005).

Characteristics of Knowledge

Knowledge is a renewable, reusable and accumulating resource of value to the organization when applied in the production of products and services. Knowledge cannot, as such, be stored in computers; it can only be stored in the human brain. Knowledge is what a knower knows; there is no knowledge without someone knowing it.

The need for a knower in knowledge existence raises the question as to how knowledge can exist outside the heads of individuals. Although knowledge cannot originate outside the heads of individuals, it can be argued that knowledge can be represented in, and often embedded in, organizational processes, routines and networks, and sometimes in document repositories. However, knowledge is seldom complete outside of an individual.

In this book, knowledge is defined as information combined with experience, context, interpretation, reflection, intuition and creativity. Information becomes knowledge once it is processed in the mind of an individual. This knowledge then becomes information again once it is articulated or communicated to others in the form of text, computer output, spoken or written words or other means. Six characteristics of knowledge can distinguish it from information: Knowledge is a human act; knowledge is the residue of thinking; knowledge is created in the present moment; knowledge belongs to communities; knowledge circulates through communities in many ways; and new knowledge is created at the boundaries of old. This definition and these characteristics of knowledge are based on current research (e.g., Poston & Speier, 2005; Ryu et al., 2005, Sambamurthy & Subramani, 2005; Tanriverdi, 2005; Wasko & Faraj, 2005).

Today, any discussion of knowledge quickly leads to the issue of how knowledge is defined. A pragmatic definition defines the topic as the most valuable form of content in a continuum starting at data, encompassing information and ending at knowledge. Typically, data is classified, summarized, transferred or corrected in order to add value, and become information within a certain context. This conversion is relatively mechanical and has long been facilitated by storage, processing and communication technologies. These technologies add place, time and form utilities to the data. In doing so, the information serves to inform or reduce uncertainty within the problem domain. Therefore, information is united with the context; that is, it only has utility within the context (Grover & Davenport, 2001).

Knowledge has the highest value, the most human contribution, the greatest relevance to decisions and actions and the greatest dependence on a specific situation or context. It is also the most difficult of content types to manage because it originates and is applied in the minds of human beings. People who are knowledgeable not only have information, but also have the ability to integrate and frame the information within the context of their experience, expertise and judgment. In doing so, they can create new information that expands the state of possibilities, and in turn allows for further interaction with experience, expertise and judgment. Therefore, in an organizational context, all new knowledge stems from people. Some knowledge is incorporated in organizational artifacts like processes, structures and technology. However, institutionalized knowledge often inhibits competition in a dynamic context, unless adaptability of people and processes (higher order learning) is built into the institutional mechanisms themselves.

Our concern with distinctions between information and knowledge is based on real differences as well as technology implications. Real differences between information and knowledge do exist, although for most practical purposes these differences are of no interest at all. Information technology implications are concerned with the argument that computers can only manipulate electronic information, not electronic knowledge. Business systems are loaded with information, but without knowledge.

Davenport and Prusak (1998) define knowledge as a fluid mix of framed experience, values, contextual information and expert insights that provides a framework for evaluating and incorporating new experiences and information. It originates and is applied in the minds of knowers. In organizations, it often becomes embedded not only in documents or repositories but also in organizational routines, processes, practices and norms. Distinctions are often made between data, information, knowledge and wisdom:

- **Data:** Letters and numbers without meaning. Data are independent, isolated measurements, characters, numerical characters and symbols.
- **Information:** Data that are included in a context that makes sense. For example, 40 degrees can have different meaning depending on the context. There can be a medical, geographical or technical context. If a person has 40 degrees Celsius in fever, that is quite serious. If a city is located 40 degrees north, we know that it is far south of Norway. If an angle is 40 degrees, we know what it looks like. Information is data that make sense, because it can be understood correctly. People turn data into information by organizing it into some unit of analysis, for example, dollars, dates or customers. Information is data endowed with relevance and purpose.
- **Knowledge:** Information combined with experience, context, interpretation and reflection. Knowledge is a renewable resource that can be used over and

over, and that accumulates in an organization through use and combination with employees' experience. Humans have knowledge; knowledge cannot exist outside the heads of individuals in the company. Information becomes knowledge when it enters the human brain. This knowledge transforms into information again when it is articulated and communicated to others. Information is an explicit representation of knowledge; it is in itself not knowledge. Knowledge can both be truths and lies, perspectives and concepts, judgments and expectations. Knowledge is used to receive information by analyzing, understanding and evaluating; by combining, prioritizing and decision-making; and by planning, implementing and controlling.

- **Wisdom:** Knowledge combined with learning, insights and judgmental abilities. Wisdom is more difficult to explain than knowledge, since the levels of context become even more personal, and thus the higher-level nature of wisdom renders it more obscure than knowledge. While knowledge is mainly sufficiently generalized solutions, wisdom is best thought of as sufficiently generalized approaches and values that can be applied in numerous and varied situations. Wisdom cannot be created like data and information, and it cannot be shared with others like knowledge. Because the context is so personal, it becomes almost exclusive to our own minds and incompatible with the minds of others without extensive transaction. This transaction requires not only a base of knowledge and opportunities for experiences that help create wisdom, but also the processes of introspection, retrospection, interpretation and contemplation. We can value wisdom in others, but we can only create it ourselves.

It has been argued that expert systems using artificial intelligence are able to do knowledge work. The chess-playing computer called Deep Blue by IBM is frequently cited as an example. Deep Blue can compete with the best human players because chess, though complex, is a closed system of unchanging and codifiable rules. The size of the board never varies, the rules are unambiguous, the moves of the pieces are clearly defined, and there is absolute agreement about what it means to win or lose (Davenport & Prusak, 1998). Deep Blue is no knowledge worker; the computer only performs a series of computations at extremely high speed.

While knowledge workers develop knowledge, organizations learn. Therefore, the learning organization has become a term frequently used. The learning organization is similar to knowledge development. While knowledge development is taking place at the individual level, organizational learning is taking place at the firm level. Organizational learning occurs when the firm is able to exploit individual competence in new and innovative ways. Organizational learning also occurs when the collective memory — including local language, common history and routines — expands. Organizational learning causes growth in the intellectual capital. Learning is a continuous, never-ending process of knowledge creation. A learning organization is a place where people are constantly driven to discover what has caused the current situation, and how they can change the present. To maintain competitive advantage, an organization's investment decisions related to knowledge creation are likely to be strategic in nature (Chen & Edgington, 2005).

Alavi and Leidner (2001) make the case that the hierarchy of data-information-knowledge can be of a different nature. Specifically, they claim that knowledge can be the basis for information, rather than information the basis for knowledge. Knowledge must exist before information can be formulated and before data can be measured to form information. As such, raw data do not exist — the thought or knowledge processes that led to its identification and collection have already influenced even the most elementary piece of data. It is argued that knowledge exists which, when articulated, verbalized, and structured, becomes information which, when assigned a fixed representation and standard interpretation, becomes data (Alavi & Leidner 2001, p. 109):

Critical to this argument is the fact that knowledge does not exist outside an agent (a knower): it is indelibly shaped by one's needs as well as one's initial stock of knowledge. Knowledge is thus the result of cognitive processing triggered by the inflow of new stimuli. Consistent with this view, we posit that information is converted to knowledge once it is processed in the mind of individuals and the knowledge becomes information once it is articulated and presented in the form of text, graphics, words, or other symbolic forms. A significant implication of this view of knowledge is that for individuals to arrive at the same understanding of data or information, they must share a certain knowledge base. Another important implication of this definition of knowledge is that systems designed to support knowledge in organizations may not appear radically different from other forms of information systems, but will be geared toward enabling users to assign meaning to information and to capture some of their knowledge in information and/or data.

Knowledge Value Level

It is not difficult to agree with this reasoning. In fact, our hierarchy from data via information to knowledge is not so much a road or direction, as it is a way of suggesting resource value levels. Knowledge is a more valuable resource to the organization than information, and information is a more valuable resource than data. This is illustrated in Figure 2.1. The figure illustrates that it is less the knowledge existing at any given time per se than the organization's ability to effectively apply the existing knowledge to develop new knowledge and to take action that forms the basis for achieving long-term competitive advantage from knowledge-based assets.

Figure 2.1. Value levels of resources in the organization

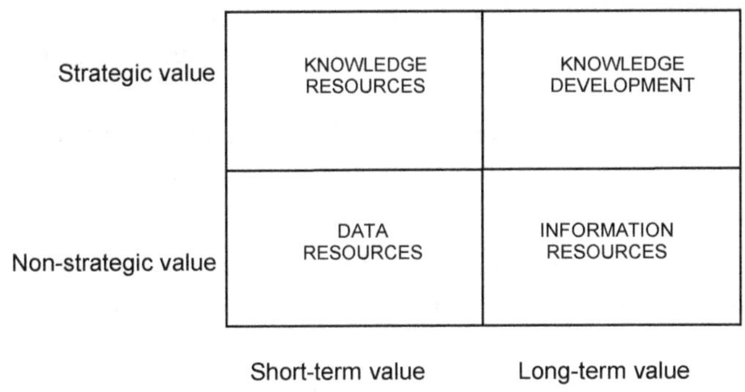

According to Grover and Davenport (2001), knowledge processes lie somewhere between information and the organization's source of revenue, its products and services. This process can be generically represented in three subprocesses: knowledge generation, knowledge codification and knowledge transfer/realization. Knowledge generation includes all processes involved in the acquisition and development of knowledge. Knowledge codification involves the conversion of knowledge into accessible and applicable formats. Knowledge transfer includes the movement of knowledge from its point of generation or codified form to the point of use.

One of the reasons that knowledge is such a difficult concept is because this process is recursive, expanding and often discontinuous. According to Grover and Davenport (2001), many cycles of generation, codification and transfer are concurrently occurring in businesses. These cycles feed on each other. Knowledge interacts with information to increase the state space of possibilities and provide new information, which can then facilitate generation of new knowledge. The knowledge process acts on information to create new information that allows for greater possibilities to fulfill old or possibly new organizational needs. This process is often discontinuous, where new needs and their fulfillment mechanism could be created.

In our resource-based perspective of knowledge, data are raw numbers and facts, information is processed data and knowledge is information combined with human thoughts. Knowledge is the result of cognitive processing triggered by the inflow of new stimuli. Information is converted to knowledge once it is processed in the mind of individuals, and the knowledge becomes information once it is articulated and presented to others. A significant implication of this view of knowledge is that for individuals to arrive at the same understanding of information, they must share the same knowledge framework.

In Figure 2.1, we can imagine that data are assigned meaning and become information, that information is understood and interpreted by individuals and becomes knowledge and that knowledge is applied and develops into new knowledge. We can also imagine the opposite route. Knowledge develops in the minds of individuals. This knowledge development causes an increase in knowledge resources. When the new knowledge is articulated, verbalized and structured, it becomes information and causes an increase in information resources. When information is assigned a fixed representation and standard interpretation, it becomes data and causes an increase in data resources.

There are alternatives to our perspective of knowledge as a resource in the organization. Alavi and Leidner (2001) list the following alternatives: knowledge is state of mind, knowledge is an object to be stored, knowledge is a process of applying expertise, knowledge is a condition of access to information and knowledge is the potential to influence action.

This book applies the resource-based theory of the organization, where the knowledge-based perspective identifies the primary role of the organization as integrating the specialist knowledge resident in individuals into goods and services. The task of management is to establish the coordination necessary for this knowledge integration. The knowledge-based perspective serves as a platform for a view of the organization as a dynamic system of knowledge production and application.

Identification of Knowledge Needs

To classify knowledge as a resource, there has to be a need for that knowledge. Hence, identification of knowledge needs in an organization is important. Three supplementary methods exist to identify needs for knowledge as illustrated in Figure 2.2:

- **Problem decision analysis:** This method aims at identifying and specifying problems that knowledge workers have, solutions they can find, decisions they have to make and what knowledge they need to solve problems and make decisions. For a lawyer, the problem can be an insurance claim by a client, the decision can be how to approach the insurance company and the knowledge need can be outcomes of similar cases handled by the law firm.
- **Critical success factors:** This method aims at identifying and specifying what factors cause success. Success can be at the firm , individual or individual case level. For a lawyer, critical success factors at the individual case level can be quality of legal advice and service level of advice delivery. Critical knowledge in this case includes legal knowledge as well as procedural knowledge.

Figure 2.2. Methods to identifyu knowledge needs

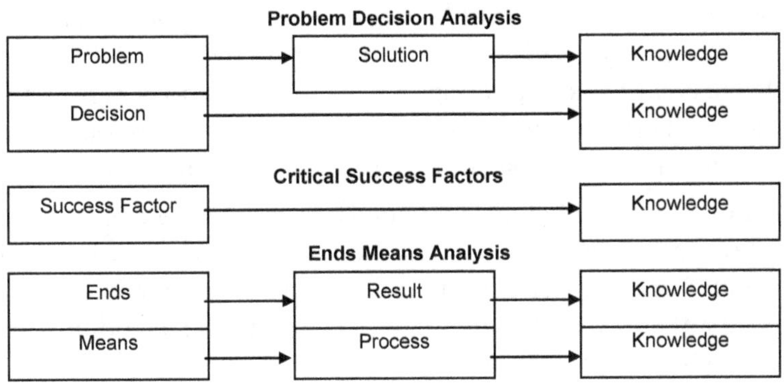

- **Ends means analysis:** This method aims at identifying and specifying external demands and expectations to goods and services from the firm. For a lawyer, the client expectation might be that she or he wins the case. The end is winning the case. Knowledge needs associated with winning a case include legal, procedural and analytical knowledge of successful cases in the past. The means for winning a case might be access to resources of various kinds, such as client documents and client funds. Knowledge needs associated with means include historical records and analysis of legal client practice.

Knowledge Categories

Many researchers have tried to define categories and dimensions of knowledge. A common distinction is made between explicit and tacit knowledge. *Explicit knowledge* can be expressed in words and numbers and shared in the form of data, scientific formulae, specifications, manuals and the like. This kind of knowledge can be readily transmitted between individuals both formally and systematically. *Tacit knowledge* is, on the other hand, highly personal and hard to formalize, making it difficult to communicate or share with others. Subjective insights, intuitions and hunches fall into this category of knowledge. Tacit knowledge is deeply rooted in an individual's actions and experience as well as in the ideals, values or emotions he or she embraces. Tacit knowledge is embedded in the human brain and cannot be expressed easily, while explicit knowledge can be easily codified. Both types of knowledge are important, but Western firms have focused largely on managing explicit knowledge (Grover & Davenport, 2001).

Tacitness may be considered as a variable, with the degree of tacitness being a function of the extent to which the knowledge is, or can be, codified and abstracted. Knowledge may dynamically shift between tacit and explicit over time, although some knowledge always will remain tacit. Nonaka et al. (2000) have suggested that knowledge creation is a spiraling process of interactions between explicit and tacit knowledge. This spiraling process consists of socialization, externalization, combination and internalization, as we will see later in this chapter.

The concept of tacit knowledge corresponds closely to the concept of knowledge with a low level of codification. Codification is the degree to which knowledge is fully documented or expressed in writing at the time of transfer between two persons. The complexity of knowledge increases with lower levels of codification. A similar distinction which scholars frequently make is between practical, experience-based knowledge and the theoretical knowledge derived from reflection and abstraction from that experience.

A distinction is sometimes made between codification and personalization. This distinction is related to the tacit vs. explicit concept. It involves an organization's approach to knowledge transfer. Companies using codification approaches rely primarily on repositories of explicit knowledge. Personalization approaches imply that the primary mode of knowledge transfer is direct interaction among people. Both are necessary in most organizations, but an increased focus on one approach or the other at any given time within a specific organization may be appropriate (Grover & Davenport, 2001).

Explicit knowledge is sometimes called articulable knowledge (Hitt et al., 2001). Articulable knowledge can be codified and thus can be written and easily transferred. Tacit knowledge is not articulable and therefore cannot be easily transferred. Tacit knowledge is often embedded in uncodified routines and in a firm's social context. More specifically, it is partially embedded in individual skills and partially embedded in collaborative working relationships within the firm. Tacit knowledge is integral to professional skills. As a result, tacit knowledge is often unique, difficult to imitate and uncertain. It has a higher probability of creating strategic value than articulable knowledge.

Distinctions can be made between core, advanced and innovative knowledge. These knowledge categories indicate different levels of knowledge sophistication. Core knowledge is that minimum scope and level of knowledge required for daily operations, advanced knowledge enables a firm to be competitively viable and innovative knowledge is the knowledge that enables the firm to lead its industry and competitors:

- **Core knowledge:** The basic knowledge required to stay in business. This is the type of knowledge that can create efficiency barriers for entry of new companies, as new competitors are not up to speed in basic business processes.

Since core knowledge is present at all existing competitors, the firm must have this knowledge even though it will provide the firm with no advantage that distinguishes it from its competitors. Core knowledge is that minimum scope and level of knowledge required just to play the game. Having that level of knowledge and capability will not assure the long-term competitive viability of the firm, but does present a basic industry knowledge barrier to entry. Core knowledge tends to be commonly held by members of an industry and therefore provides little advantage other than over nonmembers (Zack, 1999).

In a law firm, examples of core knowledge include knowledge of the law, knowledge of the courts, knowledge of clients and knowledge of procedures. For a student in the business school, core knowledge includes knowledge of what subjects to study this term and where the lectures take place.

According to Tiwana (2002), core knowledge is the basic level of knowledge required just to play the game. This is the type of knowledge that creates a barrier for entry of new companies. Since this level of knowledge is expected of all competitors, you must have it even though it will provide your company with no advantage that distinguishes it from its competitors. Let's take two examples: One from the consumer electronics (hard product) business and one from Internet programming (soft product). To enter the modem manufacturing market, a new company must have extensive knowledge of these aspects: a suitable circuit design, all electronic parts that go into a modem, fabricating surface mount (SMD) chip boards, how to write operating system drivers for modems and familiarity with computer telephony standards. Similarly, a company developing Web sites for, say, florists, needs server hosting capabilities, Internet programming skills, graphic design skills, clearly identified target markets and necessary software. In either case, just about any competitor in those businesses is assumed to have this knowledge in order to compete in their respective markets; such essential knowledge therefore provides no advantage over other market players.

- **Advanced knowledge:** What makes the firm competitively visible and active. Such knowledge allows the firm to differentiate its products and services from that of a competitor through the application of superior knowledge in certain areas. Such knowledge allows the firm to compete head on with its competitors in the same market and for the same set of customers. Advanced knowledge enables a firm to be competitively viable. The firm may have generally the same level, scope or quality of knowledge as its competitors although the specific knowledge content will often vary among competitors, enabling knowledge differentiation. Firms may choose to compete on knowledge head-on in the same strategic position, hoping to know more than a competitor. They instead may choose to compete for that position by differentiating their knowledge (Zack, 1999).

In a law firm, examples of advanced knowledge include knowledge of law applications, important court rulings and successful procedural case handling. For a student in the business school, advanced knowledge includes knowledge of important articles and books, which are compulsory literature in subjects this term.

According to Tiwana (2002), advanced knowledge is what makes your company competitively viable. Such knowledge allows your company to differentiate its product from that of a competitor, arguably through the application of superior knowledge in certain areas. Such knowledge allows your company to compete head on with its competitors in the same market and for the same set of customers. In the case of a company trying to compete in modem manufacturing markets, superior or user-friendly software or an additional capability in modems (such as warning online users of incoming telephone calls) represents such knowledge. In the case of a Web site development firm, such knowledge might be about international flower markets and collaborative relationships in Dutch flower auctions that the company can use to improve Web sites delivered to its customers.

- **Innovative knowledge:** Allows a firm to lead its entire industry to an extent that clearly differentiates it from competition. Such knowledge allows a firm to change the rules of the game by introducing new business practices. Such knowledge enables a firm to expand its market share by winning new customers and by increasing service levels to existing customers. Innovative knowledge is that knowledge that enables a firm to lead its industry and competitors and to significantly differentiate itself from its competitors. Innovative knowledge often enables a firm to change the rules of the game itself (Zack, 1999).

  In a law firm, examples of innovative knowledge include knowledge of standardizing repetitive legal cases, knowledge of successful settlements and knowledge of modern information technology to track and store vast amounts of information from various sources. For a student in the business school, innovative knowledge includes knowledge of important topics within subjects, links between subjects, typical exam questions and knowledge of business cases where theory can be applied.

  According to Tiwana (2002), innovative knowledge allows a company to lead its entire industry to an extent that clearly differentiates it from competition. Innovative knowledge allows a company to change the rules of the game. Patented technology is an applicable example of changing the rules. Innovative knowledge cannot always be protected by patents, as the lawsuit between Microsoft and Apple in the 1980s should serve to remind us. Apple sued Microsoft for copying the look and feel of its graphical user interface (GUI). The Supreme Court ruled that things like look and feel cannot be patented;

they can only be copyrighted. Microsoft won the case, since it copied the look and feel but used entirely different code to create it in the first place.

Many more categories and dimensions of knowledge have been suggested by researchers. The problem with most of these classifications is that they do not seem to satisfy three important criteria for classification. The first requirement is that a classification should always be complete, there should be no category missing. The second requirement is that each category should be different from all other categories, i.e., there should be no overlap between categories. The final requirement is that each category should be at the same level; there should be no category including another category. Consider the following categories suggested by researchers: formal knowledge, instrumental knowledge, informal knowledge, tacit knowledge, meta knowledge and context-independent knowledge. These categories seem to violate some of the classification rules. For example, there seems to be an overlap between informal knowledge and tacit knowledge. Maybe Long and Fahey's (2000) classification into human knowledge, social knowledge and structured knowledge satisfies our requirements:

- **Human knowledge:** This constitutes the know-what, know-how and know-why of individuals. Human knowledge is manifested in individual skills (e.g., how to interview law firm clients) or expertise (e.g., why this case is similar to a previous case). Individual knowledge usually combines explicit and tacit knowledge. This type of knowledge may be located in the body, such as knowing how to touch-type on a PC or how to ride a bicycle. This type of knowledge may be cognitive, that is, largely conceptual and abstract.
- **Social knowledge:** This kind of knowledge exists only in relationships between individuals or within groups. For example, high-performing teams of tax lawyers share certain collective knowledge that is more than the sum of the individual knowledge of the team's members. Social or collective knowledge is mainly tacit knowledge, shared by team members, and develops only as a result of team members working together. Its presence is reflected by an ability to collaborate effectively.
- **Structured knowledge:** This is embedded in an organization's systems, processes, tools, routines and practices. Knowledge in this form is explicit and often rule-based. A key distinction between structured knowledge and the first two types of knowledge is that structured knowledge is assumed to exist independently of individual knowers. It is, instead, an organizational resource. However, to be complete, this knowledge has to be in the heads of individuals.

Figure 2.3. Dimensions of individual knowledge

I do know	I know that I know	I don't know that I know
I don't know	I know that I don't know	I don't know that I don't know

Two dimensions have been introduced to classify knowledge. The first dimension is concerned with whether an individual knows. The second dimension is concerned with whether an individual knows whether he or she knows. This is illustrated in Figure 2.3. I can either have the knowledge (I do know) or not have the knowledge (I don't know). I can either be aware of it (I know it) or not be aware of it (I don't know it).

Some researchers have argued that the real tacit knowledge is found in the right upper quadrant. In this dimension, I do know, but I don't know that I know. Tacit knowledge in this sense is also called hidden, or nonaccessible, knowledge. In this book, we do not use this extremely limited definition of tacit knowledge. We define tacit knowledge as personal and difficult, but not impossible, to communicate.

Classification of knowledge into categories and dimensions may depend on industry. For example, there are likely to be different knowledge categories in a bank compared to a law firm. At the same time, there will be certain generic knowledge categories such as market intelligence and technology understanding in most companies independent of industry. When classifying knowledge in a firm, it is important to do the analysis without the organization chart. If you classify knowledge into technology knowledge, production knowledge, marketing knowledge and financial knowledge, it may be because the firm, according to the organization chart, consists of a development department, production department, marketing department and financial department. It might be more useful to introduce new knowledge categories such as product knowledge, which includes knowledge of development, production, marketing and finance. By identifying cross-sectional knowledge categories and dimensions, solutions for improved knowledge flows in the organization will emerge.

A law firm is a good example. A law firm is organized according to legal disciplines. Some lawyers work in the tax department, while others work in the department for mergers and acquisitions. The types of knowledge involved in the practice of law can be categorized as administrative, declarative, procedural and analytical (Edwards & Mahling, 1997):

- **Administrative knowledge:** Includes all the nuts-and-bolts information about firm operations, such as hourly billing rates for lawyers, client names and matters, staff payroll data and client invoice data.
- **Declarative knowledge:** Knowledge of the law, the legal principles contained in statutes, court opinions and other sources of primary legal authority; law students spend most of their law school time acquiring this kind of knowledge.
- **Procedural knowledge:** Involves knowledge of the mechanisms of complying with the law's requirements in a particular situation: how documents are used to transfer an asset from Company A to Company B, how forms must be filed or where to create a new corporation. Declarative knowledge is sometimes labeled know-that and know-what, while procedural knowledge is labeled know-how.
- **Analytical knowledge:** Pertains to the conclusions reached about the course of action a particular client should follow in a particular situation. Analytical knowledge results, in essence, from analyzing declarative knowledge (i.e., substantive law principles) as it applies to a particular fact setting.

Classification of knowledge into categories and dimensions has important limitations. For example, the classification into explicit and tacit knowledge may create static views of knowledge. However, knowledge development and sharing are dynamic processes, and these dynamic processes cause tacit knowledge to become explicit, and explicit knowledge to become tacit over time. Tacit and explicit knowledge depend on each other, and they influence each other. In this perspective, Alavi and Leidner (2001) argue that whether tacit or explicit knowledge is the more valuable may indeed miss the point. The two knowledge categories are not dichotomous states of knowledge, but mutually dependent and reinforcing qualities of knowledge: Tacit knowledge forms the background necessary for assigning the structure to develop and interpret explicit knowledge.

According to Alavi and Leidner (2001), the linkage of tacit and explicit knowledge suggests that only individuals with a requisite level of shared knowledge are able to exchange knowledge. They suggest the existence of a shared knowledge space that is required in order for individual A to understand individual B's knowledge. The knowledge space is the underlying overlap in knowledge base of A and B. This overlap is typically tacit knowledge. It may be argued that the greater the shared knowledge space, the less the context needed for individuals to share knowledge within the group and, hence, the higher the value of explicit knowledge. For example, in a law firm, lawyers in the maritime law department may have a large knowledge space so that even a very limited piece of explicit knowledge can be of great value. Alavi and Leidner (2001, p. 112) discuss knowledge space in the following way:

> Whether tacit or explicit knowledge is the more valuable may indeed miss the point. The two are not dichotomous states of knowledge, but mutually dependent and reinforcing qualities of knowledge: tacit knowledge forms the background necessary for assigning the structure to develop and interpret explicit knowledge. The inextricable linkage of tacit and explicit knowledge suggests that only individuals with a requisite level of shared knowledge can truly exchange knowledge: if tacit knowledge is necessary to the understanding of explicit knowledge, then in order for Individual B to understand Individual A's knowledge, there must be some overlap in their underlying knowledge bases (a shared knowledge space). However, it is precisely in applying technology to increase weak ties in organizations, and thereby increase the breadth of knowledge sharing, that IT holds promise. Yet, absent a shared knowledge space, the real impact of IT on knowledge exchange is questionable. This is a paradox that IT researchers have somewhat eschewed, and that organizational researchers have used to question the application of IT to knowledge management. To add to the paradox, the very essence of the knowledge management challenge is to amalgamate knowledge across groups for which IT can play a major role. What is most at issue is the amount of contextual information necessary for one person or group's knowledge to be readily understood by another.

It may be argued that the greater the shared knowledge space, the less the context needed for individuals to share knowledge within the group and, hence, the higher the value of explicit knowledge and the greater the value of IT applied to knowledge management. On the other hand, the smaller the existing shared knowledge space in a group, the greater the need for contextual information, the less relevant will be explicit knowledge, and hence the less applicable will be IT to knowledge management.

Some researchers are interested in the total knowledge within a company, while others are interested in individual knowledge. Dixon (2000) was interested in the knowledge that knowledge workers develop together in the organization. Employees gain this knowledge from doing the organization's tasks. This knowledge is called common knowledge to differentiate it from book knowledge or lists of regulations or databases of customer information. Some examples of common knowledge are what medical doctors in a hospital have learned about how to carry out certain kinds of surgery, what an organization has learned about how to introduce a new drug into the diabetes market, how to reduce cost on consulting projects and how to control the amount of analysis in maritime law cases. These examples all include the how-to rather than the know-what of school learning. Moreover, it is know-how that is unique to a specific company. In the law firm example, procedural knowledge was classified as know-how.

Questions for Discussion

1. What are characteristics of innovative knowledge for each primary activity in the value shop?
2. Identify some business and public organizations and discuss important knowledge for improved performance in each of them.
3. How would you estimate the value of knowledge?

List of References

Alavi, M., & Leidner, D. E. (2001). Knowledge management and knowledge management systems: Conceptual foundations and research issues. *MIS Quarterly, 25*(1), 107-136.

Chen, A. N. K., & Edgington, T. M. (2005). Assessing value in organizational knowledge creation: Considerations for knowledge workers. *MIS Quarterly, 29*(2), 279-309.

Davenport, T. H., & Prusak, L. (1998). *Working knowledge*. Boston: Harvard Business School Press.

Dixon, N. M. (2000). *Common knowledge*. Boston, MA: Harvard Business School Press.

Edwards, D. L., & Mahling, D. E. (1997). Toward knowledge management systems in the legal domain. *Proceedings of the International ACM SIGGROUP Conference on Supporting Group Work Group '97*, The Association of Computing Machinery ACM (pp. 158-166).

Garud, R., & Kumaraswamy, A. (2005). Vicious and virtuous circles in the management of knowledge: The case of Infosys technologies. *MIS Quarterly, 29*(1), 9-33.

Grover, V., & Davenport, T. H. (2001). General perspectives on knowledge management: Fostering a research agenda. *Journal of Management Information Systems, 18*(1), 5-21.

Hitt, M. A., Bierman, L., Shumizu, K., & Kochhar, R. (2001). Direct and moderating effects of human capital on strategy and performance in professional service firms: A resourced-based perspective. *Academy of Management Journal, 44*(1), 13-28.

Kankanhalli, A., Tan, B. C. Y., & Wei, K. K. (2005). Contributing knowledge to electronic knowledge repositories: An empirical investigation. *MIS Quarterly, 29*(1), 113-143.

Long, D. W., & Fahey, L. (2000). Diagnosing cultural barriers to knowledge management. *Academy of Management Executive, 14*(4), 113-127.

Malhotra, A., Gosain, S., & El Sawy, O. A. (2005). Absorptive capacity configurations in supply chains: Gearing for partner-enabled market knowledge creation. *MIS Quarterly, 29*(1), 145-187.

Nonaka, I., Toyama, R., & Konno, N. (2000). SECI, ba and leadership: A unified model of dynamic knowledge creation. *Long Range Planning, 33*(1), 5-34

Poston, R. S., & Speier, C. (2005). Effective use of knowledge management systems: A process model of content ratings and credibility indicators. *MIS Quarterly, 29*(2), 221-244.

Ryu, C., Kim, Y. J., Chaudhury, A., & Rao, H. R. (2005). Knowledge acquisition via three learning processes in enterprise information portals: Learning-by-investment, learning-by-doing, and learning-from-others. *MIS Quarterly, 29*(2), 245-278.

Sambamurthy, V., & Subramani, M. (2005). Special issue on information technologies and knowledge management. *MIS Quarterly, 29*(1), 1-7; and *29*(2), 193-195.

Tanriverdi, H. (2005). Information technology relatedness, knowledge management capability, and performance of multibusiness firms. *MIS Quarterly, 29*(2), 311-334.

Tiwana, A. (2002). *The knowledge management toolkit — Practical techniques for building a knowledge management system* (2nd ed.). Upper Saddle River, NJ: Prentice Hall.

Wasko, M. M., & Faraj, S. (2005). Why should I share? Examining social capital and knowledge contribution in electronic networks of practice. *MIS Quarterly, 29*(1), 35-57.

Zack, M. H. (1999). Developing a knowledge strategy. *California Management Review, 41*(3), 125-145.

Chapter III

Knowledge Management Systems

Introduction

As we trace the evolution of computing technologies in business, we can observe their changing level of organizational impact. The first level of impact was at the point work got done and transactions (e.g., orders, deposits and reservations) took place. The inflexible, centralized mainframe allowed for little more than massive number crunching, commonly known as electronic *data* processing. Organizations became data heavy at the bottom and data management systems were used to keep the data in check. Later, the management *information* systems were used to aggregate data into useful information reports, often prescheduled, for the control level of the organization — people who were making sure that organizational resources like personnel, money and physical goods were being deployed efficiently. As information technology (IT) and information systems (IS) started to facilitate data and information overflow, and corporate attention became a scarce resource, the concept of *knowledge* emerged as a particularly high-value form of information (Grover & Davenport, 2001).

Information technology can play an important role in successful knowledge management initiatives. However, the concept of coding and transmitting knowledge in organizations is not new: training and employee development programs, organizational policies, routines, procedures, reports and manuals have served this function for many years. What is new and exciting in the knowledge management area is the potential for using modern information technology (e.g., the Internet, intranets, extranets, browsers, data warehouses, data filters, software agents and expert systems) to support knowledge creation, sharing and exchange in an organization and between organizations. Modern information technology can collect, systematize, structure, store, combine, distribute and present information of value to knowledge workers (Nahapiet & Ghoshal, 1998).

According to Davenport and Prusak (1998), more and more companies have instituted knowledge repositories, supporting such diverse types of knowledge as best practices, lessons learned, product development knowledge, customer knowledge, human resource management knowledge and methods-based knowledge. Groupware and intranet-based technologies have become standard knowledge infrastructures. A new set of professional job titles — the knowledge manager, the chief knowledge officer (CKO), the knowledge coordinator and the knowledge-network facilitator — affirms the widespread legitimacy that knowledge management has earned in the corporate world.

The low cost of computers and networks has created a potential infrastructure for knowledge sharing and opened up important knowledge management opportunities. The computational power, as such, has little relevance to knowledge work, but the communication and storage capabilities of networked computers make computational power an important enabler of effective knowledge work. Through e-mail, groupware, the Internet and intranets, computers and networks can point to people with knowledge and connect those who need to share knowledge independent of time and place.

For example, electronic networks of practice are computer-mediated discussion forums focused on problems of practice that enable individuals to exchange advice and ideas with others based on common interests. Electronic networks make it possible to share information quickly, globally and with large numbers of individuals. Electronic networks that focus on knowledge exchange frequently emerge in fields where the pace of technological change requires access to knowledge unavailable within any single organization (Wasko & Faraj, 2005).

In the knowledge-based view of the firm, knowledge is the foundation of a firm's competitive advantage and, ultimately, the primary driver of a firm's value. Inherently, however, knowledge resides within individuals and, more specifically, in the employees who create, recognize, archive, access and apply knowledge in carrying out their tasks. Consequently, the movement of knowledge across individual and organizational boundaries, into and from repositories and into organizational routines and practices is ultimately dependent on employees' knowledge-sharing behaviors (Bock et al., 2005).

According to Grover and Davenport (2001), most knowledge management projects in organizations involve the use of information technology. Such projects fall into relatively few categories and types, each of which has a key objective. Although it is possible, and even desirable, to combine multiple objectives in a single project, this was not normally observed in a study of 31 knowledge management projects in

1997 (Davenport & Prusak, 1998). Since that time, it is possible that projects have matured and taken on more ambitious collections of objectives.

Regardless of the definition of knowledge as the highest value of content in a continuum starting at data, encompassing information and ending at knowledge itself, knowledge managers often take a highly inclusive approach to the content with which they deal. In practice, what companies actually manage under the banner of knowledge management is a mix of knowledge, information and unrefined data — in short, whatever anyone finds that is useful and easy to store in an electronic repository. In the case of data and information, however, there are often attempts to add more value and create knowledge. This transformation might involve the addition of insight, experience, context, interpretation or a myriad of other activities in which human brains specialize (Grover & Davenport, 2001).

Identifying, nurturing and harvesting knowledge is a principal concern in the information society and the knowledge age. Effective use of knowledge-facilitating tools and techniques is critical, and a number of computational tools have been developed. While numerous techniques are available, it remains difficult to analyze or compare specific tools. In part, this is because knowledge management is a young discipline. The arena is evolving rapidly as more people enter the fray and encounter new problems (Housel & Bell, 2001).

In addition, new technologies support applications that were impossible before. Moreover, the multidisciplinary character of knowledge management combines several disciplines, including business and management, computer science, cybernetics and philosophy. Each of these fields may lay claim to the study of knowledge management, and the field is frequently defined so broadly that anything can be incorporated. Finally, it is difficult to make sense of the many knowledge management tools available; it is not difficult to perform a search to produce a list of more than one hundred software providers. Each of the software packages employ unique visions and aims to capture its share of the market (Housel & Bell, 2001).

Ward and Peppard (2002) find that there are two dominant and contrasting views of IS/IT in knowledge management: the engineering perspective and the social process perspective. The engineering perspective views knowledge management as a technology process. Many organizations have taken this approach in managing knowledge, believing that it is concerned with managing pieces of intellectual capital. Driving this view is the belief that knowledge can be codified and stored; in essence that knowledge is explicit and therefore is little more than information.

The alternative view is that knowledge is a social process. As such, it asserts that knowledge resides in people's heads and that it is tacit. As such, it cannot be easily codified and only revealed through its application. As tacit knowledge cannot be directly transferred from person to person, its acquisition occurs only through practice. Consequently, its transfer between people is slow, costly and uncertain.

Technology, within this perspective, can only support the context of knowledge work. It has been argued that IT-based systems used to support knowledge management can only be of benefit if used to support the development and communication of human meaning. One reason for the failure of IT in some knowledge management initiatives is that the designers of the knowledge management systems fail to understand the situation and work practices of the users and the complex human processes involved in their work.

While technology can be used with knowledge management initiatives, Ward and Peppard (2002) argue that it should never be the first step. Knowledge management is to them primarily a human and process issue. Once these two aspects have been addressed, then the created processes are usually very amenable to being supported and enhanced by the use of technology.

What, then, is knowledge management technology? According to Davenport and Prusak (1998), the concept of knowledge management technology is not only broad but also a bit slippery to define. Some infrastructure technology that we don't ordinarily think of in this category can be useful in facilitating knowledge management. Examples are video conferencing and the telephone. Both of these technologies don't capture or distribute structured knowledge, but they are quite effective at enabling people to transfer tacit knowledge.

Our focus here, however, is on technology that captures, stores and distributes structured knowledge for use by people. The goal of these technologies is to take knowledge that exists in human heads, and partly in paper documents, and make it widely available throughout an organization. Similarly, Alavi and Leidner (2001) argue that information systems designed to support knowledge in organizations may not appear radically different from other forms of IT support, but will be geared toward enabling users to assign meaning to information and to capture some of their knowledge in information. Therefore, the concept of knowledge management technology in this book is less concerned with any degree of technology sophistication and more concerned with the usefulness in performing knowledge work in and between organizations.

Moffett and McAdam (2003) illustrate the variety of knowledge management technology tools by distinguishing between collaborative tools, content management and business intelligence. Collaborative tools include groupware technology, meeting support systems, knowledge directories and intranets/extranets. Content management includes the Internet, agents and filters, electronic publishing systems, document management systems and office automation systems. Business intelligence includes data warehousing, decision support systems, knowledge-based systems and workflow systems. In addition to technologies, we also present techniques in this book. The term technique is defined as a set of precisely described procedures for achieving a standard task (Kettinger et al., 1997).

Knowledge Management Processes

Alavi and Leidner (2001) have developed a systematic framework that will be used to analyze and discuss the potential role of information technology in knowledge management. According to this framework, organizations consist of four sets of socially enacted knowledge processes: (1) creation (also referred to as construction), (2) storage and retrieval, (3) transfer and (4) application. The knowledge-based view of the firm represents here both the cognitive and social nature of organizational knowledge and the embodiment of this knowledge in the individual's cognition and practices as well as the collective (i.e., organizational) practices and culture. These processes do not represent a monolithic set of activities, but an interconnected and intertwined set of activities.

Knowledge Creation

Organizational knowledge creation involves developing new content or replacing existing content within the organization's tacit and explicit knowledge. Through social and collaborative processes, as well as individual's cognitive processes (e.g., reflection), knowledge is created. The model developed by Nonaka et al. (2000) involving SECI, ba and knowledge assets, views organizational knowledge creation as involving a continual interplay between the tacit and explicit dimensions of knowledge, and a growing spiral flow as knowledge moves through individual, group and organizational levels. Four modes of knowledge creation have been identified: socialization, externalization, internalization and combination (SECI), and these modes occur at "ba," which means place.

Nonaka et al. (2000) suggest that the essential question of knowledge creation is establishing an organization's ba, defined as a common place or space for creating knowledge. Four types of ba corresponding to the four modes of knowledge creation are identified: (1) originating; (2) interacting; (3) cyber; and (4) exercising ba. Originating ba entails the socialization mode of knowledge creation and is the ba from which the organizational knowledge creation process begins. Originating ba is a common place in which individuals share experiences primarily through face-to-face interactions and by being at the same place at the same time. Interacting ba is associated with the externalization mode of knowledge creation and refers to a space where tacit knowledge is converted to explicit knowledge and shared among individuals through the process of dialogue and collaboration. Cyber ba refers to a virtual space of interaction and corresponds to the combination mode of knowledge creation. Finally, exercising ba involves the conversion of explicit to tacit knowledge through the internalization process. Thus, exercising ba involves the conversion of explicit to tacit knowledge through the internalization process.

Understanding the characteristics of various ba and the relationship with the modes of knowledge creation is important to enhancing organizational knowledge creation. For example, the use of IT capabilities in cyber ba is advocated to enhance the efficiency of the combination mode of knowledge creation. Data warehousing and data mining, document management systems, software agents and intranets may be of great value in cyber ba. Considering the flexibility of modern IT, other forms of organizational ba and the corresponding modes of knowledge creation can be enhanced through the use of various forms of information systems. For example, information systems designed for support or collaboration, coordination and communication processes as a component of the interacting ba, can facilitate teamwork and thereby increase an individual's contact with others.

Electronic mail and group support systems have the potential of increasing the number of weak ties in organizations. This, in turn, can accelerate the growth of knowledge creation. Intranets enable exposure to greater amounts of online organizational information, both horizontally and vertically, than may previously have been the case. As the level of information exposure increases, the internalization mode of knowledge creation, wherein individuals make observations and interpretations of information that result in new individual tacit knowledge, may increase. In this role, an intranet can support individual learning (conversion of explicit knowledge to personal tacit knowledge) through provision of capabilities such as computer simulation (to support learning-by-doing) and smart software tutors.

Computer-mediated communication may increase the quality of knowledge creation by enabling a forum for constructing and sharing beliefs, for confirming consensual interpretation and for allowing expression of new ideas. By providing an extended field of interaction among organizational members for sharing ideas and perspectives, and for establishing dialogue, information systems may enable individuals to arrive at new insights and/or more accurate interpretations than if left to decipher information on their own.

Although most information repositories serve a single function, it is increasingly common for companies to construct an internal portal so that employees can access multiple repositories and sources from one screen. It is also possible, and increasingly popular, for repositories to contain not only information, but also pointers to experts within the organization on key knowledge topics. It is also feasible to combine stored information with lists of the individuals who contributed the knowledge and could provide more detail or background on it (Grover & Davenport, 2001).

According to Grover and Davenport (2001), firms increasingly view attempts to transform raw data into usable knowledge as part of their knowledge management initiatives. These approaches typically involve isolating data in a separate "warehouse" for easier access, and the use of statistical analysis or data mining and visualization tools. Since their goal is to create data-derived knowledge, the initiatives are increasingly addressed as a part of knowledge management. Some vendors have already begun to introduce e-commerce tools in this area. They serve to customize the menu of available knowledge to individual customers, allowing sampling of information before buying and carrying out sales transactions for knowledge purchases. Online legal services are typical examples where clients can sample legal information before buying a lawyer's time.

For knowledge creation there is the current emergence of *idea-generation software.* Idea-generation software is designed to help stimulate a single user or a group to produce new ideas, options and choices. The user does all the work, but the software encourages and pushes, something like a personal trainer. Although idea-generation software is relatively new, there are several packages on the market. IdeaFisher, for example, has an associative lexicon of the English language that cross-references words and phrases. These associative links, based on analogies and metaphors, make it easy for the user to be fed words related to a given theme. Some software packages use questions to prompt the user toward new, unexplored patterns of thought. This helps users to break out of cyclical thinking patterns and conquer mental blocks.

Knowledge Storage and Retrieval

According to Alavi and Leidner (2001), empirical studies have shown that while organizations create knowledge and learn, they also forget (i.e., do not remember or lose track of the acquired knowledge). Thus, the storage, organization and retrieval of organizational knowledge, also referred to as organizational memory, constitute an important aspect of effective organizational knowledge management. Organizational memory includes knowledge residing in various component forms, including written documentation, structured information stored in electronic databases, codified human knowledge stored in expert systems, documented organizational procedures and processes and tacit knowledge acquired by individuals and networks of individuals.

Advanced computer storage technology and sophisticated retrieval techniques, such as query languages, multimedia databases and database management systems, can be effective tools in enhancing organizational memory. These tools increase the speed at which organizational memory can be accessed.

Groupware enables organizations to create intra-organizational memory in the form of both structured and unstructured information and to share this memory across time and space. IT can play an important role in the enhancement and expansion of both semantic and episodic organizational memory. Semantic memory refers to general, explicit and articulated knowledge, whereas episodic memory refers to context-specific and situated knowledge. Document management technology allows knowledge of an organization's past, often dispersed among a variety of retention facilities, to be effectively stored and made accessible. Drawing on these technologies, most consulting firms have created semantic memories by developing vast repositories of knowledge about customers, projects, competition and the industries they serve.

Grover and Davenport (2001) found that by far the most common objective of knowledge management projects in Western organizations involves some sort of knowledge repository. The objective of this type of project is to capture knowledge for later and broader access by others within the same organization. Common repository technologies include Lotus Notes, web-based intranets and Microsoft's Exchange, supplemented by search engines, document management tools and other tools that allow editing and access. The repositories typically contain a specific type of information to represent knowledge for a particular business function or process, such as:

- "Best practices" information within a quality or business process management function;
- Information for sales purposes involving products, markets and customers;
- Lessons learned in projects or product development efforts;
- Information around the implementation of information systems;
- Competitive intelligence for strategy and planning functions; and
- "Learning histories" or records of experience with a new corporate direction or approach.

The mechanical generation of databases, Web sites and systems that process data are good and have the potential to take us to a higher plane in the organization, help us understand workflows better and aid in dealing with organizational pathologies and problems. The data-to-information transition often involves a low level mechanical process that is well within the domain of contemporary information technologies, though humans are helpful in this transition as well. This information could exist in different forms throughout the organization and could even form the basis of competitive advantage or information products. For example, provision of information to customers about their order or shipment status is something that companies like Baxter and FedEx have been doing for years. But unlike knowledge, mechanically supplied information cannot be the source of sustained competitive advantage, particularly when the architectures on which it is based are becoming more open and omnipresent.

IT in knowledge management can be used to store various kinds of information. For example, information about processes, procedures, forecasts, cases and patents in the form of working documents, descriptions and reports can be stored in knowledge management systems. TietoEnator, a Scandinavian consulting firm, has a knowledge base where they store methods, techniques, notes, concepts, best practices, presentations, components, references, guidelines, quality instructions, process descriptions, routines, strategies and CVs for all consultants in the firm (Halvorsen & Nguyen, 1999).

Knowledge retrieval can find support in content management and information extraction technology, which represent a group of techniques for managing and extracting knowledge from documents, ultimately delivering a semantic meaning for decision makers and learners alike. These types of computer applications are targeted at capturing and extracting the content of free-text documents. There are several tasks that fall within the scope of content management and information extraction (Wang et al., 2001):

- **Abstracting and summarizing:** This task aims at delivering shorter, informative representations of larger (sets of) documents.
- **Visualization:** Documents can often be visualized according to the concepts and relationships that they play a role among. Visualization can be either in an introspective manner, or using some reference model/view of a specific topic.
- **Comparison and search:** This task finds semantically similar pieces of information.
- **Indexing and classification:** This considers (partial) texts, usually according to certain categories.
- **Translation:** Context-driven translation of texts from one language into another. Language translation has proven to be highly context specific, even among closely related languages. Some kind of semantic representation of meaning is needed in order to be able to make good translations.
- **Question formulation and query answering:** This is a task in human-computer interaction systems.
- **Extraction of information:** This refers to the generation of additional information that is not explicit in the original text. This information can be more or less elaborate.

A group of computational techniques are available to alleviate the burden of these tasks. They include fuzzy technology, neural networks and expert systems. On a more application-oriented level, there are several approaches that apply one or more of the general techniques. The field is currently dynamic, and new advances are made continuously. One novel approach is the CORPORUM system, presented in the section on expert systems.

Knowledge Transfer

Knowledge transfer can be defined as the communication of knowledge from a source so that it is learned and applied by a recipient (Ko et al., 2005). Knowledge transfer occurs at various levels in an organization: transfer of knowledge between individuals, from individuals to explicit sources, from individuals to groups, between groups, across groups and from the group to the organization. Considering the distributed nature of organizational cognition, an important process of knowledge management in organizational settings is the transfer of knowledge to locations where it is needed and can be used. However, this is not a simple process, in that organizations often do not know what they know and have weak systems for locating and retrieving knowledge that resides in them. Communication processes and information flows drive knowledge transfer in organizations.

Depending on the completeness or incompleteness of the sender and the receiver's information sets, there are four representative types of information structure in knowledge transfer according to Lin et al. (2005): symmetric complete information, sender-advantage asymmetric information, symmetric incomplete information and receiver-advantage asymmetric information. Lin et al. (2005) found that because of asymmetry and incompleteness, parties seeking knowledge may not be able to identify qualified knowledge providers, and the appropriate experts may fail to be motivated to engage in knowledge transfer.

Knowledge transfer channels can be informal or formal, personal or impersonal. IT can support all four forms of knowledge transfer, but has mostly been applied to informal, impersonal means (such as discussion databases) and formal, impersonal means (such as corporate directories). An innovative use of technology for transfer is use of intelligent agent software to develop interest profiles of organizational members in order to determine which members might be interested recipients of point-to-point electronic messages exchanged among other members. Employing video technologies can also enhance transfer.

IT can increase knowledge transfer by extending the individual's reach beyond the formal communication lines. The search for knowledge sources is usually limited to immediate coworkers in regular and routine contact with the individual. However, individuals are unlikely to encounter new knowledge through their close-knit work networks because individuals in the same clique tend to possess similar information. Moreover, individuals are often unaware of what their cohorts are doing. Thus, expanding the individual's network to more extended — although perhaps weaker-connections is central to the knowledge diffusion process because such networks expose individuals to more new ideas.

Computer networks and electronic bulletin boards and discussion groups create a forum that facilitates contact between the person seeking knowledge and those who may have access to the knowledge. Corporate directories may enable individuals to rapidly locate the individual who has the knowledge that might help them solve a current problem. For example, the primary content of such a system can be a set of expert profiles containing information about the backgrounds, skills and expertise of individuals who are knowledgeable in various topics. Often such metadata (knowledge about where knowledge resides) proves to be as important as the original knowledge itself. The provision of taxonomies or organizational knowledge maps enables individuals to rapidly locate either the knowledge, or the individual who has the needed knowledge, more rapidly than would be possible without such IT-based support.

Communication is important in knowledge management, because technology provides support for both intra-organizational as well as inter-organizational knowledge networks. Knowledge networks need technology in the form of technical infrastructure, communication networks and a set of information services. Knowledge networks enable knowledge workers to share information from various sources.

Traditional information systems have been of importance to vertical integration for a long time. Both customers and suppliers have been linked to the company through information systems. Only recently has horizontal integration occurred. Knowledge workers in similar businesses cooperate to find optimal solutions for customers. IT has become an important vertical and horizontal interorganizational coordination mechanism. This is not only because of the availability of broadband and standardized protocols. It is also caused by falling prices for communication services and by software programs' abilities to coordinate functions between firms.

One way to reduce problems stemming from paper workflow is to employ document-imaging systems. Document imaging systems are systems that convert paper documents and images into digital form so they can be stored and accessed by a computer. Once the document has been stored electronically, it can be immediately retrieved and shared with others. An imaging system requires indexes that allow users to identify and retrieve a document when needed (Laudon & Laudon, 2005).

Knowledge Application

An important aspect of the knowledge-based view of the firm is that the source of competitive advantage resides in the application of the knowledge rather than in the knowledge itself. Information technology can support knowledge application by embedding knowledge into organizational routines. Procedures that are culture-bound can be embedded into IT so that the systems themselves become examples of organizational norms. An example according to Alavi and Leidner (2001) is Mrs. Field's use of systems designed to assist in every decision from hiring personnel to when to put free samples of cookies out on the table. The system transmits the norms and beliefs held by the head of the company to organizational members.

Technology enforced knowledge application raises a concern that knowledge will continue to be applied after its real usefulness has declined. While the institutionalization of best practices by embedding them into IT might facilitate efficient handling of routine, linear and predictable situations during stable or incrementally changing environments, when change is radical and discontinuous, there is a persistent need for continual renewal of the basic premises underlying the practices archived in the knowledge repositories. This underscores the need for organizational members to remain attuned to contextual factors and explicitly consider the specific circumstances of the current environment.

Although there are challenges with applying existing knowledge, IT can have a positive influence on knowledge application. IT can enhance knowledge integration and application by facilitating the capture, updating and accessibility of organizational directives. For example, many organizations are enhancing the ease of access and maintenance of their directives (repair manuals, policies and standards) by making them available on corporate intranets. This increases the speed at which changes can be applied. Also, organizational units can follow a faster learning curve by accessing the knowledge of other units having gone through similar experiences. Moreover, by increasing the size of individuals' internal social networks and by increasing the amount of organizational memory available, information technologies allow for organizational knowledge to be applied across time and space.

IT can also enhance the speed of knowledge integration and application by codifying and automating organizational routines. Workflow automation systems are examples of IT applications that reduce the need for communication and coordination and enable more efficient use of organizational routines through timely and automatic routing of work-related documents, information, rules and activities. Rule based expert systems are another means of capturing and enforcing well-specified organizational procedures.

To summarize, Alavi and Leidner (2001) have developed a framework to understand IS/IT in knowledge management processes through the knowledge-based view of the firm. One important implication of this framework is that each of the four knowledge processes of creation, storage and retrieval, transfer and application can be facilitated by IT:

- **Knowledge creation:** Examples of supporting information technologies are data mining and learning tools, which enable combining new sources of knowledge and just-in-time learning.
- **Knowledge storage and retrieval:** Examples of supporting information technologies are electronic bulletin boards, knowledge repositories and databases, which provide support of individual and organizational memory as well as inter-group knowledge access.

- **Knowledge transfer:** Examples of supporting information technologies are electronic bulletin boards, discussion forums and knowledge directories, which enable a more extensive internal network, more available communication channels and faster access to knowledge sources.
- **Knowledge application:** Examples of supporting information technologies are expert and workflow systems, which enable knowledge application in many locations and more rapid application of new knowledge through workflow automation.

Knowledge Management Systems

There is no single information system that is able to cover all knowledge management needs in a firm. This is evident from the widespread potential of IT in knowledge management processes. Rather, knowledge management systems (KMS) refer to a class of information systems applied to managing organizational knowledge for use at the individual, group and organizational level. These systems are IT applications to support and enhance the organizational processes of knowledge creation, storage and retrieval, transfer and application.

Knowledge management systems can be classified as illustrated in Figure 3.1. Systems are exemplified along the axis of internal support vs. external support and along the axis of technology support vs. content support for knowledge workers. As an example of a knowledge management system, we find customer relationship management (CRM) systems in the upper left quadrant. CRM systems support knowledge exchange between the firm and its customers.

Despite widespread belief that information technology enables knowledge management, and knowledge management improves firm performance, researchers have only recently found empirical evidence of these relationships. For example, Tanriverdi (2005) used data from 250 Fortune 1000 firms to provide empirical support for these relationships.

Figure 3.1. Classification of knowledge management systems

Tools	**Information**	
Tools for external communications such as customer relationship management services	Information for external electronic cooperation such as Web-based	**External**
Tools for internal work by knowledge workers	Information for internal work by knowledge workers	**Internal**

Knowledge management systems are becoming ubiquitous in today's organizations. Knowledge management systems facilitate the efficient and effective sharing of an organization's intellectual resources. To ensure effective usage, a knowledge management system must be designed such that knowledge workers can readily find high-quality content without feeling overwhelmed (Poston & Speier, 2005).

Requirements from Knowledge Management

The critical role of information technology and information systems lies in the ability to support communication, collaboration and those searching for knowledge, and the ability to enable collaborative learning (Ryu et al., 2005). We have already touched on important implications for information systems:

1. **Interaction between information and knowledge:** Information becomes knowledge when it is combined with experience, interpretation and reflection. Knowledge becomes information when assigned an explicit representation. Sometimes information exists before knowledge, sometimes knowledge exists before information. One important implication of this two-way direction between knowledge and information is that information systems designed to support knowledge in organizations may not appear radically different from other forms of IT support, but will be geared toward enabling users to assign meaning to information and to capture some of their knowledge in information (Alavi & Leidner, 2001).
2. **Interaction between tacit and explicit knowledge:** Tacit and explicit knowledge depend on each other, and they influence each other. The linkage of tacit and explicit knowledge suggests that only individuals with a requisite level of shared knowledge are able to exchange knowledge. They suggest the existence of a shared knowledge space that is required in order for individual A to understand individual B's knowledge. The knowledge space is the underlying overlap in the knowledge bases of A and B. This overlap is typically tacit knowledge. It may be argued that the greater the shared knowledge space, the less the context needed for individuals to share knowledge within the group and, hence, the higher the value of explicit knowledge. IT is both dependent on the shared knowledge space and is itself an important part of the shared knowledge space. IT is dependent on the shared knowledge space because knowledge workers need to have a common understanding of available information contained in information systems in the organization. If common understanding is missing, then knowledge workers are unable to make use of information. IT is an important part of the shared knowledge space because information systems make common information available to all knowledge workers in the organization. One important implication of this two-way relationship between knowledge

space and information systems is that a minimum knowledge space has to be present; IT can contribute to growth in the knowledge space (Alavi & Leidner, 2001).

3. **Knowledge management strategy:** Efficiency-driven businesses may apply the stock strategy where databases and information systems are important; effectiveness-driven businesses may apply the flow strategy where information networks are important; and Expert-driven businesses may apply the growth strategy where networks of experts, work processes and learning environments are important (Hansen et al., 1999).
4. **Combination in SECI process:** The SECI process consists of four knowledge conversion modes. These modes are not equally suited for IT support. Socialization is the process of converting new tacit knowledge to tacit knowledge. This takes place in the human brain. Externalization is the process of converting tacit knowledge to explicit knowledge. The successful conversion of tacit knowledge into explicit knowledge depends on the sequential use of metaphors, analogy and model. Combination is the process of converting explicit knowledge into more complex and systematic sets of explicit knowledge. Explicit knowledge is collected from inside and outside the organization and then combined, edited and processed to form new knowledge. The new explicit knowledge is then disseminated among the members of the organization. According to Nonaka et al. (2000), creative use of computerized communication networks and large-scale databases can facilitate this mode of knowledge conversion. When the financial controller collects information from all parts of the organization and puts it together to show the financial health of the enterprise, that report is new knowledge in the sense that it synthesizes explicit knowledge from many different sources in one context. Finally, internalization in the SECI process converts explicit knowledge into tacit knowledge. Through internalization, the explicit knowledge created is shared throughout an organization and converted into tacit knowledge by individuals.
5. **Explicit transfer of common knowledge:** If management decides to focus on common knowledge as defined by Dixon (2000), knowledge management should focus on the sharing of common knowledge. Common knowledge is shared in the organization using five mechanisms: serial transfer, explicit transfer, tacit transfer, strategic transfer and expert transfer. Management has to emphasize all five mechanisms for successful sharing and creation of common knowledge. For serial transfer, management has to stimulate meetings and contacts between group members. For explicit transfer, management has to stimulate documentation of work by the previous group. For tacit transfer, management has to stimulate contacts between the two groups. For strategic transfer, management has to identify strategic knowledge and knowledge gaps. For expert transfer, management has to create networks where experts can transfer their knowledge. These five mechanisms are not equally suited

for IT support. Explicit transfer seems very well suited for IT support as the knowledge from the other group is transferred explicitly as explicit knowledge in words and numbers and shared in the form of data, scientific formulae, specifications, manuals and the like. Expert transfer also seems suited for IT support when generic knowledge is transferred from one individual to another person to enable the person to solve new problems with new methods.

6. **Link knowledge to its uses:** One of the mistakes in knowledge management presented by Fahey and Prusak (1998) was disentangling knowledge from its uses. A major manifestation of this error is that knowledge management initiatives become ends in themselves. For example, data warehousing can easily degenerate into technological challenges. The relevance of a data warehouse for decisions and actions gets lost in the turmoil spawned by debates about appropriate data structures.
7. **Treat knowledge as an intellectual asset in the economic school:** If management decides to follow the economic school of knowledge management, then intellectual capital accounting should be part of the knowledge management system. The knowledge management system should support knowledge markets where knowledge buyers, knowledge sellers and knowledge brokers can use the system.
8. **Treat knowledge as a mutual resource in the organizational school:** The potential contribution of IT is linked to the combination of intranets and groupware to connect members and pool their knowledge, both explicit and tacit.
9. **Treat knowledge as a strategy in the strategy school:** The potential contribution of IT is manifold once knowledge as strategy is the impetus behind knowledge management initiatives. One can expect quite an eclectic mix of networks, systems, tools and knowledge repositories in this scenario.
10. **Value configuration determines knowledge needs in primary activities:** Knowledge needs can be structured according to primary and secondary activities in the value configuration. Depending on the firm being a value chain, a value shop or a value network, the knowledge management system must support more efficient production in the value chain, adding value to the knowledge work in the value shop, and more value by use of IT infrastructure in the value network.
11. **Incentive alignment:** The first dimension of information systems design is concerned with software engineering (error-free software, documentation, portability, modularity and architecture, development cost, maintenance cost, speed and robustness). The second dimension is concerned with technology acceptance (user friendliness, user acceptance, perceived ease-of-use, perceived usefulness, cognitive fit and task-technology fit). The third dimension

that is particularly important to knowledge management systems is concerned with incentive alignment. Incentive alignment includes incentives influencing user behavior and the user's interaction with the system, deterrence of use for personal gain, use consistent with organizational goals and robustness against information misrepresentation (Ba et al., 2001).

Expert Systems

Expert systems can be seen as extreme knowledge management systems on a continuum representing the extent to which a system possesses reasoning capabilities. Expert systems are designed to be used by decision makers who do not possess expertise in the problem domain. The human expert's representation of the task domain provides the template for expert system design. The knowledge base and heuristic rules, which are used to systematically search a problem space, reflect the decision processes of the expert. A viable expert system is expected to perform this search as effectively and efficiently as a human expert. An expert system incorporates the reasoning capabilities of a domain expert and applies them in arriving at a decision. The system user needs little domain specific knowledge in order for a decision or judgment to be made. The user's main decision is whether to accept the system's result (Dillard & Yuthas, 2001).

Decisions or judgments made by an expert system can be an intermediate component in a larger decision context. For example, an audit expert system may provide a judgment as to the adequacy of loan loss reserves that an auditor would use as input for making an audit opinion decision. The fact that the output supports or provides input for another decision does not make the system any less an expert system, according to Dillard and Yuthas (2001). The distinguishing feature of an expert system lies in its ability to arrive at a non-algorithmic solution using processes consistent with those of a domain expert.

Curtis and Cobham (2002) define an expert system as a computerized system that performs the role of an expert or carries out a task that requires expertise. In order to understand what an expert system is, then, it is worth paying attention to the role of an expert and the nature of expertise. It is then important to ascertain what types of expert and expertise there are in business and what benefits will accrue to an organization when it develops an expert system.

For example, a doctor having a knowledge of diseases arrives at a diagnosis of an illness by reasoning from information given by the patient's symptoms and then prescribes medication on the basis of known characteristics of available drugs together with the patient's history. The lawyer advises the client on the likely outcome of litigation based on the facts of the particular case, an expert understanding of the law and knowledge of the way the courts work and interpret this law in practice. The accountant looks at various characteristics of a company's performance and makes a judgment as to the likely state of health of that company.

All of these tasks involve some of the features for which computers traditionally have been noted — performing text and numeric processing quickly and efficiently — but they also involve one more ability: reasoning. Reasoning is the movement from details of a particular case and knowledge of the general subject area surrounding that case to the derivation of conclusions. Expert systems incorporate this reasoning by applying general rules in an information base to aspects of a particular case under consideration (Curtis & Cobham, 2002). Expert systems are computer systems designed to make expert level decisions within complex domains. The business applications of this advanced information technology have been varied and broad reaching, directed toward making operational, management and strategic decisions. Audit expert systems are such systems applied in the auditing environment within the public accounting domain. Major public accounting firms have been quite active in developing such systems, and some argue that these tools and technologies will be increasingly important for survival as the firms strive to enhance their competitive position and to reduce their legal and business risk.

Dillard and Yuthas (2001) find that the implementation and use of these powerful systems raise a variety of significant ethical questions. As public accounting firms continue to devote substantial resources to the development of audit expert systems, dealing with the ethical risks and potential consequences to stakeholders takes on increasing significance. For example, when responsible behavior of an auditor is transferred to an audit expert system, then the system is incapable of being held accountable for the consequences of decisions.

Expert systems can be used in all knowledge management processes described earlier. For knowledge retrieval, content management and information extraction technology represent a useful group of techniques. An example of an expert system for knowledge retrieval is the CORPORUM system. There are three essential aspects of this system (Wang et al., 2001).

First, the CORPORUM system interprets text in the sense that it builds ontologies. Ontologies describe concepts and relationships between them. Ontologies can be seen as the building blocks of knowledge. The system captures ontologies that reflect world concepts as the user of the system sees and expresses them. The ontology produced constitutes a model of a person's interest or concern. Second, the interest model is applied as a knowledge base in order to determine contextual and thematic correspondence with documents available in the system. Finally, the interest model and the text interpretation process drive an information search and extraction process that characterizes hits in terms of both relevance and content. This new information can be stored in a database for future reference.

The CORPORUM software consists of a linguistic component, taking care of tasks such as lexical analysis and analysis at the syntactical level. At the semantic level the software performs word sense disambiguation by describing the context in which a particular word is being used. This is naturally closely related to knowledge representation issues. The system is able to augment meaning structures with concepts that are invented from the text. The core of the system is also able to extract information most pertinent to a specific text for summary creation, extract the so-called core concept area from a text and represent results according to ranking which is based on specified interest for a specific contextual theme set by the user. In addition, the system generates explanations, which will allow the user to make an informed guess about which documents to look at and which to ignore. The system can point to exactly those parts of targeted documents that are most pertinent to a specific user's interest (Wang et al., 2001).

Like all software, CORPORUM is continuously improved and revised. The content management support (CMS) was introduced in 2005 (www.cognit.no). It is based on technology that applies linguistics to characterize and index document content. The ontology based approach focuses on semantics rather than shallow text patterns. The software can be applied for intelligent search and indexing, structure content in portals, annotation of documents according to content, summary and compression of information and extraction of names and relations from text.

Another software introduced in 2005, CORPORUM Best Practice, enables organizations to structure their business and work processes and improve value creation. It is a software tool and associated methodology to build organization-wide Best Practice. In operation, the Web part of the system is a work portal. It embraces an ontology based set of templates that helps to publish work-related documentation. Company resources like check lists, control plans, MS Word templates, images and e-learning material that is relevant for any process or activity described can be linked in where it is useful and intuitive (www.cognit.no).

A final software to be mentioned is CORPORUM Intranet Search & Navigation (SLATEWeb), which indexes and categorizes corporate information sources. Featuring language detection and find-related concept search, this tool lets companies find documents that would otherwise be hard to locate. Categories are available to dynamically classify documents into a taxonomy or group structure (www.cognit.no).

Analysis and design necessary for building an expert system differ from those needed for a traditional data processing or information system. There are three major points of distinction that prevent expert systems development being subsumed under general frameworks of systems development (Curtis & Cobham, 2002):

1. **The subject matter is knowledge and reasoning as contrasted with data and processing:** Knowledge has both form and content, which need investigation.

Form is connected with the mode of representation chosen — for instance, rules, semantic networks or logic. Content needs careful attention, as once the form is selected it is still a difficult task to translate the knowledge into the chosen representation form.

2. **Expert systems are expert/expertise orientated whereas information systems are decision/function/organization directed:** The expert system encapsulates the abilities of an expert or expertise and the aim is to provide a computerized replica of these facilities.
3. **Obtaining information for expert systems design presents different problems from those in traditional information systems design:** Many expert systems rely, partly at least, on incorporating expertise obtained from an expert. Few rely solely on the representation of textbook or rulebook knowledge. It is difficult generally to elicit this knowledge from an expert. In contrast, in designing an information system, the analyst relies heavily on existing documentation as a guide to the amount, type and content of formal information being passed around the system. In the development of an expert system the experts are regarded as repositories of knowledge.

Expert systems and traditional information systems have many significant differences. While processing in a traditional information system is primarily algorithmic, processing in an expert system includes symbolic conceptualizations. Input must be complete in a traditional system, while input can be incomplete in an expert system. Search approach in a traditional system is frequently based on algorithms, while search approach in an expert system is frequently based on heuristics. Explanations are usually not provided in a traditional system. Data and information is the focus of a traditional system, while knowledge is the focus of an expert system.

Expert systems can deliver the right information to the right person at the right time if it is known in advance what the right information is, who the right person to use or apply that information would be, and, what would be the right time when that specific information would be needed. Detection of non-routine and unstructured change in business environment will, however, depend upon sense-making capabilities of knowledge workers for correcting the computational logic of the business and the data it processes (Malhotra, 2002).

Questions for Discussion

1. What kind of knowledge is created in each primary activity of the value shop?

2. How can expert systems support each primary activity of the value shop?
3. Why is efficient and effective interaction between information and knowledge so important for successful knowledge management systems?

List of References

Alavi, M., & Leidner, D. E. (2001). Knowledge management and knowledge management systems: Conceptual foundations and research issues. *MIS Quarterly, 25*(1), 107-136.

Ba, S., Stallaert, J., & Whinston, A. B. (2001). Research commentary: Introducing a third dimension in information systems design — The case of incentive alignment. *Information Systems Research, 12*(3), 225-239.

Bock, G. W., Zmud, R. W., & Kim, Y. G. (2005). Behavioral intention formation in knowledge sharing: Examining the roles of extrinsic motivators, social-psychological forces, and organizational climate. *MIS Quarterly, 29*(1), 87-111.

Curtis, G., & Cobham, D. (2002). *Business information systems: Analysis, design and practice*. Prentice Hall.

Davenport, T. H., & Prusak, L. (1998). *Working knowledge*. Boston, MA: Harvard Business School Press.

Dillard, J. F., & Yuthas, K. (2001). Responsibility ethic for audit expert systems. *Journal of Business Ethics, 30,* 337-359.

Dixon, N. M. (2000). *Common knowledge*. Boston: Harvard Business School Press.

Fahey, L., & Prusak, L. (1998). The eleven deadliest sins of knowledge management. *California Management Review, 40*(3), 265-276.

Grover, V., & Davenport, T. H. (2001). General perspectives on knowledge management: Fostering a research agenda. *Journal of Management Information Systems, 18*(1), 5-21.

Halvorsen, K., & Nguyen, M. (1999, June 17-19). A successful software knowledge base. *Proceedings of the 11th International Conference on Software Engineering and Knowledge Engineering*. Germany: Kaiserslautern.

Hansen, M. T., Nohria, N., & Tierney, T. (1999, March-April). What's your strategy for managing knowledge? *Harvard Business Review*, 106-116.

Housel, T., & Bell, A. H. (2001). *Measuring and managing knowledge*. Irwin, NY: McGraw-Hill.

Kettinger, W. J., Teng, J. T. C., & Guha, S. (1997, March). Business process change: A study of methodologies, techniques, and tools. *MIS Quarterly*, 55-79.

Ko, D. G., Kirsch, L. J., & King, W. R. (2005). Antecedents of knowledge transfer from consultants to clients in enterprise system implementations. *MIS Quarterly, 29*(1), 59-85.

Laudon, K. C., & Laudon, J. P. (2005). *Essentials of management information systems: Managing the digital firm* (6th ed.). Upper Saddle River, NJ: Prentice Hall.

Lin, L., Geng, X., & Whinston, A. B. (2005). A sender-receiver framework for knowledge transfer. *MIS Quarterly, 29*(2), 197-219.

Malhotra, A., Gosain, S., & El Sawy, O. A. (2005). Absorptive capacity configurations in supply chains: Gearing for partner-enabled market knowledge creation. *MIS Quarterly, 29*(1), 145-187.

Moffett, S., & McAdam, R. (2003). Contributing and enabling technologies for knowledge management. *International Journal of Information Technology and Management, 2*(1/2), 31-49.

Nahapiet, J., & Ghoshal, S. (1998). Social capital, intellectual capital, and the organizational advantage. *Academy of Management Review, 23*(2), 242-266.

Nonaka, I., Toyama, R., & Konno, N. (2000). SECI, ba and leadership: A unified model of dynamic knowledge creation. *Long Range Planning, 33*(1), 5-34.

Poston, R.S., & Speier, C. (2005). Effective use of knowledge management systems: A process model of content ratings and credibility indicators. *MIS Quarterly, 29*(2), 221-244.

Ryu, C., Kim, Y. J., Chaudhury, A., & Rao, H. R. (2005). Knowledge acquisition via three learning processes in enterprise information portals: Learning-by-investment, learning-by-doing, and learning-from-others. *MIS Quarterly, 29*(2), 245-278.

Tanriverdi, H. (2005). Information technology relatedness, knowledge management capability, and performance of multibusiness firms. *MIS Quarterly, 29*(2), 311-334.

Wang, K., Hjelmervik, O. R., & Bremdal, B. (2001). *Introduction to knowledge management*. Trondheim, Norway: Tapir Academic Press.

Ward, J., & Peppard, J. (2002). *Strategic planning for information systems*. UK: Wiley.

Wasko, M. M., & Faraj, S. (2005). Why should I share? Examining docial vapital and knowledge vontribution in electronic networks of practice. *MIS Quarterly, 29*(1), 35-57.

Chapter IV

Knowledge Technology Stages

Introduction

Knowledge management systems refer to a class of information systems applied to manage organizational knowledge. These systems are IT applications to support and enhance the organizational processes of knowledge creation, storage and retrieval, transfer and application (Alavi & Leidner, 2001).

The knowledge management technology stage model presented in this chapter is a multistage model proposed for organizational evolution over time. Stages of knowledge management technology is a relative concept concerned with IT's ability to process information for knowledge work. The knowledge management technology stage model consists of four stages (Gottschalk, 2005). When applied to law enforcement in the following chapters, the stages are labeled officer-to-technology, officer-to-officer, officer-to-information and officer-to-application.

Knowledge Technology Stages

Stages of growth models have been used widely in both organizational research and information technology management research. According to King and Teo (1997), these models describe a wide variety of phenomena — the organizational life cycle, product life cycle, biological growth, and so forth . These models assume that predictable patterns (conceptualized in terms of stages) exist in the growth of organizations, the sales levels of products and the growth of living organisms. These stages are: (1) sequential in nature; (2) occur as a hierarchical progression that is not easily reversed; and (3) involve a broad range of organizational activities and structures.

Benchmark variables are often used to indicate characteristics in each stage of growth. A one-dimensional continuum is established for each benchmark variable. The measurement of benchmark variables can be carried out using Guttman scales (Frankfort-Nachmias & Nachmias, 2002). Guttman scaling is a cumulative scaling technique based on ordering theory that suggests a linear relationship between the elements of a domain and the items on a test.

In the following main part of this chapter, a four-stage model for the evolution of information technology support for knowledge management is proposed and empirically tested. The purpose of the model is both to understand the current situation in an organization in terms of a specific stage and to develop strategies for moving to a higher stage in the future. We are concerned with the following question: Do organizations move through various stages of growth in their application of knowledge management technology over time, and is each theoretical stage regarded as an actual stage in an organization?

Stages of Growth Models

Various multistage models have been proposed for organizational evolution over time. These models differ in the number of stages. For example, Nolan (1979) introduced a model with six stages for IT maturity in organizations, which later was expanded to nine stages. Earl (2000) suggested a stages of growth model for evolving the e-business, consisting of the following six stages: external communication, internal communication, e-commerce, e-business, e-enterprise, and transformation. Each of these models identifies certain characteristics that typify firms in different stages of growth. Among these multistage models, models with four stages seem to have been proposed and tested most frequently (King & Teo, 1997).

In the area of knowledge management, Housel and Bell (2001) described a knowledge management maturity model. The knowledge management maturity (KMM) model is used to assess the relative maturity of a company's knowledge management efforts. The KMM model defines the following five levels (Housel & Bell 2001, p. 136):

1. **Level one:** The default stage in which there is low commitment to managing anything other than essential, necessary survival-level tasks. At level one formal training is the main mechanism for learning, and all learning is taken

to be reactive. Moreover, level-one organizations fragment knowledge into isolated pockets that are not explicitly documented.

2. **Level two:** Organizations share only routine and procedural knowledge. Need-to-know is characteristic, and knowledge awareness rises with the realization that knowledge is an important organizational resource that must be managed explicitly. Databases and routine tasks exist but are not centrally compiled or managed.
3. **Level three:** Organizations are aware of the need for managing knowledge. Content fit for use in all functions begins to be organized into a knowledge life cycle, and enterprise knowledge-propagation systems are in place. However, general awareness and maintenance are limited.
4. **Level four:** Characterized by enterprise knowledge-sharing systems. These systems respond proactively to the environment and the quality, currency, utility, and usage of these systems is improved. Knowledge processes are scaled up across the organization, and organization knowledge boundaries become blurred. Benefits of knowledge sharing and reuse can be explicitly quantified, and training moves into an ad hoc basis as the technology infrastructure for knowledge sharing is increasingly integrated and seamless.
5. **Level five:** Where knowledge sharing is institutionalized and organizational boundaries are minimized. Human know-how and content expertise are integrated into a seamless package, and knowledge can be most effectively leveraged. Level-five organizations have the ability to accelerate the knowledge life cycle to achieve business advantage.

According to Kazanjian and Drazin (1989), the concept of stages of growth is widely employed. A number of multistage models have been proposed which assume that predictable patterns exist in the growth of organizations, and that these patterns unfold as discrete time periods, best thought of as stages. These models have different distinguishing characteristics. Stages can be driven by the search for new growth opportunities or as responses to internal crises. Some models suggest that firms progress through stages while others argue that there may be multiple paths through the stages.

Kazanjian (1988) applied dominant problems to stages of growth. Dominant problems imply that there is a pattern of primary concerns that firms face for each theorized stage. In the area of IT maturity, dominant problems can shift from lack of skills to lack of resources to lack of strategy associated with different stages of growth.

Kazanjian and Drazin (1989) argue that either implicitly or explicitly stage of growth models share a common underlying logic. Organizations undergo transformations in their design characteristics, which enable them to face the new tasks or problems that growth elicits. The problems, tasks or environments may differ from model to model, but almost all suggest that stages emerge in a well-defined sequence, so that the solution of one set of problems or tasks leads to the emergence of a new set of problems or tasks that the organization must address. Growth in areas such as IT maturity can be viewed as a series of evolutions and revolutions precipitated by internal crises related to leadership, control and coordination. The striking characteristic of this view is that the resolution of each crisis sows the seeds for the next crisis. Another view is to consider stages of growth as responses to the firm's search for new growth opportunities once prior strategies have been exhausted.

Stages of growth models may be studied through organizational innovation processes. Technological innovation is considered the primary driver of improvements in many businesses today. Information technology represents a complex organizational technology, that is, technology that when first introduced imposes a substantial burden on would-be adopters in terms of the competence needed to use it effectively (Levina & Vaast, 2005). According to Fichman and Kemerer (1997), such technology typically has an abstract and demanding scientific base, it tends to be fragile in the sense that it does not always operate as expected, it is difficult to test in a meaningful way and it is unpackaged in the sense that adopters cannot treat the technology as a black box.

Embodying such characteristics, organizational learning and innovation diffusion theory can be applied to explain stages of growth models. Organizational learning is sometimes placed at the center of innovation diffusion theory through a focus on institutional mechanisms that lower the burden of organizational learning related to IT adoption. Organizations may be viewed, at any given moment, as possessing some bundle of competence related to their current operational and managerial processes. In order to successfully assimilate a new process technology, an organization must somehow reach a state where its bundle of existing competence encompasses those needed to use the new technology (Fichman & Kemerer, 1997).

Innovations through stages of growth can be understood in terms of technology acceptance over time. Technology acceptance has been studied for several decades in information systems research. Technology acceptance models explain perceived usefulness and usage intentions in terms of social influence and cognitive instrumental processes. For example, Venkatesh and Davis (2000) found that social influence processes (subjective norm, voluntariness and image) and cognitive instrumental processes (job relevance, output quality, result demonstrability and perceived ease of use) significantly influenced user acceptance. Similarly, Venkatesh (2000) identified determinants of perceived ease of use, a key driver of technology acceptance, adoption and usage behavior.

Stages of growth models have been criticized for a lack of empirical validity. Benbasat et al. (1984) found that most of the benchmark variables for stages used by Nolan (1979) were not confirmed in empirical studies. Based on empirical evidence, Benbasat et al. (1984) wrote the following critique of Nolan's stage hypothesis:

The stage hypothesis on the assimilation of computing technology provides one of the most popular models for describing and managing the growth of administrative information systems. Despite little formal evidence of its reliability or robustness, it has achieved a high level of acceptance among practitioners. We describe and summarize the findings of seven empirical studies conducted during the past six years that tested various hypotheses derived from this model. The accumulation of evidence from these studies casts considerable doubt on the validity of the stage hypothesis as an explanatory structure for the growth of computing in organizations.

For example, Nolan (1979) proposed that steering committees should be constituted in later stages of maturity. However, an empirical study showed that of 114 firms, 64 of which had steering committees, the correlation between IT maturity and steering committees was not significant. In practice, organizations adopt steering committees throughout the development cycle rather than in the later stages.

Another example is charge-back methods. In a survey, approximately half of the firms used charge-back systems and the other half did not. In the Nolan (1979) structure, as firms mature through later stages, they should have adopted charge-back systems. Yet, in the empirical analysis, there were no significant correlations between maturity indicators and charge-back system usage, according to Benbasat et al. (1984). Benchmark variables such as steering committees and charge-back systems have to be carefully selected and tested before they are applied in survey research.

The concept of stages of growth has created a number of skeptics. Some argue that the concept of an organization progressing unidirectionally through a series of predictable stages is overly simplistic. For example, organizations may evolve through periods of convergence and divergence related more to shifts in information technology than to issues of growth for specific IT. According to Kazanjian and Drazin (1989), it can be argued that firms do not necessarily demonstrate any inexorable momentum to progress through a linear sequence of stages, but rather that observed configurations of problems, strategies, structures and processes will determine firms' progress.

Kazanjian and Drazin (1989) addressed the need for further data-based research to empirically examine whether organizations in a growth environment shift according to a hypothesized stage of growth model, or whether they follow a more random pattern of change associated with shifts in configurations that do not follow such a progression. Based on a sample of 71 firms, they found support for the stage hypothesis.

To meet the criticism of lacking empirical validity, this research presentation describes the careful development, selection and attempted testing of a variety of instrument parts to empirically validate a knowledge management technology stage model.

Guttman Scaling for Cumulative Growth

Benchmark variables in stages of growth models indicate the theoretical characteristics in each stage of growth. The problem with this approach is that not all indicators of a stage may be present in an organization, making it difficult to place the organization in any specific stage.

Guttman scaling is also known as cumulative scaling or scalogram analysis. Guttman scaling is based on ordering theory that suggests a linear relationship between the elements of a domain and the items on a test. The purpose of Guttman scaling is to establish a one-dimensional continuum for a concept in order to measure it. We would like a set of items or statements so that a respondent who agrees with any specific question in the list will also agree with all previous questions. This is the ideal for a stage model — or for any progression. By this we mean that it is useful when one progresses from one state to another, so that upon reaching the higher stage one has retained all the features of the earlier stage (Trochim, 2002).

For example, a cumulative model for knowledge transfer could consist of six stages: awareness, familiarity, attempt to use, utilization, results and impact. Byers and Byers (1998) developed a Guttman scale for knowledge levels consisting of stages by order of learning difficulty. Trochim (2002) developed the following cumulative six-stage scale for attitudes towards immigration:

1. I believe that this country should allow more immigrants in;
2. I would be comfortable with new immigrants moving into my community;
3. It would be fine with me if new immigrants moved onto my block;
4. I would be comfortable if a new immigrant moved next door to me;
5. I would be comfortable if my child dated a new immigrant; and
6. I would permit a child of mine to marry an immigrant.

Guttman (1950) used scalogram analysis successfully during the war in investigating morale and other problems in the United States Army. In scalogram analysis, items are ordered such that, ideally, organizations that answer a given question favorably all have higher ranks than organizations that answer the same question unfavorably. According to Guttman (1950, p. 62), the ranking of organizations provides a general approach to the problem of scaling:

We shall call a set of items of common content a scale if an organization with a higher rank than another organization is just as high or higher on every item than the other organization.

Kline (1998, p. 75) discusses three problems with Guttman scales, which may, he claims, render them of little scientific value:

1. **The underlying measurement model:** The first problem concerns the fact that items correlate perfectly with the total scale score or the attribute being measured. This is unlikely of any variable in the real world. In general terms, it means the measurement model does not fit what is being measured. This is not dissimilar to the difficulty that in psychological measurement it is simply assumed that the attribute is quantitative.
2. **Unidimensionality of the scale:** It has been argued that all valid measuring instruments must be unidimensional. Now the construction of a Guttman scale does not ensure unidimensionality. It would be perfectly possible to take items from different scales, each item of a considerably different level of difficulty, and these could form a Guttman scale. This is because the scaling characteristics of Guttman scales are dependent only on difficulty levels. Thus, Guttman scales may not be unidimensional. The only practical way around the problem is to factor the items first, but then it may prove difficult to make a Guttman scale with so restricted an item pool.
3. **Ordinal measurement:** The construction of Guttman scales may only permit ordinal measurement. This severely restricts the kinds of statistical analyses which can be used with Guttman scales.

These problems also occurred in the empirical tests of the knowledge management technology stage model conducted in Norway and Australia, as is evident in the book by Gottschalk (2005).

The KMT Stage Model

Stages of knowledge management technology is a relative concept concerned with IT's ability to process information for knowledge work. IT at later stages is more useful to knowledge work than IT at earlier stages. The relative concept implies that IT is more directly involved in knowledge work at higher stages, and that IT is able to support more advanced knowledge work at higher stages.

The knowledge management technology (KMT) stage model consists of four stages. The first stage is general IT support for knowledge workers. This includes word processing, spreadsheets and e-mail. The second stage is information about knowledge sources. An information system stores information about who knows what within the firm and outside the firm. The system does not store what they actually know. A

Figure 4.1. The knowledge management technology stage model

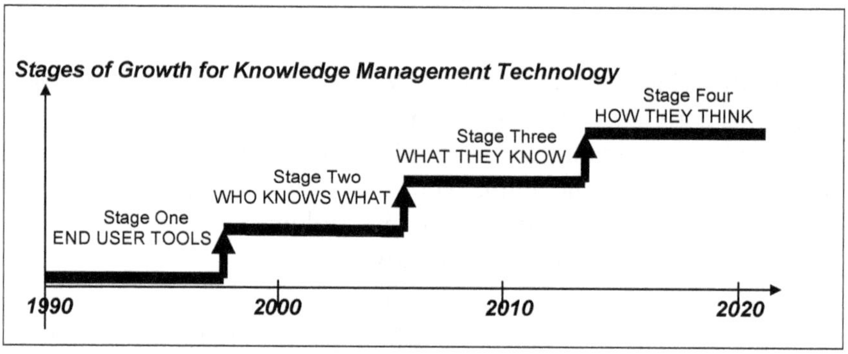

typical example is the company intranet. The third stage is information representing knowledge. The system stores what knowledge workers know in terms of information. A typical example is a database. The fourth, and final, stage is information processing. An information system uses information to evaluate situations. A typical example here is an expert system.

The contingent approach to firm performance implies that Stage One may be right for one firm, while Stage Four may be right for another firm. Some firms will evolve over time from Stage One to higher stages as indicated in Figure 4.1. The time axis ranging from 1990 to 2020 in Figure 4.1 suggests that it takes time for an individual firm and a whole industry to move through all stages. As an example applied later in this chapter, the law firm industry, is moving slowly in its use of information technology.

Stages of IT support in knowledge management are useful for identifying the current situation as well as planning for future applications in the firm. Each stage is described in the following:

1. **Tools for end users:** Made available to knowledge workers. in the simplest stage, this means a capable networked PC on every desk or in every briefcase, with standardized personal productivity tools (word processing and presentation software) so that documents can be exchanged easily throughout a company. More complex and functional desktop infrastructures can also be the basis for the same types of knowledge support. Stage One is recognized by widespread dissemination and use of end-user tools among knowledge workers in the company. For example, lawyers in a law firm will in this stage use word processing, spreadsheets, legal databases, presentation software and scheduling programs.

Stage One can be labeled *end-user-tools* or *people-to-technology* as information technology provides knowledge workers with tools that improve personal efficiency.

2. **Information about who knows what is made available to all people in the firm and to selected outside partners:** Search engines should enable work with a thesaurus, since the terminology in which expertise is sought may not always match the terms the expert uses to classify that expertise.

   According to Alavi and Leidner (2001), the creation of corporate directories, also referred to as the mapping of internal expertise, is a common application of knowledge management technology. Because much knowledge in an organization remains uncodified, mapping the internal expertise is a potentially useful application of technology to enable easy identification of knowledgeable persons.

   Here we find the cartographic school of knowledge management (Earl, 2001), which is concerned with mapping organizational knowledge. It aims to record and disclose who in the organization knows what by building knowledge directories. Often called Yellow Pages, the principal idea is to make sure knowledgeable people in the organization are accessible to others for advice, consultation or knowledge exchange. Knowledge-oriented directories are not so much repositories of knowledge-based information as gateways to knowledge, and the knowledge is as likely to be tacit as explicit.

   Information about who knows what is sometimes called metadata, representing knowledge about where the knowledge resides. Providing taxonomies or organizational knowledge maps enables individuals to rapidly locate the individual who has the needed knowledge more rapidly than would be possible without such IT-based support.

   One starting approach in Stage Two is to store curricula vitae (CV) for each knowledge worker in the firm. Areas of expertise, projects completed and clients helped may, over time, expand the CV. For example, a lawyer in a law firm works on cases for clients using different information sources that can be registered on yellow pages in terms of an intranet.

   At Stage Two, firms apply the personalization strategy in knowledge management. According to Hansen et al. (1999), the personalization strategy implies that knowledge is tied to the person who developed it and is shared mainly through direct person-to-person contact. This strategy focuses on dialogue between individuals: Knowledge is transferred mainly in personal e-mail, meetings and one-on-one conversations.

   The creation of a knowledge network is an important part of Stage Two. Unless specialists can communicate easily with each other across platform types, expertise will deteriorate. People have to be brought together both virtually and face-to-face to exchange and build their collective knowledge in each of the specialty areas. The knowledge management effort is focused on bringing the experts together so that important knowledge can be shared and amplified, rather than on the mapping expertise or benchmarking which occurs in Stage Three.

Electronic networks of practice are computer-mediated discussion forums focused on problems of practice that enable individuals to exchange advice and ideas with others based on common interests. Electronic networks have been found to support organizational knowledge flows between geographically dispersed coworkers and distributed research and development efforts. These networks also assist cooperative open-source software development and open congregation on the Internet for individuals interested in a specific practice. Electronic networks make it possible to share information quickly, globally and with large numbers of individuals (Wasko & Faraj, 2005).

The knowledge network is built on modern communication technology. Advances in portable computers such as palmtops and laptops, in conjunction with wireless network technologies, has engendered mobile computing. In mobile computing environments, users carrying portable computers are permitted to access the shared computing resources on the network through wireless channels regardless of their physical locations.

According to Earl (2001), knowledge directories represent more of a belief in personalized knowledge of individuals than the codified knowledge of knowledge bases and may demonstrate organizational preferences for human, not technology-mediated, communication and exchange. The knowledge philosophy of firms that settle in Stage Two can be seen as one of people connectivity. Consequently, the principal contribution from IT is to connect people via intranets and to help them locate knowledge sources and providers using directories accessed by the intranet. Extranets and the Internet may connect knowledge workers to external knowledge sources and providers.

Communication competence is important at Stage Two. Communication competence is the ability to demonstrate skills in the appropriate communication behavior to effectively achieve one's goals. Communication between individuals requires both the decoding and encoding of messages (Ko et al., 2005). Lin et al. (2005) found that knowledge transfer depends on the completeness or incompleteness of the sender and the receiver's information sets.

The dramatic reduction in electronic communication costs and ease of computer-to-computer linkages has resulted in opportunities to create new channel structures, fueling interest in inter-organizational systems. Inter-organizational systems are planned and managed ventures to develop and use IT-based information exchange systems to support collaboration and strategic alliances between otherwise independent actors. These systems allow for the exchange of information between partners for the purpose of coordination, communication and cooperation (Malhotra et al., 2005).

Stage Two can be labeled *who-knows-what,* or *people-to-people,* as knowledge workers use information technology to find other knowledge workers.

3. **Information from knowledge workers:** Stored and made available to everyone in the firm and to designated external partners. Data mining techniques can be applied here to find relevant information and combine information in data warehouses. On a broader basis, search engines are Web browsers and server software that operate with a thesaurus, since the terminology in which expertise is sought may not always match the terms used by the expert to classify that expertise.

   One starting approach in Stage Three is to store project reports, notes, recommendations and letters from each knowledge worker in the firm. Over time, this material will grow fast, making it necessary for a librarian or a chief knowledge officer (CKO) to organize it. In a law firm, all client cases will be classified and stored in databases using software such as Lotus Notes.

   An essential contribution that IT can make is the provision of shared databases across tasks, levels, entities and geographies to all knowledge workers throughout a process (Earl, 2001). For example, Infosys Technologies — a US$1 billion company with over 23,000 employees and globally distributed operations — created a central knowledge portal called KShop. The content of KShop was organized into different content types, for instance, case studies, reusable artifacts and downloadable software. Every knowledge asset under a content type was associated with one or more nodes (representing areas of discourse) in a knowledge hierarchy or taxonomy (Garud & Kumaraswamy, 2005).

   According to Alavi and Leidner (2001), one survey found that 74% of respondents believed that their organization's best knowledge was inaccessible and 68% thought that mistakes were reproduced several times. Such a perception of failure to apply existing knowledge is an incentive for mapping, codifying and storing information derived from internal expertise.

   However, sifting though the myriad of content available within knowledge management systems can be challenging, and knowledge workers may be overwhelmed when trying to find the content most relevant for completing a new task. To address this problem, system designers often include rating schemes and credibility indicators to improve users' search and evaluation of knowledge management system content (Poston & Speier, 2005).

   According to Alavi and Leidner (2001), one of the most common applications is internal benchmarking, with the aim of transferring internal best practices. To be successful, best practices have to be coded, stored and shared among knowledge workers.

In addition to (1) best practices knowledge within a quality or business process management function, other common applications include: (2) knowledge for sales purposes involving products, markets and customers; (3) lessons learned in projects or product development efforts; (4) knowledge around implementation of information systems; (5) competitive intelligence for strategy and planning functions; and (6) learning histories or records of experience with a new corporate direction or approach (Grover & Davenport, 2001).

In Stage Three, access both to knowledge (expertise, experience and learning) and to information (intelligence, feedback and data analyses) is provided by systems and intranets to operatives, staff and executives. The supply and distribution of knowledge and information are not restricted. Whereas we might say in Stage One, "give knowledge workers the tools to do the job," we now add, "give knowledge workers the knowledge and information to do the job." According to Earl (2001), this is another way of saying that the philosophy is enhancing the firm's capabilities with knowledge flows.

Although most knowledge repositories serve a single function, Grover and Davenport (2001) found that it is increasingly common for companies to construct an internal portal so that employees can access multiple different repositories and sources from one screen. It is also possible and increasingly popular for repositories to contain information as well as pointers to experts within the organization on key knowledge topics. Often called Knowledge Yellow Pages, these systems facilitate contact and knowledge transfer between knowledgeable people and those who seek their knowledge. Stored, codified knowledge is combined with lists of individuals who contributed the knowledge and could provide more detail or background on it.

An enterprise information portal is viewed as a knowledge community. Enterprise information portals are of multiple forms, ranging from Internet-based data management tools that bring visibility to previously dormant data so that their users can compare, analyze and share enterprise information, to a knowledge portal, which enables its users to obtain specialized knowledge related to their specific tasks (Ryu et al., 2005).

Individuals' knowledge does not transform easily into organizational knowledge, even with the implementation of knowledge repositories. According to Bock et al. (2005), individuals tend to hoard knowledge for various reasons. Empirical studies have shown that the greater the anticipated reciprocal relationships are, the more favorable the attitude toward knowledge sharing will be.

Electronic knowledge repositories are electronic stores of content acquired about all subjects for which the organization has decided to maintain knowledge. Such repositories can comprise multiple knowledge bases as well as the mechanisms for acquisition, control and publication of the knowledge.

The process of knowledge sharing through electronic knowledge repositories involves people contributing knowledge to populate repositories (e.g., customer and supplier knowledge, industry best practices and product expertise) and people seeking knowledge from repositories for use (Kankanhalli et al., 2005).

In Stage Three, firms apply the codification strategy in knowledge management. According to Hansen et al. (1999), the codification strategy centers on information technology: Knowledge is carefully codified and stored in knowledge databases and can be accessed and used by anyone. With a codification strategy, knowledge is extracted from the person who developed it, made independent from the person and stored in form of interview guides, work schedules, benchmark data, and so forth, and then searched and retrieved and used by many employees.

According to Grover and Davenport (2001), firms increasingly view attempts to transform raw data into usable knowledge as part of their knowledge management initiatives. These approaches typically involve isolating data in a separate warehouse for easier access and the use of statistical analysis or data mining and visualization tools. Since their goal is to create data-derived knowledge, they are increasingly addressed as part of knowledge management in Stage Three.

Stage Three can be labeled *what-they-know,* or *people-to-docs,* as information technology provides knowledge workers with access to information that is typically stored in documents. Examples of documents are: contracts and agreements, reports, manuals and handbooks, business forms, letters, memos, articles, drawings, blueprints, photographs, e-mail and voicemail messages, video clips, script and visuals from presentations, policy statements, computer printouts and transcripts from meetings.

Sprague (1995) argues that concepts and ideas contained in documents are far more valuable and important to organizations than facts traditionally organized into data records. A document can be described as a unit of recorded information structured for human consumption. It is recorded and stored, so a speech or conversation for which no transcript is prepared is not a document. A document is a snapshot of some set of information that can incorporate many complex information types, exist in multiple places across a network, depend on other documents for information, change as subordinate documents are updated and be accessed and modified by many people simultaneously.

4. **Informati on systems solving knowledge problems:** Made available to knowledge workers and solution seekers. Artificial intelligence is applied in these systems. For example, neural networks are statistically oriented tools that excel at using data to classify cases into one category or another. Another

example is expert systems that can enable the knowledge of one or a few experts to be used by a much broader group of workers requiring the knowledge.

According to Alavi and Leidner (2001), an insurance company was faced with the commoditization of its market and declining profits. The company found that applying the best decision-making expertise via a new underwriting process, supported by a knowledge management system based on best practices, enabled it to move into profitable niche markets and, hence, to increase income.

According to Grover and Davenport (2001), artificial intelligence is applied in rule-based systems, and, more commonly, case-based systems are used to capture and provide access to resolutions of customer-service problems, legal knowledge, new product development knowledge and many other types of knowledge.

Biodiversity is a data-intense science, drawing as it does on data from a large number of disciplines in order to build up a coherent picture of the extent and trajectory of life on earth. Bowker (2000) argues that as sets of heterogeneous databases are made to converge, there is a layering of values into the emergent infrastructure. This layering process is relatively irreversible, and it operates simultaneously at a very concrete level (fields in a database) and at a very abstract one (the coding of the relationship between the disciplines and the production of a general ontology).

Knowledge is explicated and formalized during the knowledge codification phase that took place in Stage Three. Codification of tacit knowledge is facilitated by mechanisms that formalize and embed it in documents, software and systems. However, the higher the tacit elements of the knowledge, the more difficult it is to codify. Codification of complex knowledge frequently relies on information technology. Expert systems, decision support systems, document management systems, search engines and relational database tools represent some of the technological solutions developed to support this phase of knowledge management. Consequently, advanced codification of knowledge emerges in Stage Four, rather than in Stage Three, because expert systems and other artificial intelligence systems have to be applied to be successful.

Stage Four can be labeled *how-they-think,* or *people-to-systems,* where the system is intended to help solve a knowledge problem. The label "how-they-think" does not mean that the systems, as such, think. Rather, it means that the thinking of people has been implemented in the systems.

Stage One is a *technology-centric* stage, while Stage Two is a *people-oriented* stage; Stage Three is a *technology-driven* stage, while Stage Four is a *process-centric* stage. A people-oriented perspective draws from the work of Nonaka et al. (2000). Essential to this perspective of knowledge sharing and knowledge creation is that people create knowledge, and that new knowledge, or the increasing of the extant knowledge base, occurs as a result of human cognitive activities and the effecting of specific knowledge transformations (Wasko and Faraj, 2005). A technology-driven perspective to knowledge management at Stage Three is often centered on the computerized technique of data mining and the many mathematical and statistical methods available to transform data into information and then meaningful knowledge (e.g., Poston & Speier, 2005). A process-centric approach tries to combine the essentials of both the people- and technology-centric and technology-driven perspectives in the earlier stages. It emphasizes the dynamic and ongoing nature of the process, where artificial intelligence might help people understand how to proceed in their tasks. Process-centered knowledge generation is concerned with extraction of critical and germane knowledge in a decision-making perspective (Bendoly, 2003).

The stages of growth model for knowledge management technology is mainly a sequential and accumulative model. However, in practice the model can also be applied in a cyclical mode. For example, when a firm reaches 2020 in Figure 4.1, the firm might return to Stage Three from Stage Four to improve information sources and information access at Stage Three that will improve the performance of systems applied at Stage Four. Therefore, in a short-term perspective, the stages model is sequential, while in a long-term perspective it consists of several cycles.

When companies want to use knowledge in real-time, mission-critical applications, they have to structure the information base for rapid, precise access. A Web search yielding hundreds of documents will not suffice when a customer is waiting on the phone for an answer. Representing and structuring knowledge is a requirement that has long been addressed by artificial intelligence researchers in the form of expert systems and other applications. Now these technologies are being applied within the context of knowledge management. Rule-based systems and case-based systems are used to capture and provide access to customer service problem resolution, legal knowledge, new product development knowledge and many other types of knowledge. Although it can be difficult and labor-intensive to author a structured knowledge base, the effort can pay off in terms of faster responses to customers, lower cost per knowledge transaction and lessened requirements for experienced, expert personnel (Grover & Davenport, 2001).

Expert systems are in Stage Four in the proposed model. Stewart (1997) argues for Stage Two, stating that knowledge grows so fast that any attempt to codify all is ridiculous; but the identities of in-house experts change slowly. Corporate yellow pages should be easy to construct, but it's remarkable how few companies have actually done this. A simple system that connects inquirers to experts saves time, reduces error and guesswork and prevents the reinvention of countless wheels.

What may be stored in Stage Three, according to Stewart (1997), are lessons learned and competitor intelligence. A key way to improve knowledge management is to bank lessons learned — in effect, prepare checklists of what went right and wrong, together with guidelines for others undertaking similar projects. In the area of competitor intelligence, companies need to organize knowledge about their suppliers, customers and competitors.

Information technology can be applied at four different levels to support knowledge management in an organization, according to the proposed Stages of Growth. At the first level, end-user tools are made available to knowledge workers. At the second level, information on who knows what is made available electronically. At the third level, some information representing knowledge is stored and made available electronically. At the fourth level, information systems capable of simulating human thinking are applied in the organization. These four levels are illustrated in Figure 4.2, where they are combined with knowledge management tasks. The entries in the figure only serve as examples of current systems.

One reason for Stage Three emerging after Stage Two is the personalization strategy vs. the codification strategy. The individual barriers are significantly lower with the personalization strategy, because the individual professional maintains the control through the whole knowledge management cycle. According to Disterer (2001), the individual is recognized as an expert and is cared for.

Knowledge management strategies focusing on personalization could be called communication strategies, because the main objective is to foster personal communication between people. Core IT systems with this strategy are yellow pages (directories of experts, who-knows-what systems and people-finder database) that show inquirers

Figure 4.2. Examples of IS/IT in different knowledge management stages

STAGES **TASKS**	**I** **END USER TOOLS** **People-to-technology**	**II** **WHO KNOWS WHAT** **People-to-people**	**III** **WHAT THEY KNOW** **People-to-docs**	**IV** **WHAT THEY THINK** **People-to-systems**
Distribute Knowledge	Word Processing Desktop Publishing Web Publishing Electronic Calendars Presentations	Word Processing Desktop Publishing Web Publishing Electronic Calendars Presentations	Word Processing Desktop Publishing Web Publishing Electronic Calendars Presentations	Word Processing Desktop Publishing Web Publishing Electronic Calendars Presentations
Share Knowledge		Groupware Intranets Networks E-mail	Groupware Intranets Networks E-mail	Groupware Intranets Networks E-mail
Capture Knowledge			Databases Data Warehouses	Databases Data Warehouses
Apply knowledge				Expert systems Neural networks Intelligent agents

who they should talk to regarding a given topic or problem. The main disadvantages of personalization strategies are a lack of standards and the high dependence on communication skills and the will of the professionals. Such disadvantages make firms want to advance to Stage Three. In Stage Three, independence in time among knowledge suppliers and knowledge users is achieved (Disterer, 2002).

When we look for available computer software for the different stages, we find a variety of offers from software vendors. At Stage One, we find Microsoft software such as Word, Outlook, Excel, and Powerpoint. At Stage Two, we find knowledge software such as Knowledger from Knowledge Associates (www.knowledgeassociates.com). The Knowledger 4.0 helps companies collect and categorize internal and external information. It allows individuals to capture information together with its context into a knowledge repository.

At Stage Three, we find Novo Knowledge Base Enterprise (www.novosolutions.com), Confluence the Enterprise Wiki (www.atlassian.com) and Enterprise Edition X1 Technologies (www.x1.com). While Novo's KnowledgeBase provides Web support and documentation solutions, Atlassian's JIRA tracks and managing the issues and bugs that emerge during a project.

Finally, at Stage Four we find DecisionScript by Vanguard Software Corporation (www.vanguardsw.com) and CORVID Knowledge Automation Expert System Software by Xsys (www.exsys.com). Vanguard provides decision-support system software ranging from desktop tools for managing decision-making to server-based systems that help the entire organization work smarter. Vanguard's desktop software, DecisionPro, is designed for managers, consultants and analysts who make business decisions based on uncertain estimates and imperfect information. Exsys argues that their software and services enable businesses, government and organizations to distribute a company's most valuable asset — expert knowledge — to the people who need it, through powerful, interactive Web-enabled systems.

Benchmark variables have been developed for the stages of growth model by Gottschalk (2005). Benchmark variables indicate the theoretical characteristics in each stage of growth. Examples of benchmark variables include trigger of IT, management participation, critical success factor and performance indicator.

Questions for Discussion

1. At what stage of the growth model do you find a data warehouse?
2. What kinds of systems are found at the fourth stage of the growth model?
3. How can systems at different stages support knowledge work in each primary and secondary activity of the value shop?

List of References

Alavi, M., & Leidner, D. E. (2001). Knowledge management and knowledge management dystems: Conceptual foundations and research issues. *MIS Quarterly, 25*(1), 107-136.

Benbasat, I., Dexter, A. S., Drury, D. H., & Goldstein, R. C. (1984). A critique of the stage hypothesis: Theory and empirical evidence. *Communications of the ACM, 27*(5), pp. 476-485.

Bendoly, E. (2003). Theory and support for process frameworks of knowledge discovery and data mining from ERP systems. *Information & Management, 40,* 639-647.

Bock, G. W., Zmud, R. W., & Kim, Y. G. (2005). Behavioral intention formation in knowledge sharing: Examining the roles of extrinsic motivators, social-psychological forces, and organizational climate. *MIS Quarterly, 29*(1), 87-111.

Bowker, G. C. (2000). Biodiversity datadiversity. *Social Studies of Science, 30*(5), 643-683.

Byers, C., & Byers, W. A. (1998, June). Sliding scale: A technique to optimize the assessment of knowledge level through ordering theory. *Annual Conference of the International Personnel Management Association Assessment Council,* Chicago. Retrieved from http://www.ipmaac.org/conf98/byers.pdf

Disterer, G. (2001). Individual and social barriers to knowledge transfer. *Proceedings of the 34th Hawaii International Conference on Systems Sciences (HICSS-34),* IEEE, USA.

Disterer, G. (2002). *Veränderungen der rechtsberufe durch neue technologien. Beispiel: wissensmanagement bei anwälten.* Arbeidspapier 68/2002, Fachbereich Wirtschaft, Fachhochschule Hannover, Germany.

Earl, M. J. (2000). Evolving the e-nusiness, *Business Strategy Review, 11*(2), 33-38.

Earl, M. J. (2001). Knowledge management strategies: Toward a taxonomy. *Journal of Management Information Systems, 18*(1), 215-233.

Fichman, R. G., & Kemerer, C. F. (1997). The assimilation of software process innovations: An organizational learning perspective. *Management Science, 43*(10), 1345-1363.

Frankfort-Nachmias, C., & Nachmias, D. (2002). Research methods in the social sciences (5th ed.). UK: Arnold.

Garud, R., & Kumaraswamy, A. (2005). Vicious and virtuous circles in the management of knowledge: The case of Infosys Technologies. *MIS Quarterly, 29*(1), 9-33.

Gottschalk, P. (2005). *Strategic knowledge management technology.* Hershey, PA, USA: Idea Group Publishing.

Grover, V., & Davenport, T. H. (2001). General perspectives on knowledge management: Fostering a research agenda. *Journal of Management Information Systems, 18*(1), 5-21.

Guttman, L. (1950). The basis for scalogram analysis. In S. A. Stouffer, L. Guttman, E. A.Suchman, P. F.Lazardsfeld, S. A.Star, & J. A. Clausen (Eds.), *Measurement and prediction*, studies in social psychology in World War II, Volume IV, (pp. 60-90), USA: Princeton University Press.

Hansen, M.T., Nohria, N., & Tierney, T. (1999, March-April). What's your strategy for managing knowledge? *Harvard Business Review*, 106-116.

Housel, T., & Bell, A. H. (2001). *Measuring and managing knowledge*. McGraw-Hill Irwin, New York.

Kankanhalli, A., Tan, B. C. Y., & Wei, K. K. (2005). Contributing knowledge to electronic knowledge repositories: An empirical investigation. *MIS Quarterly, 29*(1), 113-143.

Kazanjian, R. K. (1988). Relation of dominant problems to stages of growth in technology-based new ventures. *Academy of Management Journal, 31*(2), 257-279.

Kazanjian, R. K., & Drazin, R. (1989). An empirical test of a stage of growth progression model. *Management Science, 35*(12), 1489-1503.

King, W. R., & Teo, T. S. H. (1997). Integration between business planning and information systems planning: Validating a stage h ypothesis. *Decision Sciences, 28*(2), 279-307.

Kline, P. (1998). *The new psychometrics: Science, psychology and measurement.* UK: Routledge.

Ko, D. G., Kirsch, L. J., & King, W. R. (2005). Antecedents of knowledge transfer from consultants to clients in enterprise system implementations. *MIS Quarterly, 29*(1), 59-85.

Levina, N., & Vaast, E. (2005). The emergence of boundary spanning competence in practice: Implications for implementation and use of information systems. *MIS Quarterly, 29*(2), 335-363.

Lin, L., Geng, X., & Whinston, A. B. (2005). A sender-receiver framework for knowledge transfer. *MIS Quarterly, 29*(2), 197-219.

Malhotra, A., Gosain, S., & El Sawy, O. A. (2005). Absorptive capacity configurations in supply chains: Gearing for partner-enabled market knowledge creation. *MIS Quarterly, 29*(1), 145-187.

Nolan, R. L. (1979, March-April). Managing the crises in data processing. *Harvard Business Review*, pp. 115-126.

Nonaka, I., Toyama, R., & Konno, N. (2000). SECI, ba and leadership: A unified model of dynamic knowledge creation. *Long Range Planning, 33*(1), 5-34.

Poston, R. S., & Speier, C. (2005). Effective use of knowledge management systems: A process model of content ratings and credibility indicators. *MIS Quarterly, 29*(2), 221-244.

Sprague, R. H. (1995, March). Electronic document management: Challenges and opportunities for information systems managers. *MIS Quarterly*, 29-49.

Stewart, T. A. (1997). *Intellectual capital: The new wealth of organizations*. UK: Nicholas Brealy Publishing.

Trochim (2002). *Guttman Scaling*. Retrieved from http://trochim.human.cornell.edu/kb/scalgutt.htm

Venkatesh, V. (2000). Determinants of perceived ease of use: Integrating control, intrinsic motivation, and emotion into the technology acceptance model. *Information Systems Research, 11*(4), 342-365.

Venkatesh, V., & Davis, F. D. (2000). A theoretical extension of the technology acceptance model: Four longitudinal field studies. *Management Science, 46*(2), 186-204.

Wasko, M. M., & Faraj, S. (2005). Why should I share? Examining social capital and knowledge contribution in electronic networks of practice. *MIS Quarterly, 29*(1), 35-57.

Zack, M. H. (1999). Developing a knowledge strategy. *California Management Review, 41*(3), 125-145.

Section II: Knowledge-Intensive Value Shop Activities

The second section of this book is concerned with knowledge management systems in information technology management. Chapter V is about knowledge management in electronic business, and chapter VI is about knowledge management in IT outsourcing relationships. Chapter VII presents a reversal of Chapter VI that some organizations are doing: They move from outsourcing to insourcing. It is interesting to see how outsourcing theories and frameworks can be mirrored to discuss the termination strategy of insourcing. Finally, in this second part of the book, IT governance is presented.

The idea of this second section is to link knowledge management to the field of MIS (management information systems), where successful IT applications and management are dependent on the systematic and continuous availability of knowledge. Knowledge management is often the most important factor for e-business success. Similarly, knowledge management is required for an outsourcing relationship to survive and improve over time. When outsourcing is mirrored into insourcing, the importance of knowledge management emerges. In IT governance, where the use of information technology is linked to strategy and decision rights, knowledge management is again a critical success factor.

Chapter V

E-Business Knowledge

Introduction

This chapter documents some of the links between e-business and knowledge management systems that might be explored in future empirical research. The research propositions in this chapter illustrate the need for a contingent approach to knowledge management systems that are to support e-business. Knowledge management systems successfully supporting and improving e-business performance have to satisfy several requirements. First, they have to support the chosen e-business model(s). Second, they have to cause improvements through redesign of e-business processes. Furthermore, in terms of codification strategy, more advanced stages of knowledge management technology will be more powerful and successful. These are some of the research propositions presented in this chapter, which represents a rich knowledge base for future empirical studies.

The main objective of a knowledge management system (KMS) is to support the creation, transfer and application of knowledge in organizations (Feng et al., 2005). Electronic business (e-business) is marketing, buying, selling, delivering, servicing and paying for products, services and information across networks linking an enterprise and its prospects, customers, agents, suppliers, competitors, allies and complementors (Weill & Vitale, 2002).

Several researchers emphasize the important role of knowledge management systems in e-business (e.g., El Sawy, 2001; Fahey et al., 2001; Holsapple & Singh, 2000; Malhotra, 2000, 2002; Plessis & Boon, 2004; Singh et al., 2004; Tsai et al., 2005). Garud and Kumaraswany (2005) argue that knowledge has emerged as a strategically significant resource for the firm. Accordingly, knowledge creation and transfer become key factors to gain and sustain a competitive advantage (Sambamurthy & Subramani, 2005). E-business processes can create additional customer value through knowledge creation with customers (Kodama, 2005).

Plessis and Boon (2004) argue that the knowledge management value proposition with reference to e-business is not very different from the generic value proposition of knowledge management. There are, however, subtle differences in focus and areas of importance, for example, the scale of knowledge sharing over geographical, divisional and organizational boundaries, consolidation of knowledge to provide one view of organizational knowledge and the role of technology in providing platforms for sharing knowledge internal and external to the organization.

We are in an era of knowledge economy and knowledge-based competition. In this era, an organization must be able to secure various types of knowledge assets and maximize their strategic value. To do so, many organizations have begun to reexamine and rearrange their business strategies, process, information technologies and organizational structures from a knowledge perspective. This task has been complicated in the Internet-enabled business environment. With the advances of Internet-related technologies, the intricacy of the worldwide economy is fast changing. Lower cost, customized product/service and quick response have become the critical success factors for most businesses. More and more competing firms are adopting collaborative work and knowledge management to create and maintain these critical success factors. Collaborative works within an organization and between organizations can not only share the work based on each member's expertise, but also achieve a seamless information flow among the collaborative team members. Such sharing of knowledge has proven to improve productivity and decision quality of the participating organizations. In order to have effective collaborative work in electronic business, the management of knowledge is essential and critical (Li & Lai, 2005).

The purpose of this chapter is to discuss how knowledge management systems (KMS) can support and improve electronic business (e-business). Based on a review of the research literature, research propositions are developed in this chapter. Each proposition is concerned with relationships between knowledge management and e-business. Perspectives from the research literature applied in this chapter include: drivers for digital transformation, evolving the e-business, e-business models, e-business process redesign, value configurations, knowledge transfer, knowledge management technology stages and intangible assets.

This chapter makes an important contribution to the field, as there has been a missing link between know-what and know-how concerning cause and effect relationships between knowledge management systems and e-business. Know-what has stressed the importance of knowledge in e-business. This chapter makes a much-needed contribution to know-how, as it explores how knowledge management systems and e-business performance influence each other.

In the past, developing e-business systems were often given priority according to technical criteria rather than business imperatives. From the viewpoint of knowledge management, Tsai et al. (2005) found that e-business is an important process by which an enterprise wisely uses knowledge to create value. However, many companies use models of knowledge management that suit the industrial epoch. Far from benefiting these organizations, Malhotra (2000) found that these outdated models seriously undermine their information strategies. Their research findings make the following research propositions even more important to future successful support from knowledge management systems in e-business.

Knowledge Management as Key for E-Business Competitiveness

Allard and Holsapple (2002) argue that knowledge is the lifeblood of e-commerce. Processes and activities involved in e-commerce are technological means that contribute to managing knowledge.

There are several definitions of e-commerce, depending on perspective or view. The trading view focuses on market-based activities, such as buying and selling through utilization of computer-based technologies. The information exchange view holds that information itself may be a commodity that is bought and sold. The activity view acknowledges a wide range of business activities beyond trading that are accomplished with the use of technology. The effects view concentrates on the goals, reasons and effects of e-commerce. The value chain view revolves around the value configuration of a value chain.

Because e-commerce involves knowledge-based organizations, and because the manipulation of knowledge is the essence of what networked computer systems do, Allard and Holsapple (2002) argue that the definition of e-commerce should include knowledge as a basic concept, as well as noting the existence of technology that facilitates its manipulation. Therefore, they suggest the following definition (p. 21):

An approach to achieving business goals in which technology for managing knowledge enables or facilitates execution of activities in and across value chains as well as supporting decision making underlying those activities.

This definition is presented both for e-commerce in a broad sense and for e-business. In this perspective, e-business refers to the way businesses are adapting to the new environment by utilizing electronic technologies in their activities as well as the mindset they adopt to make these changes.

Here, technology for managing knowledge lies in the core of the e-business definition. In order to systematically study, develop and apply such technology for e-business, it is essential to adopt a perspective that gives a fairly comprehensive portrayal of KM. Several types of knowledge are involved in the conduct of e-business. Descriptive knowledge reflects know-what, because it describes the state of a specific domain including the items themselves, the relationships among those items and the context in which they exist. Procedural knowledge refers to know-how, because it specifies the steps by which a task can be accomplished or a goal can be achieved. Reasoning knowledge focuses on know-why, because it identifies why things happen the way they do in specific situations and the conditions that allow certain conclusions to be drawn.

A practical example of the KM view of e-commerce is Ernie, an online consulting system from Ernst & Young (ernie.ey.com). Organizations that cannot afford in-house experts or consultants on a topic can use the Ernie Web site to acquire needed knowledge. Ernie serves as a direct interface to Ernst & Young knowledge in such forms as proprietary databases, professional resources and human knowledge providers (Holsapple & Singh, 2000).

When a client accesses Ernie to acquire knowledge, he or she is asked to formulate a question, assign it to a consultation category and offer some background information as to how results are to be used. If a client has trouble formulating a question or simply does not know what to ask, he or she can access an extensive FAQ database for help. Based on the question submitted, Ernie selects relevant knowledge from knowledge repositories that may be human- or computer based. The knowledge selected could be descriptive (know-what), procedural (know-how) or reasoning (know-why), in the form of advice suggesting what to conclude about various circumstances. If needed knowledge is not in an available repository, Ernie may attempt to generate it (Holsapple & Singh, 2000).

Knowledge management as a key for e-business competitiveness is not just a question of supplying knowledge to a client, as illustrated in the case of Ernie. Often, a consulting firm also has something to learn from its clients. Fosstenløkken et al. (2003) studied knowledge development through client interaction. They identified several knowledge development processes. The process of professionals learning from clients occurs when sophisticated, knowledgeable clients are considered a key factor in knowledge development.

An interesting example of knowledge management as a key for e-business competitiveness is Web services for knowledge management in e-marketplaces, as discussed by Singh et al. (2004). A common strategic initiative of organizations engaged in e-business is the development of synergistic relations with collaborating value-chain partners to deliver their value proposition to customers. This requires the transparent flow of problem-specific knowledge to partner organizations over highly integrated information systems. Transparent exchange of information and knowledge across collaborating organizations requires technological foundations for integrating business processes using software architectures built upon industry standards. The unambiguously interpretable flow of knowledge to inform online business processes is a challenging task with significant competitive benefits for organizations that take technical initiatives. Infomediary organizations can serve the e-business need for exchange of knowledge and information through value-added knowledge services to participating firms in the value chain through intelligent software systems integrated with Web service architecture.

In this context, Singh et al. (2004) define knowledge services as the exchange of problem domain-specific knowledge to inform decision activities of specific e-business processes, facilitated by an infomediary using intelligent software systems and a Web services architecture. Knowledge services are provided by the knowledge agent to users, through their agents, over heterogeneous information platforms using Web services as a foundation.

Malhotra (2002) studied ways of enabling knowledge exchanges for e-business communities, arguing that unsuccessful attempts of e-commerce models have increased interest in online communities as critical enablers of e-business success. Collaborative technologies need to account for the dual nature of knowledge management processes. The dual nature defines KM in terms of KM by design (such as corporate intranets) and KM by emergence (such as communities of practice). Applications of traditional collaborative systems such as group support systems, shared calendaring applications and document management systems belong to KM by design.

Malhotra (2002) argues that there is a greater need for understanding how collaborative technology applications can support KM by emergence that is necessary for business model innovation. KM by emergence is characterized by creation of cultural infrastructure for enabling continuous knowledge sharing, knowledge renewal and knowledge creation.

Malhotra (2000) also posits that advancing IT strategy to Internet time is needed. Strategic IT planning must focus on knowledge management for e-business performance. There is a need for synergy between capabilities of advanced information technologies and human creativity and innovation to realize the agility demanded by emerging business environments.

Knowledge in Drivers for Digital Transformation

The digital transformation of traditional businesses is occurring. New information technologies, such as broadband networks, mobile communications and the Internet, have well known, but often unrealized, potential to transform businesses and industries. The key to success is understanding how and when to apply technologies. According to Andal-Ancion et al. (2003), companies should look at 10 specific drivers to help determine their best strategy.

The ten drivers are: (1) electronic deliverability; (2) information intensity; (3) customizability; (4) aggregation effects; (5) search costs; (6) real-time interface; (7) contracting risk; (8) network effects; (9) standardization benefits; and (10) missing competencies. These drivers determine the competitive advantage of deploying new information technology (Andal-Ancion et al., 2003):

1. **Electronic deliverability:** Some products have a large component that can be delivered electronically. Airline companies, for instance, enable customers to book reservations online, after which the confirmations and tickets can be delivered efficiently through e-mail.
2. **Information intensity:** Nearly all products have some information content, but the amount varies dramatically. Cars come with volumes of operating instructions; ice cream bought from a street vendor comes with no information except the name of its flavor.
3. **Customizability:** New information technologies allow many companies to tailor an overall offering to the specific needs and preferences of individual customers. In the past, newspapers were a one-size-fits-all product. Today, online editions can be customized to include just the news and information that a particular subscriber is likely to want.
4. **Aggregation effects:** Products and services differ in the way they can be aggregated or combined. In the past, UK customers dealt with a bank for their savings and day-to-day transactions, a building society for their mortgages, an insurance agent for life and property policies and an independent financial adviser for their investments. Thanks to new IT (and deregulation), institutions can offer customers bundled services (with attractive interest rates and better terms) to handle all those financial needs through one account.
5. **Search costs:** Before the advent of companies like Amazon.com, finding an out-of-print book could require considerable time and effort. Now, the Web provides people with vast amounts of information, regardless of their location or time zone, lowering the search costs for finding exactly the product or service they want.
6. **Real-time interface:** A real-time interface is necessary for companies and customers dealing with important information that changes suddenly and unpredictably. A good example is online trading, in which rapid fluctuations in the stock market can be devastating for those who lack instantaneous access to that information.

7. **Contracting risk:** Buying new books online has little contracting risk for customers: Prices are relatively low; specifying the exact titles is straightforward; the physical quality of books varies little; and merchants are motivated to fulfill each order efficiently to encourage customers to return. Buying cars online is a completely different matter: Prices are substantially higher; specifying the exact product is difficult; the physical quality of the vehicles can be different from the descriptions on a Web site; and sellers do not typically expect repeat purchases, so they might be less motivated to deliver premium service.
8. **Network effects:** In many industries, the utility of a good or service increases with the number of people who are using it. A key benefit of using Microsoft Office, for instance, is that the suite of programs is ubiquitous in the business world, enabling people to share Word, PowerPoint and Excel documents easily.
9. **Standardization benefits:** New IT has enabled companies to synchronize and standardize certain processes, resulting in greater efficiency in business-to-business transactions as well as increased convenience for customers. On the Web, the extensible markup language (XML) family of standards significantly increases a company's ability to broadcast a message to a wide audience in the most efficient and powerful way.
10. **Missing competencies:** New IT can facilitate company alliances in which partners use each other to fill in missing competencies.

We find that nine out of ten drivers, except contracting risk, derive from one of three knowledge processes: knowledge creation, storage and retrieval and transfer. According to Alavi and Leidner (2001), organizations have four knowledge processes: creation, storage and retrieval, transfer and application. Knowledge application is not included in the drivers for digital transformation because knowledge application represents the procedures that turn knowledge management processes into drivers of the digital transformation.

The remaining nine drivers are either about interaction between a company and its external environment or about characteristics of products in terms of goods and services. For example, aggregation effects are only obtainable if a knowledge management system records the customer's demand for bundled services. Hence, our first research proposition:

P1: Successful applications of drivers for digital transformation are dependent upon knowledge management systems.

Knowledge in Evolving the E-Business

For most firms, becoming an e-business is an evolutionary development (Porter, 2001). Earl (2000) has described a typical six-stage journey that corporations are likely to experience. The six stages are not necessarily definite periods of evolution, as companies may have activities at several neighboring stages at the same time. The six stages are illustrated in Figure 5.1.

While the early stages of evolution are concerned with simple applications of Internet technology for external and internal communication, later stages involve redesigning business processes and introducing new electronic business processes.

P2: Knowledge management systems are more important in later stages of evolving the e-business.

Knowledge in E-Business Models

A business model can be defined as the method by which a firm builds and uses its resources to offer its customers better value than its competitors and to take money

Figure 5.1. Stages of growth model for evolving the e-business

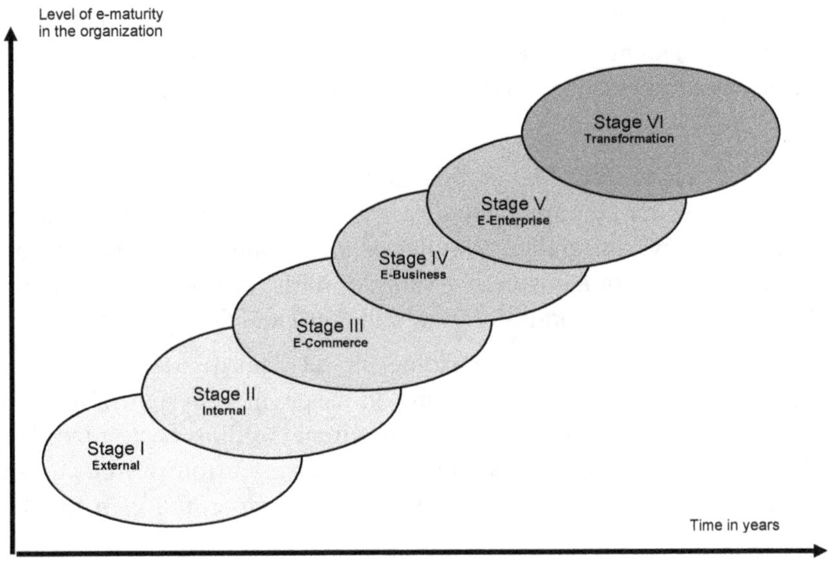

doing so. Weill and Vitale (2002) identified eight atomic e-business model, each of which describes the essence of conducting business electronically: (1) direct to customer, (2) full-service provider, (3) whole of enterprise, (4) intermediary, (5) shared infrastructure, (6) virtual community, (7) value net integrator and (8) content provider.

In their discussion of IT infrastructure services needed for each e-business model, Weill and Vitale (2002) identified knowledge management system as the most critical service for content providers. A content provider is a firm that creates and provides content (information, products or services) in digital form to customers.

P3: Knowledge management systems are more important in content providers than in other atomic e-business models.

A business model details how a firm makes money now and how it plans to do so in the long run. The model is what enables a firm to have a sustainable competitive advantage, to perform better than its rivals in the long term. A business model can be conceptualized as a system that is made up of components, linkages between the components and dynamics.

Weill and Vitale (2001) define an e-business model as a description of the roles and relationships among a firm's consumers, customers, allies and suppliers that identifies the major flows of product, information, and money, and the major benefits to participants. There are many different ways to describe and classify e-business models. Weill and Vitale (2001) proposed that there are a finite number of atomic e-business models, each of which captures a different way to conduct e-business. Firms can combine atomic e-business models as building blocks to create tailored e-business models and initiatives, using their competencies as their guide. Weill and Vitale (2001) identified the following eight atomic e-business models, each of which describes the essence of conducting business electronically:

1. **Direct to customer:** The distinguishing characteristic of this model is that buyer and seller communicate directly, rather than through an intermediary. The seller may be a retailer, a wholesaler or a manufacturer. The customer may be an individual or a business. Examples of the direct-to-customer model are Dell Computer Corporation (www.dell.com) and Gap, Inc. (www.gap.com).

   Infrastructure. The direct-to-customer model requires extensive electronic connection with the customer, including online payment systems. Many direct-to-customer implementations include an extranet to allow customized Web pages for major B2B customers. Operating a direct-to-customer e-business requires significant investment in the equivalent of the store: the Web site. Direct-to-customer businesses spend millions of dollars developing easy-to-navigate and easy-to-use Web sites with the goal of improving the B2B or B2C shopping experience online. Lands' End (www.landsend.com) has devised a feature by which women can build and store a three-dimensional model of themselves to "try on" clothes electronically. In their field research, Weill and Vitale (2001) found that firms with e-business initiatives containing the direct-to-customer e-business model needed and were investing more heavily in three areas of infrastructure services: application infrastructure, communications and IT management.

Direct-to-customer firms particularly needed payment transaction processing to process online customer payments, enterprise-wide resource planning (ERP) to process customer transactions, workflow infrastructure to optimize business process performance, communication network services linking all points in the enterprise to each other and the outside world (often using TCP/IP protocol), the installation and maintenance of workstations and local area networks supporting the large number of people required to operate a direct-to-customer model and service-level agreements between the business and the IT group or outsourcer to ensure, monitor and improve the systems necessary for the model.

Sources of revenue. The main source of revenue in the direct-to-customer model is usually direct sales to customers. Supplemental revenues come from advertising, the sale of customer information and product placement fees.

Critical success factors. Critical success factors are the things a firm must do well to flourish. The following list shows the critical success factors for the direct-to-customer model: create and maintain customer awareness, in order to build a critical mass of users to cover the fixed cost of building an electronic presence; reduce customer acquisition costs; strive to own the customer relationship and understand individual customer needs; increase repeat purchases and average transaction size; provide fast and efficient transaction processing, fulfillment and payment; ensure adequate security for the organization and its customers; and provide interfaces that combine ease of use with richness of experience, integrating multiple channels.

2. **Full-service provider:** A firm using the full-service provider model provides total coverage of customer needs in a particular domain, consolidated via a single point of contact. The domain could be any major area of customer needs requiring multiple products and services, for example, financial services, health care or industrial chemicals. The full-service provider adds value by providing a full range of products, sourced both internally and externally, and consolidating them using the channel chosen by the customer. Examples of the full-service provider are the Prudential Advisor (www.prusec.com) and GE Supply Company (www.gesupply.com).

Infrastructure. Virtually all businesses aspire to getting 100% of their customers' business, or at least to getting as much of that business as they can profitably handle. Yet the number of full-service providers remains small. Part of the reason for this is the required infrastructure. The missing piece of infrastructure in many businesses is often a database containing information about the customer and the products that the customer owns. Without owning these data, a provider does not own the customer relationship, and therefore some of the customer's transactions are likely to take place directly with other providers. All of the important interactions with customers occurring across any channel or business unit must be recorded in the firmwide customer database.

Weill and Vitale (2001) identified in their field research databases and data warehouses as some of the most important infrastructure services associated with the full-service provider model. Other important infrastructure services included the following: the ability to evaluate proposals for new information systems initiatives to coordinate IT investments across a multi-business-unit firm with the goal of a single point of contact for the customer; centralized management of IT infrastructure capacity to integrate across multiple business units within the firm and third-party providers (the full-service provider model is not readily workable if each business unit optimizes its own IT needs); installation and maintenance of workstations and local area networks to operate the online business linking all the business units and third-party providers; electronic support for groups to coordinate the cross-functional teams required to implement this model; and the identification and testing of new technologies to find cost-effective ways to deliver this complex business model to the customer across multiple channels.

Sources of revenue. A full-service provider gains revenues from selling its own products and those of others, and possibly also from annual membership fees, management fees, transaction fees, commissions on third-party products, advertising or listing fees from third-party providers and fees for selling aggregated data about customers.

Critical success factors. One important critical success factor is the brand, credibility and trust necessary for a customer to look to the firm for its complete needs in an area. Another is owning the customer relationship in one domain and integrating and consolidating the offering of many third parties into a single channel or multiple channels. A third factor is owning more of the customer data in the relevant domain than any other player. A final factor is enforcement of policies to protect the interests of internal and external suppliers, as well as customers.

3. **Whole of enterprise:** The single point of contact for the e-business customer is the essence of the whole-of-enterprise atomic business model. Although many of this model's breakthrough innovations have occurred in public-sec-

tor organizations, the model is applicable in both the for-profit and the public sectors. An example of this model is the Australian state of Victoria with its Business Channel (www.business.channel.vic.gov.au) and Health Channel (www.betterhealth.vic.gov.au).

Infrastructure. For the whole-of-enterprise model, infrastructure needs to link the different systems in the various business units and provide a firmwide perspective for management. The field research by Weill and Vitale (2001) revealed that the following infrastructure services are the most important for implementing this model: centralized management of infrastructure capacity to facilitate integration and capture economies of scale; identification and testing of new technologies to find new ways to integrate the often different systems in many business units into a single point of customer contact; management of key data independent of applications and the creation of a centralized repository for firmwide information; electronic means of summarizing data from different applications and platforms to manage the complexity arising from a single point of contact for multiple business units; development of an ERP service to process the transactions instigated by customers interacting with several different business units, often requiring consolidating or linking several ERPs in the firm; payment transaction processing, either on a firmwide basis or by linking several systems across the business units; large-scale data-processing facilities to process transactions from multiple business units, often centralized to achieve economies of scale; and integrated mobile computing applications, which provide another channel to the customer.

Sources of revenue. In the for-profit sector, revenues are generated by provision of goods and services to the customer by the business units. There may also be the opportunity to charge an annual service or membership fee for this level of service. In the government sector, the motivation is usually twofold: improved service and reduced cost. Service to the community is improved through continuous, round-the-clock operation and faster service times. Sharing more infrastructure and eliminating the need to perform the same transaction in multiple agencies can potentially reduce government costs.

Critical success factors. The following list details the critical success factors for the whole-of-enterprise model: changing customer behavior to make use of the new model, as opposed to the customer continuing to interact directly with individual units; reducing costs in the individual business units as the direct demands on them fall, and managing the transfer pricing issues that will inevitably arise; altering the perspective of the business units to take an enterprise-wide view, which includes broad product awareness, training, and cross-selling; in the integrated implementation, reengineering the business processes to link into life events at the front end and existing legacy processes and systems at the back end; and finding compelling and practical life events that customers can use as triggers to access the enterprise.

4. **Intermediaries:** These are portals, agents, auctions, aggregators and other intermediaries. E-business is often promoted as an ideal way for sellers and buyers to interact directly, shortening old-economy value chains by disintermediating some of their members. Yet some of the most popular sites on the Internet, both for consumers and for business users, are in fact intermediaries — sites that stand between the buyer and the seller. The services of intermediaries include search (to locate providers of products and services), specification (to identify important product attributes), price (to establish the price, including optional extras such as warranties), sale (to complete the sales transaction, including payment and settlement), fulfillment (to fulfill the purchase by delivering the product or service), surveillance (to conduct surveillance of the activities of buyers and sellers in order to report aggregate activity and prices and to inform and regulate the market) and enforcement (to enforce proper conduct by buyers and sellers). Examples of intermediaries are electronic malls, shopping agents, specialty auctions, electronic markets, electronic auctions and portals.

    Infrastructure. Intermediaries generate value by concentrating information and bringing together buyers and sellers, operating entirely in space and thus relying on IT as the primary infrastructure. Weill and Vitale (2001) found in their field interviews that the most important infrastructure services for firms pursuing the intermediary atomic business model are the following: knowledge management, including knowledge databases and contact databases that enable the codification and sharing of knowledge in this highly information-intensive business; enforcing Internet and e-mail policies to ensure proper and consistent use of electronic channels to buyers, sellers and intermediaries; workstation networks to support the products and services of this all-electronic business model; centralized management of e-business applications, ensuring consistency and integration across product offerings; information systems planning to identify the most effective uses of IT in the business; and information systems project management to ensure that business value is achieved from IT investments.

    Sources of revenue. An intermediary may earn revenues from buyers, sellers or both. Sellers may pay a listing fee, a transaction fee, a sales commission or some combination. Similarly, buyers may pay a subscription fee, a success fee or a sales commission.

    Critical success factors. The chief requirement for survival as an intermediary is sufficient volume of usage to cover the fixed costs of establishing the business and the required infrastructure. Attracting and retaining a critical mass of customers is therefore the primary critical success factor. Another important critical success factor is building up infrastructure just quickly enough to meet demand as it increases.

5. **Shared infrastructure:** The firm provides infrastructure shared by its owners. Other suppliers, who are users of the shared infrastructure but not owners, can also be included. Customers who access the shared infrastructure directly are given a choice of suppliers and value propositions. The owner and the nonowner suppliers are generally represented objectively. In some situations, goods or services flow directly from the shared infrastructure to the customer. In other situations, a message is sent by the shared infrastructure to the supplier, who then completes the transaction by providing the goods or services to the customer.

   An example illustrating the features of the shared-infrastructure business model is the system from 2000 by America's largest automakers, some of their dealers and IBM, Motorola and Intel. The initiative was named Covisint (collaboration vision integrity). General Motors, Ford and DaimlerChrysler see stronger potential benefits from cooperating on supply-chain logistics than from competing.

   Infrastructure. The shared-infrastructure business model requires competitors to cooperate by sharing IT infrastructure and information. This level of cooperation requires agreement on high-level IT architectures as well as operational standards for applications, data communications and technology. Effective implementation of the shared-infrastructure model also requires enforcement of these standards, and most shared-infrastructure models have a joint committee to set and enforce standards. Another role of these committees is to implement the policies of the shared infrastructure about what information, if any, is shared and what information is confidential to partner firms. Weill and Vitale (2001) found in their field research that the most important infrastructure services required by firms implementing the shared-infrastructure atomic business model all concerned architectures and standards: specification and enforcement of high-level architectures for data, technology, applications, communications and work that are agreed to by alliance partners, and specification and enforcement of detailed standards for the high-level architectures.

   Sources of revenue. Revenues can be generated both from membership fees and from transaction fees. The alliance may be run on a nonprofit basis or on a profit-making basis. Not-for-profit shared infrastructures are typically open to all eligible organizations and distribute any excess revenues back to their members. The for-profit models are typically owned by a subset of the firms in a given segment, which split up any profits among themselves.

   Critical success factors. Critical success factors for the shared-infrastructure model include the following: no dominant partner that gains more than any other partner; an unbiased channel and objective presentation of product and service information; critical mass of both alliance partners and customers;

management of conflict among the ongoing e-business initiatives of the alliance partners; compilation and delivery of accurate and timely statements of the services and benefits provided to each member of the alliance; and interoperability of systems.

6. **Virtual community:** Virtual communities deserve our attention, and not only because they are the clearest, and perhaps the last, surviving embodiment of the original intent of the Internet. By using IT to leverage the fundamental human desire for communication with peers, virtual communities can create significant value for their owners as well as for their members. Once established, a virtual community is less susceptible to competition by imitation than any of the other atomic business models. In this business model, the firm of interest — the sponsor of the virtual community — sits in the center, positioned between members of the community and suppliers. Fundamental to the success of this model is that members are able, and in fact are encouraged, to communicate with one another directly. Communication between members may be via e-mail, bulletin boards, online chat, Web-based conferencing or other computer-based media, and it is the distinguishing feature of this model. Examples of this model are Parent Soup (www.parentsoup.com), a virtual community for parents, and Motley Fool (www.motleyfool.com), a virtual community of investors.

   Infrastructure. Virtual communities depend on IT to exist. In particular, the creation and continual enhancement of an Internet site is essential if a virtual community is to survive. Many virtual-community sites include not just static content and links, but also tools of interest to potential members. Weill and Vitale (2001) found in their field research that the infrastructure services most important for the virtual-community business model are the following: training in the use of IT for members of the community; application service provision (ASP) to provide specialized systems virtual communities need such as bulletin boards, e-mail, and ISP access; IT research and development, including infrastructure services for identifying and testing new technologies and evaluating proposals for new information systems initiatives; information systems planning to identify and prioritize potential investments in IT in this completely online business; and installation and maintenance of workstations and local area networks to support the electronic world of the virtual community.

   Sources of revenue. A sponsoring firm can gain revenue from membership fees, direct sales of goods and services, advertising, click-throughs and sales commissions. A firm sponsoring a virtual community as an adjunct to its other activities may receive no direct revenue at all from the virtual community. Rather, the firm receives less tangible benefits, such as customer loyalty and increased knowledge about its customer base.

Critical success factors. The critical success factors for a virtual community include finding and retaining a critical mass of members; building and maintaining loyalty with an appropriate mix of content and features; maintaining privacy and security for member information; balancing commercial potential and members' interests; leveraging member profile information with advertisers and merchants; and engendering a feeling of trust in the community by its members.

7. **Value net integrator:** Traditionally, most firms operate simultaneously in two worlds: the physical and the virtual. In the physical world, goods and services are created in a series of value-adding activities connecting the supply side (suppliers, procurement and logistics) with the demand side (customers, marketing and shipping). In the virtual world, information about the members of the physical value chain are gathered, synthesized and distributed along the virtual value chain. E-business provides the opportunity to separate the physical and virtual value chains. Value net integrators take advantage of that split and attempt to control the virtual value chain in their industries by gathering, synthesizing and distributing information. Value net integrators add value by improving the effectiveness of the value chain by coordinating information. A pure value net integrator operates exclusively in the virtual value chain, owning a few physical assets. To achieve the gathering, synthesizing and distributing of information, the value net integrator receives and sends information to all other players in the model. The value net integrator coordinates product flows form suppliers to allies and customers. The product flows from the suppliers to customers may be direct or via allies. In some cases the value net integrator may sell in formation or other products to the customer. The value net integrator always strives to own the customer relationship with the other participants in the model, thus knowing more about their operations than any other player. Examples of value net integrators are Seven-Eleven Japan and Cisco Systems (www.cisco.com).

   Infrastructure. The value net integrator succeeds in its role by gathering, synthesizing and distributing information. Thus, for a value net integrator, data and electronic connectivity with allies and other players are very important assets. Field research carried out by Weill and Vitale (2001) suggests that the most important infrastructure services required for a value net integrator include middleware, linking systems on different platforms across the many players in the value net; a centralized data warehouse that collects and summarizes key information for analysis from decentralized databases held by several players across the value net; specification and enforcement of high-level architectures and detailed standards for data, technology, applications and communications to link together different technology platforms owned by different firms; call centers to provide advice and guidance for partners and allies in getting the most value from the information provided by the value net generator; and high-capacity communications network service to support the high volumes of information flowing across the value net.

Sources of revenue. In this model, revenues are generally earned by fees or margins on the physical goods that pass through the industry value net. By using information about consumers, the value net integrator is able to increase prices by meeting consumer demand. By using information about suppliers, the value net integrator reduces costs by cutting inventories and lead times.

Critical success factors. The critical success factors for the value net integrator atomic business model are as follows: reducing ownership of physical assets while retaining ownership of data; owning or having access to the complete industry virtual value chain; establishing a trusted brand recognized at all places in the value chain; operating in markets where information can add significant value, such as those that are complex, fragmented, regulated, multilayered, inefficient and large with many sources of information; presenting the information to customers, allies, partners and suppliers in clear and innovative ways that provide value; and helping other value chain participants capitalize on the information provided by the value net integrator.

8. **Content provider:** Like many terms associated with e-business, content provider has different meanings to different people. We define content provider as a firm that creates and provides content (information, products or services) in digital form to customers via third parties. The physical-world analogy of a content provider is a journalist, recording artist or stock analyst. Digital products such as software, electronic travel guides and digital music and video are examples of content. A virtual-world example of a content provider is weather forecasters such as Storm Weather Center (www.storm.no).

   Infrastructure. Content providers must excel at tailoring and manipulating their core content to meet the specific needs of customers. Content providers must categorize and store their content in well-indexed modules so it can be combined and customized to meet customer needs via a wide variety of channels. Customers and transactions tend to be relatively few, at least compared with the number of end consumers and their transactions. Often complex and unique IT infrastructures are needed to support the particular needs of the specialized professionals employed by the content provider. Field research by Weill and Vitale (2001) identified the most important infrastructure services: multimedia storage farms or storage area network infrastructures to deal with large amounts of information; a strong focus on architecture, including setting and enforcing standards particularly for work; detailed data architectures to structure, specify, link manipulate and manage the core intellectual property; workstation network infrastructures to enable the fundamentally online business of a content provider; and a common systems development environment to provide compatible and integrated systems, ensuring the systems can provide content across multiple channels to their customers.

Sources of revenue. The primary source of revenue for a content provider is fees from its third parties or allies. These fees may be based on a fixed price per month or year, or on the number of times the third party's own custom-

Figure 5.2. E-business models integration with customers and partners

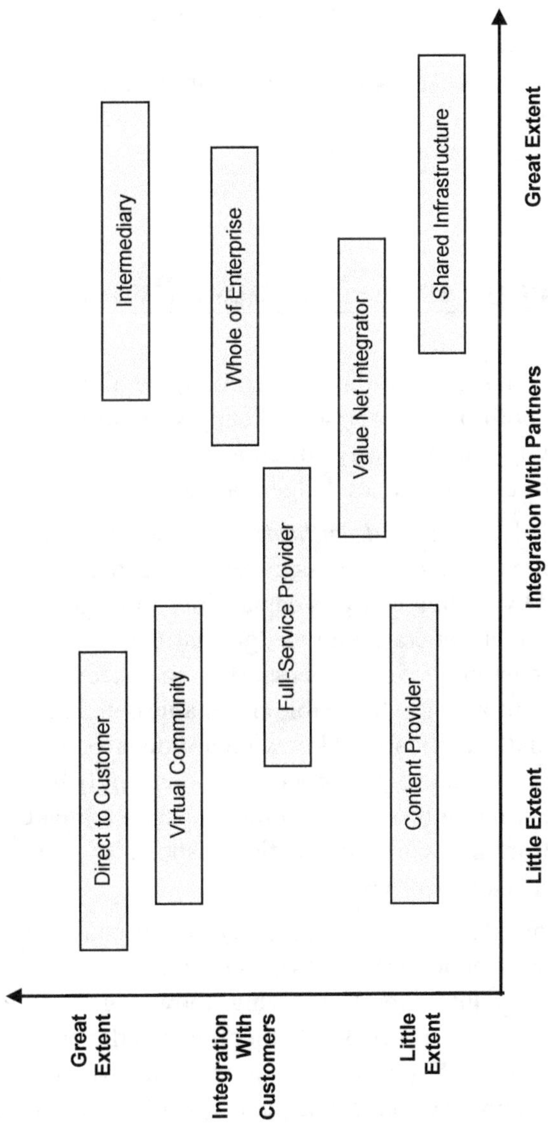

ers access the content. In some situations, the fees paid are lower for content branded by the provider, and higher for unbranded content, which then appears to the customer to have been generated by the third party itself.

Critical success factors. To succeed, a content provider must provide reliable, timely content in the right format and at the right price. The critical success factors for this model include the following: branding (the value of content is due in part to reputation), recognized as best in class (the business of content provision will be global and competitive) and network (establishing and maintaining a network of third parties through which content is distributed.

One way of comparing these e-business models is to analyze to what extent each model creates integration with customers and to what extent each model creates integration with partners. As illustrated in Figure 5.2, the business model of direct-to-customer creates mainly integration with customers, while Shared Infrastructure creates mainly integration with partners.

Knowledge in E-Business Process Redesign

Business process redesign for e-business involves rethinking and redesigning business processes at both the enterprise and supply chain level to take advantage of Internet connectivity and new ways of creating value. El Sawy (2001) developed three principles for changing knowledge management around a process.

The first principle of *analyze and synthesize* emphasizes the interactive analysis and synthesis capabilities around a process to generate added value. A business process can be redesigned by adding analysis capabilities through software and intelligent information feeds that generate knowledge that can become a major part of the deliverable to the customer of the process. Both the executors and the customers of the process become more knowledgeable and enable better outcomes for the process. This tactic is especially applicable in knowledge-intensive processes where the value proposition to the customers of the process is increasingly based on providing good advice to customers and improving customer capacity to make intelligent decisions that they are comfortable with. This tactic is especially powerful in the provision of complex products and services.

The second principle of *connect, collect, and create* emphasizes growing intelligently reusable knowledge around the process through all who touch it. A business process can be redesigned by intelligently growing knowledge around it through all the people who take part in the process, whether they are the doers of the process or the customers of the process. Superior executions of the process are identified and best practices and tips shared so that subsequent executions are improved. Eventually, this learning can be used to further change the design of the process. A knowledge management infrastructure can be viewed as having three aspects: a connect aspect, a collect aspect and a create aspect. The connect aspect includes ways of mapping connections to sources of expertise and specific knowledge. This is often done in a yellow pages format that lists sources of expertise around a process sorted by topic and issue rather than by job function or job title. The collect aspect includes ways of capturing and organizing knowledge so that it can be intelligently reused. This is done by setting up procedures through which knowledge can be captured, classified, filtered and synthesized in meaningful ways that are directly relevant to the business process and can add value to its execution. The create aspect of knowledge management infrastructure involves setting up technological platforms, institutional forms and physical or virtual spaces for shared knowledge creation. It allows the people who are involved with the process to exchange knowledge and jointly create it through informal conversations and ad hoc exchanges that contribute to expertise needed around a process, whether to execute it, reconfigure it or improve it. A successful knowledge management infrastructure needs to have all three connect, collect and create aspects.

The third and final knowledge principle of *personalize* emphasizes making the process intimate with the preferences and habits of participants. A business process can be redesigned by increasing its capabilities to learn about the preferences and habits of the customers and doers of the process. A knowledge base with customer profiles and preferences is built based on repeat executions of the process. The knowledge about preferences is then used in subsequent process executions to make the outcomes of the process more personalized to the customer or doer of the process. Taking advantage of this knowledge can add value to the process participants and speed up the process on subsequent executions. This knowledge can also be used to provide new process offerings and to redesign the process.

Three core business processes have to be redesigned for e-business: customer relationship management (CRM), supply chain management (SCM) and product development management (PDM). According to Fahey et al. (2001), the customer relationship management process is concerned with the creation and leveraging of linkages and relationships to external marketplace entities, especially channels and end users. Know-what needed for CRM includes answers to questions such as: What are your customers' wants and needs? Know-how needed includes answers to questions such as: How can you collect relevant information that can be used to accurately fulfill customer wants and needs? Know-why needed includes answers to questions such as: Why is the CRM process changing?

The supply chain management process is concerned with the acquisition of solution inputs and their transformation into desired customer benefits, while the product development management process is concerned with the development of new customer solutions and/or the invigoration of existing solutions. As for CRM, both SCM and PDM need answers to know-what, know-how and know-why questions

(Fahey et al., 2001). Know-what is describing current and future e-business change and its implications for strategy, operations and competitive context. Know-how is what an organization does or must do to adapt and leverage e-business for strategic and operational purposes. Know-why is knowledge about why e-business is evolving as it is and what accounts for its impacts on competitive context, strategy and operations.

Both El Sawy (2001) and Fahey et al. (2001) emphasize the importance of knowledge management systems in e-business process redesign.

P4: Successful redesign of business processes for e-business is dependent upon knowledge management systems.

Fahey et al. (2001) define e-business as an ability of a firm to electronically connect, in multiple ways, many organizations, both internal and external, for many different purposes. It allows an organization to execute electronic transactions with any individual entity along value creation processes. Along the value chain, for instance, suppliers, logistics providers, wholesalers, distributors, service providers and end customers, electronic transactions are executed. Managers can build pockets of know-what around specific domains of current, emerging and potential change. Managers can learn from stories to identify critical know-how, for example, how customers could interact electronically with various entities in the value creation. Considerations of know-what and know-why about a competitive context years into the future unavoidably give rise to know-why issues, such as why are customers shifting from one form of electronic connection to another. Knowledge management emphasizes design and interaction among groups to enable the development and sharing of information, ideas and perspectives on how e-business can transform processes.

Knowledge in Value Configurations

To comprehend the value that information technology provides to organizations, we must understand the way a particular organization conducts business and how information systems affect the performance of various component activities within the organization. A value configuration describes how value is created in a company for its customers. Value chain, value shop and value network are alternative value configurations.

P5: Knowledge management systems are more important in value shops doing e-business than in value chains or value networks doing e-business.

The value shop is a company that creates value by solving unique problems for customers and clients (Stabell & Fjeldstad, 1998). Knowledge is the most important resource, and reputation is critical to firm success. A value shop is characterized by five primary activities: problem finding and acquisition, problem solving, choice, execution and control and evaluation, as illustrated again in Figure 5.3.

Understanding how firms differ is a central challenge for both theory and practice of e-business. For a long time, the value chain was the only value configuration known to e-managers, focusing on supply chain management. Recently, the problem-solving activities of value shops have emerged as more knowledge-intensive and hence in greater need of knowledge management systems.

One of the e-business models presented earlier, the content provider, has the value configuration of a value shop. It solves the knowledge needs of its customers by applying knowledge management systems such as data warehouses, electronic storage farms, case-based reasoning and expert systems.

The value shop moves through the stages of growth for knowledge management systems to take advantage of end-user tools, communication networks, information sources and intelligent applications. These systems are at the core of the e-business in the value shop, while they are mostly only supporting and improving business processes in value chains and value networks.

Figure 5.3. Value configuration of value shop

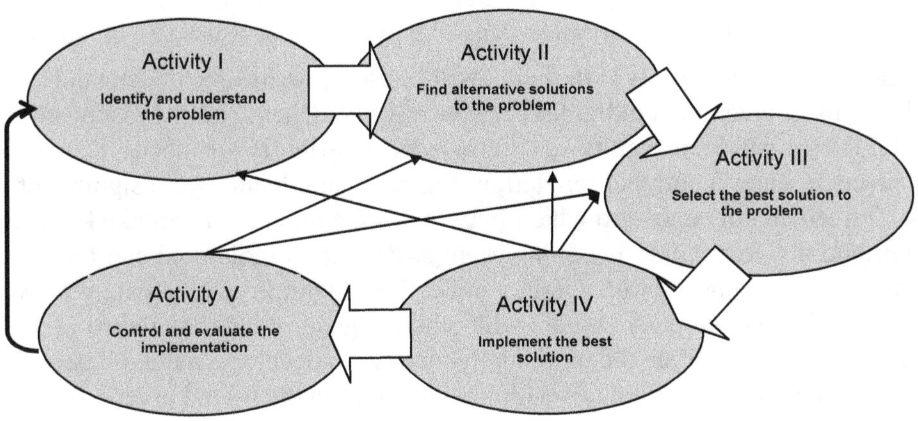

Knowledge Transfer in E-Business

According to Alavi and Leidner (2001), organizations have four knowledge processes: creation, storage and retrieval, transfer and application. In electronic business, the requirements on a KMS to support creation, storage and retrieval and application of knowledge will not change dramatically. However, the requirements concerning support for knowledge transfer will change significantly.

P6: Knowledge transfer is the most important knowledge process in e-business.

The problem of knowledge transfer is often faced by individuals or groups once an appropriate source of knowledge is located (Sambamurthy & Subramani, 2005). The new challenge lies mostly in how to transfer knowledge between the vendor and the customer. The environment for communication in certain areas of a company will be drastically altered as a consequence of e-business. Knowledge, which earlier could be transferred between people in the same organization, now has to be transferred across two different organizations. Consequently, the channels for transferring knowledge will be more formal and impersonal. A KMS has to find a way to transfer all relevant information through more formal and impersonal channels or to find a new creative way of making the communication channel less formal and/or impersonal.

According to Ko et al. (2005), some researchers have defined knowledge transfer as dyadic exchanges of organizational knowledge between a source and a recipient unit in which the identity of the recipient matters. Others also focus on the resulting changes to the recipient. For example, knowledge transfer can be seen as the process through which one unit (e.g., group, department or division) is affected by the experience of another. Other researchers go further by arguing that knowledge transfer occurs when a contributor shares knowledge that is used by an adopter.

Knowledge is in the heads of individuals. Therefore, we have to understand knowledge transfer in terms of individual behavior (Liu & Chen, 2005). Wasko and Faraj (2005) examined social capital and knowledge contribution in electronic networks of practice. They found that reputation, centrality and tenure were significant factors influencing the extent to which individuals are motivated to make knowledge contributions. Reputation is an important asset that an individual can leverage to achieve and maintain status within a collective. Centrality is the extent to which the individual is in regular contact with others; the more individuals are in regular contact with one another, the more likely they are to develop a habit of cooperation and act collectively. Individuals with longer tenure in the shared practice are likely to better understand how their expertise is relevant, and are thus better able to share knowledge with others.

Given the multiple objectives of knowledge transfer in e-business, only a sophisticated operationalization of the concept will suffice here. Since the literature suggests that key aspects of knowledge transfer are knowledge movement and the application of knowledge, Ko et al. (2005) captured both of these ideas by defining knowledge transfer as the communication of knowledge from a source so that it is learned and applied by a recipient. Knowledge is taken to be transferred when learning takes place and when the recipient understands the intricacies and implications associated with that knowledge so that he or she can apply it. For example, the vendor may transfer knowledge about testing procedures to the client, who learns and applies this knowledge, as evidenced by clients developing test scripts, conducting tests of individual modules and running integration tests to ascertain whether data are correctly passed between two or more modules.

Similarly, Inkpen and Tsang (2005) define knowledge transfer as a process through which one relationship partner is affected by the experience of another. Knowledge transfer manifests itself through changes in knowledge or performance of the recipient unit.

Stages of Knowledge Management Technology

The ambition level using knowledge management systems can be defined in terms of stages of knowledge management technology as illustrated again in Figure 5.4.

Stage I is labeled "end-user-tool systems" or "person-to-technology," as information technology provides people with tools that improve personal efficiency. Examples are word processing, spreadsheets and presentation software. Stage II is labeled "who-knows-what systems" or "person-to-person," as people use information technology to find other knowledge workers. Examples are yellow-page systems, CVs and intranets. Stage III is labeled "what-they-know systems" or "person-to-information," as information technology provides people with access to information that is typically stored in documents. Examples of documents are contracts, articles, drawings, blueprints, photographs, e-mails, presentations and reports (Kankanhalli et al., 2005). Stage IV is labeled "how-they-think systems" or "person-to-system," in which the system is intended to help solve a knowledge problem. Examples are expert systems and business intelligence.

In e-business, the electronic exchange of information requires that information is stored in electronic form. Therefore, we suggest the following proposition:

P7: Higher stages of knowledge management technology provide more effective support for electronic business.

In a different empirical setting, Ko et al. (2005) studied antecedents of knowledge transfer from consultants to clients in enterprise system implementations. They found that the greater the shared understanding between a consultant and a client, the greater the knowledge transfers. Furthermore, the greater the absorptive capacity of a client, the more intrinsically motivated the client and the consultant, the more credible the consultant, the greater a client's communication decoding competence, the greater a consultant's communication encoding competence and the greater the knowledge transfer.

The stages of growth model can be interpreted as alternative strategies, where the alternative strategies are person-to-tools strategy, person-to-person strategy, person-to-information strategy and person-to-system strategy. A comparison of these four alternatives can be made to the classification into personalization vs. codification strategy by Hansen et al. (1999). In this comparison, S tages I and II represent personalization, while Stages III and IV represent codification.

Figure 5.4. Stages of growth model for knowledge management technology

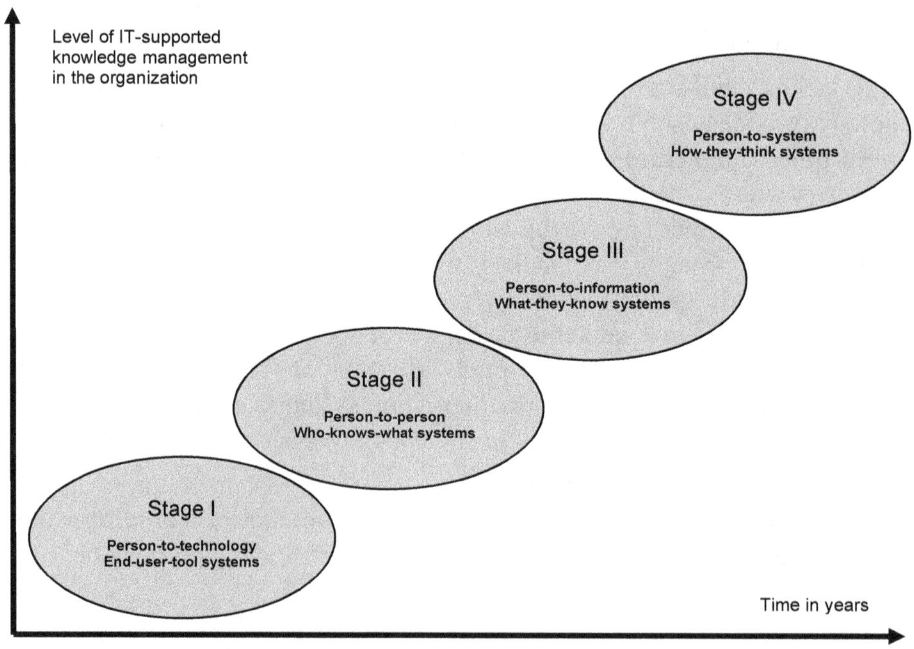

P8: The codification strategy for knowledge management systems is more effective for e-business than the personalization strategy.

Stages of knowledge management technology is a relative concept concerned with IT's ability to process information for knowledge work. IT at later stages is more useful to knowledge work than IT at earlier stages. The relative concept implies that IT is more directly involved in knowledge work at higher stages, and that IT is able to support more advanced knowledge work at higher stages.

Some benchmark variables for the stages of growth model for knowledge management technology are listed in Figure 5.5.

In knowledge management technology, the intelligence continuum is an interesting concept. The intelligence continuum is a collection of key tools, techniques and processes. Examples are data mining and business intelligence. Taken together, they represent a system for refining the data raw material stored in data marts and/or data warehouses and maximizing the value and utility of these data assets for any organization. The first component at one end of the continuum is a generic information system, which generates data that is then captured in a data repository.

In order to maximize the value of the data and use it to improve processes, the techniques and tools of data mining, business intelligence and analytics must be applied to the data warehouse. Once applied, the results become part of the data set that are reintroduced into the system and combined with the other inputs of people, processes and technology to develop an improvement continuum. Thus, the intelligence continuum includes the generation of data, the analysis of these data to provide a diagnosis and the reintroduction into the cycle as a prescriptive solution. In terms of the stages of growth model, a prescriptive solution from a system typically occurs at Stage IV.

An important application in the intelligence continuum is data mining, which occurs at Stage III. Due to the immense size of the data sets in most organizations, computerized techniques are essential to help knowledge workers understand relationships and associations between data elements. Data mining is closely associated with databases and shares some common ground with statistics since both strive toward discovering structure in data. However, while statistical analysis starts with some kind of hypothesis about relationships in data, data mining does not. Data mining deals with heterogeneous databases, data sets and data fields. Data mining, then, is the nontrivial process of identifying valid, novel, potentially useful and ultimately understandable patterns from data.

Another technology-driven technique like data mining connected to knowledge management is the area of business intelligence and the now newer term of business analytics. The business intelligence term has become synonymous with an umbrella

Figure 5.5. Characteristics of each stage of knowledge management technology

	Stage I Tools	**Stage II Sources**	**Stage III Contents**	**Stage IV Systems**
Trigger of IT for KM	Knowledge worker's need for end-user tools	Organization's need for information	Knowledge worker's need for information automation	Organization's need for work automation
Focus when applying IT to KM	Make IT available to knowledge workers	Enable knowledge sharing among knowledge workers	Enable sharing of electronic information among knowledge workers	Replace knowledge workers by information systems
Dominating strategy for KMT	Tool strategy	Flow strategy	Stock strategy	Growth strategy
Attitude toward IT in KM	Skeptics	Conservatives	Early adopters	Innovators

description for a wide range of decision-support tools, some of which target specific user audiences. At the bottom of the business intelligence hierarchy are extractions and formatting tools, which are also known as data-extraction tools. The next level is known as warehouses and marts.

Human intelligence tools form the final level in the hierarchy and involve human expertise, opinions and observations recorded to create a knowledge-based repository. These tools are the very top of business intelligence and represent business analytics specifically focused on analytic aspects. Here we find rule-based expert systems, fuzzy logic and system dynamics modeling.

System dynamics modeling is an analytical tool to study business dynamics. The modeling process starts with sketching a model, then writing equations and specifying numerical quantities. Numerical quantities can be the result of data mining. Next, the model is simulated with simulation output automatically saved as a dataset. Finally, the simulation data can be examined with analysis tools to discover the dynamic behavior of variables in the model. Normal model construction follows a pattern of create, examine and recreate, iterating until the model meets users' requirements. Debugging (making a model simulate properly) and model analysis (investigating output behavior) both play a part in refining the model. Reality check is another analytic to aid in the construction and refinement of a system dynamics model (Sterman, 2000).

Wickramasinghe and Silvers (2003) suggest that the orthopedic room represents an ideal environment for the application of a continuous improvement cycle that is dependent upon the intelligence continuum. For those patients with advanced degeneration of their hips and knees, arthtroplasty of the knee and hip represent an opportunity to regain their function. Before the operation ever begins in the operating room, there are a large number of interdependent individual processes that must be completed. Each process requires data input and produces a data output such as patient history, diagnostic test and consultations. The interaction between these data elements is not always maximized in terms of operating room scheduling and completion of the procedure.

The entire process of getting a patient to the operating room for a surgical procedure can be represented by three distinct phases: preoperative, intraoperative and post-operative. The diagnostic evaluation of data and the re-engineering of each of the potentially deficient processes will lead to increased efficiency. For example, many patients are allergic to the penicillin family of antibiotics that are often administered preoperative in order to minimize the risk of infection. For those patients who are allergic, a substitute drug requires a 45 minute monitored administration time as opposed to the much shorter administration time of the default agent. Since the antibiotic is only effective when administered prior to starting the procedure, this often means that a delay is experienced (Wickramasinghe & Silvers, 2003).

Intangible Assets in E-Business

Knowledge management systems support knowledge transfer within and between intangible assets. One approach to defining intangible assets in e-business is to distinguish between three families; the external structure, the internal structure and the individual structure, as proposed by Sveiby (2001).

The external structure consists of the external environment. For the customer, the vendor is in the external environment. For the vendor, the customer is in the external environment. The internal structure consists of models, regulations and information systems. The individual structure consists of staff competence. Knowledge transfer occurs within and between these three structures.

P9: The external structure is the most important structure for successful knowledge transfer in e-business.

Knowledge transfer from individual to external structure concerns how the organization's employees transfer their knowledge to the organization's environment. The strategic question in relation to e-business would then be: How can employees use KMS to transfer knowledge and improve the competence of their customer? This is illustrated in Figure 5.6 by arrow 1.

Knowledge transfer from external structure to individuals occurs when employees learn from the customer, where the strategic question would be: How can the customer improve the competence of the employees using KMS? This is illustrated in Figure 5.6 by arrow 2.

Knowledge transfer within the external structure concerns what the customers tell each other about the service of an organization. For example, Kodama and Ohiro (2005) studied customer value creation through customer-as-innovator approach in the case of video processing LSI development. The strategic question would be: How can we secure and enable knowledge exchange between customers using KMS so our customers improve their competence?

Knowledge transfer from the external to internal structure concerns what knowledge the organization can gain from the external environment and how the learning can be converted into action. The strategic question would be: How can competence from the customers improve the organization's systems, processes and products, using KMS?

Knowledge transfer from internal to external structure is the counterpart from the above, and the strategic question would then be: How can the organization's systems, tools and processes improve the competence of the customers using KMS?

One of the key authors in the area of intellectual capital is Sveiby (2001), who has developed a knowledge-based theory of the firm to guide in strategy formulation. He distinguished between three families of intangible assets with the outsourcing vendor. The *external structure* family consists of relationships with customers and suppliers and the reputation (image) of the firm. Some of these relationships can be converted into legal property such as trademarks and brand names. The value of such assets is primarily influenced by how well the company solves its customers' problems, and there is always an element of uncertainty here.

The *internal structure* family consists of patents, concepts, models and computer and administrative systems. These are created by the employees and are thus generally owned by the organization. The structure is partly independent of individuals and some of it remains even if a large number of the employees leave. *The individual competence* family consists of the competence of the professional staff, the experts, the research and development people, the factory workers, sales and marketing — in short, all those that have a direct contact with customers and whose work is within the business idea.

Competence is a term introduced here. Competence can be defined as the sum of knowledge, skills and abilities at the individual level. With this definition, we say that

Figure 5.6. Knowledge transfer within and between families of intangible assets

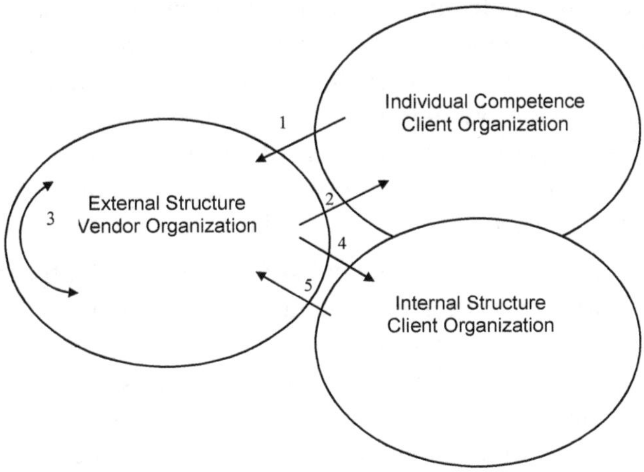

knowledge is part of competence, and competence is part of intellectual capital.

These three families of intangible resources have slightly different definitions when compared to the capital elements. The external structure seems similar to relational capital; the internal structure seems similar to structural capital, while the individual competence seems similar to human capital.

To appreciate why a knowledge-based theory of the firm can be useful for strategy formulation, Sveiby (2001) considers some of the features that differentiate knowledge transfers from tangible goods transfers. In contrast to tangible goods, which tend to depreciate in value when they are used, knowledge grows when used and depreciates when not used. Competence in a language or a sport requires huge investments in training to build up — managerial competence takes a long time on-the-job to learn. If one stops speaking the language it gradually dissipates.

Given three families of intangible assets, it is possible to identify nine knowledge transfers. These knowledge transfers can occur within a family and between families as illustrated in Figure 1.13. Each of the nine knowledge transfers in Figure 1.13 can be explained as follows (Sveiby, 2001):

1. **Knowledge transfers between individuals:** Concern how to best enable the communication between employees within the organization. The strategic question is: How can we improve the transfer of competence between people in the organization? Activities for intellectual capital management focus on

trust building, enabling team activities, induction programs, job rotation and master/apprentice scheme.

2. **Knowledge transfers from individuals to external structure:** Concern how the organization's employees transfer their knowledge to the outer world. The strategic question is: How can the organization's employees improve the competence of customers, suppliers and other stakeholders? Activities for intellectual capital management focus on enabling the employees to help customers learn about the products, getting rid of red tape, enabling job rotation with customers, holding product seminars and providing customer education.
3. **Knowledge transfers from external structure to individuals:** Occur when employees learn from customers, suppliers and community feedback through ideas, new experiences and new technical knowledge. The strategic question is: How can the organization's customers, suppliers and other stakeholders improve the competence of the employees? Activities for intellectual capital management focus on creating and maintaining good personal relationships between the organization's own people and the people outside the organization.
4. **Knowledge transfers from competence to internal structure:** Concern the transformation of human capital into more permanent structural capital through documented work routines, intranets and data repositories. The strategic question is: How can we improve the conversion of individually held competence to systems, tools and templates? Activities for intellectual capital management

Figure 5.7. Knowledge transfer within and between families of intangible assets

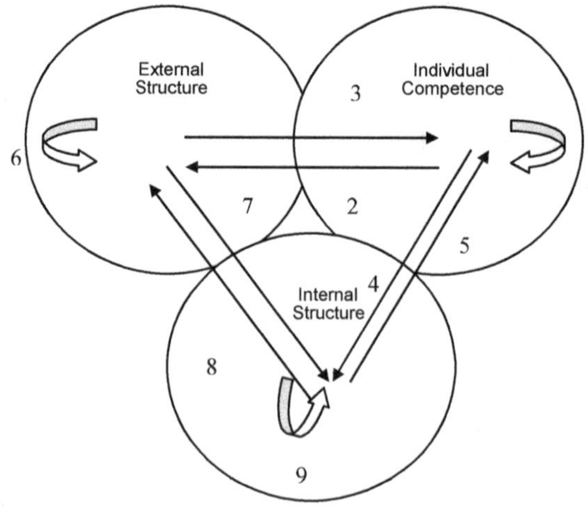

focus on tools, templates, process and systems so they can be shared more easily and efficiently.

5. **Knowledge transfers from internal structure to individual competence:** The counterpart of the above. Once competence is captured in a system, it needs to be made available to other individuals in such a way that they improve their capacity to act. The strategic question is: How can we improve individuals' competence by using systems, tools and templates? Activities for intellectual capital management focus on improving the human-computer interface of systems, action-based learning processes, simulations and interactive e-learning environments.
6. **Knowledge transfers within the external structure:** Concern what customers and others tell each other about the services of an organization. The strategic question is: How can we enable the conversations among the customers, suppliers and other stakeholders so they improve their competence? Activities for intellectual capital management focus on partnering and alliances, improving the image of the organization and the brand equity of its products and services, improving the quality of the offering, conducting product seminars and alumni programs.
7. **Knowledge transfers from external to internal structure:** Concern what knowledge the organization can gain from the external world and how the learning can be converted into action. The strategic question is: How can competence from the customers, suppliers and other stakeholders improve the organization's systems, tools and processes and products? Activities for intellectual capital management focus on empowering call centers to interpret customer complaints, creating alliances to generate ideas for new products and research and development alliances.
8. **Knowledge transfers from internal to external structure:** The counterpart of the above. The strategic question is: How can the organization's systems, tools and processes and products improve the competence of the customers, suppliers and other stakeholders? Activities for intellectual capital management focus on making the organization's systems, tools and processes effective in servicing the customer, extranets, product tracking, help desks and e-business.
9. **Knowledge transfers within the internal structure:** Where the internal structure is the backbone of the organization. The strategic question is: How can the organization's systems, tools and processes and products be effectively integrated? Activities for intellectual capital management focus on streamlining databases, building integrated information technology systems and improving the office layout.

In addition to these nine knowledge transfer mechanisms, the client has to retain several core capabilities. These ensure the elicitation and delivery of business requirements, the development of technical/business architecture, the managing of external supply and the coordination and governance of these tasks.

The Case of Law Firms

Law firms are examples of content providers that lately have discovered the advantages of e-business. According to Weill and Vitale (2002), content providers must categorize and store their content in well-indexed modules so it can be combined and customized to meet client needs via a wide variety of channels. They argue that to succeed, a content provider must provide reliable, timely content in the right format and at the right price.

Legaliz (www.legaliz.no) is an example of a Norwegian law firm offering their services on the Internet as a content provider. They claim that they can offer legal advice faster, cheaper and with greater availability (24x7x54) than their traditional competitors. Even though there are important advantages for clients using the Internet for legal services, it is crucial that the clients are offered the same quality in content as in traditional law firms. The main difference from a KM perspective in e-business is how knowledge is transferred from the law firm to its clients.

According to Mountain (2001), legal Web advisors were pioneered in London in 1994 when the law firm Linklaters introduced a browser-based product called Blue Flag. Blue Flag is now a suite of products covering regulatory compliance, derivatives documentation, employee share plans, funds, share disclosure and transaction management. Within months, another London law firm, Clifford Chance, followed with NextLaw, a Web-accessible online service that helps assess the legal and regulatory risks of e-commerce and reportedly required an investment of more than one million pounds sterling. Today, there are approximately a dozen online legal services in the UK, and the pace of their introduction is accelerating.

For a law firm, e-business is a new way to provide clients with the knowledge they possess and develop. Based on the client's problem, a solution can be delivered either by creating or by using existing knowledge. An example of a knowledge management system at Stage IV of the stage model is case-based reasoning. The client types in certain characteristics of the problem and answers questions from the knowledge management system. The system then searches similar cases in its database and develops a recommended solution to the problem based on earlier cases.

Generally, law firms belong to the industry of professional service firms. Knowledge development has been found to occur through client interaction in such firms (Fosstenløkken et al., 2003). The value-creation processes include both service-delivery processes, which create value directly for clients, and knowledge-development processes, which are indirectly value creating, in that they enhance the value-creation potential of the firm, and thereby also the value of the firm itself to owners and other stakeholders. As value shops (Stabell & Fjeldstad, 1998) being content providers (Weill & Vitale, 2002), professional service firms can improve both business processes using the principles suggested by El Sawy (2001).

The Case of Supply Chains

The need for continual value innovation is driving supply chains to evolve from a pure transactional focus to leveraging interorganizational partnerships for sharing information and, ultimately, market knowledge creation. Supply chain partners are engaging in interlinked processes that enable (1) rich (broad-ranging, high quality and privileged) information sharing, and (2) building information technology infrastructures that allow them to process information obtained from their partners to create new knowledge.

A study by Malhotra et al. (2005) uncovered and examined the variety of supply chain partnership configurations that exist based on differences in capability platforms, reflecting varying processes and information systems. They identified five partnership configurations that were labeled collector, connector, cruncher, coercer and collaborator.

The uncovering and characterization of supply chain configurations enabled Malhotra et al. (2005) to better understand how partner-enabled knowledge creation and operational efficiency can both be affected by shortcomings in organizational capability platforms and the nature of information exchanged.

Organizational capability platforms can be improved using two distinct types of partner interface-directed information systems that enable assimilation and transformation: memory systems for interorganizational activities and interpretation systems for interorganizational information.

Memory systems for interorganizational activities represent use of IT-based systems by an enterprise to store and retrieve information related to previous exchanges with its supply chain partners. Organizational memory is the means by which knowledge from the past can be utilized to understand and influence current activities. Information systems that support organizational memory store information from past activities and outcomes. Supporting organizational memory through information systems can play a significant role in the creation of new knowledge. Memory systems can manifest themselves as databases that store and enable retrieval of the history of events related to the formal interactions or informal information exchanges with business partners, both in terms of the processes that ensued as well as the outcomes. Such systems allow enterprises to bring previously stored information to bear on information received from external sources in order to create new knowledge as well as create operational efficiency. Memory systems are applications of information technology at Stage III of the knowledge management technology stage model.

Interpretation systems for interorganization information represent use of IT-based systems by an enterprise to manipulate and interpret information received from its supply chain partners. Employees and teams within enterprises are conduits for knowledge creation and sharing. Their diverse cognitive needs require the use of information systems that are able to represent information in multiple ways — from global to minute — and allow dynamic configuration of interpretation. Use of IT-based interpretation systems enables information obtained from supply chain partners to be organized, rearranged and processed to create new knowledge. A manifestation of such a system is data analysis and mining software that can help uncover patterns in data and enable insights to be generated by processing large quantities of raw data. IT-based interpretation systems have been shown to enable more effective knowledge creation and generation of insights that lead to improved performance outcomes. Interpretation systems are applications of information technology at Stage IV of the knowledge management technology stage model.

Malhotra et al. (2005) conducted their research study in the context of the RosettaNet B2B initiative (www.rosettanet.org). RosettaNet is a consortium of major IT, electronic components, semiconductor manufacturing, telecommunications and logistics enterprises working to create and implement industry-wide, open electronic business process standards for supply chain collaboration. RosettaNet helped the researchers identify their supply chain partners, restricted to three supply chain tiers: manufacturers, distributors and retailers. This resulted in identifying 91 partnerships, which the researchers grouped into five partnership configurations.

Enterprises structuring their supply chain partnerships as collectors appeared to focus their resources on deploying standard electronic business interfaces with partners for supporting interorganizational process linkages and information exchange. In the second configuration, connector, the focus was the structuring of interorganizational processes. Cruncher supply chain partnerships seem to be a polar opposite of connector configurations. While connector enterprises are externally focused (structuring their interorganizational processes), cruncher enterprises appear to focus on partner interface-directed information systems for storage and processing of information.

Coercive supply chain partnership was the fourth configuration identified. Here we typically find a very large enterprise with much power in the supply chain and a much smaller enterprise, where relative dependence determines the power that can be exerted by enterprises specifically for adoption of interorganizational information sharing systems. The fifth and final configuration was collaborator supply chain partnership. This configuration indicates advanced capabilities in the structuring of their interorganizational integrative processes.

The Case of Seven-Eleven Japan

Seven-Eleven Japan is a company that has invested aggressively and successfully in information technology for many years. Tsai et al. (2005) argue that the company's strong performance rests on its information technology investments. The company developed an electronic ordering system (EOS) and a point-of-sales data-collection system (POS) to reduce the average turnover time of its stock and acquire information regarding the sales of its products. It used information technology to gain competitive advantage. Now, Seven-Eleven Japan is the largest and most profitable retailer in Japan. When it was designed, the POS system was able to gather customer information regarding age and gender, and was also able to make cross comparisons in regard to the different types and quantities of products, as well as the time when they were bought.

In this way the enterprise was able to extend the knowledge level of knowing "which products sold well" to the level of knowing "who is buying these products." The POS comprises the design and implementation of the system's hardware and software. However, from the standpoint of knowledge management, the system is the construction of the knowledge about product sales analysis. After this enterprise determines the knowledge of product sales analysis as the enterprise's key ability (knowledge identification, selection and acquisition), they translated this tacit knowledge that was formerly stored within the experienced sales specialists in the company's head office into the POS system (knowledge construction, which is also knowledge externalization).

This system is installed into each franchise, thereby allowing each franchise operator to learn how to use the system gathering and analyzing product sales (knowledge learning and culture, which is also knowledge externalization), thereby demonstrating the effectiveness of implementing such a system. In other words, this enterprise, through building and implementing a POS system, has achieved knowledge of product sales analysis being disseminated throughout the whole of the enterprise, thus allowing this knowledge to be retained, used and revised for the benefit of the whole organization (Tsai et al., 2005).

South African Case Study Findings

Plessis and Boon (2004) investigated the role of knowledge management in e-business in practice through questionnaires administered to selected South African corporations. They found that South African organizations understand the strategic importance of knowledge and knowledge management, but only apply knowledge management on an operational level. This is supported by the fact that knowledge management is not integrated into business, for example, into the business process value chain, but is implemented as an administrative function.

E-business did not explode as anticipated in the years 1998-2000 globally, but even less so in South Africa. The role that knowledge management played in e-business in South Africa will thus be smaller compared to other countries like the U.S. and UK, simply because there is more e-business activity than in South Africa, according to Plessis and Boon (2004). Nevertheless, the survey showed that knowledge management was rated in as having an important role in e-business.

Plessis and Boon (2004) suggest that South African organizations should expose their knowledge workers to international knowledge management programs with an e-business focus where possible, for example, through exchange programs to ensure they get adequate exposure to developments internationally.

Discussion

Businesses operate in a knowledge-driven economy and increasingly function as knowledge-based organizations. In such knowledge-rich environments, e-businesses must explicitly recognize knowledge and the processes and technologies for knowledge management and exchange across participants in the marketplace (Singh et al., 2004). To this end, Allard and Holsapple (2002) suggest KM audits. They give a way to assess and analyze effectiveness of e-business knowledge handling processes. Results of these audits can be a foundation for finding ways to enhance e-business competitiveness through KM improvements and to improve business innovation capability.

In this chapter, we have documented some of the links between e-business and KMS that need to be explored in future empirical research. With the growing importance of pooling knowledge resources, knowledge management will have to transcend organizational boundaries to include customers, vendors and other partners using electronic information. However, the focus of previous research studies has mainly been on intra-organizational knowledge management. In this study, we have attempted to direct the attention of knowledge management researchers toward interorganizational interfaces.

In a different empirical setting, Malhotra et al. (2005) attempted to direct the attention of knowledge management researchers toward interorganizational interfaces. They studied absorptive capacity configurations in supply chains. Their study indicates that enterprises have to build requisite absorptive capacity to prepare for collaborative knowledge creation with their supply chain partners. Absorptive capacity in this context is the ability of enterprises to acquire and assimilate information from their supply chain partners and to transform and exploit this information to achieve superior operational and strategic outcomes.

Similarly, Allard and Holsapple (2002) attempted to direct the attention of knowledge management researchers toward interorganizational interfaces. They studied knowledge management as a key for e-business competitiveness. In their knowledge chain model, knowledge externalization describes the embedding of knowledge into organizational outputs that are then released into the external environment.

The research propositions in this chapter illustrate the need for a contingent approach to knowledge management systems that are to support e-business. We have seen different situations that require different KMS. For example, the business model of a content provider has knowledge at its core, while the business model of direct to customer is less dependent on knowledge management.

Implementation is an important issue for knowledge management systems in e-business. Critical success factors for KMS implementation will typically include resources for the implementation, user involvement in implementation and management support for implementation. Such critical success factors can be studied in future research.

Conclusion

Knowledge management systems successfully supporting e-business and improving e-business performance have to satisfy several requirements. First, they have to support the chosen e-business model(s). Second, they have to cause improvements through redesign of e-business processes. Furthermore, more advanced stages of knowledge management technology in terms of codification strategy will be more powerful and successful. These are some of the research propositions presented in this chapter, which represents a rich knowledge base for future empirical studies. The avenue opened up through this chapter is for future research to look for situations, rather than generalizations, in terms of the contingent approach to management.

As a conclusion, some important causal influences between knowledge management and IT outsourcing relationships are mapped in the causal loop diagram in Figure 5.8. Causal loop diagramming is described by Sterman (2000) and presented as a tool by www.vensim.com.

More knowledge sharing will increase customer satisfaction, leading to higher e-business success. Learning from the success, new knowledge is created, causing modifications and extensions to the e-business model. The revised e-business model requires process redesign, and one important aspect of redesign will be more knowledge management technology. More technology for knowledge management improves knowledge sharing, leading to even higher customer satisfaction.

Figure 5.9 illustrates two positive feedback loops from Figure 5.8. When knowledge sharing increases, customer satisfaction increases, leading to greater e-business success, making it more attractive to continue the digital transformation, leading to even more knowledge sharing. The other loop says that when knowledge sharing increases, more know-what, know-how and know-why lead to greater process redesign, making new applications of knowledge management technology, leading to even more knowledge sharing.

Effective knowledge management in electronic business is dependent on a knowledge-centered culture. Organizational culture is believed to be the most significant input to effective knowledge management and organizational learning in that corporate culture determines values, beliefs and work systems that could encourage or impede learning (knowledge creation) as well as knowledge sharing (Janz & Prasarnphanich, 2003). Therefore, an organization's culture should provide sup-

Figure 5.8. Causal loop diagram for knowledge management in e-business

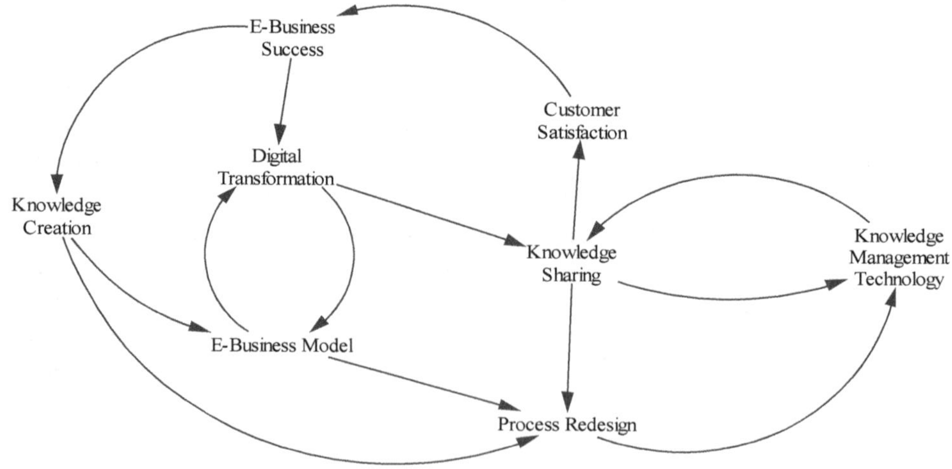

Figure 5.9. Positive feedback loops in the causal loop diagram

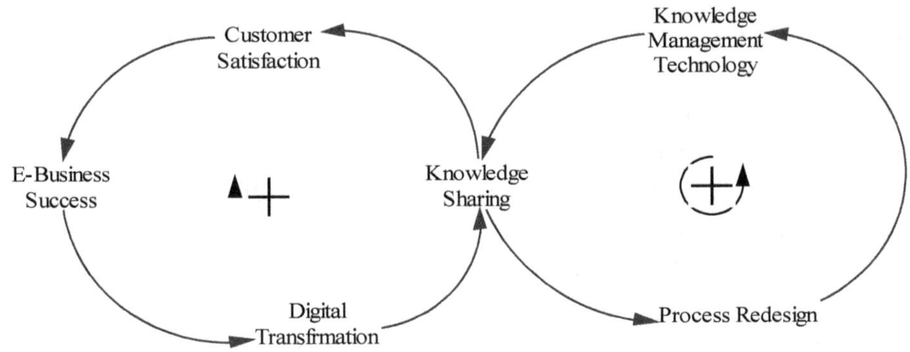

port and incentives as well as encourage knowledge-related activities by creating environments for knowledge exchange and accessibility.

Questions for Discussion

1. What is the value configuration of each of the eight e-business models?
2. How can knowledge management systems improve the performance of an e-business?
3. Which IT infrastructure services are needed when a content provider wants to improve knowledge sharing with customers?

List of References

Alavi, M., & Leidner, D. E. (2001). Knowledge management and knowledge management systems: Conceptual foundations and research issues. *MIS Quarterly, 25*(1), 107-136.

Allard, S., & Holsapple, C. W. (2002). Knowledge management as a key for e-business competitiveness: From the knowledge chain to KM audits. *Journal of Computer Information Systems (JCIS), 42*(5), 19-25.

Andal-Ancion, A., Cartwright, P. A., & Yip, G. S. (2003, Summer). The digital transformation of traditional businesses. *Sloan Management Review*, 34-41.

Earl, M. J. (2000). Evolving the e-business. *Business Strategy Review, 11*(2), 33-38.

El Sawy, O. A. (2001). *Redesigning enterprise processes for e-business*. Boston, MA: McGraw-Hill.

Fahey, L., Srrivastava, R., Sharon, J. S., & Smith, D. E. (2001). Linking e-business and operating processes: The role of knowledge management. *IBM Systems Journal, 40*(4), 889-907.

Feng, K., Chen, E. T., & Liou, W. (2005). Implementation of knowledge management systems and firm performance: An empirical investigation. *Journal of Computer Information Systems (JCIS), 45*(2), 92-104.

Fosstenløkken, S. W., Løwendahl, B. R., & Revang, Ø. (2003). Knowledge development through client interaction: A comparative study. *Organization Studies, 24*(6), 859-879.

Garud, R., & Kumaraswamy, A. (2005). Vicious and virtuous circles in the management of knowledge: The case of Infosys Technologies. *MIS Quarterly, 29*(1), 9-33.

Hansen, M. T., Nohria, N., & Tierney, T. (1999, March-April). What's your strategy for managing knowledge? *Harvard Business Review*, 106-116.

Holsapple, C. W., & Singh, M. (2000). Electronic commerce: From a definitional taxonomy toward a knowledge-management view. *Journal of Organizational Computing and Electronic Commerce, 10*(3), 149-170.

Inkpen, A. C., & Tsang, E. W. K. (2005). Social capital, networks, and knowledge transfer. *Academy of Management Review, 30*(1), 146-165.

Janz, B. D., & Prasarnphanich, P. (2003). Understanding the antecedents of effective knowledge management: The importance of a knowledge-centered culture. *Decision Sciences, 34*(2), 351-384.

Kankanhalli, A., Tan, B. C. Y., & Wei, K. K. (2005). Contributing knowledge to electronic knowledge repositories: An empirical investigation. *MIS Quarterly, 29*(1), 113-143.

Ko, D. G., Kirsch, L. J., & King, W. R. (2005). Antecedents of knowledge transfer from consultants to clients in enterprise system implementations. *MIS Quarterly, 29*(1), 59-85.

Kodama, M. (2005). Customer value creation through knowledge creation with customers: Case studies of IT and multimedia businesses in Japan. *International Journal of Innovation and Learning, 2*(4), 357-385.

Kodama, M., & Ohira, H. (2005). Customer value creation through customer-as-innovator approach: A case study of video processing LSI development. *International Journal of Innovation and Learning, 2*(2), 175-185.

Li, E., & Lai, H. (2005). Collaborative work and knowledge management in electronic business. *Decision Support Systems*, 39, 545-547.

Liu, C. C., & Chen, S. Y. (2005). Determinants of knowledge sharing of e-learners. *International Journal of Innovation and Learning, 2*(4), 434-445.

Malhotra, A., Gosain, S., & El Sawy, O. A. (2005). Absorptive capacity configurations in supply chains: Gearing for partner-enabled market knowledge creation. *MIS Quarterly, 29*(1), 145-187.

Malhotra, Y. (2000, Summer). Knowledge management for e-business performance: Advancing information strategy to 'Internet time.' *Information Strategy: The Executive's Journal*, 5-16.

Malhotra, Y. (2002, Spring). Enabling knowledge exchanges for e-business communities. *Information Strategy: The Executive's Journal*, 26-31.

Mountain, D. (2001). Could new technologies cause great law firms to fail?, *Journal of Information, Law and Technology*, (1), 9 pages. Retrieved from http://elj.warwick.ac.uk/jilt/

Plessis, M., & Boon, J. A. (2004). Knowledge management in eBusiness and customer relationship management: South African case study findings. *International Journal of Information Management, 24,* 73-86.

Porter, M. E. (2001, March), Strategy and the Internet. *Harvard Business Review*, 63-78.

Sambamurthy, V., & Subramani, M. (2005). Special issue on information technologies and knowledge management. *MIS Quarterly, 29*(1), 1-7.

Singh, R., Iyer, L., & Salam, A. F. (2004). Web service for knowledge management in e-marketplaces. *e-Service Journal*, 32-52.

Stabell, C. B., & Fjeldstad, Ø. D. (1998). Configuring value for competitive advantage: On chains, shops, and networks. *Strategic Management Journal, 19,* 413-437.

Sterman, J. D. (2000). *Business dynamics: Systems thinking and modeling for a complex world.* Boston: McGraw-Hill.

Sveiby, K. E. (2001). A knowledge-based theory of the firm to guide in strategy formulation. *Journal of Intellectual Capital, 2*(4), 344-358.

Tsai, M. T., Yu, M. C., & Lee, K. W. (2005, March). Developing e-business systems based on KM process perspective — A case study of Seven-Eleven Japan. *The Journal of American Academy of Business*, 285-289.

Wasko, M. M., & Faraj, S. (2005). Why should I share? Examining social capital and knowledge contribution in electronic networks of practice. *MIS Quarterly, 29*(1), 35-57.

Weill, P., & Vitale, M. R. (2001). *Place to space, migrating to eBusiness models.* Boston: Harvard Business School Press.

Weill, P., & Vitale, M. R. (2002). What IT infrastructure capabilities are needed to implement e-business models? *MIS Quarterly Executive, 1*(1), 17-34.

Wickramasinghe, N., & Silvers, J. B. (2003). IS/IT prescription to enable medical group practices to manage managed care. *Health Care Management Science*, 6, 75-86.

Chapter VI

Outsourcing Knowledge

Introduction

With changing business environments, the locus of value creation is no longer within the boundaries of a single firm, but occurs instead at the nexus of relationships between parties. With the growing importance of pooling knowledge resources, knowledge management will have to transcend organizational boundaries. Based on current research literature, this chapter develops research propositions to study causal aspects of knowledge management systems supporting IT outsourcing relationships. Perspectives from the research literature applied in this chapter include knowledge transfer, strategic intent, knowledge management technology stages, intangible assets, resource-based theory, vendor value proposition, value shop and knowledge strategy (Gottschalk & Solli-Sæther, 2006).

Research propositions in this chapter suggest that knowledge transfer is the most important knowledge process in an IT outsourcing relationship. Increase in knowledge transfer between vendor and client will improve partnership quality in IT outsourcing relationships; a higher level of strategic intent for IT outsourcing requires a higher stage of knowledge management systems, and vendor and client need to be at the same technology stage of growth to be able to successfully communicate with each other through knowledge management systems.

Furthermore, a codification strategy is more dependent on knowledge management systems than a personalization strategy in knowledge transfer between vendor and client in an IT outsourcing relationship; the external structure is the most important structure for successful knowledge transfer in IT outsourcing relationships. The need for knowledge management systems in an IT outsourcing relationship increases as vendor and client mobilize strategic resources in their relationship, and the need for knowledge management systems in an IT outsourcing relationship increases as the vendor increases his complementary competencies. Finally, vendor value shop performance in selecting and implementing the best solution for the client is dependent on the extent of client knowledge transfer, and knowledge management systems in outsourcing relationships are less important when the client is an expert-driven business.

With changing business environments, the locus of value creation is no longer within the boundaries of a single firm, but occurs instead at the nexus of relationships between parties (Malhotra et al., 2005). Enterprises have to rely on business partners to share knowledge and continually respond to change. With the growing importance of pooling knowledge resources, knowledge management will have to transcend organizational boundaries to include sourcing partners. However, the focus of previous research studies has mainly been on intraorganizational knowledge management. This chapter attempts to direct the attention of knowledge management researchers toward interorganizational interfaces.

As mentioned in the previous chapter, several researchers emphasize the important role of knowledge for interorganizational learning and innovation (e.g., Alard & Holsapple, 2002; Inkpen & Tsang, 2005; Ko et al., 2005; Malhotra et al., 2005; Wasko & Faraj, 2005). Garud and Kumaraswany (2005) argue that knowledge has emerged as a strategically significant resource for the firm. Accordingly, knowledge creation and transfer becomes a key factor to gain and sustain a competitive advantage (Sambamurthy & Subramani, 2005). The main objective of a knowledge management system is to support the creation, transfer and application of knowledge in organizations (Feng et al., 2005).

An IT outsourcing relationship is an interorganizational arrangement for the exchange of IT services after the transfer of IT assets from the client to the vendor (Koh et al., 2004). In an outsourcing setting, knowledge, which earlier existed internally in an organization, is moved to an external organization (Bahli & Rivard, 2005). Accordingly, changes in the knowledge transfer requirements are viewed as the single most important challenge to knowledge management systems in an outsourcing arrangement. Therefore, the focus of this chapter is how the requirements for knowledge management systems change when an organization has entered into an IT outsourcing relationship with another organization.

This chapter makes an important contribution to the field, as there has been a missing link between know-what and know-how concerning cause and effect relationships between knowledge management systems and IT outsourcing arrangement. Know-what has stressed the importance of knowledge in outsourcing relationships. Knowledge can be descriptive (know-what), procedural (know-how) or reasoning (know-why) (Fahey et al., 2001; Holsapple & Singh, 2000). This chapter makes a much-needed contribution to know-how, as it explores how knowledge management systems and IT outsourcing arrangements influence each other.

The outsourcing promise for the client is to explore and exploit the supplier's superior technical know-how (human capital), superior management practices (structural capital), economies of scale and, increasingly, access to strategic and business advice. This should enable the client to refocus on strategic, core capability and knowledge areas. But the research of Willcocks et al. (2004) into IT outsourcing has shown consistently over the past decade that the prospects have been disappointing for meaningful knowledge management, and therefore value creation. Their research findings make the following research propositions even more important to future successful support from knowledge management systems in IT outsourcing relationships.

Outsourcing Management Competence

In the knowledge-based view of the firm, IT outsourcing can be seen as a mechanism to integrate IT knowledge from IT vendors. Further, IT outsourcing may encourage the generation of new ways to use IT for better organizational performance through positive interactions. Finally, some executives have concerns regarding the potential loss of internal know-how through IT outsourcing. Shi et al. (2005) believe that a knowledge management-based perspective of IT outsourcing can help determine ways of avoiding loss of important knowledge and nurturing an organizational learning capability.

Shi et al. (2005) studied IT outsourcing management competence. They identified four IT outsourcing management competence dimensions:

- **Informed buying:** The capability of IT purchasing personnel to manage the IT outsourcing strategy that meets the interests of the business.
- **Contract facilitation:** The mechanism through which IT services can be coordinated and synchronized, conflicts between users and suppliers resolved in a collaborated fashion, lessons learned from one buyer-supplier relationship can be documented and applied to other situations and both excessive user demands and cost overruns by vendors can be managed and limited.
- **Contract monitoring:** The capability of a firm to protect its contractual position over time.
- **Vendor development:** The capability of organizations looking beyond existing contractual arrangements to explore the long-term potential for suppliers to

create win-win situations in which the supplier increases revenues by providing services that increase business benefits.

In successful outsourcing management, Shi et al. (2005) found continuously interacting relationships among informed buying, contract management and relationship management. They measured informed buying in terms of IT personnel having the capability to select the right IT sourcing strategy, making decisions based on business needs and understanding the firm's technological criteria. Contract management was measured on items such as processes to ensure agreements, accountability, achievements and meetings. Relationship management was measured on items such as single point of contact, confidence in conflict resolution and coordination.

Knowledge Transfer in Outsourcing Relationships

In an IT outsourcing relationship, the requirements on a KMS to support creation, storage and retrieval and application of knowledge will not change dramatically. However, the requirements concerning support for knowledge transfer will change significantly.

P1: Knowledge transfer is the most important knowledge process in an IT outsourcing relationship.

The problem of knowledge transfer is often faced by individuals or groups once an appropriate source of knowledge is located (Sambamurthy & Subramani, 2005). The new challenge lies mostly in how to transfer knowledge between the vendor and the client. The environment for communication in certain areas of a company will be drastically altered as a consequence of an outsourcing decision. Knowledge, which earlier could be transferred between people in the same organization, now has to be transferred across two different organizations. Consequently, the channels for transferring knowledge will be more formal and impersonal. A KMS has to find a way to transfer all relevant information through more formal and impersonal channels or to find a new creative way of making the communication channel less formal and/or impersonal.

According to Ko et al. (2005), some researchers have defined knowledge transfer as dyadic exchanges of organizational knowledge between a source and a recipient unit in which the identity of the recipient matters. Others also focus on the resulting changes to the recipient. For example, knowledge transfer can be seen as the process through which one unit (e.g., group, department or division) is affected by the experience of another. Other researchers go further by arguing that knowledge transfer occurs when a contributor shares knowledge that is used by an adopter.

Knowledge is in the heads of individuals. Therefore, we have to understand knowledge transfer in terms of individual behavior. Wasko and Faraj (2005) examined social capital and knowledge contribution in electronic networks of practice. They found that reputation, centrality and tenure were significant factors influencing the extent to which individuals are motivated to make knowledge contributions. Reputation is an important asset that an individual can leverage to achieve and maintain status within a collective. Centrality is the extent to which the individual is in regular contact with others; the more individuals are in regular contact with one another, the more likely they are to develop a habit of cooperation and act collectively. Individuals with longer tenure in the shared practice are likely to better understand how their expertise is relevant, and are thus better able to share knowledge with others.

Given the multiple objectives of knowledge transfer in IT outsourcing relationships, only a sophisticated operationalization of the concept will suffice here. Since the literature suggests that key aspects of knowledge transfer are knowledge movement and the application of knowledge, Ko et al. (2005) captured both of these ideas by defining knowledge transfer as the communication of knowledge from a source so that it is learned and applied by a recipient. Knowledge is taken to be transferred when learning takes place and when the recipient understands the intricacies and implications associated with that knowledge so that he or she can apply it. For example, the vendor may transfer knowledge about testing procedures to the client, who learns and applies this knowledge, as evidenced by clients developing test scripts, conducting tests of individual modules and running integration tests to ascertain whether data are correctly passed between two or more modules.

Similarly, Inkpen and Tsang (2005) define knowledge transfer as a process through which one relationship partner is affected by the experience of another. Knowledge transfer manifests itself through changes in knowledge or performance of the recipient unit. Partnerships can create a competitive advantage through the strategic sharing of organizations' key information and knowledge. Close relationships result from more frequent and more relevant information and knowledge transferred between high performance partners. By transferring knowledge between the client and vendor, organizations are able to sustain a more effective outsourcing relationship over time. Lee (2001) found that the association between the degree of knowledge sharing and outsourcing success is mediated by the quality of the partnership. Therefore, we suggest the following proposition:

P2: Increase in knowledge transfer between vendor and client will improve partnership quality in IT outsourcing relationships.

Figure 6.1. Knowledge transfer influencing outsourcing success

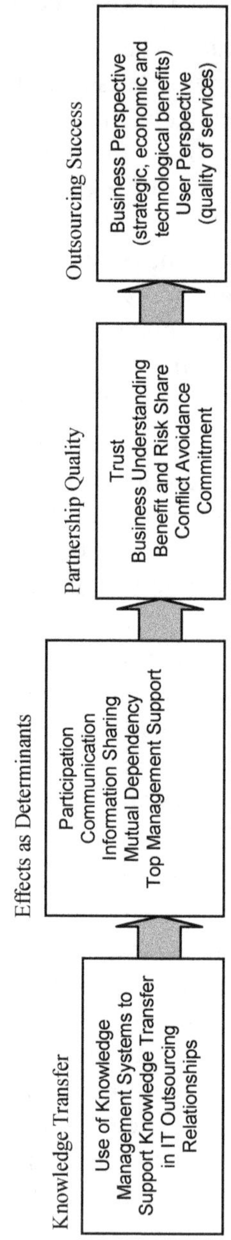

According to Lee and Kim (1999), there is a significant positive relationship between partnership quality and outsourcing success. In their research, they identified five factors that make up partnership quality: trust, business understanding, benefit-risk share, conflict avoidance and commitment. A successful partnership enables participants to achieve organizational objectives and build a competitive advantage that each organization could not easily attain by itself.

The links and causalities are presented in Figure 6.1. First, the use of knowledge management systems to support knowledge transfer in IT outsourcing relationships has effects on the relationships. Next, these effects are determinants of partnership quality. Finally, partnership quality influences outsourcing effects.

For example, participation is important in a partnership. From a social perspective, participation is prescribed as a remedy when there is conflict, frustration and vacillation in the group. Active participation of the partnership members plays a major part in enhancing the sustainability of their partnership over time (Lee & Kim, 1999). Knowledge transfer using knowledge management systems can be an enabler of easier and more comprehensive participation. Hence, participation is influenced by knowledge transfer, and participation influences partnership quality, as illustrated in Figure 6.1.

The shift to more distributed forms of organizations and the growth of interorganizational relationships, such as outsourcing relationships, have led to an increase in the transfer of knowledge between parties with asymmetric and incomplete information about each other. Because of this asymmetry and incompleteness, parties seeking knowledge may not be able to identify qualified knowledge providers, and the appropriate experts may fail to be motivated to engage in knowledge transfer.

Therefore, Lin et al. (2005) proposed a sender-receiver framework for studying knowledge transfer under asymmetric and/or incomplete information. In developing the sender-receiver framework, they first introduced the market view of knowledge transfer, where knowledge is treated as a good that moves in a knowledge market where parties may have incomplete and asymmetric information about other participants and the knowledge itself.

A knowledge market exists within organizations when knowledge buyers and sellers within a firm expect to gain from a knowledge transaction (Davenport & Prusak, 1998). This market view is consistent with empirical studies, which show that an effective internal knowledge sharing and transfer system provides motivations to both the provider and the seeker. Knowledge markets also exist across organizations. Consulting firms are hired to provide strategic advice; companies sign licensing agreements and technology development contracts; services and business processes are outsourced to vendors (Lin et al., 2005).

There are two groups of participants in a knowledge transfer: senders who are knowledge sellers, and receivers who are knowledge buyers. The knowledge sender as well as the knowledge receiver can be an individual, a team, a firm or a unit (subsidiary) within a firm. It can be assumed that each participant focuses on maximizing his or her own benefits, and their interests are generally not aligned. This applies to both the external knowledge market where the sender and receiver belong to two different organizations and the internal knowledge market where they belong to the same organization but care primarily about their own interests.

Each sender is endowed with a piece of knowledge in which a receiver is interested. Specifically, the receiver hopes to derive benefits in terms of value from utilizing the knowledge. The value of knowledge is realized when the receiver has assimilated and put the knowledge in use, which has brought about outcomes attributable to the knowledge use. Because knowledge transfer precedes knowledge utilization, the sender and the receiver cannot measure the realized value of knowledge when deciding on the transfer. Instead, the sender and the receiver form expectations of the value of knowledge based on their information.

The expected value of knowledge for the client in an outsourcing relationship is based on the client's information about available knowledge from the vendor. Ultimately, the value of knowledge can be realized when the client has assimilated and put in use the knowledge by achieving more efficient, more effective and more competitive use of information technology in the organization. Such improved application of information technology based on knowledge transfer from vendor to client creates added value that the client might be willing to share with the vendor.

All of the information available to the sender and used by him to evaluate the knowledge is called the sender's information set. The receiver's information set is defined similarly. To derive the expected value of the knowledge transfer, the sender's and the receiver's information sets should contain at least the following five components (Lin et al., 2005, p. 200):

1. The nature of the knowledge, such as the knowledge being tacit or explicit, proven or unproven;
2. The sender's knowledge capability, such as his/her area and level of expertise;
3. The context in which the knowledge is put to use (whether the context has idiosyncratic features);
4. The fit between the knowledge and the receiver based on the receiver's declared usage of the knowledge; and
5. The ties between the sender and receiver, such as their frequency of interactions and trust.

Since we are interested in whether the vendor (sender) and the receiver (client) have sufficient information to estimate the value of the knowledge to be transferred, instead of studying the individual elements of a sender or a receiver's information set, Lin et al. (2005) introduce the notion of completeness of an information set. One party's information set is considered complete if it contains sufficient information for its owner to reach the correct expected value of the knowledge transferred; otherwise, it is incomplete. The completeness or incompleteness of the sender and the receiver's information sets is called the information structure of knowledge transfer.

Lin et al. (2005) identified four different information structures. Depending on the completeness or incompleteness of the sender and the receiver's information sets, there are four possible combinations: (1) symmetric complete information; (2) sender-advantage asymmetric information; (3) symmetric incomplete information; and (4) receiver-advantage asymmetric information.

An outsourcing relationship typically starts with the third structure of symmetric incomplete information. Neither the potential knowledge sender (vendor) nor the knowledge receiver has complete information about the knowledge transfer. One challenge in this structure is for the sender and the receiver to find mechanisms to alleviate information incompleteness for both before knowledge transfer. One surprising aspect of this structure is that, although no party holds information advantage over the other, strategic distortion in communication still happens (Lin et al., 2005).

Strategic Intent for IT Outsourcing

Research on IT outsourcing has identified several crucial ways in which clients relate to their IT outsourcing providers that influence outsourcing success (Lee et al., 2004). How can a KMS support knowledge transfer to make IT outsourcing successful in different IT outsourcing settings? In order to answer this question, we use the concept of strategic intent to identify different IT outsourcing arrangements. DiRomualdo and Gurbaxani (1998) discovered that beside information systems (IS) improvement that was purely driven by a singular focus on costs reduction and service improvement, there are two more kinds of strategic intent for IT outsourcing: business impact and commercial exploitation. Business impact refers to improving information technology's contribution to company performance within its existing lines of business, while commercial exploitation focuses on leveraging technology-related assets — applications, operations, infrastructure and know-how — in the marketplace to generate new revenue and profit.

These three categories of strategic intent are cumulative, which means that focusing on business impact also incorporates a focus on IS improvement, and commercial exploitation encompasses both of the other elements. Therefore, we suggest the following proposition:

P3: A higher level of strategic intent for IT outsourcing requires a higher stage of knowledge management systems.

The higher stage of knowledge management systems can be defined in terms of the stages of growth model for knowledge management technology as described in the next section.

The findings of DiRomualdo and Gurbaxani (1998) establish the importance of understanding the different types of strategic intent for IT:

- **IS improvement:** Companies that want better performance from their core IS resources — the hardware, software, networks, people and processes involved in managing and operating the technology and supporting users — have the strategic intent of IS improvement. Their objectives typically include cost reduction, service quality improvement and acquisition of new technical skills and management competencies. They believe that outside specialists who are better able to keep pace with new technologies and skills, and who use superior processes and management methods, should manage some, if not all, of their IT services.
- **Business impact:** Many IS organizations are struggling to develop the right mix of technical and business skills to exploit technology. As a result, many companies are looking to the IT outsourcing market for help, on the premise that outsourcing vendors' state-of-the-art skills, capabilities and proficiency at recruiting and managing technologists make them better than internal IS organizations at using IT to improve business results. This strategic intent is deploying IT to significantly improve critical aspects of business performance. Realizing this goal requires an understanding of the business and the link between IT and business processes, and the ability to implement new systems and business change simultaneously. This form of outsourcing brings new skills and capabilities that link IT to business results rather than those related purely to technology.
- **Commercial exploitation:** Outsourcing information technology with the strategic intent of commercial exploitation aims to improve the return on IT investment by generating new revenue and profit or by offsetting costs. The means by which IT assets can be leveraged commercially range from licensing systems and technologies developed initially for internal use, through selling IS products and services to other firms, to launching new IT-based businesses. Companies pursuing commercial exploitation are often those with innovative information systems. Many come from technology-intensive industries, such as air transport and financial services, and have mission-critical systems that are expensive to maintain and enhance.

Based on the different types of strategic intent, DiRomualdo and Gurbaxani (1998), conclude that there is no "one size fits all" approach to IT outsourcing. Each type of strategic intent for IT outsourcing requires different approaches and tactics to be realized successfully. And last, but not least, each type requires different approaches to knowledge management to be successful.

Stages of Knowledge Management Technology

The ambition level using knowledge management systems can be defined in terms of stages of knowledge management technology as was illustrated in Chapter IV. Stage I was labeled end-user-tool systems, or person-to-technology, as information technology provides people with tools that improve personal efficiency. Examples are word processing, spreadsheets and presentation software. Stage II was labeled who-knows-what systems, or person-to-person, as people use information technology to find other knowledge workers. Examples are yellow-page systems, CVs and intranets. Stage III was labeled what-they-know systems or person-to-information, as information technology provides people with access to information that is typically stored in documents. Examples of documents are contracts, articles, drawings, blueprints, photographs, e-mails, presentations and reports (Kankanhalli et al., 2005). Stage IV was labeled how-they-think systems, or person-to-system, in which the system is intended to help solve a knowledge problem. Examples are expert systems and business intelligence.

The first stage is general support for knowledge workers to improve their individual efficiency. The second stage is to locate knowledge sources. The third stage is information representing knowledge, that is, to store what knowledge workers know in terms of information. The fourth, and final, stage is information processing. The stage model was originally designed to describe to what extent a company has utilized

Figure 6.2. Contingent approach to knowledge management systems in IT outsourcing relationships

Strategic Intent/ Stage of KMS	IS Improvement	Business Impact	Commercial Exploitation
Person-to-Tools	End user tools to improve efficiency		
Person-to-Person	Efficient access to knowledge workers	Joint efforts for business process reengineering	Joint exploitation of assets
Person-to-Information	Efficient access to shared databases	Joint efforts for performance monitoring	Joint exploitation of resources
Person-to-System			

knowledge management technology, while here we use these categories to describe at which level the KMS should be in order to meet the changes in requirements from various IT outsourcing relationships on knowledge management systems. Our third proposition is illustrated in Figure 6.2.

An IS improvement strategy requires KMS to provide each knowledge worker with appropriate and standardized tools such as Word, Excel and e-mail at stage I. At stage II, an address book is needed, so that the client can find the updated information or the expert with the appropriate knowledge. At Stage III, the client needs access to the vendor's technical database. In general, KMS in the IS improvement should use all the possible methods to facilitate the timely flow of expertise from the vendor to the client when required.

A business impact strategy is needed to leverage the client's business processes. The challenge of the person-to-person systems is two-way communication between client and vendor. Joint contribution in the knowledge exchange is found a necessity. The KMS must enable both parties to interact through letting them share both explicit and tacit knowledge. Collaboration tools are a possible way to deal with this challenge, although, as Alavi and Leidner (2001) see it, to make use of tacit knowledge through a KMS is a real challenge.

A commercial exploitation strategy has the purpose of making money on the organizations' IT assets. In addition to supporting knowledge transfer from vendor to client, the KMS has to effectively facilitate knowledge transfer from client to vendor. The vendor needs free access to the acquired IT assets to fully exploit it. This is also important to the client, as he or she will get better deals from selling their IT assets. In addition, the client needs continuous access to the IT assets that have been sold. This makes client and vendor mutually dependent on each other. A good KMS for this type of outsourcing arrangement has to include information about who knows what as well as what they know from vendor and client as well.

The stages model for knowledge management technology can be applied to develop another research proposition concerned with knowledge management in IT outsourcing relationships. As knowledge management systems to be applied in an outsourcing relationship involve two parties, both parties will have to be capable of using such applications.

P4: Vendor and client need to be at the same technology stage of growth to be able to successfully communicate with each other through knowledge management systems.

In a different empirical setting, Ko et al. (2005) studied antecedents of knowledge transfer from consultants to clients in enterprise system implementations. They found that the greater the shared understanding between a consultant and a client, the greater the knowledge transfers. Furthermore, the greater the absorptive capacity of a client, the more intrinsically motivated the client and the consultant, the more credible the consultant, the greater a client's communication decoding competence, the greater a consultant's communication encoding competence and the greater the knowledge transfer.

The stages of growth model can be interpreted as alternative strategies, where the alternative strategies are person-to-tools, person-to-person, person-to-information, and person-to-system. A comparison of these four alternatives can be made to the classification into personalization vs. codification strategy by Hansen et al. (1999). In this comparison, Stages I and II represent personalization, while stages III and IV represent codification. Therefore, it can be argued that the need for KMS is greater when the outsourcing relationship is supported by a codification strategy rather than a personalization strategy.

P5: A codification strategy is more dependent on knowledge management systems than a personalization strategy in knowledge transfer between vendor and client in an IT outsourcing relationship.

Intangible Assets in an Outsourcing Relationship

Knowledge management systems support knowledge transfer within and between intangible assets. One approach to defining intangible assets in an outsourcing relationship is to distinguish between three families: the external structure, the internal structure and the individual structure, as proposed by Sveiby (2001).

The external structure consists of the external environment. For the client, the vendor is in the external environment. For the vendor, the client is in the external environment. The internal structure consists of models, regulations and information systems. The individual structure consists of staff competence. Knowledge transfer occurs within and between these three structures.

P6: The external structure is the most important structure for successful knowledge transfer in IT outsourcing relationships.

Knowledge transfer from individual to external structure concerns how the organization's employees transfer their knowledge to the organization's environment.

The strategic question in relation to outsourcing would then be: How can employees use KMS to transfer knowledge and improve the competence of their outsourcing partner? This was illustrated in Chapter V.

Knowledge transfer from external structure to individuals occurs when employees learn from the outsourcing, where the strategic question would be: How can the outsourcing partner improve the competence of the employees using KMS? This was illustrated in Chapter V.

Knowledge transfer within the external structure concerns what the vendors tell each other about the service of an organization. The strategic question would be: How can we secure and enable knowledge exchange between vendors using KMS so our outsourcing vendor improves his competence?

Knowledge transfer from the external to internal structure concerns what knowledge the organization can gain from the external environment and how the learning can be converted into action. The strategic question would be: How can competence from the outsourcing vendor improve the organization's systems, processes and products, using KMS?

Knowledge transfer from internal to external structure is the counterpart from the above, and the strategic question would then be: How can the organization's systems, tools and processes improve the competence of the outsourcing vendor using KMS?

Resource-Based Theory for Knowledge

In this chapter we apply the knowledge-based view of the firm that has established itself as an important perspective in strategic management (Bock et al., 2005; Garud & Kumaraswamy, 2005). This perspective builds on the resource-based theory of the firm. According to the resource-based theory of the firm, performance differences across firms can be attributed to variances in the firms' resources and capabilities. Resources are considered strategic resources if they are: (1) valuable; (2) unique; (3) nonimitable; (4) nontransferable; (5) nonsubstitutable; (6) exploitable; and (7) combinable.

P7: The need for knowledge management systems in an IT outsourcing relationship increases as vendor and client mobilize strategic resources in their relationship.

The central tenet in resource-based theory is that unique organizational resources of both tangible and intangible nature are the real source of competitive advantage.

With resource-based theory, organizations are viewed as a collection of resources that are heterogeneously distributed within and across industries. Accordingly, what makes the performance of an organization distinctive is the unique bland of the resources it possesses. A firm's resources include not only its physical assets, such as plant and location, but also its competencies. The ability to leverage distinctive internal and external competencies relative to environmental situations ultimately affects the performance of the business.

Exploring competencies in the context of the management of information technology is a relatively recent development in the evolution of the information systems discipline. The importance of developing competencies that allow organizations to successfully take advantage of information in their specific context has been noted. The concept of competence in the information systems literature is predominantly focused upon individual competence in the form of IT skill sets rather than treated as an organizational construct. The focus has been on the technology supply side and individuals' skills, emphasizing the requirement for IT professionals to have not just technical skills but also business and interpersonal skills. More recently, change agentry as a skill for IT professionals has been proposed. The implication of this literature stream is that the solution to the problem of lacking benefits from IT can be solved by equipping IT specialists with additional skills. The inference is that the inability to deliver value from information arises from shortcomings in the IT function and among IT professionals.

Outsourcing gives a client organization access to resources in the vendor organization as the vendor handles IT functions for the client. Vendor resources can produce innovation, which is essential for long-term survival of the client. Quinn (2000) argues that the time is right for outsourcing innovation. Four powerful forces are currently driving the innovation revolution. First, demand is growing fast in the global economy, creating a host of new specialist markets sufficiently large to attract innovation. Second, the supply of scientists, technologists and knowledge workers has skyrocketed, as have knowledge bases and the access to them. Third, interaction capabilities have grown. Fourth, new incentives have emerged.

Transformational outsourcing is an emerging practice to bring new capabilities to the organization. Resources are required to bring new capabilities, and resources bringing new capabilities can be found in an outsourcing vendor. In this context we apply the knowledge-based view of the firm that has established itself as an important perspective in strategic management. This perspective builds on the resource-based theory of the firm. According to the resource-based theory of the firm, performance differences across firms can be attributed to the variance in the firms' resources and capabilities. Resources that are valuable, unique and difficult to imitate can provide the basis for firms' competitive advantages. In turn, these competitive advantages produce positive returns. According to Hitt et al. (2001), most of the few empirical tests of the resource-based theory that have been conducted have supported positive, direct effects of resources.

The essence of the resource-based theory of the firm lies in its emphasis on the internal resources available to the firm, rather than on the external opportunities and threats dictated by industry conditions. Firms are considered to be highly heterogeneous, and the bundles of resources available to each firm are different. This is both because firms have different initial resource endowments and because managerial decisions affect resource accumulation and the direction of firm growth as well as resource utilization (Løwendahl, 2000).

The resource-based theory of the firm holds that, in order to generate sustainable competitive advantage, a resource must provide economic value and must be presently scarce, difficult to imitate, nonsubstitutable and not readily obtainable in factor markets. This theory rests on two key points. First, that resources are the determinants of firm performance and second, that resources must be rare, valuable, difficult to imitate and nonsubstitutable by other rare resources. When the latter occurs, a competitive advantage has been created. Resources can simultaneously be characterized as valuable, rare, nonsubstitutable and inimitable. To the extent that an organization's physical assets, infrastructure and workforce satisfy these criteria, they qualify as resources. A firm's performance depends fundamentally on its ability to have a distinctive, sustainable competitive advantage, which derives from the possession of firm-specific resources (Priem & Butler, 2001). The resource-based theory is a useful perspective in strategic management. Research on the competitive implications of such firm resources as knowledge, learning, culture, teamwork and human capital, was given a significant boost by resource-based theory — a theory that indicated it was these kinds of resources that were most likely to be sources of sustainable competitive advantage for firms (Barney, 2001).

Firms' resource endowments, particularly intangible resources, are difficult to change except over the long term. For example, although human resources may be mobile to some extent, capabilities may not be valuable for all firms or even for their competitors. Some capabilities are based on firm-specific knowledge, and others are valuable when integrated with additional individual capabilities and specific firm resources. Therefore, intangible resources are more likely than tangible resources to produce a competitive advantage. In particular, intangible firm-specific resources such as knowledge allow firms to add value to incoming factors of production (Hitt et al., 2001). Resource-based theory attributes advantage in an industry to a firm's control over bundles of unique material, human, organizational and locational resources and skills that enable unique value-creating strategies. A firm's resources are said to be a source of competitive advantage to the degree that they are scarce, specialized, appropriable, valuable, rare and difficult to imitate or substitute.

Vendor Value Proposition

The value generation potential of an outsourcing relationship consists of three factors: client characteristics, the vendor-client relationship and vendor characteristics. A key client characteristic is an understanding of how to manage resources that a firm does not own. A key in the vendor-client relationship is formal (contractual) aspects of the relationship.

The third factor shaping the outsourcing value proposition is the vendor's own capabilities. According to Levina and Ross (2003), the concepts of complementarities and competencies explain that outsourcing vendors can increase productivity and reduce costs on client projects by applying a set of complementary application management competencies. This is the vendor value proposition.

P8: The need for knowledge management systems in an IT outsourcing relationship increases as the vendor increases his or her complementary competencies.

The concept of complementarity posits that firms can improve productivity by engaging in complementary activities where benefits from doing more of one activity increase if the firm is also doing more of the other activity. This concept of complementarity has been used in studies of manufacturing to show that modern manufacturing approaches work as a system, rather than as a set of independent factors. Those firms that invest simultaneously in several complementary activities perform better than those firms that increase the level of some of these activities, but not others. In fact, literature on complementarity argues that firms that increase one factor without also increasing complementary factors may be worse off than firms that keep the factors at the same lower level.

An outsourcing vendor may develop different competencies. In the case study by Levina and Ross (2003), the vendor developed a set of three competencies to respond to client needs and market demands: personnel development, methodology development and dissemination and customer relationship management:

- **IT personnel development:** Addressed existing IT labor market constraints by the vendor in ways that the client had not. The vendor replaced experienced, high-cost client staff with mostly lower-cost, junior programmers and then developed their skills through training, mentoring and team-based project work. Junior staff valued the professional growth while their mentors often relished opportunities to watch somebody take off. As a professional services firm, the vendor viewed maintenance work as a first step in a career development path, which involved rotating professionals within engagements, assigning personnel development managers and creating both technical and management hierarchies.

- **Methodology development and dissemination:** Was necessary for consistent delivery of best of breed solutions to client problems. Whereas the client's staff focused on addressing users' immediate needs, the vendor introduced methodologies that focused on overall operational improvements on projects. The vendor had a long history of methodology development. The methodologies not only specified processes, they also standardized project documentation through forms and templates such as change request forms, lost time logs and weekly status report forms, to closely monitor project status.
- **Customer relationship management:** Was formalized through level of service agreements. Each agreement set a fixed price for agreed-upon services. The major philosophy of outsourcing was that the vendor is taking a risk. The vendor is responsible for whatever is defined in that client interface document as being the vendor's responsibility. While agreements might not lead to greater user satisfaction with the level of IT services, it did reduce uncertainty, thereby creating clearer expectations and an acceptance of limits. As users accepted these limits, they recognized and appreciated services that exceeded contract requirements.

These three competencies turned out to be complementary by being mutually reinforcing. Management practices targeted at one competency tended to enhance the other competencies as well. This reinforcing pattern was apparent in all three pairings of the competencies:

- **Personnel development and methodology development and dissemination are complementary competencies:** The methodology competency reinforced personnel development by helping junior staff learn quickly what they were expected to do. While methodologies were sometimes viewed as constraining individual initiative, one junior consultant argued that the methodology empowered her and others to challenge management directives that might be inconsistent with documented practices. In addition, standardization of practices around methodology facilitated staff rotations and scheduling. In the same way, personnel development practices, such as skill development, rotations and promotion policies provided training, encouragement and incentives that led to consistent use and improvement of methodologies across the organization.
- **Methodology development and dissemination and customer relationships are complementary competencies:** When methodology delivered operational improvements, the vendor could sometimes increase service levels with no

added cost to the client. In some cases, the vendor had been able to pull people off a project and had elected to share the savings with the client. These very visible improvements in IT service levels reinforced the customer relationship. Methodological approaches also improved customer relationship management practices by defining and standardizing best practices for creating and managing level of service agreements. The customer relationship management competence similarly reinforced the methodology competence. The vendor regularly communicated with the client to discuss issues and expectations, and one outcome was to help the client managers understand the methodologies so that they could facilitate, rather than hinder, the vendor's ability to meet expectations. Thus, client managers shared their knowledge of systems with the vendor and provided early warnings, where possible, when business or corporate IT changes might have an impact on the vendor's responsibilities.

- **Personnel development and customer relationships are complimentary competencies:** Personnel development practices reinforced customer relationships by ensuring that staff understood and accepted accountability for meeting contractual obligations. Personnel development practices also developed communication skills to help staff establish customer expectations and build trust. At the same time, strong customer relationships led to better buy-in on the customer's part and to personnel development policies that required release time or movement of personnel, such as training programs, mentoring, and job rotations.

The concepts of complementariness and core competencies explain that the vendor can increase productivity and reduce costs on client projects by applying this set of complementary application management competencies. Levina and Ross (2003) examined how the vendor delivers value to clients as a result of its ability to develop complementary competencies. First, they went beyond neoclassical economics theory to explain why potential clients are unlikely to develop these complementary competencies internally. They then explored the mechanisms that ensure that the benefits of the vendor's competencies are, in part, passed on to clients.

- **Why clients do not replicate and apply vendors' competencies:** Typically, clients have a different set of market structures and resource constraints than the IT services industry. Accordingly, clients have a different organization and different business processes. Clients have hired personnel to address the market conditions and customer demands of their industry. Clients can attempt to build IT application competencies rather than outsource to vendors, but, unlike vendors, they may find that optimizing the development and application of IT competencies will conflict with optimizing core business activities. Vendors, on the other hand, can shield themselves from these conflicts through the structure provided by contracts, which specify deliverables rather than levels of investment in competencies.

For example, to address labor market constraints, clients could increase the compensation of technical specialists, but non-IT workers might perceive the inflated IT salaries as unfair. Similarly, clients are typically not as well positioned as vendors to institute an IT personnel career development office or a practice of IT personnel rotation and promotion.

- **Why vendors share productivity gains with clients:** From the client perspective, the vendor's value proposition would not exist if the benefits of complementary competencies accrued solely to the vendor. Contract-based, interpersonal and reputation-based mechanisms encourage vendors to share advantages with clients. Clients may deploy some contract-based mechanisms including pilot projects, multiphase contracting with penalties, interpersonal relationship building, carrot and stick incentives and short-term contracts and competent contract monitoring. All of these mechanisms increase client control and motivate vendors to demonstrate value to the client. Since the value of outsourcing to the client is very hard to measure, most researchers have focused on client satisfaction.

  Reputation-based mechanisms provide vendors with a strong incentive to share productivity gains with clients. IT service vendors' focus on reputation-building in their relationships with clients. In addition to their current contracting structure, vendors care about their long-term market position. Thus, the vendor is inclined to share benefits with the client so that the information about the vendor's contribution enables it to win future contracts. Developing a solid industry reputation helps a vendor win new, and extend existing, engagements, which lead to the acquisition of, and control over, more projects.

  Knowledge-intensive service firms, like outsourcing vendors, are typical value shops, and such firms depend on reputation for success, as reputation is a key driver of firm value creation. Reputation is a relational concept, in the sense that firms are judged by their stakeholders relative to their competitors. Reputation is what is generally said or believed about an entity by someone, it is the net perception of a firm held by stakeholders judged relative to other firms. According to Sheehan (2002), there are four conditions which must be present for reputation to work. First, rents earned from maintaining a good reputation must be greater than not. Second, there must be a minimum of contact among stakeholders to allow for the changes in reputation to be communicated. Third, there needs to be a possibility of repeat business. And last, there must be some uncertainty regarding the firm's type and/or behavior.

  Reputation is related to the asymmetry of information, which is a typical feature of knowledge-intensive service firms. Asymmetry is present when clients believe the firm knows something that the clients do not and believe it is necessary to know to solve their problems.

Reputation can be classified as a strategic resource in knowledge-intensive firms. To be a strategic resource, it has to be valuable, rare, costly to imitate and possible to organize. Reputation is valuable as it increases the value received by the client. Reputation is rare, as by definition only a few firms can be considered best in the industry. Reputation is costly to imitate, as it is difficult

Figure 6.3. Vendor's value proposition

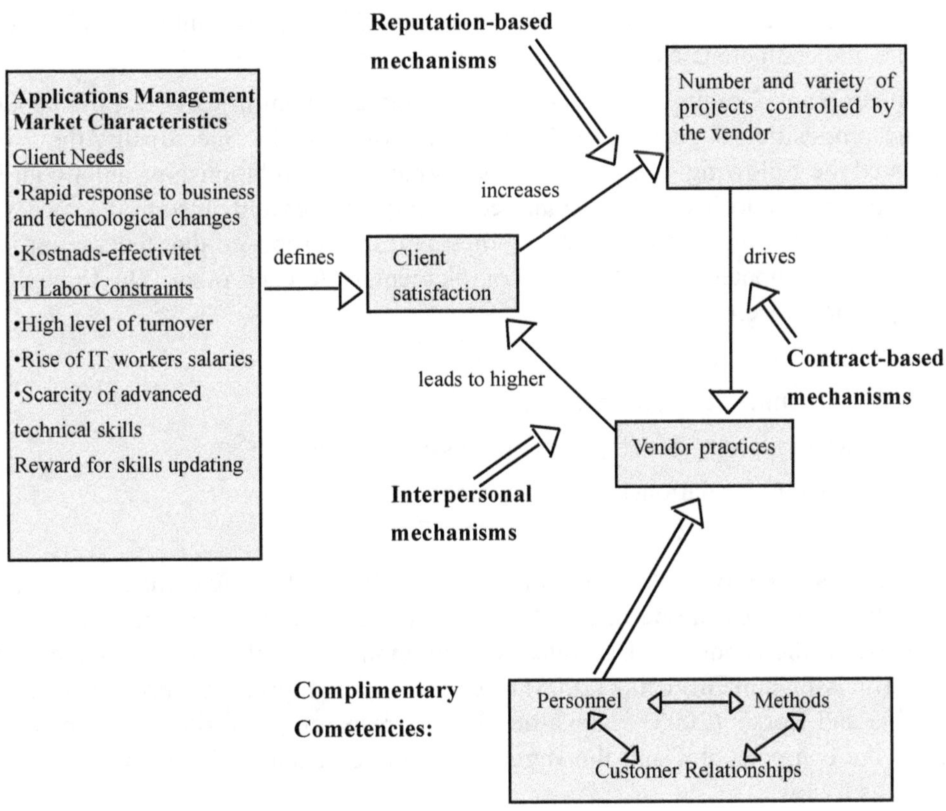

to build a reputation in the short run. Reputation is possible to organize in the general sense of controllability, which implies that a firm can be organized to take advantage of reputation as a resource.

The vendor's strategy and practices are depicted in Figure 6.3. This model of the IT vendor's value proposition suggests that client needs, as shaped by market constraints, specify the requirements for client satisfaction. Client satisfaction results from services provided by vendors through the application of a complementary set of core competencies targeted at delivering higher service at a lower marginal cost.

Client satisfaction is achieved in Figure 6.3 when the application of core competencies to projects is enabled by a healthy client-vendor relationship, which is in part influenced by the vendor's expertise in managing client relationships. Competencies, in turn, grow through the vendor's firm-wide experience gained from controlling a large number and variety of projects, which, in turn grow due to the reputation the vendor, and develop through its ability to satisfy customers. The model represents a set of positive feedback loops, which will result in negative outcomes if, for example, the competencies do not match client needs.

Erlingsson and Grødem (2005) conducted research to empirically test the vendor value proposition suggested by Levina and Ross (2003). Specifically, they formulated the following research question: What are the relationships among an IT outsourcing vendor's complementary core competencies and outsourcing success? In line with Levina and Ross (2003), their research proposed that the vendor has three core competencies which are complementary to each other. The three core competencies are:

- Personnel development
- Methodology development and dissemination
- Customer relationship management

These are argued to create more value as mutually reinforcing competencies than as individual, stand alone ones. Thus, benefits from doing more of one activity increases if the vendor is also doing more of another complementary competency. As Erlingsson and Grødem's (2005) research was attempting to empirically verify Levina and Ross's (2003) claims, the first six research propositions are made up from the competencies and the suggested complementary relationships between them as follows:

1. Will increased personnel development lead to more methodology development and dissemination?

2. Will increased methodology development and dissemination lead to more personnel development?
3. Will increased personnel development lead to more customer relationship management?
4. Will increased customer relationship management lead to more personnel development?
5. Will increased methodology development and dissemination lead to more customer relationship management?
6. Will increased customer relationship management lead to more methodology development and dissemination?

The final three propositions address the direct relationship between core competencies and outsourcing success. It can be reasoned that in order for the competencies to be complementary to each other and to have an effect on outsourcing success, both competencies must have an impact. If one competency does not have a relationship to outsourcing success, there is no mutuality. Therefore the direct impact of each competency on outsourcing success contributes the last three propositions as follows:

7. Will more personnel development lead to increased IT outsourcing success?
8. Will more methodology development and dissemination lead to increased IT outsourcing success?
9. Will more customer relationship management lead to increased IT outsourcing success?

In Erlingsson and Grødem's (2005) research, outsourcing success was measured by customer benefits, customer satisfaction and vendor benefits. Customer benefits are the extent of economical, technical and strategic benefits attained. Customer satisfaction is the extent of overall satisfaction with the contract and desire to retain with the outsourcing partner. Vendor benefits are the degree of economical, business development and organizational benefits attained.

In their empirical study of outsourcing relationships, Erlingsson and Grødem (2005) tested the first six propositions using simple regression and found that all relationships between core competencies were statistically significant. This implies that the assumed complementarities between personnel development, methodology development and dissemination and customer relationship management found initial support.

However, when applying multiple regression analysis, not all relationships were significant anymore. Relationships three to six were still statistically significant. The final complementary relationship, between customer relationship and methodology development, was not found to be present anymore. No statistical significance in either direction was shown. This contradicts the theory suggested by Levina and Ross (2003).

The last three propositions (7, 8, and 9) did find support in the empirical research. Personnel development, customer relationship management and methodology development and dissemination all influence outsourcing success. In our knowledge management perspective, such findings imply that improved knowledge management by the vendor in terms of personnel development, customer relationship management and methodology development and dissemination will increase outsourcing success.

However, when applying multiple regression analysis, not all relationships were significant anymore. Based on their empirical research, Erlingsson and Grødem (2005) developed a new model of significant relationships between vendor competencies and outsourcing success as illustrated in Figure 6.4.

Figure 6.4. Empirical relationships for vendor competencies

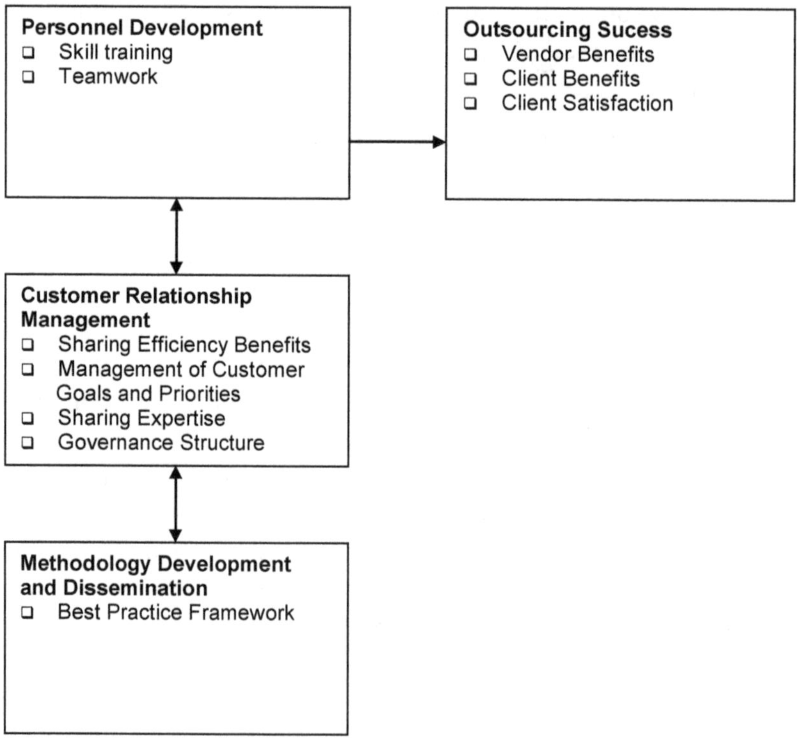

Personnel development in Figure 6.4 can be substituted with the more common term of human resource development. Human resource development is a process of developing and freeing up human potential and expertise through organizational development and personnel training and development in order to improve performance. Training is an important part of human resource development. There are two paths of skill training — formal and informal. Teamwork is another part of human resource development with an emphasis on cooperation rather than competition, on open disclosure of information and on building loyalty to the firm as significant underpinnings of success. Norms of interaction for teamwork include willingness to value and respond to diversity, openness to criticism and tolerance for failure.

Customer relationship management in Figure 6.4 is defined in terms of sharing efficiency benefits, management of customer goals and priorities, sharing expertise and governance structure. Efficiency can be defined as the internal perspective to metrics like cost reduction and productivity enhancement. Management of customer goals and priorities is concerned with the vendor organization's ability to understand and satisfy the customer's needs and objectives by becoming better at meeting requirements. Sharing expertise with client's staff requires the vendor to have the right policies and procedures in order to transfer knowledge effectively to the client organization. Governance structure is the framework for assigning decision rights concerning principles, architecture and infrastructure so that both vendor and customer have powers that match responsibilities.

Finally, methodology development and dissemination in Figure 6.4 is concerned with best practice framework. Best practice is the best of breed solutions to customer problems. For example, ITIL (Information Technology Infrastructure Library) provides a set of best practice guidelines and architectures to ensure that IT processes are closely aligned to business processes (Erlingsson & Grødem, 2005).

Value Shop as Vendor Value Configuration

When solving client problems, the vendor has the value configuration of value shop. The value shop is a company that creates value by solving unique problems for customers and clients (Stabell & Fjeldstad, 1998). Knowledge is the most important resource, and reputation is critical to firm success. A value shop is characterized by five primary activities: problem finding and acquisition, problem solving, choice, execution and control and evaluation, as illustrated in Chapter I.

Problem finding and acquisition involves working with the customer to determine the exact nature of the problem or need. It involves deciding on the overall plan of approaching the problem. Problem solving is the actual generation of ideas and action (or treatment) plans. Choice represents the decision of choosing between alternatives. While the least important primary activity of the value shop in terms of time and effort, it is also the most important in terms of customer value. Execution represents communicating, organizing and implementing the decision, or performing the treatment. Control and evaluation activities involve monitoring and measurement of how well the solution solved the original problem or met the original need. This may feed back in the first activity, problem finding and acquisition, for two reasons. First, if the proposed solution is inadequate or did not work, it feeds back into learning why it was inadequate and begins the problem-solving phase anew. Second, if the problem solution was successful, the firm might enlarge the scope of the problem-solving process to solve a bigger problem related to or dependent upon the first problem being solved.

P9: Vendor value shop performance in selecting and implementing the best solution for the client is dependent on the extent of client knowledge transfer.

Knowledge Strategy

Stock, flow and growth strategies are alternative knowledge strategies (Hansen et al., 1999). Approaches to knowledge management are dependent on knowledge focus in the client organization. Distinctions can be made between expert-driven, experience-driven and efficiency-driven businesses. An expert-driven business solves new problems with new methods. An experience-driven business solves new problems with experienced methods. An efficiency-driven business solves known problems with known methods.

The knowledge management strategy of an efficiency-driven business will be the stock strategy, while the flow strategy is more appropriate for the experience-driven business and the growth strategy is more appropriate for the expert-driven business.

P10: Knowledge management systems in outsourcing relationships are less important when the client is an expert-driven business.

Approaches to knowledge management are dependent on knowledge focus in the organization. Distinctions can be made between expert-driven, experience-driven and efficiency-driven businesses:

- Expert-driven business solves large, complex, risky, new and unusual problems for customers. Competitive advantage is achieved through continuous improvisation and innovation. Knowledge workers apply general high-level knowledge to understand, solve and learn. Learning from problem solving is important to be able to solve the next new and unknown problem for customers. An expert-driven business is characterized by both new problems and new methods for solution.
- Experience-driven business solves large and complicated problems for customers. The problems are new, but they can be solved with existing methods in a specific context every time. Competitive advantage is achieved through effective adaptation of existing problem solving methodologies and techniques. Continuous improvement in effectiveness is important to be able to solve the next problem for customers. An experience-based business is characterized by new problems and existing methods for solution.
- Efficiency-driven business solves known problems. The quality of the solution is found in fast and inexpensive application to meet customer needs. Competitive advantage is achieved in the ability to make small adjustments in existing goods and services at a low price. An efficiency-driven business is characterized by known problems and known methods for solution.

Few knowledge-intensive firms are only active in one of these businesses. Most firms are active in several of these businesses. For example, medical doctors in a hospital are mainly in the experience-driven business of solving new problems with known methods. Sometimes, they are in the expert-driven business of solving new problems with new methods. Similarly, lawyers in a law firm are often in the expert-driven business, but most of the time in the experience-driven business. In some engineering firms, engineers are often in the efficiency-driven business, but most of the time in the experience-based business.

Knowledge focus will be different in expert-driven, experience-driven and efficiency-driven businesses. In the expert-driven business, learning is important, while previous knowledge becomes obsolete. In the experience-driven business, know-how concerning problem solutions is important, while knowledge of previous problems becomes obsolete. In the efficiency-based business, all knowledge concerning both problems and solutions is important in an accumulation of knowledge to improve efficiency. These differences lead us to make distinctions between the following three knowledge management strategies of stock strategy, flow strategy and growth strategy as suggested by Hansen et al. (1999):

- **Stock strategy:** Focused on collecting and storing all knowledge in information bases in the organization. Information is stored in databases and made available to knowledge workers in the organization and in knowledge networks. Knowledge workers use databases to keep updated on relevant problems, relevant methods, news and opinions. Information on problems and methods accumulate over time in databases. This strategy can also be called person-to-knowledge strategy.
- **Flow strategy:** Focused on collecting and storing knowledge in information bases in the organization as long as the information is used in knowledge work processes. If certain kinds of knowledge work disappear, then information for those work processes become obsolete and can be deleted from databases. This is a yellow-pages strategy where information on knowledge areas covered by individuals in the firm is registered. The link to knowledge sources in the form of individuals is made specific in the databases, so that the person source can be identified. When a knowledge worker starts on a new project, the person will search company databases to find colleagues who already have experience in solving these kinds of problems. This strategy can also be called person-to-person strategy.
- **Growth strategy:** Focused on developing new knowledge. New knowledge is developed in innovative work processes taking place when knowledge workers

Figure 6.5. Characteristics of knowledge management strategies

Characteristics	**Stock strategy**	**Flow strategy**	**Growth strategy**
Knowledge focus	Efficiency-driven business	Experience-driven business	Expert-driven business
Important persons	Chief knowledge officer Chief information officer Database engineers	Chief knowledge officer Experienced knowledge workers	Management Experts
Knowledge base	Databases and information systems	Information networks	Networks of experts, work processes and learning environments
Important elements	Access to databases and information systems	Access to knowledge space	Access to networks of experts and learning environments
Management task	Collecting information and making it available	Connecting persons to experienced knowledge workers	Providing access to networks
Learning	Efficiency training applying existing knowledge	Experience accumulation applying existing knowledge	Growth training developing new knowledge

> have to solve new problems with new methods for customers. Often, several persons are involved in the innovation, and together they have gone through a learning process. When a knowledge worker starts on a new project, the person will use the intraorganizational and interorganizational network to find information on work processes and learning environments, which colleagues have used successfully in previous innovation processes.

There is a strong link between these three knowledge management strategies and the three alternatives of expert-driven, experience-driven and efficiency-driven businesses. In Figure 6.5, characteristics of the three strategies are presented. Typically, efficiency-driven businesses will apply the stock strategy, while experience-driven businesses will apply the flow strategy and expert-driven businesses will apply the growth strategy.

Research on Leadership Roles in Outsourcing Projects

This section presents research investigating the emphasis placed on different managerial roles by IT project managers. *Please note that this section describes research carried out by the author.*

Six managerial roles were applied in this research: personnel leader, resource allocator, spokesman, entrepreneur, liaison and monitor. Two surveys were conducted in Norway to investigate these management roles. In the first survey, which focused on project management roles in internal IT projects, the respondents emphasized the personnel leader role significantly more than other managerial roles. In the second survey, which focused on project management roles in IT outsourcing projects, the respondents emphasized the spokesman role. With changing business environments, the locus of value creation is no longer within the boundaries of a single firm, but occurs instead at the nexus of relationships between parties. With the growing importance of pooling knowledge resources, knowledge management will have to transcend organizational boundaries in exchanges such as IT outsourcing relationships. We would therefore expect to find differences in our two surveys. The empirical results provide evidence that project managers in internal IT projects are more internally oriented than project managers in outsourcing projects. Future research should also take into account culture and structure dimensions as well as the specific industry of the IT project. This research concludes that project managers of both internal IT projects and outsourcing projects should be more externally oriented to meet future challenges. The contingent approach to leadership roles is applied in this research section.

Information technology (IT) functions of all sizes and in all industries face many new challenges in today's rapidly changing environment. Multiple and flexible ways of working require organizational structures to be flexible as well. Projects are a flexible and efficient way of working, whether the goal is to design, install, reengineer or reorganize technology initiatives. However, IT projects are often driven by aggressive deadlines and periods of frequent change (Murch, 2000). Projects are temporary organizational structures and unique, goal-oriented work systems where technical, procedural, organizational and human elements are integrated. To get the job done, resources must be identified and allocated, and activities must be properly organized and structured in accordance with business and technical requirements.

The project management approach to solving IT problems and opportunities involves stakeholders such as CEOs, clients, IT managers, project managers, end-users and consultants (Ko et al., 2005). Each role and responsibility of these stakeholders must be clearly defined in making the most of the potential of information technology. Information technology projects come in many different shapes and sizes. In this section we are studying two types: internal IT projects and IT outsourcing projects.

Internal IT projects are performed within the IT department. Both the project manager and the staff are members of the department (Gottschalk & Karlsen, 2002). The results of this type of project are typically used within the IT department or the user organization. Examples of internal IT projects include feasibility studies, development projects, design projects, implementation projects, upgrade projects, migration projects and support services projects.

IT outsourcing is typically organized as a project. The project is concerned with turning over all or parts of an IT activity to an outside vendor. The user organization (client) transfers property decision rights over information technology functions to an external (vendor) organization (Koh et al. 2004). The project is a process whereby an organization decided to contract-out or sell the firm's IT assets, people and/or activities to a third party supplier, who in exchange provides and manages these assets and services (Kern & Willcocks, 2002).

This section investigates project management roles in internal IT projects vs. IT outsourcing projects. We are studying how project managers in these two groups of projects perceive their leadership roles, and discuss the implications of the differences between them. The following research question is addressed: *What leadership roles are emphasized in internal IT projects vs. IT outsourcing projects?* This IT management research is important because the contingent approach to leadership roles implies that the significance of each role is dependent on the situation. This section discusses a very important and interesting aspect of leadership roles and types with IT projects.

Management Roles

A manager's job is complicated and demanding. Managers must undertake several types of activities to achieve the objectives of their organization. To better understand the manager's activities, we will use the concept of management roles, which was introduced by Mintzberg (1990, 1994).

A manager's job consists of several parallel roles. At a certain point in time, the manager may perceive one role as more important than the others. Mintzberg (1994) found that it is a peculiarity of the management literature that its best-known writers all seem to emphasize one particular part of the manager's job to the exclusion of the others. Together they cover all the parts, but even that may not describe the whole task of managing.

Mintzberg's role typology is frequently used in studies of managerial work. In the context of information technology management, Grover et al. (1993) identified the relevance of six roles from Mintzberg's role typology: personnel leader, resource allocator, spokesman, entrepreneur, liaison and monitor. In this research, the same six roles are applied, both to internal IT projects and to IT outsourcing projects. The role terminology is commonly in use and is genderless. We will employ the following role descriptions:

- **Personnel leader:** As a leader, the manager is responsible for supervising, hiring, training, organizing, coordinating and motivating a cadre of personnel to achieve the goals of the organization (which may be the IT department or the IT project). This role is mainly internal.
- **Resource allocator:** The manager must decide how to allocate human, financial and information resources to the different tasks of the project. This role emphasizes planning, organizing, coordinating and controlling tasks, and is mainly internal.
- **Spokesman:** As a spokesman, the manager extends organizational contacts to areas outside his or her own jurisdiction. This role emphasizes promoting acceptance of the IT department or the IT project within the organization of which they are part. For the IT executive, it means contact with the rest of the organization, for the project manager, contact with the base organization. Frequently, he or she must move across traditional departmental boundaries and become involved in production, distribution, marketing and financial matters.
- **Entrepreneur:** The manager identifies the users' needs and develops solutions that change business situations. A major responsibility of the manager is to ensure that rapidly evolving technical opportunities are understood, planned, implemented and strategically exploited in the organization.

Figure 6.6. Leadership roles

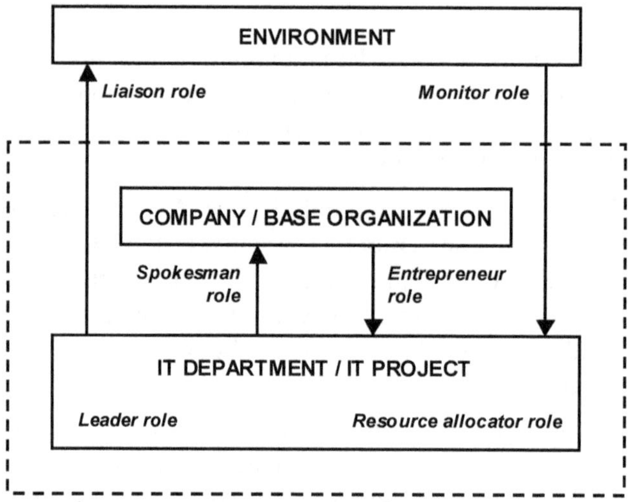

- **Liaison:** In this role, the manager communicates with the external environment, and it includes exchanging information with IS/IT suppliers, customers, buyers, market analysts and the media. This is an active, external role.
- **Monitor:** This role emphasizes scanning of the external environment to keep up with relevant technical changes and competition. The manager identifies new ideas from sources outside his or her organization. To accomplish this task, the manager uses many resources, including vendor contacts, professional relationships and a network of personal contacts.

These six leadership roles are illustrated in Figure 6.6 (Karlsen & Gottschalk, 2002). The personnel leader and resource allocator are roles internal to the project for the project manager. The spokesman and entrepreneur are roles directed toward the base organization, and the liaison and monitor roles are external to the base organization for the project manager.

Research Hypotheses

Many IT projects are internal projects carried out in the IT department. The project manager is often the IT executive or another member of the department. The challenges that face the project manager in carrying out such a project requests both project management knowledge and practice, for example, planning and scheduling systems. A dominant focus in such projects has been on internal activities within the project and the base organization. Very often, little or no attention is given to the project environment and other stakeholders. Most of the project-planning models currently available consider the project as though it was developed in a vacuum. The project manager is responsible for planning, organizing, coordinating and controlling tasks to ensure successful project completion. In order to do this, the project manager has to allocate human, financial and information resources to the project.

According to Mintzberg's (1990) role typology, we expect the internal roles — personnel leader and resource allocator — to be more emphasized in internal IT projects than in outsourcing projects, since outsourcing projects have an external emphasis (Lee et al., 2004; Willcocks et al., 2004). From the above discussion, we find it reasonable to propose the following hypotheses:

H1: Internal roles are more important in internal IT projects than in outsourcing projects.

H1a: The personnel leader role is more important in internal IT projects than in outsourcing projects.

H1b: The resource allocator role is more important in internal IT projects than in outsourcing projects.

Project managers responsible for outsourcing projects in client organizations will have to focus on managing client characteristics, while project managers responsible for outsourcing projects from the vendor side will have to focus on both vendor-client relationships and the vendor's value proposition (Levina & Ross, 2003). Hence, we argue that the job of the project managers in outsourcing projects is oriented towards external roles.

According to this line of reasoning, we should expect that the most external roles (monitor and liaison) are more emphasized and important among project managers in outsourcing projects than among project managers in internal IT projects. From the above discussion, we propose the following hypotheses:

H2: External roles are more important in outsourcing projects than in internal IT projects.

H2a: The liaison role is more important in outsourcing projects than in internal IT projects.

H2b: The monitor role is more important in outsourcing projects than in internal IT projects.

The last two management roles defined by Mintzberg (1990) — spokesman and entrepreneur — are somewhat difficult to classify in our research context, since they are external to the IT department/IT project and internal to the organization.

However, according to Grover et al. (1993) we should to some degree expect that the role of spokesman (with internal orientation to the organization and other departments) to be more emphasized by project managers in internal IT projects than project managers in outsourcing projects. The role of spokesman is a management role that incorporates activities that require the project manager to extend organizational interactions outside the department to other areas of the organization and top executives as well. Frequently, the spokesman must communicate across traditional departmental boundaries and become involved in matters concerning production, distribution, marketing and finance. The spokesman role requires that the project manager acts as an information disseminator and politician (Inkpen & Tsang, 2005), ensuring that IT projects are properly connected to the top level of the firm and to key decision-makers in other departments. Hence, we propose the following hypothesis:

H3: The spokesman role is more important in internal IT projects than in outsourcing projects.

According to Frame (1995), the clients and users' needs are the driving force behind projects. If articulating needs is done insufficiently, the project will be built on a poor foundation, and major problems will arise when implementing the changes. As an entrepreneur, it is the project manager's role in outsourcing projects to identify the users' needs and develop a fully acceptable solution. This project management role is further emphasized by Edum-Fotwe and McCaffer (2000), who state that the project manager is required to provide innovative solutions, as well as the business processes involved in the achievement of the project's outcome.

Client consultation, communication, listening, feedback activity and client acceptance are critical project success factors (Bahli & Rivard, 2005). We will therefore expect that the role of entrepreneur is more emphasized by project managers in outsourcing projects than project managers in internal IT projects. Hence, the fourth hypothesis is as follows:

H4: The entrepreneur role is more important in outsourcing projects than in internal IT projects.

Research Method

The Grover et al. (1993) instrument, which operationalized the managerial roles identified by Mintzberg (1990) and adapted them to the IT context, was used as a basis to investigate the roles in internal IT projects and outsourcing projects. The rationale for choosing this instrument was based upon the high validity and reliability they and others have obtained within each of the managerial roles.

The present study consists of two surveys conducted in Norway in 2002/2004 to investigate the leadership roles. The survey instrument contains six five-point Likert scales, and the respondent is asked to rate the importance of each item as it relates to the management role.

The first questionnaire focused on internal IT project and was mailed to 673 companies selected from the listing of members of the Norwegian Computing Society. It was assumed that these firms would tend to have internal IT projects and project managers with job attributes consistent with our management role classification. Based on the availability of correct addresses, 591 questionnaires reached their destinations. Questionnaires with incomplete responses were deleted. After two mailings, a total sample of 80 was returned, representing a response rate of 14%.

The second questionnaire focused on outsourcing projects. It was distributed at an internal seminar for project managers in IT outsourcing projects. Eighty-four responses were received.

In both surveys the objective of the study was explained and respondents were assured of the confidentiality of their answers. We have no indications of nonresponse bias. There is little reason to suspect that nonresponding project managers perceived their firm or project differently than those project managers who did respond, since the respondents included all sectors within the industry and the public sector.

Statistical Data and Results

Figures 6.7 to 6.15 present the results of statistical analysis (both descriptive statistics and ANOVA) of the comparisons between internal IT projects and outsourcing projects.

Figure 6.7 shows descriptive statistics regarding management roles in internal IT projects, where the response scale ranged from 1 to 5 (1 = not important and 5 = very important). Means and t-tests (to assess statistical significance of the difference between two independent sample means) were used to examine the data from the survey.

Figure 6.7. Statistics for internal IT projects

Leadership role	Mean	t-values				
		2	3	4	5	6
1 Personnel leader	4.33	2.65*	2.56*	4.38**	8.22**	9.12**
2 Resource allocator	4.04		0.30	2.20*	5.63**	6.33**
3 Spokesman	4.00			2.04*	4.88**	5.79**
4 Entrepreneur	3.70				2.30*	4.45**
5 Liaison	3.34					-1.54
6 Monitor	3.11					

*Note: The statistical significance of the t-values is ** for p<.01 and * for p<.05*

As can be seen from Figure 6.7, project managers in internal IT projects emphasize the internal roles, personnel leader and resource allocator as the most important management roles. The management roles of monitor and liaison, which have a focus outside the project and base organization, are the least important roles. Using a t-test procedure, we found that there are thirteen significant differences between the management roles. Most interesting is the fact that the personnel leader role is significantly more important than all the other management roles. From Figure 6.7 we can observe that the internal management role of personnel leader is considered to be significantly more important than the two external roles, monitor ($t = 9.12$, $p = 0.00$) and liaison ($t = 8.22$, $p = 0.00$). Statistical analysis also indicates that the resource allocator role is significantly more important than the monitor role ($t = 6.33$, $p = 0.00$) and the liaison role ($t = 5.63$, $p = 0.00$).

Figure 6.8 shows the descriptive statistics for project managers in IT outsourcing projects. As we can see from the table, project managers in outsourcing projects choose the spokesman role as a top priority role. A t-test between the six different leadership roles gives seven significant t-values. The results indicate that the spokesman role is significantly more important than the other roles. Surprisingly, the liaison and monitor roles, which focus on contacts and personal relationships with people outside the project and scanning of the external environment, are given lowest priority.

The statistical technique used for testing the research hypotheses was the univariate analysis of variance (ANOVA). The principal consideration in the use of the two-group ANOVA is the sample size in each of the groups. In this study, one group had 80 responses, while the other group had 84 responses. Testing of the assumptions for using ANOVA was conducted, and the criteria were met.

Figure 6.8. Statistics for IT outsourcing projects

Leadership role	Mean	t-values				
		2	3	4	5	6
1 Personnel leader	3.29	-1.76	-4.03**	-2.23*	0.37	0.06
2 Resource allocator	3.59		-2.41*	-0.97	1.81	1.66
3 Spokesman	4.04			1.61	4.70**	4.59**
4 Entrepreneur	3.77				2.83**	3.03**
5 Liaison	3.28					0.35
6 Monitor	3.23					

*Note: The statistical significance of the t-values is ** for p<.01 and * for p<.05*

Figure 6.9. Analysis of variance: Personnel leader role

Source	*DF*	*SS*	*MS*	*F*	*P*
Factor	1	43.25	43.25	37.85**	0.00
Error	162	185.11	1.14		
Total	163	228.36			

*Note: The statistical significance of the F-values is ** for p<0.01 and * for p<0.05*

Hypothesis 1 examines whether project managers in internal IT projects are more internally oriented than project managers in outsourcing projects. This hypothesis had two sub-hypotheses (H1a and H1b).

In Figure 6.9, statistical results of the test of hypothesis H1a are shown. The analysis of variance (ANOVA) gives sufficient statistical evidence to conclude that project managers in internal IT projects emphasize the leader role significantly more than project managers in outsourcing projects. The hypothesis is supported (F = 37.85, p = 0.00).

The statistical test of hypothesis H1b is shown in Figure 6.10. As we can see from the data, project managers in internal IT projects emphasize the resource allocator role significantly more than project managers in outsourcing projects. The hypothesis is significant at the 0.01 level of significance (F = 8.41, p = 0.00).

Figure 6.10. Analysis of variance: Resource allocator role

Source	*DF*	*SS*	*MS*	*F*	*P*
Factor	1	7.95	7.95	8.41**	0.00
Error	160	151.12	0.95		
Total	161	159.07			

*Note: The statistical significance of the F-values is ** for p<0.01 and * for p<0.05*

Figure 6.11. Analysis of variance: Liaison role

Source	*DF*	*SS*	*MS*	*F*	*P*
Factor	1	0.54	0.54	0.42	0.52
Error	161	208.48	1.30		
Total	162	209.02			

*Note: The statistical significance of the F-values is ** for p<0.01 and * for p<0.05*

Figure 6.12. Analysis of variance: Monitor role

Source	*DF*	*SS*	*MS*	*F*	*P*
Factor	1	1.20	1.20	0.95	0.33
Error	161	203.12	1.26		
Total	162	204.32			

*Note: The statistical significance of the F-values is ** for p<0.01 and * for p<0.05*

The second main hypothesis (H2) proposed in this section was whether project managers in outsourcing projects are more externally oriented than project managers in internal IT projects. The main hypothesis was de-composed into two sub-hypotheses (H2a and H2b).

The results of the ANOVA analysis of hypothesis H2a are presented in Figure 6.11. The hypothesis is not supported ($F = 0.42$, $p = 0.52$).

The results of the testing of hypothesis H2b are shown in Figure 6.12. The results conclude that project managers in outsourcing projects do not emphasize the monitor role significantly more than project managers in internal IT projects. Thus, the hypothesis is not supported ($F = 0.95$, $p = 0.33$).

Figure 6.13. Analysis of variance: Entrepreneur role

Source	***DF***	***SS***	***MS***	***F***	***P***
Factor	1	0.25	0.25	0.19	0.66
Error	161	205.41	1.28		
Total	162	205.66			

*Note: The statistical significance of the F-values is ** for p<0.01 and * for p<0.05*

Figure 6.14. Analysis of variance: Spokesman role

Source	***DF***	***SS***	***MS***	***F***	***P***
Factor	1	0.05	0.05	0.05	0.82
Error	162	164.89	1.02		
Total	163	164.94			

*Note: The statistical significance of the F-values is ** for p<0.01 and * for p<0.05*

Figure 6.15. Leadership roles (statistical results for internal vs. outsourcing projects)

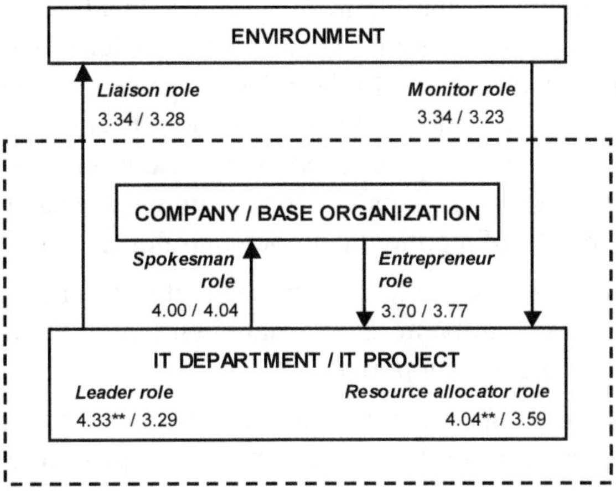

Hypothesis 3 examines whether the spokesman role is more important in internal IT projects than in outsourcing projects. Figure 6.13 displays that this hypothesis did not find support (F = 0.19, p = 0.66).

Hypothesis 4 examines whether the entrepreneur role is more important in outsourcing projects than in internal IT projects. Figure 6.14 displays that this hypothesis did not find support (F = 0.05, p = 0.82).

To summarize, we have illustrated the importance of each management role in Figure 6.15. The first number is the mean score of project managers in internal IT projects, and the second number is the mean score of project managers in outsourcing projects. The response scale ranged from 1 to 5 (1 = not important and 5 = very important). The statistical significant values are shown with ** for p<0.01 and * for p<0.05.

Summary

IT functions and tasks are typically organized as projects. IT management is largely a project-driven exercise. IT projects differ in their goals. An internal IT project has the objective of improving IT systems using internal resources. An IT outsourcing project has the objective of improving IT systems using external resources. Therefore, we expected to find differences in leadership roles in these two kinds of IT projects.

We found that personnel leader and resource allocator roles are the most important in internal IT projects, as expected. Also as expected, we found that spokesman and entrepreneur roles were the most important leadership roles in IT outsourcing projects.

One explanation for the latter finding is the substantial risks involved in information systems outsourcing. According to a study by Gonzales et al. (2005), the main concern in relation to IT outsourcing is the excessive dependence on the provider of this type of contracted services. In the roles of spokesman and entrepreneur, the project manager is able to collect information about needs and expectations from the users and managers to be implemented in an outsourcing contract. Especially in common situations of organizations lacking a computer usage policy (Foltz et al., 2005), the establishment of a policy in an outsourcing arrangement is important.

In our testing of hypotheses, we found support that personnel leader and resource allocator roles are significantly more important in internal vs. outsourcing projects. Further hypotheses were not supported.

One reason for lack of support is that external roles are becoming more important in all kinds of projects. It is not feasible anymore for a project to be an island in the organization. Project managers have learned that one day at the end of the project, the base organization is to gain from project outcomes. The only way to enable project results transfer to the base organization is to stay in contact with it during project work.

IT outsourcing is a make-or-buy decision of information technology services that includes both operations of information systems and development of new systems. In this perspective, Perrons and Platts (2004) found that the make decision may be more suited to either extremely fast or extremely slow rate of technological change, while a buy strategy might be more appropriate in market sectors where technologies evolve at a medium pace. This perspective emphasizes the monitor role, which is concerned with monitoring the external environment concerning technological and other changes. Based on this perspective, it is surprising that the monitor role achieves the lowest score among leadership roles.

IT outsourcing is an arrangement where a vendor takes over work from the client. In this perspective, systems and routines have to be implemented at the vendor's premises. Successful implementation becomes crucial issue. We know from IT that there are many implementation barriers (Ko et al., 2005). In the roles of spokesman and entrepreneur, the project manager will enable communications with the user community for successful implementation of the outsourcing arrangement.

With changing business environments, the locus of value creation is no longer within the boundaries of a single firm, but occurs instead at the nexus of relationships between parties (Malhotra et al., 2005). Enterprises have to rely on business partners to share knowledge and continually respond to change. With the growing importance of pooling knowledge resources, the project manager has the role of knowledge manager in the project. This argument stresses the roles of spokesman and entrepreneur in IT outsourcing projects. To avoid reluctance to share knowledge, as discussed by Wasko and Faraj (2005) and also by Kankanhalli et al. (2005), the project manager has to be active as both entrepreneur and spokesman in the organization.In our perspective of knowledge management, we can identify some leadership roles that are more knowledge management intensive than others. For example, both spokesman and entrepreneur roles are knowledge management intensive.

As introduced in the last section, future research on leadership roles in different kinds of IT projects can apply the knowledge management perspective from the resource-based theory of the firm (Garud & Kumaraswamy, 2005). Furthermore, projects can be studied in terms of their value configuration, which will typically be a value shop. A project solves problems, and problem solving occurs in the five primary activities like the value shop as illustrated in Chapter I.

A comparison of leadership roles in internal IT projects vs. outsourcing projects leads to different importance of roles in the value shop. An external partner, the (potential) vendor of IT services, will get involved in all five primary activities. Future research can apply this framework to study the importance of leadership roles depending on the extent to which the project solves an internal problem, an external problem or a mixed problem, as is the case in an IT outsourcing project.

Future research should also take into account culture and structure dimensions as well as the specific industry of the IT project. For example, it is unrealistic to believe that an IT project in healthcare would require the same type of leadership roles as an IT project in a manufacturing environment. It is only by cross-industry data analysis that a more robust methodology can be developed. Further, one must look at the type of IT project (e.g., SAP implementation vs. PACS implementation) and its local, national or international impact on the organization.

This research applied the contingent approach to leadership roles. It was assumed that internal IT projects would emphasize internal leadership roles, while IT outsourcing projects would emphasize external leadership roles. Generally, empirical tests of research hypotheses provided support for this assumption.

Specifically, project managers in internal IT projects emphasize the personnel leader role significantly more than project managers in outsourcing projects. Also, project managers in internal IT projects emphasize the resource allocator role significantly more than project managers in outsourcing projects. However, we found no support for the hypothesis that the liaison and monitor roles would be more important in outsourcing projects. The same lack of significant results was found concerning the spokesman and entrepreneur roles.

Maturity Model for IT Outsourcing Relationships

Stages of growth models have been used widely in both organizational research and information technology management research. According to King and Teo (1997), these models describe a wide variety of phenomena — the organizational life cycle, product life cycle, biological growth and so forth. These models assume that predictable patterns (conceptualized in terms of stages) exist in the growth of organizations and in the growth of relationships among organizations.

In this section, a three-stage model for the evolution of an outsourcing relationship is proposed. The purpose of the model is both to understand the current situation in the relationship in terms of a specific stage and to develop strategies for moving to a higher stage in the future. The model is based on several management theories.

The first stage is the cost stage. This stage is based on transaction cost theory, neoclassical economic theory, contractual theory, theory of firm boundaries and agency theory. The second stage is the resource stage. This stage is based on core competencies theory, resource-based theory and relational exchange theory. The third and final stage is the partnership stage, which is based on partnership and alliance theory, stakeholder theory and social exchange theory.

P10: Knowledge management systems are more important at higher stages of maturity in an outsourcing relationship.

Cost Stage

Initially, IT outsourcing is driven by cost concerns. According to neoclassical economic theory, firms outsource IT to attain cost advantages from assumed economies of scale and scope possessed by vendors (Ang & Straub, 1998). Neoclassical economic theory regards every business organization as a production function (Williamson, 2000), and where their motivation is driven by profit maximization. This means that companies offer products and services to the market where they have a cost or production advantage. They rely on the marketplace where they have disadvantages. According to neoclassical economic theory, companies will justify their sourcing strategy based on evaluating possibilities for production cost savings. Thus, the question whether to outsource, is a question whether the marketplace can produce products and services at a lower price than internal production. In the context of IT outsourcing, a company will keep its IT function internally if this has production cost advantages, and it will outsource when the marketplace can offer production cost savings.

However, IT outsourcing causes additional costs to occur that are labeled transaction costs. Transaction costs occur in the exchange between client and vendor. According to transaction cost theory, transaction costs are positively associated with (1) the necessity of investments in durable, specific assets, (2) infrequency of transacting, (3) task complexity and uncertainty, (4) difficulty in measuring task performance and (5) independencies with other transactions.

Hancox and Hackney (2000) interviewed IT managers to find support for the transaction cost theory in IT outsourcing. Many of the features of transaction cost economics could be identified in the outsourcing arrangements.

When entering an IT outsourcing arrangement, vendor and client sign a contract. An outsourcing contract provides a legally bound, institutional framework in which each party's rights, duties and responsibilities are codified and the goals, policies and strategies underlying the arrangement are specified. Every outsourcing contract has the purpose of facilitating exchange and preventing opportunism.

Luo (2002) examined how contract, cooperation and performance are associated with each other. He argues that contract and cooperation are not substitutes but complements in relation to performance. A contract alone is insufficient to guide outsourcing evolution and performance. Since outsourcing involves repeated inter-organizational exchanges that become socially embedded over time, cooperation is an important safeguard mechanism mitigating external and internal hazards and overcoming adaptive limits of contracts, as we will see at higher levels of relationship maturity.

In an outsourcing relationship, the cooperating parties engage in an agency relationship defined as a contract under which one organization (the principal) engage another organization (the agent) to perform some service on its behalf which involves delegating some decision-making authority to the agent. Agency theory describes the relationship between the two parties.

According to Eisenhardt (1985), agency theory is concerned with resolving two problems that can occur in agency relationships. The first is the agency problem that arises when the desires or goals of the principal and agent conflict, and it is difficult or expensive for the principal to verify what the agent is actually doing. The second is the problem of risk sharing that arises when the principal and agent have different risk preferences. These problems are well known in IT outsourcing. An example might be that the client organization wants to reduce its costs, while the vendor organization wants to maximize profits.

A final theory for the cost stage is the theory of firm boundaries. Firm boundaries — defined as the scope of revenue-sharing arrangements across individuals — reflect trade-offs associated with referral problems, which are problems of matching economic opportunities to individuals' efficiency (Garicano & Hubbard, 2003). A large theoretical literature focuses on the question, "What determines firms' boundaries?" In our case of IT outsourcing, firms' boundaries are determined by the extent to which there are large markets for specialization. If there are large markets for IT services available from vendors, then a client company will tend to outsource more of its internal IT function.

When an outsourcing relationship has solved all problems at the cost stage, the parties are ready for the resource stage. Solving all problems implies that the client achieves intended cost savings, transaction costs are at acceptable level, the contract is successful in preventing opportunistic behavior, principal and agent avoid conflicts and the division of labor between client and vendor works satisfactorily.

Resource Stage

The central tenet in resource-based theory is that unique organizational resources of both tangible and intangible nature are the real source of competitive advantage. With resource-based theory, organizations are viewed as a collection of resources that are heterogeneously distributed within and across industries.

Outsourcing gives a client organization access to resources in the vendor organization as the vendor handles IT functions for the client. Vendor resources can produce innovation, which is essential for long-term survival of the client. Quinn (2000) argues that the time is right for outsourcing innovation, because demand is growing fast in the global economy, creating a host of new specialist markets sufficiently large to attract innovation.

The value generation potential of an outsourcing relationship consists of three factors: client characteristics, the vendor-client relationship and vendor characteristics. A key client characteristic is an understanding of how to manage resources that a firm does not own. A key in the vendor-client relationship is a formal (contractual) aspect of the relationship. The third factor shaping the outsourcing value proposition is the vendor's own capabilities. From an outsourcing vendor's perspective, there are many potential opportunities and benefits for the client. These opportunities and benefits can be derived from the IT outsourcing vendor's value proposition. Important vendor characteristics include capabilities such as technical competence, understanding the customer's business and relationship management.

Levina and Ross (2003) stressed the importance of vendor characteristics in terms of the vendor value proposition. The concepts of complementaries and competencies explain that outsourcing vendors can increase productivity and reduce costs on client projects by applying a set of complementary application management competencies. They identified three complementary vendor competencies: IT personnel development, methodology development and dissemination and customer relationship management.

The value generation potential from vendor resources can be significant for the client. If the vendor has strategic resources, applications of these resources for the client can provide the client organization with sustained competitive advantage. Strategic resources are characterized by being valuable, rare, nonimitable, nontransferable, nonsubstitutable, combinable and exploitable (Barney, 2002).

The resource stage is not only characterized by access to vendor resources. Also, the client will focus on internal resources at this stage. Those resources are typically concerned with core competencies. After outsourcing, the client organization will typically focus on and strengthen its core competencies. Core competencies can be defined as the skills that are the determinant resources for a firm's competitive advantage. Quinn (1999) argues that core competencies are not products or "those things we do relatively well." They are those activities — usually intellectually based service activities or systems — that the company performs better than any other enterprise. They are the set of skills and systems that a company does at best-in-the-world levels and through which a company creates uniquely high value for customers.

According to the theory of core competencies, developing best-in-the-world capabilities is crucial in designing a core competency strategy. Long-term advantage will depend on identifying the next unique combination no one else is exploiting in the marketplace; however, sustainable competitive advantage is strongest if tied to firm-specific capabilities.

When the vendor value proposition is working in terms of successful application of vendor resources for the client organization, and when the client organization is able to work on its core competencies, then the relationship is ready to move from the resource stage to the partnership stage.

Partnership Stage

Partnership appears to be a less rigorously defined analytical framework than other theories such as transaction costs, agency and core competencies. Indeed, the very word *partnership* has a more everyday ring to it and is associated with readily understood characteristics, which may be found in a relationship between two or more parties in a particular context. Partnership's treatment in the IS literature seems largely nontheoretical, perhaps reflecting a wide diversity of practical arrangements and the absence of a single commonly recognized theory. Although the sharing of risk and reward is sometimes mentioned in the IS literature, often the emphasis is on intangibles, such as trust, comfort, understanding, flexibility, cooperation, shared values, goals problem solving, good interpersonal relations and regular communication (Hancox & Hackney, 2000).

Partnership, often referred to as an alliance, has frequently been noted as a major feature of IT outsourcing. Alliances are broadly defined as collaborative efforts between two or more firms in which the firms cooperate in an effort to achieve mutually compatible goals that they could not achieve easily alone.

According to relational exchange theory, a partnership is dependent on relational norms. Norms are expectations about behavior that are at least partially shared by a group of decision-makers. Norms are important in relational exchange because they provide the governance rules of the game. Relational norms are based on the expectation of mutuality of interest, essentially prescribing stewardship behavior, and are designed to enhance the wellbeing of the relationship as a whole (Lambe et al., 2000).

Social exchange theory suggests that each party in an exchange relationship compares the social and economic outcomes from these interactions to those that are available from exchange alternatives, which determines their dependence on the exchange relationship. Positive economic and social outcomes over time increase the partners' trust of each other and commitment to maintaining the exchange relationship (Lambe et al., 2001).

A final theory that can illustrate the partnership stage is stakeholder theory. Stakeholder theory is concerned with balancing the interests of the stakeholders in an outsourcing relationship. According to Lacity and Willcocks (2000), there are four distinct client IT stakeholder groups and three distinct supplier IT stakeholder groups. The groups identified are customer senior business managers, customer senior IT managers, customer IT staff, customer IT users, supplier senior managers, supplier account managers and supplier IT staff.

Figure 6.16. Critical issues in each stage of maturity in outsourcing relationships

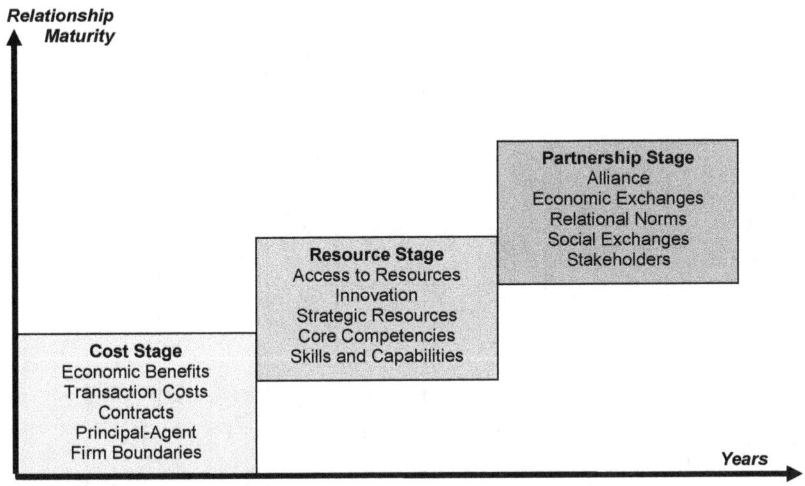

Comparison of Stages

As illustrated in Figure 6.16, the cost stage is concerned with high economic benefits, low transaction costs, effective contracts, good principal-agent cooperation and efficient division of labor from firm boundaries.

The resource stage is concerned with access to vendor resources, resources for innovation, strategic resources and development of core competencies in the client organization in terms of skills and capabilities. The third and final partnership stage is concerned with alliance work, economic exchanges, mutual relational norms, social exchanges and balancing stakeholder interests. Characteristics of each stage are listed in Figure 6.17.

As an outsourcing relationship matures, the maturity model suggests that performance measures develop beyond cost minimization and operational efficiency into business productivity and technology innovation, and further into business benefits and achievement of mutual goals for client and vendor. The outsourcing contract changes focus from specified obligations and service level agreements, to availability of strategic resources, management of key competence and critical projects, to arrangements for profit sharing and personnel exchanges between vendor and client.

Figure 6.17. Characteristics of stages in outsourcing relationships

	Stage I Cost Stage	Stage II Resource Stage	Stage III Partnership Stage
Performance measures	Cost minimization Operational efficiency	Business productivity Technology innovation	Business benefits Mutual goals
Contract focus	Specified obligations Service level agreements	Key competence Critical projects	Profit sharing People exchanges
Relationship	Division of labor Service exchanges	Resource transactions Economic exchanges	Joint projects Social exchanges
Vendor management	Account manager	Operations manager	Business manager
Client management	IT manager	Division manager	Business manager
Vendor role	Supplier Contractual partner	Agent Strategic resource	Partner
Client role	Buyer Define technology requirements	Principal Define business needs	Partner Co-developing business processes
Transplant role	Excellent operations	Technology initiatives	Complementary capabilities, skills, competences and methods
Control mechanism	Service level agreement Costs	Project performance Service quality	Strategy implementation
Governance arrangement	Duopoly IT infrastructure	Federation Applications	Monarchy Investments
Knowledge management	Information	Explicit knowledge	Tacit knowledge
Transactions	Scheduled	On demand	Continuous
Client dependency	Low	Medium	High
Vendor involvement	Low	Medium	High

Knowledge Needs

Knowledge needs will vary from stage to stage. At the cost stage, accounting and financial information is important. At the resource stage, resource information is needed. Finally, at the partnership stage, relationship support is needed. Examples of knowledge needs are listed in Figure 6.18.

Figure 6.18. Knowledge management issues depending on relationship maturity

	Stage I Cost Stage	Stage II Resource Stage	Stage III Partnership Stage
Know-what Descriptive knowledge	Financial transactions Service transactions	Resources and competences needed in business process redesign	Partner goals and strategies Partner culture
Know-how Procedural knowledge	Transaction processes Exchange processes	Business process redesign	Contributions to partner performance
Know-why Reasoning knowledge	Incidents in financial transactions Incidents in service transactions	Effects of business process redesign	Partner behavior in the relationship

Maturity Case of ABB-IBM, RR-EDS and SAS-CSC

In order to understand the inherent complexities and the underlying constructs of managing successful IT outsourcing relationships, empirical research is need. The exploratory case studies that Gottschalk and Solli-Sæther (2006) conducted had the following guiding research question: "How do client and vendor organizations manage their IT outsourcing relationships?"

The selection of cases was based on an instrumental approach, which means that the case study was carried out to provide insight into issue or refinement of theory. "The case is of secondary interest; it plays a supportive role, facilitating our understanding of something else. The choice of case is made because it is expected to advance our understanding of that other interest" (Stake, 1994, p. 237). Three cases were selected for their paradigmatic characteristics in terms of their outsourcing undertaking. In other words, the cases were selected because, the ABB-IBM was a global one; the SAS-CSC contract belonged to the largest buy-outs in Europe; and the Rolls-Royce-EDS contract was a mature one. All cases were unique with global client companies from different industries, and all vendor companies were global service providers. In all three international-based cases, more than a thousand employees were transferred from client to vendor organizations. They provided a broad base of relationship practice, suggesting that a case in each company would be of interest and value to this research study. Figure 6.19 shows some characteristics of the IT outsourcing relationships studied.

Data collection was done through a total of sixteen interviews, with questions addressing: enter and exit strategies, phases and activities, contract development, personnel issues, governance structures and relationship management and knowledge

Figure 6.19. Three international- based case studies

Client company & interviewee	*Industry*	*Origin*	*Outsourced*	*Start of deal*	*Length of deal*	*Size of deal*	*No of people transferred*	*Customer of vendor company*
Rolls-Royce	Power for civil aerospace, defense aerospace, marine and energy markets	UK	Infrastructure, application support and development	2000 (1996)	144 months	\$2.1bn	1,220	EDS
ABB	Power and automation technologies	Switzerland	Data centre, infrastructure and desktop	7/28/2003	120 months	\$1.1bn	1,200	IBM
Scandinavian Airlines	Air travel and airline related businesses	Nordic	Infrastructure management, application development and support	12/18/2003	60 months	\$1.5bn	1,150	CSC

management, with a strong emphasis on what characteristics influenced a successful IT outsourcing relationship. For each client-vendor outsourcing relationship, 2-3 interviewees were selected from each organization. All interviewees were assured anonymity to promote openness. Interviews were either personal meetings or telephone conferences, and lasted from 60 to 95 minutes. Transcripts of each interview were sent to respondents for approval. An abbreviation of each case was written and analyzed according to the theoretical perspectives. The individual cases served only as the evidentiary base for the study and were then used in a cross-case analysis. The purpose was not to portray any single one of the relationships. Rather, it was to synthesize the lessons learned from all of them, dispersed throughout separate cross-case issues.

ABB is a leader in power and automation technologies that enable utility and industry customers to improve performance while lowering environmental impact. By July 28, 2003, ABB and IBM signed a 10-year agreement to outsource close to 90% of ABB's information systems infrastructure operations, including the transfer to IBM of more than 1,200 employees. The contract is part of ABB's strategy to focus on its core industrial businesses. The deal included taking over the management of servers, operating systems, corporate networks, personal computers and help desks.

Rolls-Royce is a global power systems company providing power for land, sea and air, with leading positions in civil aerospace, defense, marine and energy markets. Until 1996, RR had its own IT operation. The first outsourcing deal with EDS was done in 1996, and was renewed in 2000 for 12 more years. RR outsourced the basic operation of the complete infrastructure — the management of networks, data centers, servers and so on. And it outsourced the application support for most of its major applications and the application development function. What was kept was development of internal software and the control level, such as control systems for jet engines.

The SAS Group serves northern Europe with air travel and airline-related businesses. SAS uses a broad range of applications — for customers, travel agencies and reservation offices, and also for crew planning and aircraft maintenance and repair. SAS started a huge cost-reduction program called "Turn Around 2005," due to the state of the airline market after September 11, 2001. SIG (Scandinavian IT Group) was owned by the SAS Group as a stand-alone company. SIG was sold to Computer Science Corporation (CSC) on December 18, 2003, and the SAS Group entered into an IT outsourcing agreement with CSC. Under the terms of the contract, CSC provides IT consulting, systems integration, application development and maintenance and IT infrastructure services for mission-critical SAS business needs, including booking and ticket reservation systems, ticket-free travel technologies, self-service check-in, flight maintenance and cargo control systems.

Research Results

In all three cases, one important driver of outsourcing was cost reduction. According to neo-classical economic theory, companies will justify their sourcing strategy based on evaluating possibilities for production cost savings. Thus, the question of whether or not to outsource is a question whether the marketplace can produce products and services at a lower price than internal production. Client companies reported reduction of costs, better cost-performance, and economies of scale, compared to internal IT function.

Due to their financial conditions, Rolls-Royce was looking for a 10% reduction of IT costs. But, the strategic issues underlying the outsourcing decision were also internal IT capabilities and the need for a change agent. Due to fact that the decision was taken several years ago, and none of the interviewees were involved in the decision-making process of that time, it is difficult to state what criteria were the most important. A large company as Rolls-Royce can generate economies of scale and scope internally by reproducing methods of vendors. And thus, defining outsourcing simply in terms of procurement activities seemed inadequate to capture the true strategic discussion of the Rolls-Royce IT outsourcing.

In the SAS-CSC case it was obvious that IT costs were an important issue. Benchmarking showed that costs and efficiency of SIG were far too high. Enquiring the market, bidders showed that SAS could benefit from economies of scale outsourcing IT to an external service provider. In neoclassical economic theories, outsourcing may be regarded as the substitution of external purchase for internal activities and an initiation of procurement from outside suppliers (Gilley & Rasheed, 2000). Selling SIG and buying services back, the outsourcing reduced SAS's involvement in successive stages of production, and thus the outsourcing could be viewed as vertical disintegration.

There was no doubt ABB had a very strong focus on reducing IT costs. They invited the largest outsourcers in the world to bid for their information technology infrastructure. The scope was defined and the goal was to obtain economies of scale. As stated by ABB's CFO: "This long-term deal allows us to significantly take down costs, while benefiting from IBM's global expertise" (source: press release of July 2003). Neo-classical economic theory suggests that all IT functions which an external vendor can operate at lower costs than the company should be outsourced. Selecting IBM as vendor, ABB would obtain better cost-performance of their IT infrastructure. Whatever service IBM provided under the contract, they were committed to provide competitiveness compared to the market.

Because production costs are objectively calculated by the accounting system, while transaction costs are assessed subjectively through indirect indicators, functional managers are likely to differ in the importance that they assign to reducing transaction costs. Consequently, the effect transaction costs have on a make-or-buy choice can partly reflect the influence exerted by the purchasing manager. Production cost differences seems more influential in sourcing decisions than transaction cost differences, and experience of the decision-maker is related to assessments of technological uncertainty. Perrons and Platts (2004) highlight the importance of industry clock speed and supplier relationships in make-or-buy decisions for new technologies. They suggest the "make" prescription may be more suited to either extremely fast or extremely slow rates of technological change, while the "buy" strategy might be more appropriate in market sectors where technologies evolve at a medium pace.

The case studies support the *cost stage* as the first stage in an outsourcing relationship. But costs were not the only reasons for the three client companies. New business strategies and restructuring of client companies were also important drivers. ABB was restructuring around two core business areas, and SAS admitted that information technology was not at the core of an airliner. Core competencies theory suggests that activities which are not core competencies should be considered for outsourcing with best-in-the-world suppliers. Their outsourcing vendors, IBM and CSC respectively, had information technology as their core competencies.

The ability to handle technological change was also reported as a major issue for outsourcing. The companies were looking for strategic resources from vendors, which supports the *resource stage* as the second stage in an outsourcing relationship. Both Rolls-Royce and SAS had a challenge, handling both cost reduction and new technologies at the same time. According to the resource-based perspective, outsourcing is a strategic decision that can be used to fill gaps in the firm's IS resources and capabilities. In the case of Rolls-Royce and SAS, it was a difference between desired and actual capabilities. Interesting to notice, the transforming of Rolls-Royce, from a manufacturing-oriented company to a service-oriented company, seemed to be a part of the plan. Vendor resources can produce innovation, which might be important for long-term survival of the client. In this specific case, the vendor's ability to do change agentry was an important criterion for vendor selection.

Rolls-Royce's initial IT outsourcing back in 1996 outsourced all IT functions, and very little IT competence was kept in-house. What Rolls-Royce emphasized was very strong business process skills, solution architecture skills and contract management skills. The ability to define IT requirements and to monitor their delivery by third parties may be some of the core IT competencies that Rolls-Royce retained in-house to outsource IT successfully.

For SAS, most business applications, for example, booking and travel planning, had become a commodity. What really gave competitive edge were electronic tickets and mobile solutions. As the CIO of SAS stated: "[I]t is appropriate for the employees of Scandinavian IT Group (SIG) to get employed by an outsourcer. CSC has got IT as their core competence." Although outsourcing IT to CSC, SAS considered IT as important and delivering competitive advantage. Beside the CIO function, SAS got a common function called Airline IT that served as a competence centre for the airline companies in SAS Group. SAS built core competencies to define IT requirements and to monitor their delivery.

ABB had enacted significant organizational changes, focusing on two core areas of business. They were selling away noncore business areas and internal support functions. Operating information technology infrastructure was outsourced to reap cost savings from suppliers with clear comparative advantages. IBM had information technology as a core competence, and people redeployed were given an opportunity to focus on their profession. ABB had been aware that the ability to define IT requirements and to monitor their delivery from IBM were regarded as important competencies for them to outsource IT successfully. ABB had kept necessary resources to follow-up both the operational and commercial sides of outsourcing.

Core competence management was found to be the most critical success factor in IT outsourcing relationships. Activities, which are not core competencies, should be considered for outsourcing with best-in-world suppliers. An organization may view IT itself as a core competence. It seems that most successful companies have a good understanding of IT's potential. However, some organizations outsource IT even though they see it as core and delivering competitive advantage. This may be because IT can be considered core at the corporate level, but some of its aspects, at lower levels, might be commodities. Thus, the complexity of IT, and it's (at least in part) core nature, may make the contracting out of IT a particularly challenging exercise. Core competencies are the collective learning in the organization, especially how to coordinate diverse production skills and integrate multiple streams of technologies.

One of the critical issues of the *partnership stage* is stakeholder management. Following stakeholder theory recommendations for successful IT, outsourcing relationships are to create efficient and effective communication with and between stakeholders to secure continued support from all stakeholders, to balance their interests and to make the IT outsourcing arrangement so that all stakeholders achieve their goals. During the case studies, several stakeholder groups were identified — client senior managers, client business managers, client retained IT managers, transferred IT employees (transplants), vendor senior managers, vendor account managers and vendor supplier IT staff — each group with their own expectations and goals. These findings are not very different from stakeholder groups defined by Lacity and Willcocks (2000). An interesting observation was that the interviewees seemed to be aware of other stakeholders' expectations and goals. What was emphasized in the case studies was the unique position of the transplants. Respecting and balancing stakeholders' interests were ranked as an important factor for successful relationship.

Next to the theory of core competencies, stakeholder theory was found important. A stakeholder is any group or individual who can affect, or is affected by, the achievement of a corporation's purpose. Stakeholders include employees, customers, suppliers, stockholders, banks, environmentalists, government and other groups who can help or hurt the corporation. Stakeholder theory is justified on the basis that firms have responsibilities to stakeholders for moral reasons, and that there is no priority of one set of interests over another. Upholding four principles: (1) honoring agreements, (2) avoiding lying, (3) respecting the autonomy of others and (4) avoiding harm to others, are necessary preconditions for a firm's efficient working. And thus, stakeholder theories of the firm establish economic relationships within a general context of moral management. Contrary to the traditional understanding of the principal-agent relationship, used in several IT outsourcing studies, a stakeholder orientation will include at least two new dimensions: (1) a number of stakeholder groups, and (2) the interpretation of the four moral principles that underlie stakeholder theory. The term stakeholders is widely used and accepted by IT outsourcing practitioners and researchers.

Critical Success Factors in IT Outsourcing Relationships

This section identifies and ranks critical issues in IT outsourcing relationships. Eleven management theories are applied in this research: core competencies, resource-based, neo-classical economic, transaction cost, contractual, agency, partnership and alliance, relational exchange, stakeholder, social exchange, and theory of firm boundaries. The main methods used are case studies and surveys. Case studies were conducted in the same three IT outsourcing relationships: ABB-IBM, SAS-CSC and RR-EDS. Core competence management and stakeholder management were found to be the most critical success factors. Future research should focus on one or two theories, explicitly laying out expectations with respect to the theories, and organizing rich data to test expectations. This section demonstrates that a holistic approach to IT outsourcing is needed that recognizes and emphasizes the combination of several critical success factors. The original value of the section is the theory-based factors having both divergent and convergent implications for management.

Information technology (IT) outsourcing is the practice of turning over all or part of an organization's IT functions to an outside vendor. Although IT functions never have been more important to business success, outsourcing is developing in an unprecedented rate. To understand this trend, we have conducted an extensive literature review. We have identified a total of eleven theories that help explain why IT outsourcing is occurring worldwide. These theories are presented first in this section. Based on these theories, we developed eleven critical success factors in IT outsourcing, one for each theory. These factors are presented next in this section. We developed the following research question: *How do practitioners rank critical success factors based on outsourcing theories?* To study this research question, we developed a survey instrument and conducted a survey among business organizations. Results from this survey and discussion of the results are presented in this section.

The eleven theoretical perspectives presented may help to understand IT outsourcing practices in different settings.

Theory of Core Competencies

Core competencies theory suggests that activities should be performed either in-house or by suppliers. Activities, which are not core competencies, should be considered for outsourcing with best-in-world suppliers. Some noncore activities may have to be retained in-house if they are part of a defensive posture to protect competitive advantage. Although some authors indicate characteristics of core competencies, most of the literature on this subject seems tautological — core equals key or critical or fundamental. Employees in noncore functions (even if not facing outsourcing) may feel excluded by the organization because they are a nondominant discipline. For example, information technology employees working on Web-based legal services in a law firm may feel excluded by lawyers in the firm. In the public sector, there may be particular uncertainty about what is core; and it has been suggested that government may aim to discover its core competencies via a residualization process–outsourcing until and unless the shoe pinches, or a political backlash is triggered (Hancox & Hackney, 2000).

An organization may view IT itself as a core competence. It seems that most successful companies have a good understanding of IT's potential. However, some organizations outsource IT even though they see it as core and delivering competitive advantage. This may be because IT can be considered core at the corporate level, but some of its aspects, at lower levels, might be commodities. Thus, the complexity of IT, and it's (at least in part) core nature, may make the contracting out of IT a particularly challenging exercise. The ability to define IT requirements and to monitor their delivery by third parties may be some of the core IT competencies that any organization must have if it is to outsource IT successfully. It can even be argued that the very acts of specifying and managing supply contracts can themselves give competitive advantage (Hancox & Hackney, 2000). Outsourcing of noncore competencies will continue to be important as such arrangements place responsibilities, for example, for IT, logistics or production functions, in the hands of the constituent most capable of performing these successfully (Chandra & Kumar, 2000).

Resource-Based Theory

According to the resource-based theory of the firm, outsourcing is a strategic decision, which can be used to fill gaps in the firm's resources and capabilities (Grover et al., 1998). Firms develop firm-specific resources and then renew these to respond to shifts in the business environment. Firms develop dynamic capabilities to adapt to changing environments. According to Pettus (2001), the term dynamic refers to the capacity to renew resource positions to achieve congruence with changing environmental conditions. A capability refers to the key role of strategic management in appropriately adapting, integrating and reconfiguring internal and external organizational skills, resources and functional capabilities to match the requirements of a changing environment.

The essence of the resource-based theory of the firm lies in its emphasis on the internal resources available to the firm, rather than on the external opportunities and threats dictated by industry conditions. Firms are considered to be highly heterogeneous, and the bundles of resources available to each firm are different. This is both because firms have different initial resource endowments and because managerial decisions affect resource accumulation and the direction of firm growth as well as resource utilization (Løwendahl, 2000). The resource-based theory of the firm holds that, in order to generate sustainable competitive advantage, a resource must provide economic value and must be presently scarce, difficult to imitate, nonsubstitutable and not readily obtainable in factor markets. This theory rests on two key points. First, that resources are the determinants of firm performance and second, that resources must be rare, valuable, difficult to imitate and nonsubstitutable by other rare resources. When the latter occurs, a competitive advantage has been created (Priem & Butler, 2001).

Transaction Cost Theory

Transaction costs arise because complete contracting is often impossible, and incomplete contracts give rise to subsequent renegotiations when the balance of power between the transacting parties shifts (Williamson, 2000). Five attributes of business exchange are positively associated with transaction costs: (1) the necessity of investments in durable, specific assets; (2) infrequency of transacting; (3) task complexity and uncertainty; (4) difficulty in measuring task performance; and (5) interdependencies with other transactions. The necessity of early investments in durable, transactions-specific assets (e.g., human and physical capital) shifts the balance of power between transaction participants, because in later renegotiations these costs are sunk costs of the party that incurs them. Infrequent transactions increase the likelihood of opportunistic behavior in later periods by reducing the threat of retribution. In situations where broader market reputations are at stake, infrequent transactions may be sustainable. However, even long-term contracts often do not provide sufficient adaptation mechanisms, and inflexibility may actually induce holdup. The five transaction attributes indicate settings in which opportunistic behavior is likely. If transactions costs offset production cost advantages of the external supplier, the firm subsumes the activity — an outcome termed vertical integration or insourcing.

Drawing on transaction cost economics theory, the sourcing decision is often seen as a rational decision made by firms that have considered transaction-related factors such as asset specificity, environmental uncertainty and other types of transaction costs (Ang & Straub, 1998). Whenever an activity is conducted under conditions of high uncertainty, or whenever an activity requires specific assets, transaction costs, the costs of writing, monitoring and enforcing contracts, are likely to be high. When transaction costs are high, outsourcing is deemed to be relatively inefficient compared with internal, hierarchical administration.

Contractual Theory

An outsourcing contract provides a legally bound, institutional framework in which each party's rights, duties and responsibilities are codified and the goals, policies and strategies underlying the arrangement are specified. Every outsourcing contract has the purpose of facilitating exchange and preventing opportunism. Appropriate contractual arrangements can attenuate the leeway for opportunism, prohibit moral hazards in a cooperative relationship and protect each party's proprietary knowledge. A complete contract reduces the uncertainty faced by organizational decision-makers and the risks stemming from opportunism on the part of one or more contracting parties. It provides a safeguard against ex post performance problems by restraining each party's ability to pursue private goals at the expense of common benefits. An incomplete contract may bring about ambiguity, which creates a breeding ground for shirking responsibility and shifting blame, raises the likelihood of conflict and hinders the ability to coordinate activities, utilize resources and implement strategies (Luo, 2002).

Third-party legal experts have for quite some time emphasized the need for a comprehensive contract, not only because it is their livelihood, but also because it basically becomes a reference point specifying how the client and vendor relate (Kern & Willcocks, 2000). Key IT outsourcing contractual issues include service level, transfer of assets, staffing, pricing and payment, warranty and liability, dispute resolution mechanisms, termination, intellectual property matters and information security (Lee, 1996).

Neoclassical Economic Theory

Neo-classical economic theory posits that firms outsource IT to attain cost advantages from assumed economies of scale and scope possessed by vendors (Ang & Straub, 1998). This theory has attained more empirical support in studies of outsourcing decisions than transaction cost economics. Neo-classical economic theory regards every business organization as a production function (Williamson, 2000), where their motivation is driven by profit maximization. This means that companies offer products and services to the market where they have a cost or production advantage. They rely on the marketplace where they have disadvantages. According to neo-classical economic theory, companies will justify their sourcing strategy based on evaluating possibilities for production cost savings. Thus, the question of whether or not to outsource is a question whether the marketplace can produce products and services at a lower price than internal production. In the context of IT outsourcing, a company will keep its IT function internally if this has production cost advantages, and it will outsource when the marketplace can offer production cost savings.

IT outsourcing is not only a purchasing decision — all firms purchase elements of their operations. This is done to achieve economic, technological and strategic advantages. However, the economies of scale and scope argument would predict that outsourcing has little to offer to larger firms, because they can generate economies of scale and scope internally by reproducing methods used by vendors. As documented by Levina and Ross (2003), there are other reasons for large firms to move into outsourcing (e.g., a vendor's efficiency is based on the economic benefits derived from the ability to develop a complementary set of core competencies).

Partnership and Alliance Theory

Partnership, often referred to as an alliance, has frequently been noted as a major feature of IT outsourcing. Partnership can reduce the risk of inadequate contractual provision, which may be comforting for clients about to outsource a complex and high-cost activity such as IT. However, in the relationship between vendor and client the latter may be overly dependent on the former, and goals are not necessarily shared. According to Lambe et al. (2002), alliances are broadly defined as collaborative efforts between two or more firms in which the firms pool their resources in an effort to achieve mutually compatible goals that they could not achieve easily alone. Resources here are defined as any tangible or intangible entity available for use by a firm to compete in its marketplace. When interfirm business relationships are collaborative, rather than adversarial in nature, a variety of these relationships may be classified as alliances, for example outsourcing.

Hancox and Hackney (2000) interviewed IT managers to find support for the partnership theory in IT outsourcing. Despite assurances found in vendors' marketing literature, most clients were skeptical about partnership. If partnership did exist, it was usually as a collection of some of the intangibles mentioned earlier, rather than as a formalized arrangement. Partnership was more likely to be claimed in the area of systems development, where vendors needed to have a greater understanding of the organization, than in outsourcing of operations and IT infrastructure support.

Relational Exchange Theory

Relational exchange theory is based on relational norms. According to this theory, the key to determining how efficiently contract governance is carried out lies in the relational norms between the transactors. For example, the degree to which transactors engage in joint planning or their extent of interfirm information sharing, are process elements that determine the costs associated with periodically renegotiating contracts. Those transactors who have established behavioral norms that can simplify and smooth the renegotiation process can reasonably expect to incur lower ex post bargaining costs than those who have not (Artz & Brush, 2000).

Many classifications of norms have been proposed, but no one is regarded as dominant. It has been proposed that relational norms are a higher order construct, consisting of three dimensions (Kern & Blois, 2002). First is flexibility, which defines a bilateral expectation of the willingness to make adaptations as circumstances change. Second is information exchange, which defines a bilateral expectation that parties will proactively provide information useful to the partner. And third is solidarity, which defines a bilateral expectation that a high value is placed on the relationship. It prescribes behaviors directed specifically towards relationship maintenance.

Social Exchange Theory

Social exchange theory was initially developed to examine interpersonal exchanges that are not purely economic. Several sociologists are responsible for the early development of this theory. These theorists view people's social behavior in terms of exchanges of resources. The need for social exchange is created by the scarcity of resources, prompting actors to engage one another to obtain valuable inputs. Social exchange can be defined as voluntary actions of individuals that are motivated by the return they are expected to bring and typically in fact bring from others. Social exchange can be viewed as an ongoing reciprocal process in which actions are contingent on rewarding reactions from others (Das & Teng, 2002).

An exchange perspective places the study of international relations, such as global outsourcing, in a framework of negotiations. Central to this perspective are issues of equivalence (fairness) and contingency (responsiveness). The challenge for international actors is to define a precise medium for exchange. The more precise the medium, the less likely actors will misperceive each other's move. But, the more precise the medium, the less likely will actors explore their relationships (Druckman, 1998). This is also a dilemma for IT outsourcing relationships. The more precise, the easier it is to follow-up service levels. And thus, value-added benefits will be difficult to achieve.

Agency Theory

According to Eisenhardt (1985), agency theory is concerned with resolving two problems that can occur in agency relationships. The first is the agency problem that arises when the desires or goals of the principal and agent conflict and it is difficult or expensive for the principal to verify what the agent is actually doing. The second is the problem of risk sharing that arises when the principal and agent have different risk preferences. These problems are well known in IT outsourcing. An example might be that the client organization wants to reduce its IT costs, while the vendor organization wants to maximize profits. The agency problem arises when the two parties do not share productivity gains. The risk-sharing problem might be the result of different attitudes towards the use of new technologies.

The technological and business complexity of IT means that there may be major problems for the principal in choosing a suitable agent and in monitoring the agent's work. Only the agent knows how hard he is working, and that can be especially important in multilateral contracting where one agent acts for several principals. This is often the case in IT outsourcing because of the market dominance of one large firm. Given the difficulties of behavior-based contracts suggested by agency theory, it is reasonable to assume that the overwhelming majority of clients would insist on outcome-based contracts when acquiring IT products and services. Such a strategy can only succeed if the client can confidently specify current and future requirements. But accurate predictions by the client may not always be in the vendor's interests, since vendor account managers often are rewarded according to contract profitability, which is principally achieved through charging the client extra for anything which is not in the contract (Hancox & Hackney, 2000).

Theory of Firm Boundaries

Some theorists have proposed that firms' boundaries reflect the division of labor across individuals (Garicano & Hubbard, 2003). Whether a set of tasks is organized within one or multiple firms depends on the extent to which individuals specialize. While the particular trade-offs these theories emphasize differ from each other, together they represent a departure from the earlier literature: There is far less emphasis on specificity and far greater emphasis on issues related to the division of labor such as specialization and job design. This class of theories is important because it has the potential to explain firms' boundaries in a wide range of contexts where specificity is unlikely to have an important effect on individuals' incentives.

Firm boundaries — defined as the scope of revenue-sharing arrangements across individuals — reflect trade-offs associated with referral problems, which are problems of matching economic opportunities to individuals' efficiency. The idea is that individuals with specialized skills sometimes have private information about economic opportunities for which others have a comparative advantage in exploiting. This can happen, for example, when a client with a legal problem involving corporate law approaches a tax lawyer. Incentive problems arise because private information about such opportunities is valuable, and transferring them involves adverse selection problems (Garicano & Hubbard, 2003).

Lonsdale and Cox (2000) note that outsourcing is just one of the means by which the boundary of the firm can be adjusted. There are a number of dimensions to the boundary of the firm issue. These dimensions include conglomeration, horizontal integration, vertical integration and the internal integration of supporting activities. It is important to consider these dimensions when considering outsourcing. Not only should it be part of a wider picture concerning the boundary of the firm, but it should also be part of a wider concern over the corporate strategies.

Stakeholder Theory

Stakeholder theory is justified on the basis that firms have responsibilities to stakeholders for moral reasons, and that there is no priority of one set of interests over another. Upholding four principles: (1) honoring agreements, (2) avoiding lying, (3) respecting the autonomy of others and (4) avoiding harm to others, are necessary preconditions for efficient working. And thus, stakeholder theories of the firm establish economic relationships within a general context of moral management. Contrary to the traditional understanding of the principal-agent relationship, used in several IT outsourcing studies, a stakeholder orientation will include at least two new dimensions: (1) a number of stakeholder groups, and (2) the interpretation of the four moral principles that underlie stakeholder theory. Neglecting these dimensions, firms will have less satisfied stakeholders and will show financial performance that is consistently below industry average (Shankman, 1999).

Stakeholders are a group of people with aligned interests (Lacity & Willcocks, 2000). The term is widely used and accepted by IT outsourcing practitioners and researchers. However, as indicated by some of the reviewed literature above, stakeholder is defined and used differently in finance (issue of CEO responsibility to shareholders or stakeholders), law (requires ownership) and gaming (person who holds the bets). According to Lacity and Willcocks (2000), there are four distinct client IT stakeholder groups and three distinct supplier IT stakeholder groups. The groups identified are customer senior business managers, customer senior IT managers, customer IT staff, customer IT users and supplier senior managers, supplier account managers and supplier IT staff. An additional group is subcontractors. All stakeholder groups are presumed to have significant differences in expectations and goals regarding IT outsourcing. Thus, it is reasonable to propose that upholding the interest of these different stakeholder groups with the principles of moral management will affect the success of IT outsourcing.

Figure 6.20. Possibilities and limitations in IT outsourcing based on theories

Theory	What should be outsourced?
Theory of core competencies	All IT functions which are peripheral to the company's production of goods and services for the market.
Resource-based theory	All IT functions where the company does not have sufficient strategic resources to perform in a competitive way. Strategic resources are unique, valuable, difficult to imitate, exploitable and difficult to substitute.
Transaction cost theory	All IT functions where benefits for the company are greater than the transaction costs. Benefits include increased revenues and reduced costs.
Contractual theory	Only IT functions where the company can expect and secure that vendor and customer will have the same contractual behavior. Common contract behavioral patterns include role integrity, reciprocity, implementation of planning, effectuation of consent, flexibility, contractual solidarity, reliance, restraint of power, proprietary of means and harmonization with the social environment.
Neoclassical economic theory	All IT functions which an external vendor can operate at lower costs than the company.
Partnership and alliance theory	Only IT functions where the company can expect and secure a partnership and alliance with the vendor that implys interdependence between the partners based on trust, comfort, understanding, flexibility, co-operation, shared values, goals and problem solving, interpersonal relations and regular communication.
Relational exchange theory	Only IT functions where the company easily can develop and secure common norms with the vendor. Norms determine behavior in three main dimensions: flexibility, information exchange and solidarity.
Social exchange theory	Only IT functions where each of the parties can follow their own self-interest when transacting with the other self-interested actor to accomplish individual goals that they cannot achieve alone and without causing hazards to the other party.
Agency theory	Only IT functions where the agent (vendor) and the principal (client) have common goals and the same degree of risk willingness and aversion.
Theory of firm boundaries	All IT functions that satisfy several of the other theories, mainly resource-based theory and transaction cost theory.
Stakeholder theory	Only IT functions where a balance can be achieved between stakeholders. Stakeholders relevant in IT outsourcing include business management, IT management, user management and key IT personnel at the client and business management, customer account management and key service providers at the vendor.

Comparison of Theories

We have introduced eleven theories concerned with outsourcing. In Figure 6.20, these theories are compared in terms of what they recommend for outsourcing. We find that some theories indicate possibilities for outsourcing (theory of core competencies, resource-based theory, transaction cost theory, neoclassical economic theory and theory of firm boundaries), while others indicate limitations (contractual theory, partnership and alliance theory, relational exchange theory, social exchange theory, agency theory and stakeholder theory).

Figure 6.21. Recommendations for managing successful IT outsourcing relationships based on theories

Theory	How to succeed in an outsourcing arrangement
Theory of core competencies	Capability to define IT needs and ability to manage IT services from the vendor represent the core competence within IT needed in the client organization to succeed in an IT outsourcing arrangement.
Resource-based theory	Capability to integrate and exploit strategic IT resources from the vendor together with own resources to produce competitive goods and services. An example of such a resource is the vendor's competence in an IT application area where the client has limited experience.
Transaction cost theory	Minimize transaction costs by reducing the need for lasting specific IT assets, increase transaction frequency, reduce complexity and uncertainty in IT tasks, improve performance measurements and reduce dependence on other transactions.
Contractual theory	A complete IT contract based on information symmetry in a predictable environment with occurrence adaptation that prevents opportunistic behavior in an efficient collaborative environment with balance of power between client and vendor, where the contract is a management instrument that grants decision rights and action duties.
Neoclassical economic theory	Capability to integrate and exploit IT services from the vendor together with own services to produce competitive goods and services. An example of such a service is the vendor's operation of the client's communication network.
Partnership and alliance theory	Develop experience with alliances, develop alliance managers and develop the ability to identify potential partners.
Relational exchange theory	Develop and secure common norms that are relevant to both parties. Norms determine behavior and are mainly concerned with flexibility, information exchange and solidarity. Norms shall secure integration in the relation, which takes place through involvement. Involvement occurs by coordination of activities, adaptation of resources and interaction between individuals. The degree of involvement in these three dimensions is called activity link, resource link and actor link.
Social exchange theory	Enable social and economic outcomes in the exchange between client and vendor such that these outcomes outperform those obtainable in alternative exchanges. Positive economic and social outcomes over time increase the partners' trust of each other and commitment to maintaining the exchange relationship. Commitment is important, as it is an exchange partner's belief that an ongoing relationship with another is so important as to warrant maximum efforts at maintaining it.
Agency theory	It must be easy and inexpensive for the principal (client) to find out what the agent (vendor) is actually doing. In addition, both outcome-based and behavior-based incentives can be used to reduce and prevent opportunistic behavior.
Theory of firm boundaries	The supply of IT services from the organization's environment should change firm boundaries between the firm that desires the competence (sourcing firm) and the firm having the technology (source firm) in a clear and unambiguous manner. This can be achieved in a strict and rigid division of labor between client and vendor.
Stakeholder theory	Create efficient and effective communication with and between stakeholders to secure continued support from all stakeholders, to balance their interests and to make the IT outsourcing arrangement so that all stakeholders achieve their goals.

Figure 6.21 lists a comparison of the theories when it comes to the next stage. The next stage is when outsourcing has occurred and both client and vendor want the outsourcing arrangement to be successful. What do the theories tell us? As is visible in Figure 2.11, the theories tell us a lot about what to do to be successful. Each theory provides recommendations for actions that will contribute to managing successful IT outsourcing relationships. Recommendations are made from different theoretical persepectives. Taken together, the list in the table represents critical success factors for an outsourcing arrangement.

Critical Success Factors

Based on this extensive literature review of outsourcing theories, we identified the following 11 critical success factors in IT outsourcing:

1. **Core competence management:** The organization has to define its IT needs and manage IT services from the vendor.
2. **Vendor resource exploitation:** The organization has to integrate and exploit strategic IT resources from the vendor together with its own resources to produce competitive goods and services.
3. **Transaction cost reduction:** The organization has to minimize transaction costs by reducing the need for lasting specific IT assets, increase transaction frequency, reduce complexity and uncertainty in IT tasks, improve performance measurements and reduce dependence on other transactions.
4. **Contract completeness:** The organization must have a complete IT outsourcing contract. The contract should prevent opportunistic behavior in an efficient collaborative environment with balance of power between client and vendor.
5. **Production cost reduction:** The organization has to integrate and exploit IT services from the vendor in a cost effective way to produce competitive goods and services.
6. **Alliance exploitation:** The organization has to develop experience with alliances, develop alliance managers and develop the ability to identify potential vendors.
7. **Relationship exploitation:** The organization has to develop and secure common norms that are relevant to both parties.
8. **Social exchange exploitation:** The organization has to enable social and economic outcomes in the exchange between the vendor and itself such that these outcomes outperform those obtainable in alternative exchanges.
9. **Vendor behavior control:** The organization has to make it easy and inexpensive for itself to find out what the vendor is actually doing. In addition,

both outcome-based and behavior-based incentives can be used to reduce and prevent opportunistic vendor behavior.

10. **Demarcation of labor:** The organization has to implement a strict and rigid division of labor between the vendor and itself.
11. **Stakeholder management:** The organization must create efficient and effective communication with and between stakeholders to secure continued support from all stakeholders, to balance their interests and to make the IT outsourcing arrangement so that all stakeholders achieve their goals.

Critical Success Factors Case of ABB-IBM, RR-EDS and SAS-CSC

Again we use case study results from research by Gottschalk and Solli-Sæther (2006), which had the following guiding research question: "How do client and vendor organizations manage their IT outsourcing relationships?"

Research Results

In this part of the outsourcing theories section, we first present survey results. Then we present findings from the case studies to illustrate the most critical success factors. On a scale from 1 (low) to 5 (high), core competence management was found to be the most critical success factors in IT outsourcing relationships, as indicated with the score of 4.67 in Figure 6.22. The score is based on the response from sixteen interviews.

Figure 6.22. Ranking of critical success factors in IT outsourcing relationships

Rank	Critical Success Factors	Score	Theory
1	Core competence management	4.67	Theory of core competencies
2	Stakeholder management	4.58	Stakeholder theory
3	Production cost reduction	3.92	Neoclassical economic theory
4	Social exchange exploitation	3.82	Social exchange theory
5	Transaction cost reduction	3.80	Transaction cost theory
6	Vendor resource exploitation	3.75	Resource-based theory
7	Contract completeness	3.75	Contractual theory
8	Relationship exploitation	3.50	Relational exchange theory
9	Vendor behavior control	3.33	Agency theory
10	Demarcation of labor	3.17	Theory of firm boundaries
11	Alliance exploitation	2.83	Partnership and alliance theory

In all three cases, one important driver of outsourcing was cost reduction. According to neo-classical economic theory, companies will justify their sourcing strategy based on evaluating possibilities for production cost savings. Thus, the question of whether or not to outsource is a question of whether the marketplace can produce products and services at a lower price than internal production. Client companies reported reduction of costs, better cost-performance and economies of scale, compared to internal IT function.

But, costs were not the only reasons for some of the client companies. New business strategies and restructuring of client companies were also important drivers. ABB was restructuring around two core business areas, and SAS admitted that information technology was not at the core of an airliner. Core competencies theory suggests that activities which are not core competencies should be considered for outsourcing with best-in-the-world suppliers. Their outsourcing vendors, IBM and CSC respectively, had information technology as their core competence.

The ability to handle technological change was also reported as a major issue for outsourcing. Both Rolls-Royce and SAS had a challenge, handling both cost reduction and new technologies at the same time. According to the resource-based perspective, outsourcing is a strategic decision that can be used to fill gaps in the firm's IS resources and capabilities. In the cases of Rolls-Royce and SAS, it was a difference between desired capabilities and actual capabilities. Interesting to notice, the transforming of Rolls-Royce, from a manufacturing-oriented company to a service-oriented company, seemed to be a part of the plan. Vendor resources can produce innovation, which might be important for long-term survival of the client. In this specific case, the vendor's ability to do change agentry was an important criterion for vendor selection.

In the following, we will present the case studies for the three most critical success factors in Figure 2.12.

Core Competence Management

Rolls-Royce's initial IT outsourcing back in 1996 outsourced all IT functions, and very little IT competence was kept in-house. What Rolls-Royce emphasized were very strong business process skills, solution architecture skills and contract management skills. The ability to define IT requirements and to monitor their delivery by third parties may be some of the core IT competencies that Rolls-Royce retained in-house to outsource IT successfully.

For SAS, most business applications, for example, booking and travel planning, had become a commodity. What really gave competitive edge were electronic tickets and mobile solutions.

As the CIO of SAS stated: "{I} it is appropriate for the employees of Scandinavian IT Group (SIG) to get employed by an outsourcer. CSC has got IT as their core competence." Although outsourcing IT to CSC, SAS considered IT as important and delivering competitive advantage. Beside the CIO function, SAS got a common function called Airline IT that served as a competence centre for the airline companies in the SAS Group. SAS built core competencies to define IT requirements and to monitor their delivery.

ABB had accomplished significant organizational changes, focusing on two core areas of business. They were selling away noncore business areas and internal support functions. Operating information technology infrastructure was outsourced to reap cost savings from suppliers with clear comparative advantages. IBM had information technology as a core competence, and people redeployed were given an opportunity to focus on their profession. ABB had been aware that the ability to define IT requirements and to monitor their delivery from IBM were regarded as important competencies for them to outsource IT successfully. ABB had kept necessary resources to follow-up both the operational and commercial sides of outsourcing.

Core competence management was found to be the most critical success factor in IT outsourcing relationships. Activities, which are not core competencies, should be considered for outsourcing with best-in-world suppliers. An organization may view IT itself as a core competence. It seems that most successful companies have a good understanding of IT's potential. However, some organizations outsource IT even though they see it as core and delivering competitive advantage. This may be because IT can be considered core at the corporate level, but some of its aspects, at lower levels, might be commodities. Thus the complexity of IT, and its (at least in part) core nature, may make the contracting out of IT a particularly challenging exercise. Core competencies are the collective learning in the organization, especially how to coordinate diverse production skills and integrate multiple streams of technologies.

Stakeholder Management

Following stakeholder theory recommendations for successful IT outsourcing relationships create efficient and effective communication with and between stakeholders to secure continued support from all stakeholders, to balance their interests and to make the IT outsourcing arrangement so that all stakeholders achieve their goals. During the case studies several stakeholder groups were identified — client senior managers, client business managers, client retained IT managers, transferred IT employees (transplants), vendor senior managers, vendor account managers and vendor supplier IT staff — each group with their own expectations and goals. These findings are not very different from stakeholder groups defined by Lacity and Willcocks

(2000). An interesting observation was that the interviewees seemed to be aware of other stakeholders' expectations and goals. What was emphasized in the case studies was the unique position of the transplants. Respecting and balancing stakeholders' interests were ranked as important factors for successful relationships.

Next to the theory of core competencies, stakeholder theory was found important. A stakeholder is any group or individual who can affect, or is affected by, the achievement of a corporation's purpose. Stakeholders include employees, customers, suppliers, stockholders, banks, environmentalists, government and other groups who can help or hurt the corporation. Stakeholder theory is justified on the basis that firms have responsibilities to stakeholders for moral reasons, and that there is no priority of one set of interests over another. Upholding four principles: (1) honoring agreements, (2) avoiding lying, (3) respecting the autonomy of others and (4) avoiding harm to others, are necessary preconditions for efficient working stakeholder relationships. And thus, stakeholder theories of the firm establish economic relationships within a general context of moral management. Contrary to the traditional understanding of the principal-agent relationship, used in several IT outsourcing studies, a stakeholder orientation will include at least two new dimensions: (1) a number of stakeholder groups, and (2) the interpretation of the four moral principles that underlie stakeholder theory. The term stakeholders is widely used and accepted by IT outsourcing practitioners and researchers.

Production Cost Reduction

Due to their financial condition, Rolls-Royce was looking for a 10% reduction of IT costs. But, the strategic issues underlying the outsourcing decision were also internal IT capabilities and the need for a change agent. Due to fact that the decision was taken several years ago, and none of the interviewees were involved in the decision-making process of that time, it is difficult to state what criteria were the most important. A large company as Rolls-Royce can generate economies of scale and scope internally by reproducing vendor methods. And thus, defining outsourcing simply in terms of procurements activities did not seem to capture the true strategic discussion of the Rolls-Royce IT outsourcing.

In the SAS-CSC case it was obvious that IT costs were an important issue. Benchmarking showed that costs compared to the efficiency of SIG were far too high. Enquiring the market, bidders showed that SAS could benefit from economies of scale outsourcing IT to an external service provider. In neoclassical economic theories, outsourcing may be regarded as the substitution of external purchase for internal activities and an initiation of procurement from outside suppliers (Gilley & Rasheed, 2000). Selling SIG and buying services back, the outsourcing reduced SAS's involvement in successive stages of production, and thus the outsourcing could be viewed as vertical disintegration.

There was no doubt ABB had a very strong focus on reducing IT costs. They invited the largest outsourcers in the world to bid for their information technology infrastructure. The scope was defined and the goal was to obtain economies of scale. As stated by ABB's CFO: "This long-term deal allows us to significantly take down costs, while benefiting from IBM's global expertise" (source: press release of July 2003). Neo-classical economic theory suggests that all IT functions which an external vendor can operate at lower costs than the company should be outsourced. Selecting IBM as vendor, ABB would obtain better cost-performance of their IT infrastructure. Whatever service IBM provided under the contract, they were committed to provide competitiveness compared to the market.

Because production costs are objectively calculated by the accounting system, while transaction costs are assessed subjectively through indirect indicators, functional managers are likely to differ in the importance that they assign to reducing transaction costs. Consequently, the effect transaction costs have on a make-or-buy choice can partly reflect the influence exerted by the purchasing manager. Production cost differences seem more influential in sourcing decisions than transaction cost differences, and experience of the decision-maker is related to assessments of technological uncertainty. Perrons and Platts (2004) highlight the importance of industry clock speed and supplier relationships in make-or-buy decisions for new technologies. They suggest the "make" prescription may be more suited to either extremely fast or extremely slow rates of technological change, while the "buy" strategy might be more appropriate in market sectors where technologies evolve at a medium pace.

Summary

Based on our interpretation of relevant theories, critical success factors for IT outsourcing relationships were developed. These factors were empirically tested and investigated in three outsourcing relationships. Although cost savings still seem to be the overriding cause of IT outsourcing, the success of outsourcing relationships depends on other factors. Both core competence management and stakeholder management, as identified in this research, are primarily noncost factors.

In this research we have addressed the question of how to successfully manage IT outsourcing relationships. Using well-established theoretical perspectives and our own experiences earned from case studies, our ambition has been to identify critical issues in the complex IT outsourcing process and emerging relationships.

Based on the findings, three managerial implications are suggested. Firstly, we argue that a holistic approach to IT outsourcing is needed that recognizes and emphasizes the combination of several critical success factors. These factors have both divergent and convergent implications for management. Being aware of these factors, managers are enabled to recognize relationship problems as they occur and to handle them before they scrutinize the IT outsourcing success. Second, we emphasize the importance of both client and vendor success in an effective IT outsourcing relationship, as the two parties are mutually dependent on each other. Finally, we recognize the complexity of IT outsourcing. When contracts expire there is a need to have an exit strategy focusing not only on the economic success of the IT outsourcing, but also to question issues such as core competence management, access to resources and the maturity of the relationship.

The current research has several shortcomings that should be addressed in future research. Future research should: (1) more carefully develop the motivation for such studies, elaborate on the specific research questions it addresses, and why these questions are important for research or practice; (2) more carefully develop and explain how critical success factors can be identified from the various theories; and (3) clarify the theoretical and empirical contributions this kind of research makes over and above the prior literature in the area. Perhaps future research should focus on one or two theories, explicitly laying out expectations with respect to the theories, and organizing rich data to test expectations. Furthermore, it would be interesting to observe theories where the predictions contradict each other, and use observational data to study conditions for one theory or another to dominate.

Discussion

With the growing importance of pooling knowledge resources, knowledge management will have to transcend organizational boundaries to include sourcing partners. However, the focus of previous research studies has mainly been on intraorganizational knowledge management. In this study, we have attempted to direct the attention of knowledge management researchers toward interorganizational interfaces.

In a different empirical setting, Malhotra et al. (2005) attempted to direct the attention of knowledge management researchers toward interorganizational interfaces. They studied absorptive capacity configurations in supply chains. Their study indicates that enterprises have to build requisite absorptive capacity to prepare for collaborative knowledge creation with their supply chain partners. Absorptive capacity in this context is the ability of enterprises to acquire and assimilate information from their supply chain partners and to transform and exploit this information to achieve superior operational and strategic outcomes.

Similarly, Allard and Holsapple (2002) attempted to direct the attention of knowledge management researchers toward interorganizational interfaces. They studied knowledge management as a key for e-business competitiveness. In their knowledge chain model, knowledge externalization describes the embedding of knowledge into organizational outputs that are then released into the external environment.

The extent of interorganizational knowledge transfer between vendor and client in an IT outsourcing relationship will depend on the extent of outsourcing. Total IT outsourcing will typically require a greater extent of interorganizational knowledge transfer (Barthélemy & Geyer, 2004). This can be explored in future research, as outsourcing choices represent alternate ways for organizations to leverage available resources to increase the value of IT in meeting corporate objectives (Lee et al., 2004).

Conclusion

Knowledge management systems successfully supporting IT outsourcing relationships have to satisfy several requirements. First, they have to enable knowledge transfer between vendor and client. Second, they have to match strategic intent and knowledge management strategy. Furthermore, vendor and client need to be at the same technology stage of growth to be able to successfully communicate with each other through knowledge management systems. These are some of the research propositions presented in this chapter, which represent a rich knowledge base for future empirical studies.

In this chapter, we have learned that:

- Knowledge transfer is the most important and most relevant knowledge management mechanism in an IT outsourcing relationship.
- Vendor and client need to be at the same technology stage of growth to be able to successfully communicate with each other through knowledge management systems.
- Strategic intent influences knowledge needs.

Furthermore, we have developed several causal links from knowledge management systems to IT. Important concepts in these links are innovation, shared understanding, cost efficiency, social interaction, partnership quality and access to vendor's intellectual capital.

Some of the important causal influences between knowledge management and IT outsourcing relationships are mapped in the causal loop diagram in Figure 2.23. Causal loop diagramming is described by Sterman (2000) and presented as a tool by www.vensim.com.

Figure 6.23 illustrates that knowledge transfer is the most important and most relevant knowledge management mechanism in an IT outsourcing relationship.

Figure 6.23. Causal loop diagram for knowledge management in outsourcing relationships

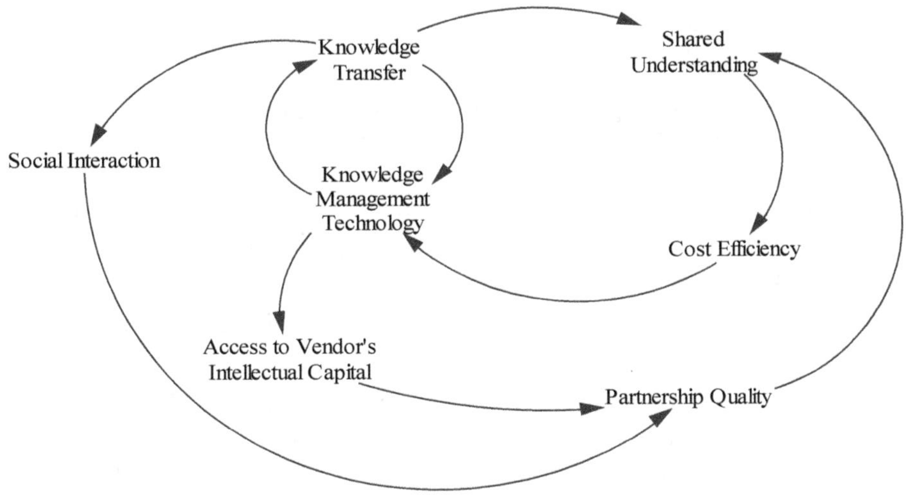

Figure 6.24. Positive feedback loop in the causal loop diagram

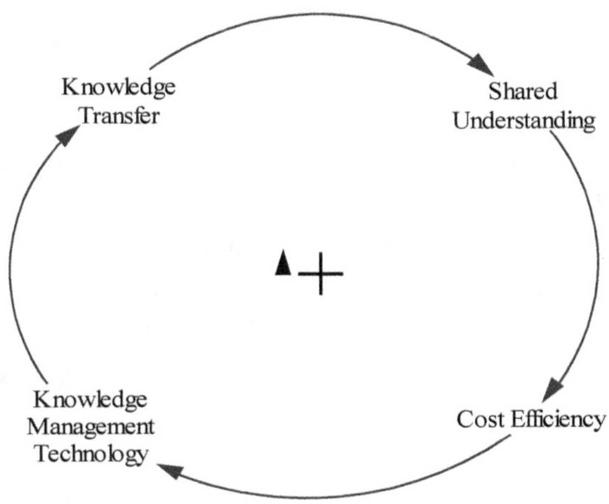

Knowledge transfer is supported by knowledge management technology. More knowledge transfer increases the extent of social interaction between vendor and client, thereby improving partnership quality. Increased knowledge transfer also improved shared understanding, which leads to higher cost efficiency in tasks that have to be performed and services that are to be delivered.

Figure 6.24 illustrates one positive feedback loop from Figure 2.23. When knowledge transfer increases, shared understanding increases, causing improved cost efficiency, leading to more investments in knowledge management technology, causing even more knowledge transfer between the IT outsourcing partners.

Questions for Discussion

1. What kind of client knowledge is critical for the vendor in an outsourcing relationship? What kind of vendor knowledge is critical for the client in an outsourcing relationship?
2. Do you find support for the vendor value proposition in the three cases of ABB-IBM, SAS-CSC and RR-EDS?
3. When the vendor organization solves IT problems for the client organization, it can be defined as a value shop. What kind of client knowledge does the vendor need in each of its primary activities?

List of References

Alavi, M., & Leidner, D. E. (2001). Knowledge management and knowledge management systems: Conceptual foundations and research issues. *MIS Quarterly, 25*(1), 107-136.

Allard, S., & Holsapple, C. W. (2002). Knowledge management as a key for e-business competitiveness: From the knowledge chain to KM audits. *Journal of Computer Information Systems (JCIS), 42*(5), 19-25.

Ang, S., & Straub, D. W. (1998). Production and transaction economics and IS outsourcing: A study of the U.S. banking industry. *MIS Quarterly, 22*(4), 535-552.

Artz, K. W., & Brush, T. H. (2000). Asset specificity, uncertainty and relational norms: An examination of coordination costs in collaborative strategic alliances. *Journal of Economic Behavior & Organization, 41*(4), 337-362.

Bahli, B., & Rivard, S. (2005). Validating measures of information technology outsourcing risk factors. *Omega*, 22, 175-187.

Barney, J. B. (2001). Is the resource-based 'view' a useful perspective for strategic management research? Yes. *Academy of Management Review, 26*(1), 41-56.

Barney, J. B. (2002). *Gaining and sustaining competitive advantage*. Upper Saddle River, NJ: Prentice Hall.

Bock, G. W., Zmud, R. W., & Kim, Y. G. (2005). Behavioral intention formation in knowledge sharing: Examining the roles of extrinsic motivators, social-psychological forces, and organizational climate. *MIS Quarterly, 29*(1), 87-111.

Chandra, C., & Kumar, S. (2000). Supply chain management in theory and practice: a passing fad or a fundamental change? *Industrial Management & Data Systems, 100*(3), 100-113.

Das, T. K., & Teng, B. S. (2002). Alliance constellations: A social exchange perspective. *Academy of Management Review, 27*(3), 445-456.

Davenport, T. H., & Prusak, L. (1998). *Working knowledge.* Boston, MA: Harvard Business School Press.

DiRomualdo, A., & Gurbaxani, V. (1998). Strategic intent for IT outsourcing. *Sloan Management Review, 39*(4), 67-80.

Druckman, M. (1998). Social exchange theory: Premises and prospects. *International Negotiation, 3*(2), 253-266.

Edum-Fotwe, F. T., & McCaffer, R. (2000). Developing project management competency: Perspectives from the construction industry. *International Journal of Project Management, 18*(2), 111-124.

Eisenhardt, K. M. (1985). Control: Organizational and economic approaches. *Management Science, 31*(2), 134-149.

Erlingsson, O. G., & Grødem, E. (2005). *Vendor's complementary core competencies and IT outsourcing success: An empirical investigation.* Master of Science thesis, Norwegian School of Management, Oslo.

Fahey, L., Srrivastava, R., Sharon, J. S., & Smith, D. E. (2001). Linking e-business and operating processes: The role of knowledge management. *IBM Systems Journal, 40*(4), 889-907.

Feng, K., Chen, E. T., & Liou, W. (2005). Implementation of knowledge management systems and firm performance: An empirical investigation. *Journal of Computer Information Systems (JCIS), 45*(2), 92-104.

Foltz, C. B., Cronan, T. P., & Jones, T. W. (2005). Have you met your organization's computer usage policy? *Industrial Management & Data Systems, 105*(2), 137-146.

Frame, J. D. (1995). *Managing projects in organizations.* San Francisco: Jossey-Bass Publishers.

Garicano, L., & Hubbard, T. N. (2003). Firms' boundaries and the division of labor: Empirical strategies. *Journal of the European Economic Association, 1*(2/3), 495-502.

Garud, R., & Kumaraswamy, A. (2005). Vicious and virtuous circles in the management of knowledge: The case of Infosys Technologies. *MIS Quarterly, 29*(1), 9-33.

Gilley, M. K., & Rasheed, A. (2000). Making more by doing less: An analysis of outsourcing and its effects on firm performance. *Journal of Management, 26*(4), 763-790.

Gonzales, R., Gasco, J., & Llopis, J. (2005). Information systems outsourcing risks: A study of large firms. *Industrial Management & Data Systems, 105*(1), 45-62.

Gottschalk, P., & Karlsen, J. T. (2002). Management roles for successful IT projects. *Project Management, 8*(1), 7-13.

Gottschalk, P. & Solli-Sæther, H. (2006). *Managing successful IT outsourcing relationships*. Hershey, PA: Idea Group Publishing.

Grover, V., Jeong, S. R., Kettinger, W. J., & Lee, C. C. (1993). The chief information officer: A study of managerial roles. *Journal of Management Information Systems, 10*(2), 107-130.

Grover, V., Teng, T. C., & Cheon, M. J. (1998). Towards a theoretically-based contingency model of information systems outsourcing. In L. P. Willcocks, & M. C. Lacity (Eds.), *Strategic sourcing of information systems: Perspectives and practices.* Chichester, UK: John Wiley & Sons.

Hancox, M., & Hackney, R. (2000). IT outsourcing: Frameworks for conceptualizing practice and perception. *Information Systems Journal, 10*(3), 217-237.

Hansen, M. T., Nohria, N., & Tierney, T. (1999, March-April). What's your strategy for managing knowledge? *Harvard Business Review*, 106-116.

Hitt, M. A., Bierman, L., Shumizu, K., & Kochhar, R. (2001). Direct and moderating effects of human capital on strategy and performance in professional service firms: A resourced-based perspective. *Academy of Management Journal, 44*(1), 13-28.

Holsapple, C. W., & Singh, M. (2000). Electronic commerce: From a definitional taxonomy toward a knowledge-management view. *Journal of Organizational Computing and Electronic Commerce, 10*(3), 149-170.

Inkpen, A. C., & Tsang, E. W. K. (2005). Social capital, networks, and knowledge transfer. *Academy of Management Review, 30*(1), 146-165.

Kankanhalli, A., Tan, B. C. Y., & Wei, K. K. (2005). Contributing knowledge to electronic knowledge repositories: An empirical investigation. *MIS Quarterly, 29*(1), 113-143.

Karlsen, J. T., & Gottschalk, P. (2002). External or internal focus? A comparison of IT executive and IT project manager roles. *Engineering Management Journal, 14*(2), 5-11.

Kern, T., & Blois, K. (2002). Norm development in outsourcing relationship. *Journal of Information Technology, 17,* 32-42.

Kern, T., & Willcocks, L. P. (2000). Contract, control and presentation in IT outsourcing: Research in thirteen UK organizations. *Journal of Global Information Management, 8*(4), 15-29.

Kern, T., & Willcocks, L. P. (2002). Exploring relationships in information technology outsourcing: The interaction approach. *European Journal of Information Systems, 11,* 3-19.

King, W. R., & Teo, T. S. H. (1997). Integration between business planning and information systems planning: Validating a stage hypothesis. *Decision Sciences, 28*(2), 279-307.

Ko, D. G., Kirsch, L. J., & King, W. R. (2005). Antecedents of knowledge transfer from consultants to clients in enterprise system implementations. *MIS Quarterly, 29*(1), 59-85.

Koh, C., Ang, S., & Straub, D. W. (2004). IT outsourcing success: A psychological contract perspective. *Information Systems Research, 15*(4), 356-373.

Lacity, M. C., & Willcocks, L. P. (2000). Relationships in IT outsourcing: A stakeholder perspective. In R. W. Zmud (Ed.), *Framing the domains of IT management: Projecting the future through the past.* Cincinnati, OH: Pinnaflex Educational Resources.

Lambe, C. J., Spekman, R. E., & Hunt, S. D. (2000). Interimistic relational exchange: Conceptualization and propositional development. *Journal of the Academy of Marketing Science, 28*(2), 212-225.

Lambe, C. J., Spekman, R. E., & Hunt, S. D. (2002). Alliance competence, resources, and alliance success: Conceptualization, measurement, and initial test. *Journal of the Academy of Marketing Science, 30*(2), 141-158.

Lambe, C. J., Wittmann, C. M., & Spekman, R. E. (2001). Social exchange theory and research on business-to-business relational exchange. *Journal of Business-to-Business Marketing, 8*(3), 1-36.

Lee, J. N. (2001). The impact of knowledge sharing, organizational capability and partnership quality on IS outsourcing success. *Information & Management, 38*(5), 323-335.

Lee, J. N., & Kim, Y. G. (1999). Effect of partnership quality on IS outsourcing success: Conceptual framework and empirical validation. *Journal of Management Information Systems, 15*(4), 29-61.

Lee, J. N., Miranda, S. M., & Kim, Y. G. (2004). IT outsourcing strategies: Universalistic, contingency, and configurational explanations of success. *Information Systems Research, 15*(2), 110-131.

Lee, M. K. O. (1996). IT outsourcing contracts: Practical issues for management. *Industrial Management & Data Systems, 96*(1), 15-20.

Levina, N., & Ross, J. W. (2003). From the vendor's perspective: Exploring the value proposition in information technology outsourcing. *MIS Quarterly, 27*(3), 331-364.

Lin, L., Geng, X., & Whinston, A. B. (2005). A sender-receiver framework for knowledge transfer. *MIS Quarterly, 29*(2), 197-219.

Lonsdale, C., & Cox, A. (2000). The historical development of outsourcing: the latest fad? *Industrial Management & Data Systems, 100*(9), 444-450.

Løwendahl, B. R. (2000). *Strategic management of professional service firms.* Copenhagen: Copenhagen Business School Press.

Luo, Y. (2002). Contract, cooperation, and performance in international joint ventures. *Strategic Management Journal,* 23, 903-991.

Malhotra, A., Gosain, S., & El Sawy, O. A. (2005). Absorptive capacity configurations in supply chains: Gearing for partner-enabled market knowledge creation. *MIS Quarterly, 29*(1), 145-187.

Mintzberg, H. (1990). The manager's job: Folklore and fact. *Harvard Business Review, 68*(2), 163-177.

Mintzberg, H. (1994). Rounding out the manager's job. *Sloan Management Review, 36*(1), 11-26.

Murch, R. (2000). *Project management: Best practices for IT professionals*. New York: Prentice Hall.

Perrons, R. K., & Platts, K. (2004). The role of clockspeed in outsourcing decisions for new technologies: Insights from the prisoner's dilemma. *Industrial Management & Data Systems, 104*(7), 624-632.

Pettus, M. L. (2001). The resourced-based view as a development growth process: Evidence from the deregulated trucking industry. *Academy of Management Journal, 44*(4), 878-896.

Priem, R. L., & Butler, J. E. (2001). Is the resourced-based view a useful perspective for strategic management research? *Academy of Management Review, 26*(1), 22-40.

Quinn, J. B. (1999, Summer). Strategic outsourcing: Leveraging knowledge capabilities. *Sloan Management Review*, 9-21.

Quinn, J. B. (2000, Summer). Outsourcing innovation: The new engine of growth. *Sloan Management Review*, 13-28.

Sambamurthy, V., & Subramani, M. (2005). Special issue on information technologies and knowledge management. *MIS Quarterly, 29*(1), 1-7.

Shankman, N. A. (1999). Reframing the debate between agency and stakeholder theories of the firm. *Journal of Business Ethics, 19*(4), 319-334.

Sheehan, N. T. (2002). *Reputation as a driver in knowledge-intensive service firms.* Series of Dissertations 4/2002, Norwegian School of Management, Sandvika, Norway.

Shi, Z., Kunnathur, A. S., & Ragu-Nathan, T. S. (2005). IS outsourcing management competence dimensions: Instrument development and relationship exploration. *Information & Management, 42*, 901-919.

Stabell, C. B., & Fjeldstad , Ø. D. (1998). Configuring value for competitive advantage: On chains, shops, and networks. *Strategic Management Journal, 19,* 413-437.

Stake, R. E. (1994). Case studies. In N. K. Denzin & Y. S. Lincoln (Eds.), *Handbook of qualitative research* (pp. 236-247). Thousand Oaks, CA: Sage Publications.

Sterman, J. D. (2000). *Business dynamics: Systems thinking and modeling for a complex world.* Boston: McGraw-Hill.

Sveiby, K. E. (2001). A knowledge-based theory of the firm to guide in strategy formulation. *Journal of Intellectual Capital, 2*(4), 344-358.

Wasko, M. M., & Faraj, S. (2005). Why should I share? Examining social capital and knowledge contribution in electronic networks of practice. *MIS Quarterly, 29*(1), 35-57.

Willcocks, L. P., Hindle, J. L., Feeny, D. F., & Lacity, M. C. (2004, Summer). IT and business process outsourcing: The knowledge potential. *Information Systems Management*, 7-15.

Williamson, O. E. (2000). The new institutional economics: Taking stock, looking ahead. *Journal of Economic Literature, 38,* 595-613.

Chapter VII

Insourcing Knowledge

Introduction

The term outsourcing can be studied further by using the opposite term of insourcing. Hirschheim and Lacity (2000) define insourcing as the practice of evaluating the outsourcing option, but confirming the continued use of internal IT resources to achieve the same objectives of outsourcing. They studied six decision factors: scope, sponsor, evaluation process, year of decision, size of the organization and outcome. Lacity et al. (1996) define total insourcing as the management and provision of at least 80% of the IT budget internally after evaluating the IT services market. The common element of the two definitions seems to be that customers evaluate the external IT services market before a sourcing decision takes place.

Four Sourcing Categories

A survey of IT outsourcing experiences in U.S. and UK organizations revealed a wide spectrum of sourcing decisions, ranging from exclusive use of internal IT functions to large-scale IT outsourcing (Lacity & Willcocks, 2000). This wide spectrum can be classified into the following four sourcing categories (Lacity et al., 1996):

Figure 7.1. Insourcing definition compared to other relevant terms

Key term	Definition
Insourcing	The practice of evaluating the outsourcing option, but confirming the continued use of internal IT resources to achieve the same objectives of outsourcing.
Offshoring	The practice of migrating business processes overseas to lower costs without significantly sacrificing quality. This practice is also called global outsourcing.
Outsourcing	A process whereby an organization decides to contract-out, or sell, the firm's IT assets, people and/or activities to a third party supplier, who in exchange provides and manages these assets and services for an agreed fee over an agreed time period.
Selective sourcing	Selected IT functions are located with external providers while still providing between 20 and 80 percent of IT budget.
Source firm	The firm that has the technology. The source firm is sometimes called a vendor, supplier or outsourcer.
Sourcing firm	The firm that desires the technology. The sourcing firm is sometimes called a client, customer or outsourcee.
Transformational outsourcing	Partnering with another company to achieve a rapid, substantial and sustainable improvement in enterprise-level performance.

1. **Total outsourcing:** The decision to transfer IT assets, leases, staff and management responsibility for delivery of IT services from an internal IT function to an external IT provider that represents more than 80% of the IT budget.
2. **Total insourcing:** The decision to retain the management and provision of more than 80% of the IT budget internally after evaluating the IT services market. Included in the definition of insourcing is the buying-in of vendor resources to meet a temporary need, such as programmers in the latter stages of a new development project or management consultants to facilitate a strategic planning process. In these cases, the customer retains responsibility for the delivery of IT services; vendor resources are brought in to supplement internally managed teams.
3. **Selective outsourcing:** The decision to source selected IT functions from external provider(s) while still providing between 20 and 80% of the IT budget internally. This strategy may include single or multiple suppliers. The vendor becomes responsible for delivering the result of the selectively outsourced IT activities, while the customer remains responsible for delivering the result of the insourced activities.
4. **De facto insourcing:** A de facto decision to use internal IT departments to provide products and services that arise from historical precedent, rather than from a reasoned evaluation of the IT services market.

With these definitions, Lacity et al. (1996) found 14 cases of total outsourcing, 15 cases of total insourcing and 33 cases of selective outsourcing, in their sample of 62 companies. In a later survey, Lacity and Willcocks (2000) found that 73% of respondents pursued selective outsourcing, while 22% of organizations exclusively use internal IT functions to provide IT services, leaving only 5% to total outsourcing.

Applications service providers (ASPs) deliver and manage applications and computer services from remote computer centers to multiple users via the Internet or a private network. Instead of buying and installing software programs, subscribing companies can rent the same functions from these services. Users pay for the use of this software either on a subscription or per transaction basis. The ASP's solution combines package software applications and all of the related hardware, system software, network and other infrastructure services that the customer otherwise would have to purchase, integrate or manage independently. The ASP customer interacts with a single entity instead of an array of technologies and service vendors. Companies are turning to this software service model as an alternative to developing their own software. Some companies will find it much easier to rent software from another firm and avoid the expense and difficulty of installing, operating and maintaining the hardware and software for complex systems, such as enterprise resource planning (ERP) systems. The ASP contracts guarantee a level of service and support to ensure that the software is available and working at all times. Today's Internet-driven business environment is changing so rapidly that getting a system up and running in three months instead of six could mean the difference between success and failure. Application service providers also enable small and medium-size companies to use applications that they otherwise could not afford.

Barthélemy and Geyer (2004) studied determinants of total IT outsourcing in French and German firms. The total vs. selective IT outsourcing dichotomy is a classic in the literature, and they reported the following findings from their study:

- For firms that outsource IT, the likelihood of total outsourcing is *higher* when the cost reduction motivation is strong.
- For firms that outsource IT, the likelihood of total outsourcing is *lower* when the IT department is large.
- For firms that outsource IT, the likelihood of total outsourcing is *lower* in IT-intensive sectors.
- For firms that outsource IT, the likelihood of total outsourcing is *higher* for French firms than for German firms.

They found no support for the hypothesis that performance improvement motivation is a significant factor nor the hypothesis that non-IT senior executives' involvement is a significant factor.

Insourcing Theories

Based on insourcing definitions explored earlier, we can identify taxonomies, or schools of IT insourcing. The primary purpose of this framework is to guide executive choices to initiate insourcing projects according to goals, organizational character and technological, behavioral or economic biases. This categorization approach is adapted from Earl (2001).

Each school or category is proposed as an ideal type based on theory. No claims are made that any one school or theory outperforms others. Each represents a particular theoretical orientation and different form of organizational intervention at IT insourcing. The theories are not mutually exclusive. Indeed, two or more of them sometimes can be observed in the same outsourcing arrangement. Also, some theories draw on other theories. An example is the theory of firm boundaries that draws on transaction cost theory.

There may be more theories and other schools that our literature review has not encountered. We identified the following theory-based schools in IT insourcing: transaction cost, neoclassical economics, contractual, core competencies, agency, resource-based, partnership and alliance, relational exchange, stakeholder, firm boundaries and the school of social exchange. Each of these 11 schools are presented in the following and compared at the end.

Transaction Cost Theory: Reduce Transaction Costs

In an outsourcing arrangement, transaction costs occur. After insourcing, such transaction costs disappear. The cost savings can be substantial, depending on transaction attributes.

Transaction costs arise because vendor and client are in an exchange relationship with each other. Transaction costs include the costs associated with writing contracts as well as the costs of opportunistic holdup at a later date. Although internal organization or hierarchies are posited to offer lower costs of coordination and control and to avert subsequent opportunistic behavior, related problems can occur in decentralized firms. A major concern is the loss of high-powered incentives when the pay-for-performance link is attenuated by internal production (Anderson et al., 2000).

Five attributes of business exchange are positively associated with transaction costs: (1) the necessity of investments in durable, specific assets; (2) infrequency of transacting; (3) task complexity and uncertainty; (4) difficulty in measuring task performance; and (5) interdependencies with other transactions.

Neoclassical Economic Theory: Reduce Production Costs

Neoclassical economic theory regards every business organization as a production function, and where their motivation is driven by profit maximization. This means that companies produce goods and services where they have a cost or production advantage. If a company has a cost advantage in producing IT services, then insourcing will improve firm profitability (Gilley & Rasheed, 2000).

In neoclassical economic theory, insourcing arises through substitution. Insourcing arises through the substitution of internal activities for external purchases. In this way, it can be viewed as a discontinuation of procurement from outside suppliers and an initiation of internal production. To the extent this type of insourcing increases a firm's involvement in successive stages of production, substitution-based insourcing may be viewed as vertical integration.

Contractual Theory: Eliminate Contract Problems

In an outsourcing arrangement, contractual arrangements occur. Contractual arrangements are both hard to agree upon and settle. After insourcing, such contracts disappear. The benefits can be substantial for the client organization, depending on the complexity of the terminated relationship with the vendor.

An outsourcing contract provides a legally bound, institutional framework in which each party's rights, duties and responsibilities are codified, and the goals, policies and strategies underlying the arrangement are specified. Every outsourcing contract has the purpose of facilitating exchange and preventing opportunism. However, there will always be leeway for opportunism, moral hazards and leakage of proprietary knowledge. An incomplete contract may bring about ambiguity, which creates a breeding ground for shirking responsibility and shifting blame, raises the likelihood of conflict and hinders the ability to coordinate activities, utilize resources and implement strategies (Luo, 2002).

An IT outsourcing contract tends to be more complicated than other business contracts, resembling as it does a hybrid between an asset purchase and sale agreement and a sale/leaseback agreement, in that there is a sale of assets or transfer of operations, transfer of employees and a leaseback to the customer of the information technology services that were divested. This legal complexity is evident in the detail and in the time typically invested in negotiating such an agreement (Kern & Willcocks, 2000).

The outsourcing contract is unlike other service contracts because of the nature of what is being contracted for and the length of the contract. This makes it extremely difficult to define and describe service provision or any other exchanges that may be needed in the future. Insourcing creates a situation without a need for contract and without a need for specification of services into the long-term future.

Theory of Core Competencies: Strengthen Core Competencies

Core competencies theory suggests activities should be performed in-house if they are core activities in the organization. An organization may view IT itself as a core competency. It seems that most successful companies have a good understanding of IT's potential. However, some organizations have outsourced IT even though they see it as core and delivering competitive advantage.

Hancox and Hackney (2000) interviewed IT managers to find support for the core competencies theory. Most organizations seemed to share the view of IT as a mix of core and noncore activities.According to Prahalad and Hamel (1990), core competencies are the collective learning in the organization, especially how to coordinate diverse production skills and integrate multiple streams of technologies. Since core competency is about harmonizing streams of technology, it is also about the organization of work and the delivery of value. Core competencies are sometimes called firm-specific competence, invisible assets and distinctive competencies. According to the theory of core competencies, IT should be insourced when IT is considered a core function. An activity that contributes to the competitive capabilities of a company is considered to be core.

Agency Theory: Avoid Goal Conflicts

In an outsourcing arrangement, the cooperating parties are engaged in an agency relationship defined as a contract under which a client organization (the principal) engages a vendor organization (the agent) to perform some service on their behalf which involves delegating some decision-making authority to the agent.

According to agency theory, two problems occur in an agency relationship. The first is the agency problem that arises when the desires or goals of the principal and agent conflict and it is difficult or expensive for the principal to verify what the agent is actually doing. The second is the risk sharing that arises when the principal and agent have different risk preferences. These problems are well known in IT outsourcing. An example might be that the client organization wants to reduce its IT costs, while the vendor organization wants to maximize profits. The agency problem arises when the two parties do not share productivity gains. The risk-sharing problem might be the result of different attitudes toward the use of new technologies (Eisenhardt, 1985). Insourcing eliminates both problems, as the cooperation between vendor and client comes to an end. The technological and business complexity of IT means that the benefits from avoiding the agent and avoiding monitoring the agent's work can be substantial.

Resource-Based Theory: Control Strategic Resources

The central tenet in resource-based theory is that unique organizational resources of both tangible and intangible nature are the real source of competitive advantage. With resource-based theory, organizations are viewed as a collection of resources that are heterogeneously distributed within and across industries. The essence of the resource-based theory of the firm lies in its emphasis on the internal resources available to the firm, rather than on the external opportunities and threats dictated by industry conditions (Hitt et al., 2001).

Insourcing enables the firm to improve internal resources, both in terms of availability and control. More resources will become available internally, and the firm establishes complete control over its resources. This is especially important for strategic resources that are characterized by being valuable, unique, non-imitable, non-transferable, non-substitutable, combinable and exploitable (Barney, 2002).

Partnership and Alliance Theory: Avoid Performance Disagreement

Hancox and Hackney (2000) found that few organizations claim to be in a strategic partnership with their IT suppliers in outsourcing relationships. The relationship is more likely to favor the vendor over time, because of greater experience in service delivery, as he or she has several clients. Despite assurances found in vendors' marketing literature, most clients are skeptical about partnership.

Alliances are broadly defined as collaborative efforts between two or more firms in which the firms pool their resources. Das and Teng (2002) studied partnerships and alliances. They found a lack of agreement concerning alliance performance. Insourcing terminates partnerships and alliances. The benefits can be substantial, as the insourcing firm can concentrate on its own goals, priorities and strategies. Furthermore, the insourcing firm no longer has to spend time and effort in cooperation with the vendor firm.

Relational Exchange Theory: Avoid Conflicting Norms

Norms are expectations about behavior that are at least partially shared by a group of decision makers. Norms are important in relational exchange because they provide the governance rules of outsourcing arrangement (Lambe et al., 2000). Relational exchange is an interactive process where commitments are made, outcomes are observed and further investments are made if outcomes meet or exceed expectations.

Kern and Blois (2002) studied the role of norms within networks by describing how BP Exploration outsourced its information technology function — a major business activity. This outsourcing venture led to the formation of a consortium of vendors. However, this attempt was found to have failed. They suggested that the issue of norms was central to the failure of the consortium as an outsourcing arrangement..

Intraorganizational norms are more easily handled than interorganizational norms, suggesting insourcing of IT functions to avoid conflicting norms. Norms are formed in different ways. Some norms' roots can be related to cultural backgrounds. Relational norms consist of flexibility, information exchange and solidarity.

Stakeholder Theory: Satisfy Internal Stakeholders

A stakeholder is any group or individual who can affect, or is affected by, the achievement of a corporations' purpose. According to Lacity and Willcocks (2000), there are four distinct client IT stakeholder groups and three distinct supplier IT stakeholder groups. The client groups identified are customer senior business managers, customer senior IT managers, customer IT staff, customer IT users, and the supplier groups are senior managers, account managers and IT staff.

Stakeholder theory is justified on the basis that firms have responsibilities to stakeholders for moral reasons, and that there is no priority of one set of interests over another. Upholding four principles is necessary as preconditions for efficient working relationships: (1) honoring agreements; (2) avoiding lying; (3) respecting the autonomy of others; and (4) avoiding harm to others. After insourcing, the number of stakeholders is reduced from seven to four. Since all stakeholder groups are presumed to have significant differences in expectations and goals regarding IT, it is reasonable to propose that reducing the number of stakeholders will have two main benefits. First, the extent of effort invested in stakeholder satisfaction can be reduced. Second, the extent of stakeholder satisfaction will increase.

Theory of Firm Boundaries: Reduce Division of Labor

In an outsourcing arrangement, work is divided between vendor and client organization. After insourcing, all work is coordinated within the client organization, reducing division of labor problems. Insourcing expands firm boundaries.

nological performance. In contrast to popular arguments suggesting that insourcing or outsourcing will lead to superior technological performance, they found that governance decisions per se do not significantly influence technological performance directly. Rather, observed differences in the performance of transactions governed by different organizational forms are driven by factors underlying governance choice. While the increasing rapidity of technological change and the increasing dispersion of knowledge suggest an increased role for outsourcing in the economy, the relationship between governance choice and performance is dependent on the distribution of relevant capabilities and the degree to which performance is driven by autonomous or systemic innovation.

Transaction Cost Theory

The five transaction attributes indicate settings in which opportunistic behavior is likely. If transaction costs offset production cost advantages of the external supplier, the firm subsumes the activity — an outcome termed vertical integration or insourcing. Empirical research indirectly tests transaction cost theory by relating observed sourcing decisions to transaction attributes that proxy for transaction costs. Evidence on the relation between transaction-specific investments, contract duration and technological uncertainty generally supports the theory. The consistency of the empirical results seems startling in light of two problems with the hypothesis that firms take sourcing decisions to minimize the sum of production and transaction costs.

P2: Knowledge management will reduce insourcing transaction costs.

First, production and transaction costs are rarely neatly separable. For example, the choice of production technology (and subsequent production costs) is often inextricably linked with production volume, which in turn depends on whether the firm produces some or all products internally. Second, decision-makers are likely to be affected by wealth effects associated with sourcing, and thus are unlikely to take decisions that strictly maximize firm profit (Anderson et al., 2000).

Insourcing Archetypes

Hirschheim and Lacity (2000) argue that the current IT sourcing research covers the motivations and consequences of outsourcing, and has neglected another important

- **Archetype 4:** Senior executives confirm the value of IT. This archetype indicates the case where the insourcing decisions did not result in significant reduction in IT costs, but the insourcing decisions were still considered a success because companies revalidated and further legitimated internal sourcing. In these companies, organizational structures and processes are implemented to demonstrate the cost effectiveness of their IT departments.

Hirschheim and Lacity (2000) contend that outsourcing evaluations often result from the frustrations caused by different stakeholder expectations and perceptions of IT performance.

P3: Knowledge management reduces management frustrations in insourcing decision-making.

This belief is based on an analysis of what IT managers can realistically achieve vs. what senior executives and users expect them to achieve. Different stakeholder perspectives set unrealistic performance expectations for IT managers, leading to frustration, loss of faith in internal IT management and hopes that outsourcing vendors will provide the solutions.

Hidden Costs

The hidden management costs in outsourcing relationships were identified in research conducted by Kern and Willcocks (2002). Three areas of hidden costs were identified, which received little attention at the outset by client companies. First, the significant costs involved in post-contract management are not planned for. The findings suggested that management resorting to develop and maintain relations is generally higher than initially anticipated and expected. The percentage split of management time on relationship management and the rest, that is, contract management is 70/30. Second, ongoing monitoring of costs generally is not considered. This arises due to the client's management agenda of assuring not only that the vendor keeps its commitment to deliver the agreed services, but also to control the costs of the deal. Finally, the renegotiation or update costs involved in ensuring the contract always reflects the current statutes of the IT outsourcing arrangement. This is essential to ensure, for example, that in the event of termination, all service levels, technological assets and staffing are listed to simplify insourcing or vendor switch. Planning a contract that caters for every contingency is generally impossible in long-term business deals. Hence, outsourcing contracts, like so many other long-term business contracts, suffer from an inherent incompleteness, and hence necessitate updating.

P4: More knowledge about hidden costs increases the likelihood of IT insourcing.

Overlooking hidden costs of outsourcing was listed as the sixth deadly sin of outsourcing by Barthélemy (2003). In a separate research article, Barthélemy (2001) discussed the various hidden costs of IT outsourcing. Most companies outsourcing IT for the first time are not aware of those costs. Companies say they entered an outsourcing agreement believing that they understood all major costs. They agree that some amount was needed for activities such as finding a vendor, drafting the contract and managing the effort, but they think the amount would be negligible — in some cases, they halved or even canceled out the company's potential savings from outsourcing. Only those companies who have a bad experience take preventive measures. Barthélemy (2001) identified four categories of hidden costs:

1. **Vendor search and contracting:** Many enterprises underestimate the expense to identify and evaluate suitable IT vendors, select a finalist and negotiate and draft the contract. Companies incur such costs before spending the first dollar on the actual work. Thus, it costs something just to think about IT outsourcing. Companies may not want to reduce their spending for search and contracting, because it can significantly lower the other hidden costs. Additional time and expense early on helps avoid problems later, such as having to renegotiate the contract or constantly monitor the vendor to get the needed performance.
2. **Transition to the vendor:** Switching in-house IT activities to a vendor presents probably the most elusive hidden cost. Most companies do not realize how much they have spent until the transition is complete. It can take months before the vendor knows as much as the internal IT department, and it is hard to say exactly when the vendor has taken over. Most managers are unable to analyze transition cost. The best they can do is report transition time; a measure offering only limited insight into what drives transition cost. The average transition period — when the organization actually incurred a cost — was about a year. Transition costs are elusive: A company incurs them as long as the vendor has not completely taken over from the internal IT department. The time that internal employees spend helping the vendor is transition costs. Costs that stem from disruption — and from the vendor's inability to react as quickly and appropriately as the internal department did at the beginning of the contract — are transition costs. The characteristics of the outsourced activity greatly influence transition cost. The more idiosyncratic the activity

(the more tailored for the specific company), the higher the cost to pass it to a vendor that must take time to learn the activity. Outsourcing commodities such as PC procurement and maintenance entail lower transition costs. Also, the more complex the outsourced activity, the harder the transition. Furthermore, outsourcing activities that require transferring many people to the vendor also increase transition costs. The transferred employees often feel betrayed. They can resist outsourcing initiatives either directly (e.g., strike) or indirectly (e.g., slow motion).

3. **Managing the effort:** Managing the effort probably represents the largest category of hidden costs because it covers three areas: monitoring to see that IT vendors fulfill their contractual obligations, bargaining with IT vendors (and sanctioning them if necessary) and negotiating any needed contract changes. Unlike outsourcing fees, vendor-management costs for IT outsourcing are not readily apparent. A company knows what it pays to the vendor. Indeed, many businesses outsource to find out how much they pay for IT. Management costs, in contrast, are purely internal. Because of the costs' relative obscurity, many companies do not take them into account until they become visible — usually when the overall outsourcing cost has noticeably escalated.
4. **Transitioning after outsourcing:** The fourth hidden cost comes form switching vendors or reintegrating IT activities internally. When activities must be redirected to a new vendor, the cost involves finding that vendor, drafting a new contract and transitioning resources. When activities must be reintegrated, the cost involves building a new internal IT activity from scratch. The time needed is roughly the same regardless of the kind of transition. Such hidden costs represent expenses that managers find hard to quantify. Most managers are reluctant to think about the end of the contract. Outsourcing IT to focus on a company's core business or to cut costs is generally meant to be permanent. Companies do not plan to reintegrate IT. Even switching vendors is a move they prefer to avoid. Thus, regardless of how the contract ends, the end signifies a failed outsourcing effort. Most managers find it hard to consider that possibility.

All too often, companies neglect the hidden costs of IT outsourcing. Overlooking hidden costs is unwise. A better approach is to manage the four costs proactively and holistically and to spend extra time and resources in the early stages of the outsourcing effort. Knowing what the company wants and spending time on the contract can help curb the cost of managing the initiative and of transitioning outsourced activities when the contract ends (Barthélemy, 2001).

Strategic Outsourcing Termination

Termination of an IT outsourcing arrangement involves strategic decision-making. General studies of strategic decision-making show how rapidly strategic decisions are made in small firms operating within high-velocity environments, and how decision speed is linked to performance. Fast decision-makers use more, not less, information than do slow decision-makers. The former also develop more, not fewer, alternatives, and use a two-tiered advice process. Conflict resolution and integration between strategic managers are also critical to the pace of decision-making. Finally, fast decisions based on this pattern of behaviors lead to superior performance (Elter, 2004).

Managers are engaged in myriad day-to-day activities in attempting to resolve various strategic and organization issues associated with internal and external uncertainty. Problems and opportunities appear unstructured and incoherent. This makes it difficult for them to define appropriate and coherent means to address the many pressing business issues. Individuals cannot absorb all the information needed to formulate a complete set of alternatives from which to choose. Information may not be available and evaluation may be subject to personal biases. This means that actors' rationality is bounded by the environment in which they operate and their own human limitations. Under such complex and uncertain conditions, typically the case in an IT outsourcing termination situation, strategic plans become of limited value.

Researchers increasingly call for a need to explore the detailed processes and practices, which constitute strategic decision-making. Understanding strategizing is a key. Strategizing refers to the continuous formation and transformation of strategic patterns through ongoing and intertwined processes of strategic thinking and strategic acting, with several actors involved on different layers of the organization. IT outsourcing termination is a strategic issue. The term *strategic issue* refers to developments or trends that emerge from an organization's internal or external environments recognized by strategic managers as trends or events with significant influence on an organization's prospect of reaching a desired future. Strategic issues can be seen as the problems that actors in an organization engage in getting resolved (Elter, 2004).

In strategic outsourcing termination, there are typically three alternatives: (a) continuation after termination, (b) continuation with a new service provider after termination or (c) insourcing after termination. The decision will be influenced by several factors, such as economic concerns, change in business needs and service quality concerns. For example, the following propositions can be made concerning strategic choices:

P5: Economic concerns influence termination strategy.

If costs in the current outsourcing arrangement exceed acceptable level, then alternative (b) may be preferred over alternative (a), which will be ranked before alternative (c). This would imply that the client has lost faith in the current vendor in terms of the vendor's ability to cut costs. An alternative vendor may be able to cut costs.

P6: Change in business needs influence termination strategy.

If there is a considerable change in business needs that cause the current IS/IT situation to be obsolete and mainly consist of legacy systems, then alternative (a) may be ranked first, alternative (c) second and alternative (b) third. This would imply a belief that major changes in the IS/IT portfolio can either be handled in-house or by the current vendor who knows and understands the client's business and business needs.

P7: Service quality influences termination strategy.

If the current vendor has been unable to provide a service according to the service level agreement, then the client can accept the lower quality, but at a lower price, which would be choice of alternative (a). However, it is more likely that the client wants and needs the required service level, causing the client to prefer alternatives (b) and (c) over (a).

The Evaluation Phase

The customer goal in this phase is to identify the best source for IT activities. The major activities during this phase include measuring baseline services and costs, creating a request for proposal, developing evaluation criteria and inviting internal and external bids.

There is a need for joint senior management and IT management participation in sourcing evaluations. The evaluation process that frequently lead to success includes creating a request for proposal and inviting both external and internal bids. This practice ensures that a supplier's bid is not merely compared with current IT performance but with IT performance that could be achieved if internal managers were empowered to behave like suppliers.

Supplier stakeholders become much more active during this phase. In addition to the supplier senior management team, a host of supplier experts may attend bid presentations. While the supplier representatives talk to senior business managers about finances, they also talk to users about service, to the IT staff about career paths and benefits and to IT managers about baseline service-level agreements.

As with the previous phase, the customer-supplier interactions — although tentative — are typically characterized by enthusiasm and optimism at the senior management level during the evaluation phase.

The customer IT users are primarily concerned with service excellence during the entire outsourcing evaluation. IT users sometimes question confidentiality and privacy of data with IT outsourcing. But in general, IT users typically support outsourcing because they perceive that suppliers — with their IT expertise — will increase service and provide new IT to the user community.

At the customer IT staff level, however, IT professionals are frequently threatened by the impending decision. Some organizations, particularly those with an IT labor union, experience significant resistance from this stakeholder groups.

In cases in which IT staff is invited to submit an alternative bid, the internal bid process often serves as a galvanizing force. In some cases, senior management grants a request for an internal bid more as a morale preserver than as a serious contender against external bidders. Once given free rein to compete based on cost efficiency, internal IT managers may surprise senior management by submitting the winning bid. Sourcing evaluations, which lead to continued insourcing of the IT function, then proceed to a transition phase. The primary activity of the insourcing transition phase is the implementation of consolidation, rationalization and standardization of the internal bid proposal.

Sourcing evaluations that result in outsourcing typically proceed through the four additional phases whose description follows. Unlike insourcing, IT outsourcing requires significant changes in duties and responsibilities of IT management, staff and users. Also, more stakeholders must adapt and learn to interact with each other to deliver a cost-effective IT service.

The Case of British Aerospace

The outsourcing decision processes at British Aerospace (BA) started during the firm's financial crises in 1992. EDS approached the Corporate Finance Director with an unsolicited bid to take IT assets off the balance sheet. Although the EDS offer was attractive, BA felt they needed more information.

A full-scale investigation of IT outsourcing commenced. The entire decision process lasted a year and a half and involved the services of outside expertise, including lawyers, financial modelers, auditors of the request for proposal (RFP), auditors of the in-house proposal and technical experts. In late 1992, the Corporate IT Director created two independent teams, a six-person outsourcing evaluation team and an insourcing team to develop an in-house proposal. The in-house proposal was not intended to be a bid to compete with other suppliers. But rather it was to inform the company what might be possible internally, and also to provide useful benchmarking information to use in the discussions with other outsourcing parties.

In December 1992, the outsourcing team sent a request for information to 20 potential suppliers. In March 1993, 10 suppliers were invited to a bidders meeting. Two weeks later, five suppliers responded with a short proposal and a three-hour presentation. By April, the outsourcing team short-listed three suppliers.

In June 1993, BA sent out a complete RFP to the short-listed suppliers. The scope of the RFP included most of the infrastructure, applications development and applications support. The RFP contained cost estimates for in-scope resources, including almost 1,500 IT people. The cost estimates were based on the insourcing proposal.

Although BA planned to outsource the majority of applications, BA felt that a supplier could not provide software cheaper because BA would have to pay their mark-up. Instead, they were looking for value-added, such as getting free software from other clients. BA planned to retain about 300 people for core IT capabilities, including IT strategy, contract administration, relationship management and strategic IT systems.

After distribution of the RFP, the outsourcing team invited the bidders for on-site tours. In return, the bidders invited BA to visit a number of supplier reference sites. These reference sites highlighted the need for BA to define a comprehensive and detailed contract. In particular, the outsourcing team needed consistent cost and service data, including standard service-level agreements for 500 services. BA also rejected the idea of a partnership, as IT suppliers and customers do not share revenue nor are they responsible for each other's debts.

In July 1993, the three short-listed suppliers submitted their final bids. BA felt that all three suppliers were committed to winning the bid because they spent a significant amount of time and resources on the bidding process. It was estimated that each supplier had 30 employees working on each bid, and spent approximately three million pounds during the process.

In August, one supplier was eliminated because its bid was 20% higher than the other two. Ironically, this supplier knew BA the best because of past business interactions. The supplier admitted that their bid was high because they simply did not believe some of the claims in the RFP.

The remaining two external bids and the in-house proposal were very similar in price (only a 1% difference). The in-house proposal showed that BA could compete with external suppliers on price. But the suppliers were able to do a number of things that BA could not achieve on their own. Suppliers would bear the initial investment costs required to implement cost reduction tactics such as data center consolidation. Outside auditors noted that initially BA would need to hire 50 people to deliver the savings. But in the end, the insourcing proposal served its purpose of increasing BA's negotiating power. At this stage, the main objective of outsourcing shifted from cost reduction to value-added.

From August 1993 to November 1993 the divisions became involved in the evaluation of the two remaining bidders. Some of the divisions would not benefit financially from outsourcing, and argued against the bids. The Corporate IT Director forcefully argued that the entire IT functionality across all business units had to be placed on the auction block to attract an external supplier, CSC

CSC won the contract. One reason was that CSC marketed IT outsourcing very hard to the divisions. CSC answered many tough questions about value-added outsourcing. This decentralized marketing strategy finally sold divisions to CSC. CSC was successful in winning the bid also because of their expertise in aerospace and their ability to talk business language.

In November 1993, the final report was made and approved at the board level. The next four months were spent in due diligence to verify RFP data. CSC could alter their bid during this time if they found any major missing items from the RFP. Also during this time, service-level agreements (SLAs) were defined for the corporate IT and 14 divisions.

Discussion

A typical analytical framework to aid in decisions concerning outsourcing is offered in Figure 7.2. The guiding parameters are the business value of a technology or application and the operational performance of the associated service. The framework suggests, for example, that outsourcing of information systems central to business strategy may be a dangerous diversion, especially if IT operations are already efficient. Insourcing in this situation is preferred. If business value is high but operational performance is weak, then market testing (or benchmarking) might make sense, at least so that a company can see what performance improvement might be possible by either internal or external sourcing. However, if operational performance is weak and the business value of the particular technology or application is low, then outsourcing is a more obvious route to improvement. Finally, smart sourcing or selective outsourcing might be a way to simplify the IT domain

Figure 7.2. IT sourcing strategies

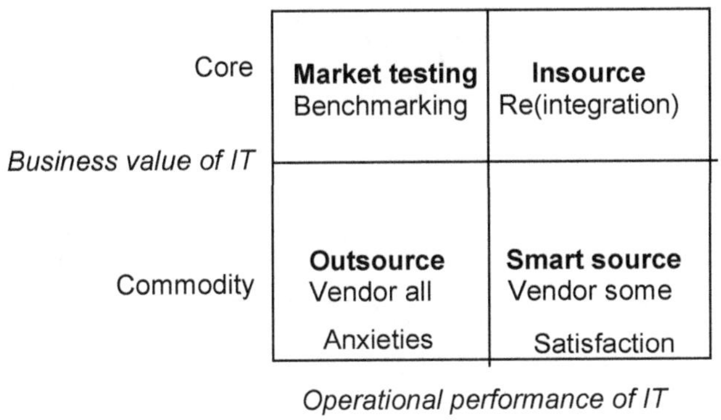

when elements of it are satisfactory for operational performance but not central to business capability or strategy.

Such arguments are intuitively appealing at an analytical and general level. The trouble is that they can be simplistic in practice. They do not account for the complexities that permeate the management of information resources. Managers should always ask themselves why does outsourcing make sense and why does it not make sense to the company in the current situation.

Conclusion

Business-oriented exit strategy can build on resource-based theory, transaction cost theory, activity theory, agency theory or other theories of the firm. The business-oriented exit strategy develops an understanding of the value configuration of the firm to understand the role of information systems in primary and secondary activities. The strategy defines vision, mission and objectives of the firm. It includes changes in electronic business and other important business areas that impact future use of information technology. The strategy analyzes distinctive IT nature in the firm, sourcing categories, IT challenges and selective outsourcing. In particular, the business-oriented exit strategy summarizes experiences from the current outsourcing arrangement and analyzes strengths and weaknesses of the current vendor. The strategy identifies and analyzes strengths and weaknesses of alternative sourcing options, including identified vendors and insourcing. The Y model can be applied

Figure 7.3. Causal loop diagram linking determinants of insourcing decisions

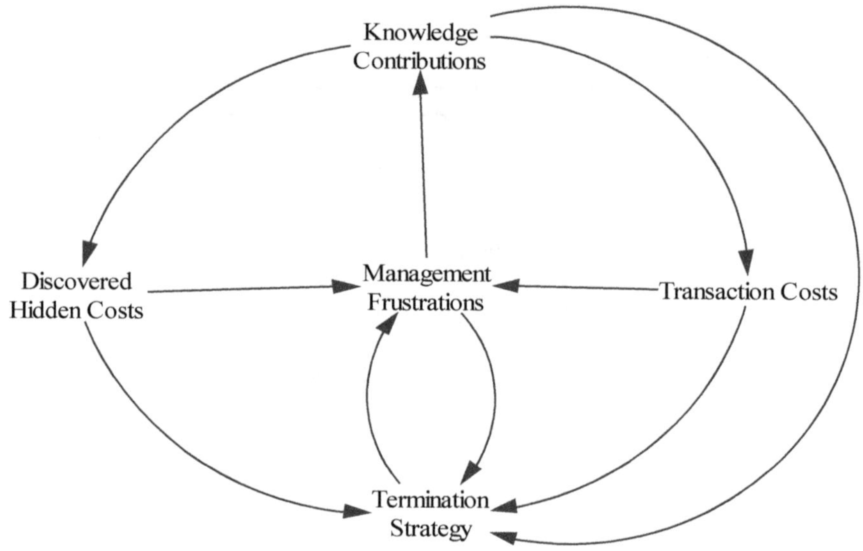

Figure 7.4. Positive feedback loop in the causal loop diagram

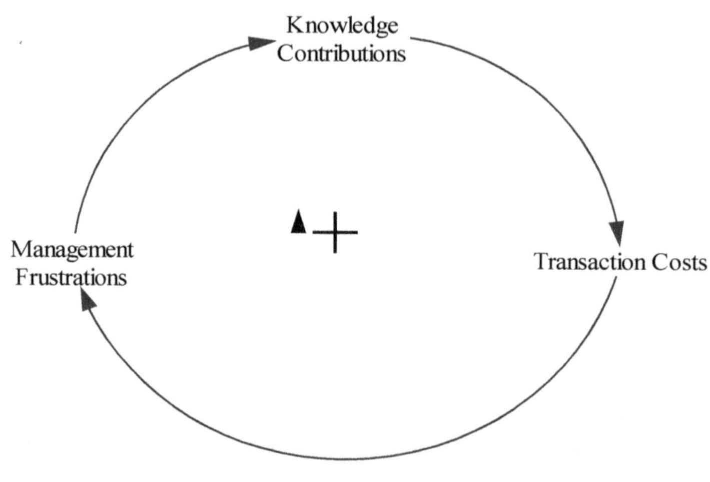

for strategic IT planning to define depth and breath of potential exit options. The result of a business-oriented exit strategy is contract termination, combined with a new sourcing decision.

Figure 7.3 illustrates some of the determinants that relate knowledge management to IT insourcing. When people contribute more knowledge about the current situation, that knowledge may cause discovery concerning hidden costs. More knowledge contributions may also cause reductions in transaction costs, as people learn how to perform transactions in a more efficient way.

An interesting feedback loop from the causal loop diagram is illustrated in Figure 7.4. Knowledge contributions reduce transaction costs. Transaction costs increase management frustration. Management frustration reduces knowledge contributions. Since there are two negative cause-and-effect relationships in this loop, in addition to one positive relationship, the whole loop becomes positive.

Questions for Discussion

1. How will knowledge management systems differ depending on executives' focus on core competencies, stakeholders or resources?
2. How will you describe insourcing in terms of the value shop?
3. What are differences between outsourcing and insourcing in terms of knowledge management systems?

List of References

Anderson, S. W., Glenn, D., & Sedatole, K. L. (2000). Sourcing parts of complex products: Evidence on transactions costs, high-powered incentives and ex-post opportunism. *Accounting, Organizations and Society, 25,* 723-749.

Barney, J. B. (2002). *Gaining and sustaining competitive advantage*. Upper Saddle River, NJ: Prentice Hall.

Barthélemy, J. (2001). The hidden costs of IT outsourcing. *Sloan Management Review, 42*(3), 60-69.

Barthélemy, J., & Geyer, D. (2004). The determinants of total IT outsourcing: An empirical investigation of French and German firms. *Journal of Computer Information Systems (JCIS), 44*(3), 91-97.

Das, T. K., & Teng, B. S. (2002). Alliance constellations: A social exchange perspective. *Academy of Management Review, 27*(3), 445-456.

Earl, M. J. (2001). Knowledge management strategies: Toward a taxonomy. *Journal of Management Information Systems, 18*(1), 215-233.

Eisenhardt, K. M. (1985). Control: Organizational and economic approaches. *Management Science, 31*(2), 134-149.

Elter, F. (2004). *Strategizing in complex contexts*. Unpublished doctoral thesis, Norwegian School of Management, Sandvika, Norway.

Garicano, L., & Hubbard, T. N. (2003). Firms' boundaries and the division of labor: Empirical strategies. *Journal of the European Economic Association, 1*(2/3), 495-502.

Gilley, M. K., & Rasheed, A. (2000). Making more by doing less: An analysis of outsourcing and its effects on firm performance. *Journal of Management, 26*(4), 763-790.

Hancox, M., & Hackney, R. (2000). IT outsourcing: Frameworks for conceptualizing practice and perception. *Information Systems Journal, 10*(3), 217-237.

Hirschheim, R., & Lacity, M. C. (2000). The myths and realities of information technology insourcing. *Communications of the ACM, 43*(2), 99-107.

Hitt, M. A., Bierman, L., Shumizu, K., & Kochhar, R. (2001). Direct and moderating effects of human capital on strategy and performance in professional service firms: A resourced-based perspective. *Academy of Management Journal, 44*(1), 13-28.

Kern, T., & Blois, K. (2002). Norm development in outsourcing relationship. *Journal of Information Technology, 17*, 32-42.

Kern, T., & Willcocks, L. P. (2000). Contract, control and presentation in IT outsourcing: Research in thirteen UK organizations. *Journal of Global Information Management, 8*(4), 15-29.

Kern, T., & Willcocks, L. P. (2002). Exploring relationships in information technology outsourcing: The interaction approach. *European Journal of Information Systems, 11*, 3-19.

Lacity, M. C., & Willcocks, L. P. (2000). Relationships in IT outsourcing: A stakeholder perspective. In R. W. Zmud (Ed.), *Framing the domains of IT management: Projecting the future through the past*. Cincinnati, OH: Pinnaflex Educational Resources.

Lacity, M. C., Willcocks, L. P., & Feeny, D. F. (1996, Spring). The value of selective IT sourcing. *Sloan Management Review*, 13-25.

Lambe, C. J., Spekman, R. E., & Hunt, S. D. (2000). Interimistic relational exchange: Conceptualization and propositional development. *Journal of the Academy of Marketing Science, 28*(2), 212-225.

Lambe, C. J., Wittmann, C. M., & Spekman, R. E. (2001). Social exchange theory and research on business-to-business relational exchange. *Journal of Business-to-Business Marketing, 8*(3), 1-36.

Leiblein, M. J., Reuer, J. J., & Dalsace, F. (2002). Do make or buy decisions matter? The influence of organizational governance on technological performance. *Strategic Management Journal, 23*, 817-833.

Luo, Y. (2002). Contract, cooperation, and performance in international joint ventures. *Strategic Management Journal, 23,* 903-991.

Prahalad, C. K., & Hamel, G. (1990). The core competence of the corporation. *Harvard Business Review, 76*(3), 79-91.

Chapter VIII

Governance Knowledge

Introduction

In many organizations, information technology has become crucial in the support, sustainability and growth of the business. This pervasive use of technology has created a critical dependency on IT that calls for a specific focus on IT governance. IT governance consists of the leadership and organizational structures and processes that ensure that the organization's IT sustains and extends its strategy and objectives (Grembergen et al., 2004).

IT governance matters because it influences the benefits received from IT investments. Through a combination of practices (such as redesigning business processes and well-designed governance mechanisms) and appropriately matched IT investments, top-performing enterprises generate superior returns on their IT investments (Weill, 2004).

IT governance can be defined as specifying decision rights and accountability framework to encourage desirable behavior in the use of IT (Weill & Ross, 2004). This is the definition we will use here.

Other definitions of IT governance are, for example: (1) an embodiment of the structures and processes that ensure that IT supports the organization's mission. The purpose is to align IT with the enterprise, maximize the benefits of IT, use IT resources responsibly and manage IT risks, (2) a structure of relationships and processes to direct and control the enterprise in order to achieve its goals by adding value while balancing risk vs. return over IT and its processes, (3) the responsibility of the board of directors and executive management. It is an integral part of enterprise governance and consists of the leadership and organizational structures and processes that ensure that the organization's IT sustains and extends is strategies and objectives, and (4) IT governance is the system by which an organization's IT portfolio is directed and controlled. IT Governance describes: (a) the distribution of decision-making rights and responsibilities among different stakeholders in the organization, and (b) the rules and procedures for making and monitoring decisions on strategic IT concerns (Peterson, 2004a).

IT governance has attracted substantial attention in recent years (e.g., Chin et al., 2004; Grembergen & Haes, 2004a, 2004b; McManus, 2004; Meyer, 2004; O'Donnell, 2004; Peterson, 2004a, 2004b; Rau, 2004; Read, 2004, Robbins, 2004; Trites, 2004; Weill & Ross, 2004, 2005). Here we will discuss IT governance in terms of resource mobilization, allocation of decision rights as well as strategic alignment.

IT Governance as Resource Mobilization

According to the resource-based theory of the firm, performance differences across firms can be attributed to the variance in the firms' resources and capabilities. The essence of the resource-based theory of the firm lies in its emphasis on the internal resources available to the firm, rather than on the external opportunities and threats dictated by industry conditions. A firm's resources are said to be a source of competitive advantage to the degree that they are scarce, specialized, appropriable, valuable, rare and difficult to imitate or substitute.

A fundamental idea in resource-based theory is that a firm must continually enhance its resources and capabilities to take advantage of changing conditions. Optimal growth involves a balance between the exploitation of existing resource positions and the development of new resource positions. Thus, a firm would be expected to develop new resources after its existing resource base has been fully utilized. Building new resource positions is important if the firm is to achieve sustained growth. When unused productive resources are coupled with changing managerial knowledge, unique opportunities for growth are created (Pettus, 2001).

The term resource is derived from Latin, resurgere, which means, *to rise* and implies an aid or expedient for reaching an end. A resource implies a potential means to achieve an end, or as something that can be used to create value. The first strategy textbooks outlining a holistic perspective focused on how resources needed to be allocated or deployed to earn rents. The interest in the term was for a long time linked to the efficiency of resource allocation, but this focus has later been expanded to issues such as resource accumulation, resource stocks and resource flows (Haanaes, 1997).

Firms develop firm-specific resources and then renew these to respond to shifts in the business environment; firms develop dynamic capabilities to adapt to changing environments. According to Pettus (2001), the term dynamic refers to the capacity to renew resource positions to achieve congruence with changing environmental conditions. A capability refers to the key role of strategic management in appropriately adapting, integrating and reconfiguring internal and external organizational skills, resources and functional capabilities to match the requirements of a changing environment.

If firms are to develop dynamic capabilities, learning is crucial. Change is costly; therefore, the ability of firms to make necessary adjustments depends upon their ability to scan the environment to evaluate markets and competitors and to quickly accomplish reconfiguration and transformation ahead of competition. However, history matters. Thus, opportunities for growth will involve dynamic capabilities closely related to existing capabilities. As such, opportunities will be most effective when they are close to previous resource use (Pettus, 2001).

According to Johnson and Scholes (2002), successful strategies are dependent on the organization having the strategic capability to perform at the level that is required for success. So the first reason why an understanding of strategic capability is important is concerned with whether an organization's strategies continue to fit the environment in which the organization is operating and the opportunities and threats that exist. Many of the issues of strategy development are concerned with changing strategic capability to fit a changing environment better. Understanding strategic capability is also important from another perspective. The organization's capability may be the leading edge of strategic developments, in the sense that new opportunities may be created by stretching and exploiting the organization's capability either in ways which competitors find difficult to match or in genuinely new directions, or both. This requires organizations to be innovative in the way they develop and exploit their capability.

In this perspective, strategic capability is about providing products or services to customers that are valued — or might be valued in the future. An understanding of what customers value is the starting point. The discussion then moves to whether an organization has the resources to provide products and services that meet these customer requirements. By a resource is meant anything that could be thought of as a strength or weakness of a given firm. More formally, a firm's resources at a given time can be defined as those (tangible and intangible) assets that are tied to the firm over a substantial period of time. Examples of resources are brand names, in-house knowledge of technology, employment of skilled personnel, trade contracts, machinery, efficient procedures, capital, and so forth. According to the economic school, resources include human capital, structural capital, relational capital and financial capital.

Priem and Butler (2001) find it problematic that virtually anything associated with a firm can be a resource, because this notion suggests that prescriptions for dealing in certain ways with certain categories of resources might be operationally valid, whereas other categories of resources might be inherently difficult for practitioners to measure and manipulate. One example of a resource that might be difficult to measure and manipulate is tacit knowledge. Some have argued for tacit knowledge — that understanding gained from experience but that sometimes cannot be expressed to another person and is unknown to oneself — as a source of competitive advantage.

Another example is the CEO resource. Prescriptions have been made to top managers of poorly performing firms that they are the cause of the problem and should think about voluntarily exiting the firm. This is a case where viewing a CEO as a resource would have more prescriptive implications for boards of directors than for the CEO (Priem & Butler, 2001).

Barney (2002) discusses how value, rarity, imitability and organization can be brought together into a single framework to understand the return potential associated with exploiting any of a firm's resources and capabilities. The framework consists of the following five steps (Barney, 2002):

1. If a resource or capability controlled by a firm is *not valuable*, that resource will not enable a firm to choose or implement strategies that exploit environmental opportunities or neutralize environmental threats. Organizing to exploit this resource will increase a firm's costs or decrease its revenues. These types of resources are weaknesses. Firms will either have to fix these weaknesses or avoid using them when choosing and implementing strategies. If firms do exploit these kinds of resources and capabilities, they can expect to put themselves at a competitive disadvantage compared to firms that either do not possess these nonvaluable resources or do not use them in conceiving and implementing strategies. Firms at a competitive disadvantage are likely to earn below-normal economic profits.
2. If a resource or capability is *valuable but not rare*, exploiting this resource in conceiving and implementing strategies will generate competitive parity and normal economic performance. Exploiting these valuable-but-not-rare resources will generally not create above-normal economic performance for a firm, but failure to exploit them can put a firm at a competitive disadvantage. In this sense, valuable-but-not-rare resources can be thought of as organizational strengths.
3. If a resource or capability is *valuable and rare but not costly to imitate*, exploiting this resource will generate a temporary competitive advantage for a firm and above-normal economic profits. A firm that exploits this kind of resource

is, in an important sense, gaining a first-mover advantage because it is the first firm that is able to exploit a particular resource. However, once competing firms observe this competitive advantage, they will be able to acquire or develop the resources needed to implement this strategy through direct duplication or substitution at no cost disadvantage compared to the first-moving firm. Over time, any competitive advantage that the first mover obtained would be competed away as other firms imitate the resources needed to compete. However, between the time a firm gains a competitive advantage by exploiting a valuable and rare but imitable resource or capability, and the time that competitive advantage is competed away through imitation, the first-moving firm can earn above-normal economic performance. Consequently, this type of resource or capability can be thought of as an organizational strength and distinctive competence.

4. If a resource is *valuable, rare and costly to imitate*, exploiting this resource will generate a sustained competitive advantage and above-normal economic profits. In this case, competing firms face a significant cost disadvantage in imitating a successful firm's resources and capabilities, and thus cannot imitate this firm's strategies. This advantage may reflect the unique history of the successful firm, causal ambiguity about which resources to imitate or the socially complex nature of these resources and capabilities. In any case, attempts to compete away the advantages of firms that exploit these resources will not generate above-normal or even normal performance for imitating firms. Even if these firms are able to acquire or develop the resources and capabilities in question, the very high costs of doing so would put them at a competitive disadvantage compared to the firm that already possessed the valuable, rare and costly to imitate resources. These kinds of resources and capabilities are organizational strengths and sustainable distinctive competencies.
5. The question of organization operates as an adjustment factor in the framework. If a firm with a resource that is *valuable, rare and costly to imitate is disorganized*, some of its potential above-normal return could be lost. If the firm completely fails to organize itself to take advantage of this resource, it could actually lead the firm that has the potential for above-normal performance to earn normal or even below-normal performance.

Barney (2001) discusses how value and rarity of resources can be determined. *Value* is a question of conditions under which resources will and will not be valuable. Models of the competitive environment within which a firm competes can determine value. Such models fall into two large categories: (1) efforts to use structure-conduct-performance-based models to specify conditions under which different firm resources will be valuable; and (2) efforts to determine the value of firm resources that apply other models derived from industrial organization models of perfect and imperfect competition.

As an example of resource value determination, Barney (2001) discusses the ability of cost leadership strategy to generate sustained competitive advantage. Several firm attributes may be associated with cost leadership, such as volume-derived economies of scale, cumulative volume-derived learning curve economies and policy choices. These firm attributes can be shown to generate economic value in at least some market settings. The logic used to demonstrate the value of these attributes is a market structure logic that is consistent with traditional microeconomics. After identifying the conditions under which cost leadership can generate economic value, it is possible to turn to the conditions under which cost leadership can be a source of competitive advantage (i.e., rare) and sustained competitive advantage (i.e., rare and costly to imitate).

The resource-based theory postulates that some resources will have a higher value for one firm than for other firms. The reasons why the value of resources may be firm-specific are multiple and include (Haanaes, 1997): the experience of working together as a team, the firm possessing superior knowledge about its resources, the bundling of the resources and the existence of co-specialized or complementary assets.

The value of a given resource may change over time as the market conditions change, for example, in terms of technology, customer preferences or industry structure. Thus, it is often argued that firms need to maintain a dynamic, as opposed to static, evaluation of the value of different resources.

Rarity is a question of how many competing firms possess a particular valuable resource. If only one competing firm possesses a particular valuable resource, then that firm can gain a competitive advantage, that is, it can improve its efficiency and effectiveness in ways that competing firms cannot. One example of this form of testable assertion is mentioned by Barney (2001). The example is concerned with organizational culture as a source of competitive advantage. If only one competing firm possesses a valuable organizational culture (where the value of that culture is determined in ways that are exogenous to the firm), then that firm can gain a competitive advantage, that is, it can improve its efficiency and effectiveness in ways that competing firms cannot. Both these assertions are testable. If a firm uniquely possesses a valuable resource and cannot improve its efficiency and effectiveness in ways that generate competitive advantages, then these assertions are contradicted. One could test these assertions by measuring the extent to which a firm uniquely possesses valuable resources, for example, valuable organizational culture, measuring the activities that different firms engage in to improve their efficiency and effectiveness, and then seeing if there are some activities a firm with the unique culture engages in to improve its effectiveness and efficiency — activities not engaged in by other competing firms.

In general, the rarity of a resource is present as long as the number of firms that possess a particular valuable resource is less than the number of firms needed to generate perfect competition dynamics. Of course, there are difficult measurement problems associated with testing assertions of this form. Barney (2001) points out that additional research work is needed to complete the parameterization of the concept of rarity.

Efficient firms can sustain their competitive advantage only if their resources can neither be extended freely nor imitated by other firms. Hence, in order for resources to have the potential to generate rents, they must be rare. Valuable, but common, resources cannot by themselves represent sources of competitive advantage because competitors can access them. Nobody needs to pay extra for obtaining a resource that is not held in limited supply.

In addition to value and rarity, inimitability has to be determined. *Inimitability* can be determined through barriers to imitation and replication. The extent of barriers and impediments against direct and indirect imitation determine the extent of inimitability. One effective barrier to imitation is that competitors fail to understand the firm's sources of advantage. The lack of understanding can be caused by tacitness, complexity and specificity that form bases for competitive advantage (Haanaes, 1997).

Several authors have categorized resources. A common categorization is tangibles vs. intangibles. Tangibles are relatively clearly defined and easy to identify. Tangible resources include plants, technology, land, geographical location, access to raw materials, capital, equipment and legal resources. Tangible resources tend to be property-based and may also include databases, licenses, patents, registered designs and trademarks, as well as other property rights that are easily bought and sold.

Intangibles are more difficult to define and also to study empirically. Intangible resources encompass skills, knowledge, organizational capital, relationships, capabilities and human capital, as well as brands, company and product reputation, networks, competences, perceptions of quality and the ability to manage change. Intangible resources are generally less easy to transfer than tangible resources, as the value of an intangible resource is difficult to measure (Haanaes, 1997).

P1: Increase in knowledge sharing will improve resource mobilization.

The resource-based view started to appear in IT research one decade ago. Now IT resources can be compared to one another and, perhaps more importantly, compared with nonIT resources. Thus, the resource-based view promotes cross-functional studies through comparisons with other firm resources.

In the beginning of resource-based studies of IT resources, IT was divided into three assets, which together with processes contribute to business value. These three IT assets were labeled human assets (e.g., technical skills, business understanding and problem-solving orientation), technology assets (e.g., physical IT assets, technical platforms, databases, architectures and standards) and relationship assets (e.g., partnerships with other divisions, client relationships, top management sponsorship, shared risk and responsibility). IT processes were defined as planning ability, cost effective operations and support and fast delivery. This categorization was later modified to include IT infrastructure, human IT resources and IT-enabled intangibles.

Wade and Hulland (2004) presented a typology of IT resources, where the IT resources held by a firm can be sorted into three types of processes: inside-out, outside-in and spanning. Inside-out resources are deployed from inside the firm in response to market requirements and opportunities, and tend to be internally focused. In contrast, outside-in resources are externally oriented, placing an emphasis on anticipated market requirements, creating durable customer relationships and understanding competitors. Finally, spanning resources, which involve both internal and external analysis, are needed to integrate the firm's inside-out and outside-in resources.

Inside-out resources include IS infrastructure, IS technical skills, IS development and cost effective IS operations:

- **IT infrastructure:** Many components of the IT infrastructure (such as off-the-shelf computer hardware and software) convey no particular strategic benefit due to lack of rarity, ease of imitation and ready mobility. Thus, the types of IT infrastructure of importance are either proprietary or complex and hard to imitate. Despite research attempts to focus on the nonimitable aspects of IT infrastructure, the IT infrastructure resource has generally not been found to be a source of sustained competitive advantage for firms.
- **IT technical skills:** IT technical skills are a result of the appropriate, updated technology skills, relating to both systems hardware and software that are held by the IS/IT employees of a firm. Such skills do not include only current technical knowledge, but also the ability to deploy, use and manage that knowledge. Thus, this resource is focused on technical skills that are advanced, complex and, therefore, difficult to imitate. Although the relative mobility of IS/IT personnel tends to be high, some IS skills cannot be easily transferred, such as corporate-level knowledge assets and technology integration skills, and, thus, these resources can become a source of sustained competitive advantage.
- **IT development:** IT development refers to the capability to develop or experiment with new technologies, as well as a general level of alertness to emerging technologies and trends that allow a firm to quickly take advantage of new advances. Thus, IT development includes capabilities associated with managing a systems development life-cycle that is capable of supporting competitive advantage, and should therefore lead to superior firm performance.

- **Cost effective IT operations:** This resource encompasses the ability to provide efficient and cost-effective IS operations on an ongoing basis. Firms with greater efficiency can develop a long-term competitive advantage by using this capability to reduce costs and develop a cost leadership position in their industry. In the context of IS operations, the ability to avoid large, persistent cost overruns, unnecessary downtime and system failure is likely to be an important precursor to superior performance. Furthermore, the ability to develop and manage IT systems of appropriate quality that function effectively can be expected to have a positive impact on performance.

Outside-in resources include external relationship management and market responsiveness:

- **External relationship management:** This resource represents the firm's ability to manage linkages between the IT function and stakeholders outside the firm. It can manifest itself as an ability to work with suppliers to develop appropriate systems and infrastructure requirements for the firm, to manage relationships with outsourcing partners or to manage customer relationships by providing solutions, support and/or customer service. Many large IT departments rely on external partners for a significant portion of their work. The ability to work with and manage these relationships is an important organizational resource leading to competitive advantage and superior firm performance.
- **Market responsiveness:** Market responsiveness involves both the collection of information from sources external to the firm as well as the dissemination of a firm's market intelligence across departments, and the organization's response to that learning. It includes the abilities to develop and manage projects rapidly and to react quickly to changes in market conditions. A key aspect of market responsiveness is strategic flexibility, which allows the organization to undertake strategic change when necessary.

Spanning resources include IS-business partnerships and IS planning and change management:

- **IS-business partnerships:** This capability represents the processes of integration and alignment between the IS function and other functional areas or departments of the firm. The importance of IS alignment, particularly with business strategy, has been well documented. This resource has variously been referred to as synergy, assimilation and partnerships. All of these studies recognize the importance of building relationships internally within the firm between the IS function and other areas or departments. Such relationships help to span the traditional gaps that exist between functions and departments, resulting in superior competitive position and firm performance. An element of this resource is the support for collaboration within the firm.

- **IS planning and change management:** The capability to plan, manage and use appropriate technology architectures and standards also helps to span these gaps. Key aspects of this resource include the ability to anticipate future changes and growth, to choose platforms (including hardware, network and software standards) that can accommodate this change and to effectively manage the resulting technology change and growth. This resource has been defined variously in previous research as "understanding the business case," "problem solving orientation" and "capacity to manage IT change." It includes the ability of IS managers to understand how technologies can and should be used, as well as how to motivate and manage IS personnel through the change process.

In order to explore the usefulness of the resource-based theory for IT resources, it is necessary to explicitly recognize the characteristics and attributes of resources that lead them to become strategically important. Although firms possess many resources, only a few of these have the potential to lead the firm to a position of sustained competitive advantage. What is it, then, that separates regular resources form those that confer a sustainable strategic benefit?

According to Wade and Hulland (2004), resource-based theorists have approached this question by identifying sets of resource attributes that might conceptually influence a firm's competitive position. Under this view, only resources exhibiting all of these attributes can lead to a sustained competitive advantage for the firm. We have already mentioned Barney's (2001) attributes of value, rareness, inimitability, nonsubstitutability, combination and exploration.

In addition, an important seventh attribute is immobile. Once a firm establishes a competitive advantage through the strategic use of resources, competitors will likely attempt to amass comparable resources in order to share in the advantage. A primary source of resources is factor markets. If firms are able to acquire the resources necessary to imitate a rival's advantage, the advantage will be short-lived. Thus, a requirement for sustained competitive advantage is that resources be imperfectly mobile or nontradable.

To govern IT resources efficiently and effectively, it is necessary to understand the strategic attributes of each resource. In Figure 8.1, the table shows an example of how strategic IT resources can be identified. The scale from 1 (little extent) to 5 (great extent) is applied.

In this example, we see that IT infrastructure is the IT resource with the greatest potential to lead to sustained competitive advantage, which would contradict the

Figure 8.1. IT resources in terms of strategic importance based on attributes

Attributes / Resources	*Valuable*	*Rare*	*Exploitable*	*Inimitable*	*Non-substitutable*	*Combinable*	*Immobile*	*TOTAL*
IT infrastructure	4	2	5	5	2	5	4	27
IT technical skills	4	2	3	3	4	4	3	23
IT development	4	3	3	3	4	3	2	22
Cost- effective IT operations	4	2	3	2	4	3	1	19

belief that the IT infrastructure resource has generally not been found to be a source of sustained competitive advantage for firms. On the other hand, cost-effective IT operations have the least potential.

Wade and Hulland (2004) suggest that some of the resources create competitive advantage, while others sustain that advantage. A distinction is made between resources that help the firm attain a competitive advantage and those that help the firm to sustain the advantage. These two types of resource attributes can be thought of as, respectively, *ex ante* and *ex post* limits to competition.

Ex ante limits to competition suggest that prior to any firm's establishing a superior resource position, there must be limited competition for that position. If any firm wishing to do so can acquire and deploy resources to achieve the position, it cannot by definition be superior. Attributes in this category include value, rarity and appropriability. *Ex post* limits to competition mean that subsequent to a firm's gaining a superior position and earning rents, there must be forces that limit competition for those rents. Attributes in this category include imitability, substitutability and mobility.

Damianides (2005) applied a different approach to identify resources. He defined the following, naturally-grouped processes of IT resources: plan and organize, acquire and implement, deliver and support and monitor and evaluate. He also developed an IT governance checklist, listing questions to uncover IT issues, questions to find out how management addresses the IT issues and questions to self-assess IT governance practices.

IT Governance as Allocation of Decision Rights

Weill and Ross (2004, p. 58) use political archetypes (monarchy, feudal, federal, duopoly and anarchy) to describe the combinations of people who have either decision rights or input to IT decisions:

1. **Business monarchy:** In a business monarchy, senior business executives make IT decisions affecting the entire enterprise. It is a group of business executives or individual executives (CxOs), including committees of senior business executives (may include CIO). It excludes IT executives acting independently.
2. **IT monarchy:** In an IT monarchy, IT professionals make IT decisions. It is a group of IT executives or individual CIOs.
3. **Feudal:** The feudal model is based on traditions where the princes and princesses or their designated knights make their own decisions, optimizing their local needs. It is business unit leaders, key process owners or their delegates.
4. **Federal:** The federal decision-making model has a long tradition in government. Federal arrangements attempt to balance the responsibilities and accountability of multiple governing bodies, such as country or states. It is C-level executives and business groups (e.g., business units or processes). It may also include IT executives as additional participants. It is the equivalent of the central and state governments working together.
5. **IT duopoly:** The IT duopoly is a two-party arrangement where decisions represent a bilateral agreement between IT executives and one other group (e.g., CxO or business unit or process leaders). The IT executives may be a central IT group or team of central and business unit IT organizations.
6. **Anarchy:** Within an anarchy, individuals or small groups make their own decisions based only on their local needs. Anarchies are the bane of the existence of many IT groups and are expensive to support and secure. It can be each individual user.

Peterson (2004a) discusses decision-makers and decision rights in terms of centralization vs. decentralization. Over the past decade, organizations have set out to achieve the best of both worlds by adopting a *federal* IT governance structure. In a federal IT governance model, IT infrastructure decisions are centralized, and IT application decisions are decentralized. The federal IT governance model thus represents a hybrid model of both centralization and decentralization.

The discussion of whether to centralize or decentralize IT governance is based on a rational perspective of the organization, in which choices are reduced to one of internal efficiency and effectiveness. This view assumes a system of goal consonance and agreement on the means for achieving goals, that is, rational and logical trade-off between (a) efficiency and standardization under centralization, vs. (b) effectiveness and flexibility under decentralization.

In general, it is assumed that centralization leads to greater specialization, consistency and standardized controls, while decentralization provides local control, ownership and greater responsiveness and flexibility to business needs. However, flexibility under decentralization may lead to variable standards, which ultimately result in lower flexibility, and specialization under centralization incurs risks due to bounded rationality and information overload (Peterson, 2004a).

A federal approach towards IT governance challenges managers in local business units to surrender control over certain business-specific IT domains for the well-being of the enterprise, and to develop business-to-corporate and business-to-IT partnerships. The potential risk in contemporary business environments is that either centralization or decentralization fit the organization into a fixed structure. The challenge is therefore to balance the benefits of decentralized decision-making and business innovation and the benefits of central control and IT standardization (Peterson, 2004a).

P2: Increase in knowledge sharing will improve allocation of decision rights.

IT Governance as Strategic Alignment

Strategy can simply be defined as principles, a broad based formula, to be applied in order to achieve a purpose. These principles are general guidelines guiding the daily work to reach business goals. Strategy is the pattern of resource allocation decisions made throughout the organization. These encapsulate both desired goals and beliefs about what are acceptable and, most critically, unacceptable means for achieving them.While the business strategy is the broadest pattern of resource allocation decisions, more specific decisions are related to information systems and information technology. IS must be seen both in a business and an IT context. IS is in the middle because IS supports the business while using IT.

Business strategy is concerned with achieving the mission, vision and objectives of a company, while IS strategy is concerned with use of IS/IT applications, and IT strategy is concerned with the technical infrastructure. A company has typically several IS/IT applications. The connection between them is also of great interest, as interdependencies should prevent applications from being separate islands. Furthermore, the arrows in the illustration in Figure 8.2 are of importance. Arrows from business strategy to IS strategy, and from IS to IT strategy, represent the alignment perspective, they illustrate the *what* before the *how*. Arrows from IT to IS strategy, and from IS to business strategy, represent the extension from *what* to *how* to *what*. This is the impact perspective, representing the potential impacts of modern information technology on future business options.

Necessary elements of a *business strategy* include mission, vision, objectives, market strategy, knowledge strategy and our general approach to the use of information, information systems and information technology.

Figure 8.2. Relationships between strategies at three levels

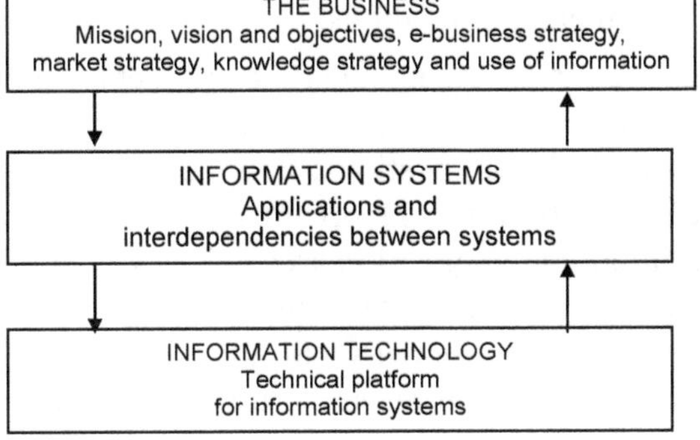

Mission describes the reason for firm existence. For example, the reason for law firm existence is client's needs for legal advice. The mission addresses the organization's basic question of "What business are we in?" This single, essential, sentence should include no quantification, but must unambiguously state the purpose of the organization and should, just as carefully, define what the organization does not do. According to Ward and Griffiths (1996), the mission is an unambiguous statement of what the organization does and its long-term, overall purpose. Its primary role is to set a direction for everyone to follow. It may be short, succinct and inspirational, or contain broad philosophical statements that tie an organization to certain activities and to economic, social, ethical or political ends. Values are also frequently stated alongside the mission. Three differing examples of missions are: to help people move from one place to another; to provide medical treatment to sick people; and to enable electronic communication between people.

Vision describes what the firm wants to achieve. For example, the law firm wants to become the leading law firm in Norway. The vision represents the view that senior managers have for the future of the organization; so it is what they want it to become. This view gives a way to judge the appropriateness of all potential activities that the organization might engage in. According to Ward and Griffiths (1996), the vision gives a picture, frequently covering many aspects, that everyone can identify with, of what the business will be in the future, and how it will operate. It exists to bring objectives to life, and to give the whole organization a destination that it can visualize, so that every stakeholder has a shared picture of the future aim.

Objectives describe where the business is heading. For example, the law firm can choose to merge with another law firm to become the leading law firm in Norway.

Objectives are the set of major achievements that will accomplish the vision. These are usually small in number, but embody the most important aspects of the vision, such as financial returns, customer service, manufacturing excellence, staff morale and social and environmental obligations.

Market strategy describes market segments and products. For example, the law firm can focus on corporate clients in the area of tax law. Necessary elements of an *IS strategy* include future IS/IT applications, future competence of human resources (IS/IT professionals) and future IS/IT organizational structure and control of the IS/IT function. An important application area is KMS. The future applications are planned according to priorities, how they are to be developed or acquired (make or buy), how they meet user requirements and how security is achieved. The future competence is planned by types of resources needed, motivation and skills needed (managers, users and IS/IT professionals), salaries and other benefits. The future IS/IT organization defines tasks, roles, management and possibly outsourcing.

Necessary elements of an *IT strategy* include selection of IT hardware, basic software and networks, as well as how these components should interact as a technological platform, and how the required security level is maintained. The IT platform consists of hardware, systems software, networks and communications, standards and support form selected vendors.

P3: Increase in knowledge sharing will improve strategic alignment.

An *IS/IT strategy* is a combined strategy including business context, the IS in a narrow sense and the technological platform. Necessary elements of an IS/IT strategy include business direction and strategy (mission, vision, objectives and knowledge strategy), applications (knowledge management systems), people (future competence of human resources), organization (future organization and control of IT function) and IT platform (future technical infrastructure). Hence, IS/IT is quite a broad term. The term is broad in order to take care of all connections and interdependencies in a strategy, as changes in one element will have effect on all other elements, as illustrated in Figure 8.3.

The same thinking is represented in a famous model called Leavitt's Diamond. Everything is connected, and changes in one element affect all the others as illustrated in Figure 8.4. Tasks are performed using systems, structure is important for support functions and people represent the competence. The Diamond can only create change in desired strategic business direction if all interdependencies between elements are taken care of over time.

Figure 8.3. IS / IT strategy elements and interdependencies

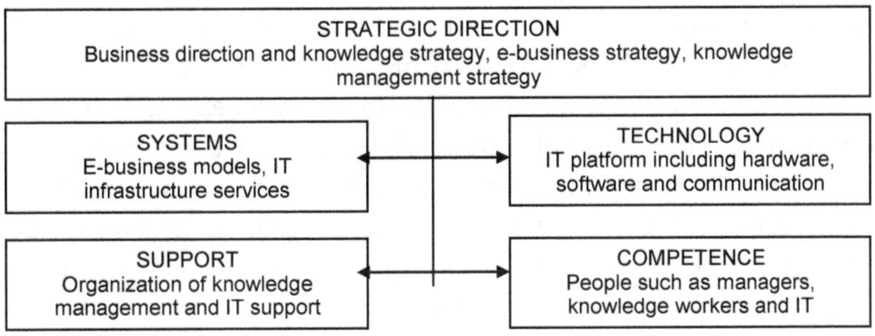

Figure 8.4. Leavitt's Diamond of elements and interrelationships

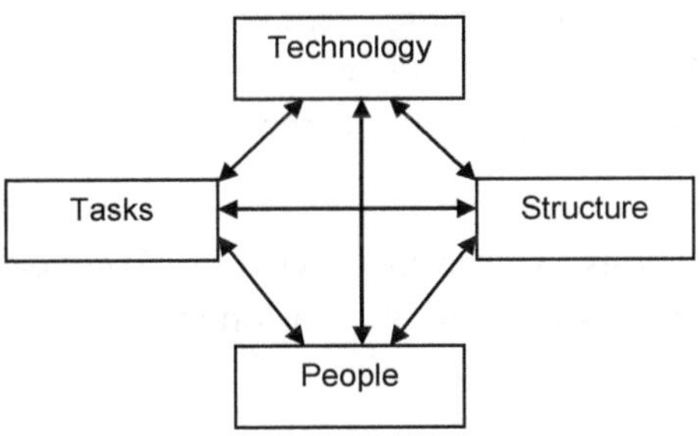

Implementing IT Governance

Enterprises implement their governance arrangements through a set of governance mechanisms — structures, processes and communications. Well-designed, well-understood and transparent mechanisms promote desirable IT behaviors. Conversely, if mechanisms are poorly implemented, then governance arrangements will fail to yield the desired results. According to Weill and Ross (2004), effective governance deploys three different types of mechanisms:

- **Decision-making structures:** Organizational units and roles responsible for making IT decisions, such as committees, executive teams and business/IT relationship managers. Decision-making structures are the most visible IT governance mechanisms. They locate decision-making responsibilities according to intended archetypes. Decision-making structures are the natural approach to generating commitment.

- **Alignment processes:** Formal processes for ensuring that daily behaviors are consistent with IT policies and provide input back to decisions. These include IT investment proposal and evaluation processes, architecture exception processes, service-level agreements, chargeback and metrics. Alignment processes are IT management techniques for securing widespread involvement in the effective management and use of IT. Alignment processes should bring everybody on board both by providing input into governance decisions and by disseminating the outputs of IT decisions.
- **Communication approaches:** Announcements, advocates, channels and education efforts that disseminate IT governance principles and policies and outcomes of IT decision-making processes. Communication mechanisms are intended spread news about IT governance decisions and processes and related desirable behaviors throughout the enterprise. Firms communicate their governance mechanisms in a variety of ways. Weill and Ross (2004) found that the more management communicated formally about the existence of IT governance mechanisms, how they worked and what outcomes were expected, the more effective was their governance.

Decision-making structures are the most visible IT governance mechanism that locate decision-making responsibilities according to the intended archetypes (Weill & Ross, 2004):

- **Business monarchy decision-making structures:** IT can enable enterprise strategy only if senior management establishes strategic direction and elaborates an operating model. Enterprises adopt a number of approaches to elicit this direction. Business monarchies — usually in the form of executive committees — often play a role. Enterprises vary considerably in the design of their executive committees. In some enterprises the CEO works with a small team of top executives to ensure that IT aligns with corporate objectives. Other enterprises focus the attention of a subset of the senior management team on IT issues. The level of senior executive involvement in IT governance evolves as enterprises become more savvy in using IT strategically.
- **IT monarchy decision-making structures:** Complementing business monarchies, IT monarchies make most of the world's IT architecture and infrastructure decisions. The two most common implementations of IT monarchies are IT leadership teams and IT architecture committees. IT leadership teams may comprise IT functional heads (operations, architecture, applications, etc.),

they may be CIOs of business units or they may be combinations of the two. Architecture committees are usually made up of technical experts. They are responsible for defining standards and, in some cases, granting exceptions. In most cases, the role of the architecture committee is to advise the IT leadership team on architectural issues, but occasionally the architecture committee is a key governance decision-making body.

- **Federal decision-making structures:** Almost 90% of enterprises in the Weill and Ross (2004) study indicated that a senior executive committee played a role in IT governance. Where these senior executive teams drew members from all business units, they implemented a federal rather than business monarchy archetype. Because federal structures overtly work to balance enterprise and business unit priorities, they can provide valuable input to IT governance decisions.
- **IT duopoly decision-making structures:** The typical role of business leaders in IT governance is to clarify business objectives and incorporate IT capabilities into strategy formulation. The typical role of IT leaders is to help envision IT-enabled strategies, clarify architectural standards and design shared infrastructures. The responsibilities of these two groups are obviously intertwined. Formal governance linkages often result in better performance. Linkages are sometimes accomplished through overlapping memberships on IT and business monarchy mechanisms. Alternatively, some enterprises establish duopoly governance arrangements that comprise joint IT and business members. One approach to ensuring business-IT interactions is through a joint decision council. Business-IT relationship managers play an important role in communicating mandates and their implications and supporting the needs of business unit managers while helping them see benefits.

Alignment processes are the next step after decision-making structures in designing IT governance. Key alignment processes include the IT investment approval process, the architecture exception process, service-level agreements, chargeback, project tracking and formal tracking of business value for IT (Weill & Ross, 2004):

- **IT investment approval process:** Has the objective of ensuring that IT investments generate significant returns to the enterprise relative to alternative investment opportunities. Most enterprises formalize their IT investment proposal process to ensure that creative ideas and strategic priorities are considered by investment decision-makers. Many enterprises use standardized IT investment approval application templates to estimate metrics such as ROI, NPV and risk for each project.

- **Architectural exception process:** Caused by the fact that few enterprises can afford to support every technical platform that the business might find useful. Technology standards are critical to IT — and business — efficiency. Enterprises use the exception process to meet unique business needs and to gauge when existing standards are becoming obsolete. Architecture committees usually have responsibility for establishing standards. In many cases the architecture committee also takes responsibility for granting exceptions to standards.
- **Service-level agreements (SLAs):** List available services, alternative quality levels and related costs. Through negotiations between the IT services unit and business units, an SLA leads to articulation of the services IT offers and the costs of the services. These negotiations clarify the requirements of the business units, thereby informing governance decisions on infrastructure, architecture and business application needs. SLAs force IT units to think like external providers.
- **Chargeback:** An accounting mechanism for allocating central IT costs to business units. Some enterprises use chargeback successfully for aligning decisions on infrastructure, business application needs and IT investment with business objectives. The purpose of chargeback is to allocate costs so that business unit IT costs reflect use of shared services while the shared services unit matches its costs with the businesses it supports.
- **Project tracking:** A critical step in implementing IT governance. It is critical to develop the discipline to track the progress of individual IT projects. Over 90% of enterprises in the Weill and Ross (2004) study indicated that they are tracking project resources consumed. Enterprises use a variety of tools to support project tracking. At top performing enterprises, tracking is just one element of a standard project management methodology.
- **Formal tracking of business value:** Meeting the challenge of assessing the value of IT. IT decision-makers make more effective decisions as they better understand the value the enterprise receives from IT. Formally tracking the business value of IT enhances organizational learning about the value of IT-enabled initiatives. Because project outcomes are difficult to isolate — particularly when projects are part of larger program goals — increasing numbers of enterprises are formalizing intermediate objectives.

Communication approaches include senior management announcements, formal committees, office of CIO or IT governance, working with nonconformists and Web-based portals (Weill & Ross, 2004):

- **Senior management announcements:** Clarifying priorities and demonstrating commitment usually get a great deal of attention throughout an enterprise. As

IT becomes more strategic in enterprises, IT governance grows more important. Developing a communication strategy to announce and explain new IT governance processes contributes to achieving the objectives of the governance design.

- **Formal committees:** Create communication between committee members. Committees often make lower-level governance decisions and carry out high-level decisions. Careful committee assignments are required to involve executives in decisions important to them. Communication within and across committees align the efforts of the committees with other governance initiatives.
- **Office of CIO or IT governance:** Often the recognized advocate, owner and organizational home for IT governance. Eighty-six percent of participants in the Weill and Ross (2004) study used an office of IT governance or the office of the CIO to communicate governance arrangements. IT governance needs an owner to ensure that individual mechanisms reinforce rather than contradict one another and to communicate governance processes and purposes.
- **Working with nonconformists:** Means working with managers who stray from desirable behaviors. Rarely do all affected managers enthusiastically embrace IT governance decisions. When managers engage in behaviors that undermine enterprise architecture, disregard IT investment guidelines, duplicate shared infrastructure or ignore project-tracking standards, they may be demonstrating lack of awareness of governance decisions or an unwillingness to adopt mandated practices.
- **Web-based portals:** Can be used for communication around IT governance to educate organizational members on IT governance processes, including specific procedures for mechanisms such as investment proposals, architectural exceptions and service-level agreements. Web-based portals provide a central communications channel for many enterprises. IT governance owners use the portals to make announcements and updates. Some portals have examples of IT investment cases with templates. Other portals have lists of approved IT software and hardware with instructions on ordering hardware and software. Portals can also support IT governance by posting metrics from project-tracking systems.

Distribution of decision rights is not sufficient to achieve successful IT governance. Peterson (2004a) argues that a holistic view emphasizes the need to view IT governance as a complex social system interacting with its environment, and consisting of a set of interdependent subsystems that produce a purposeful whole. Complex systems are characterized by reciprocal interdependence, in which decisions made by subunits are mutually dependent and influential, thereby increasing the need to exchange information. In complex governance systems, each decision-making unit presents direct decision contingencies for every other unit. Interacting subsystems in a social system imply that stakeholders are interdependent and need to work together in a coordinated fashion to achieve objectives. A systems thinking approach towards IT governance acknowledges its complex and dynamic nature, and underscores the importance of personal mastery and mental models, and team learning and shared vision.

P4: Increased knowledge sharing will improve IT governance implementation.

The manner in which responsibilities and accountabilities for the IT portfolio are organized and integrated is defined as an IT governance architecture. An IT governance architecture describes the differentiation and integration of strategic decision-making for IT. The IT governance architecture specifies the strategic policies and business rules that provide direction to strategic IT decision-making, and plots a path for achieving business objectives. The IT governance architecture describes coordination mechanisms to be applied to decisions. Decisions can be coordinated either by hierarchy or by plan (Peterson, 2004a).

Hierarchical coordination describes the hierarchical referral of infrequent situations for which standardized programs have no solution. The hierarchy achieves coordination by having one person (e.g., CxO) take responsibility for the work of others, issuing instructions and monitoring actions. If the hierarchy gets overloaded, additional levels or positions can be added to the hierarchy.

Plan-based coordination describes the use of standard programs, formal rules and procedures and the specification of outputs, goals and targets. The adoption and use of reporting forms and service-level agreements (SLAs) are typical examples of how contemporary organizations coordinate by plan. Peterson (2004a) argues that hierarchical coordination and plan-based coordination only provide limited coordination capability in complex and uncertain environments. Organizations need to develop horizontal integration mechanisms.

Peterson (2004a) classified integration strategies for IT governance according to two dimensions. Vertically, integration mechanisms can focus either on integration structures or integration processes. Horizontally, a division is made between formal positions and processes, and relational networks and capabilities. Collectively, this provides the following four types of integration strategies:

- **Formal integration structures:** Involve appointing IT executives and accounts, and institutionalizing special and standing IT committees and councils. The use of account and/or relationship managers aid IT managers to develop an improved understanding of business needs, and aid in proactive — vs. reactive — behavior by IT managers. Committees and/or executive teams can take the form of temporary task forces, for example, project steering committees, or can alternatively be institutionalized as an overlay structure in the organization in the form of executive or IT management councils.

- **Formal integration processes:** Describe the formalization and institutionalization of strategic decision-making/monitoring procedures and performance. Formal integration processes vary with levels of comprehensiveness, formalization and integration.
- **Relational integration structures:** Involve the active participation of and collaborative relationships between corporate executives, IT management and business management. Central to relational integration is the participative behavior of different stakeholders to clarify differences and solve problems in order to find integrative solutions. An example is strategic partnership that reflects a working relationship of long-term commitment.
- **Relational integration processes:** Describe strategic dialogue and shared learning between principle business and IT stakeholders. Strategic dialogue involves exploring and debating ideas and issues in depth prior to decision-making or outside the pressure of immediate IT decision-making.

We can here see a considerable overlap with the governance mechanisms suggested by Weill and Ross (2004). The three governance mechanisms do, in many ways, cover these four types of integration strategies. Formal integration structures are similar to decision structures, and formal integration processes are similar to alignment processes. Communication approaches are here divided into relational integration structures and relational integration processes.

Designing an effective IT governance architecture is dependent on both the differentiation and integration of strategic decision-making for IT. Whereas differentiation focuses on the distribution of IT decision-making rights and responsibilities among different stakeholders in the organization, integration focuses the coordination of IT decision-making processes and structures across stakeholder constituencies. The notion of an IT governance architecture emphasizes the need to define and control the interfaces between the separate components of the IT governance system. Designers of IT governance architectures thus need to consider and implement integration strategies and tactics for governing IT effectively (Peterson, 2004a).

The IT Governance Model

Our governance model is illustrated in Figure 8.5. It consists of five elements (contracts, principles, resources, activities and managers), two main links (terms-exchanges link between contracts and resources, and norms-relationships link between principles and activities) and four local links (roles between contracts and principles, capabilities between principles and resources, efficiencies between resources and activities and outcomes between activities and contracts).

Contracts provide a legally bound, institutional framework in which each party's rights, duties and responsibilities are codified and the goals, policies and strategies underlying the arrangement are specified. *Principles* define decision rights concerning general IT principles, IT infrastructure, IT architecture, business application needs and IT investments. *Resources* define decision rights concerning human assets, financial assets, physical assets, IP assets, information and IT assets and relationship assets. *Activities* define decision rights concerning transactions, projects, problem solving and reporting. *Managers* are classified into stakeholder groups of client business management, client IT management, vendor business management and vendor account management.

Exchanges of resources occur through transactions based on contracts. *Terms* for use of resources are defined in contracts. *Norms* create expectations of behavior and

Figure 8.5. IT governance model

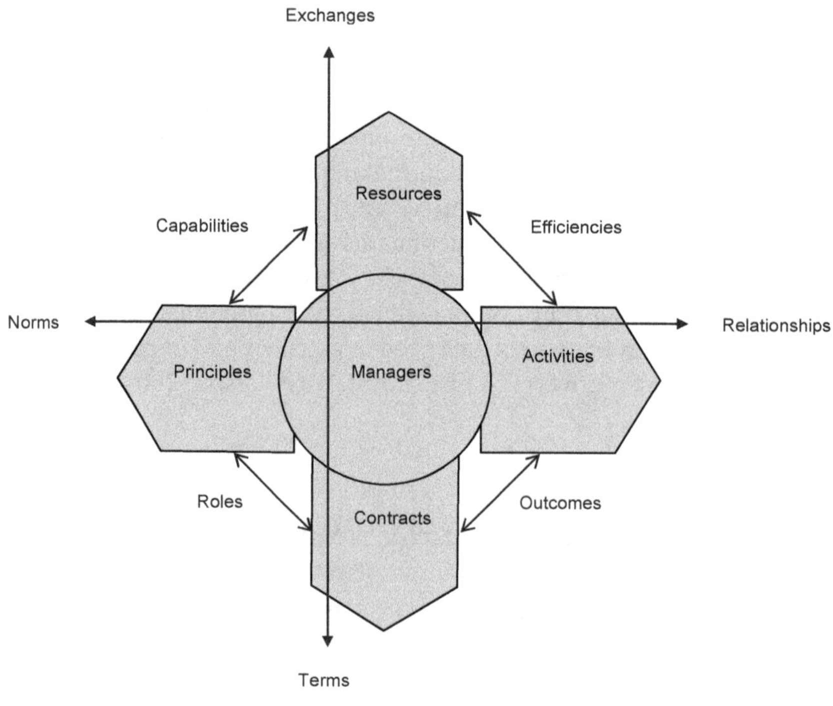

imply a certain action and are shared by the actors. Norms are based on principles and they occur in activities. Norms are concerned with flexibility, solidarity, mutuality, harmonization and power. *Relationships* frame activities based on principles and norms.

Roles are defined by contracts and carried out when making decisions about principles. Management roles include spokesperson, entrepreneur, personnel leader, resource allocator, monitor and liaison. *Capabilities* enable the use of resources

Figure 8.6. The governance model defines decision rights concerning principles

Principles/ Stakeholders	**General principles**	**IT infrastructure**	**IT architecture**	**Business application needs**	**IT investments**
Client business management	Strategic information systems planning decisions	Infrastructure capabilities decisions	Architecture performance decisions	Strategic information systems planning decisions	Financial investments decisions
Client IT management	Technology business alignment decisions	Infrastructure functions decisions	Architecture structure decisions	Information systems decisions	Investment analysis contents decisions
Vendor business management	Service level decisions	Service organization decisions	Service organization decisions	Information systems organization decisions	Financial investments decisions
Vendor account management	Technology decisions	Infrastructure integration decisions	Architecture integration decisions	Technology decisions for information systems	Investment analysis contents decisions

based on principles. *Efficiencies* are determined by the use of resources in activities. *Outcomes* occur in activities that are performance results from contracts.

P5: Increased knowledge sharing will improve links between elements in IT governance.

Figure 8.6 illustrates how managers and principles are related through decision rights in an IT outsourcing relationship. *General principles* are high-level statements about how IT is used in the business. *IT infrastructure* describes strategies for the base foundation of budgeted-for IT capability (technical and human), shared throughout the firm as reliable services, and centrally coordinated such as network, help desk and shared data. *IT architecture* is an integrated set of technical choices to guide the organization in satisfying business needs. The architecture is a set of policies and rules that govern the use of IT and plot a migration path to the way business will be done (includes data, technology and applications). *Business application needs* are concerned with business applications to be acquired and built. *IT investment* and prioritization are decisions about how much and where to invest in IT, including project approvals and justification techniques (Weill & Ross, 2004).

Research Model for IT Governance

Knowledge has long been recognized as a valuable resource for organizational growth and sustained competitive advantage, especially for organizations competing in uncertain environments.

Recently, some researchers have argued that knowledge is an organization's most valuable resource because it represents intangible assets, operational routines and creative processes that are hard to imitate (Wasko & Faraj, 2005).

IT Governance

In many organizations, information technology has become crucial in the support, sustainability and growth of the business. This pervasive use of technology has created a critical dependency on IT that calls for a specific focus on IT governance. IT governance consists of the leadership and organizational structures and processes that ensure that the organization's IT sustains and extends its strategy and objectives (Grembergen et al., 2004).

IT governance matters because it influences the benefits received from IT investments. Through a combination of practices (such as redesigning business processes and well-designed governance mechanisms) and appropriately matched IT investments, top-performing enterprises generate superior returns on their IT investments (Weill, 2004).

IT governance can be defined as specifying decision rights and accountability framework to encourage desirable behavior in the use of IT (Weill & Ross, 2004). This is the definition we will use here.

Other definitions are for example: (1) IT governance is the structures and processes that ensure that IT supports the organization's mission. The purpose is to align IT with the enterprise, maximize the benefits of IT, use IT resources responsibly and manage IT risks, (2) A structure of relationships and processes to direct and control the enterprise in order to achieve the enterprise's goals by adding value while balancing risk vs. return over IT and its processes, (3) IT governance is the responsibility of the board of directors and executive management. It is an integral part of enterprise governance and consists of the leadership and organizational structures and processes that ensure that the organization's IT sustains and extends the organization's strategies and objectives, and (4) IT governance is the system by which an organization's IT portfolio is directed and controlled. IT Governance describes (a) the distribution of decision-making rights and responsibilities among different stakeholders in the organization, and (b) the rules and procedures for making and monitoring decisions on strategic IT concerns (Peterson, 2004a).

Strategic IT Resources

According to the resource-based theory of the firm, performance differences across firms can be attributed to the variance in the firms' resources and capabilities. The essence of the resource-based theory of the firm lies in its emphasis on the internal resources available to the firm, rather than on the external opportunities and threats dictated by industry conditions. A firm's resources are said to be a source of competitive advantage to the degree that they are scarce, specialized, appropriable, valuable, rare and difficult to imitate or substitute.

A fundamental idea in resource-based theory is that a firm must continually enhance its resources and capabilities to take advantage of changing conditions. Optimal growth involves a balance between the exploitation of existing resource positions and the development of new resource positions. Thus, a firm would be expected to develop new resources after its existing resource base has been fully utilized. Building new resource positions is important if the firm is to achieve sustained growth. When unused productive resources are coupled with changing managerial knowledge, unique opportunities for growth are created (Pettus, 2001).

Leadership Roles

Managers undertake activities to achieve the objectives of the organization. A number of different and sometimes conflicting views of a manager's role can be noted. Often, one particular aspect of the manager's job is emphasized to the exclusion of others. In sum, they perhaps cover all the aspects. A role typology is frequently used in studies of managerial work and is genderless (Mintzberg, 1994).

In the context of IT management, the relevance of six management roles can be identified — personnel leader, resource allocator, spokesman, entrepreneur, liaison and monitor (Grover et al., 1993). The following role descriptions can be used (Karlsen & Gottschalk, 2002): personnel leader, resource allocator, spokesman, entrepreneur, liaison, and monitor. These roles were described earlier in this chapter.

In terms of decision-making for IT governance, two management roles are visible. First, the resource allocator role is mainly concerned with decisions. The manager must decide how to allocate human, financial and information resources to the activities of the IT function. Second, the entrepreneur role is mainly concerned with decisions. The manager identifies the users' needs and management expectations and makes decisions concerning solutions that change business situations.

Research Model and Hypotheses

Figure 8.7 depicts our research model. Intention to share knowledge is the dependent variable in the model.

Grembergen et al. (2004) argue that an important prior mechanism for IT governance is an effective two-way communication and a good participation/collabora-

Figure 8.7. Research model for knowledge sharing influencing governance performance

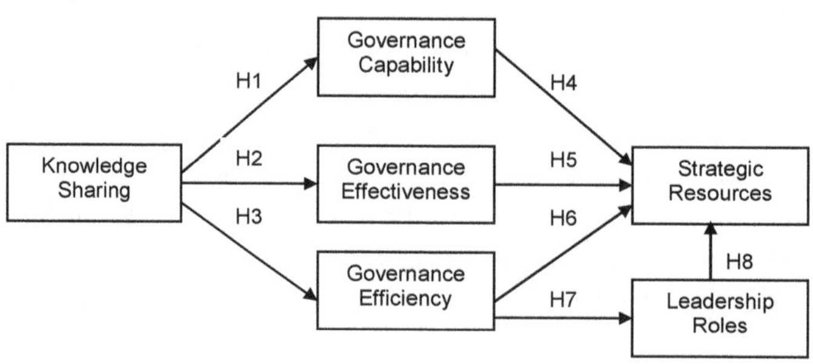

tion relationship between the business and the IT department, because there is little business awareness on the part of IT or little IT appreciation on the part of the business. Ensuring ongoing knowledge sharing across departments and organizations is paramount for attaining and sustaining business-IT alignment. According to Callahan et al. (2004), it is important to facilitate the sharing and the management of knowledge. Sharing knowledge will improve IT governance capability, effectiveness and efficiency (Fairchild, 2004).

IT Governance Capability

IT governance capability is the capability to integrate IS/IT effort with business purpose and activity. The ability to deal with interdependencies that arise between the business and IS function falls into this category. Being a management capability, it is typically developed between the IT manager or CIO (chief information officer) and the general manager or CEO (chief executive officer), but also between the CIO and the management of other business departments (Heijden, 2001).

Four behaviors reflect this capability. The first indicator refers to the quality of the executive relationship between the CIO and the other executives. High-performance CIOs build and develop good quality relationships with their peer executives in the firm. Another behavior associated with this capability is the ability to arrive at shared objectives and visions. Shared objectives involve the alignment between business and IT objectives. The alignment can be intellectual, social or both. The intellectual dimension refers to whether IS and business executives understand each other's objectives and plans.

Fostering an appropriate culture in the IT department is a third behavior associated with IS/IT governance. There is often a cultural gap between IT and business departments. This gap is often fostered by "hard" elements (power and control structures), but also by the rituals, routines, stories, myths and symbols that set the IT department apart from the other departments. Therefore, strong IS/IT governance capabilities are associated with cultural alignment between IT and business departments (Heijden, 2001).

The fourth and final behavior is the behavior of incorporating best practices in management with this capability. Best practices, which is a broad term originating from the total quality management movement, is usually defined as the acquisition and implementation of (management) processes with superior performance on a continuous basis. Thus, the search for continuous improvement of processes is associated with strong IS/IT governance capability (Heijden, 2001).

Hypothesis 1: Knowledge sharing is positively related to governance capability.

IT Governance Effectiveness

All enterprises have IT governance. The difference is that enterprises with effective governance have actively designed a set of IT governance mechanisms that encourage behaviors consistent with the organization's mission, strategy, values, norms and culture. Effective IT governance encourages and leverages the ingenuity of all enterprise personnel in using IT, while ensuring compliance with the enterprise's overall vision and principles. As a result, good IT governance can achieve a management paradox: simultaneously empowering and controlling (Weill, 2004).

IT governance encompasses five major decision areas (Weill & Ross, 2005, p. 30):

1. IT Principles
   - How do the business principles translate to IT principles that guide IT decision making?
   - What is the role of IT in the business?
   - What are desirable IT behaviors?
   - How will IT be funded?
2. IT Architecture
   - What are the core business processes of the enterprise? How are they related?
   - What information drives these core processes? How must this data be integrated?
   - What technical capabilities should be standardized enterprise-wide to support IT efficiencies and facilitate process standardization and integration?
   - What activities must be standardized enterprise-wide to support data integration?
   - What technology choices will guide the enterprise's approach to IT initiatives?
3. IT Infrastructure Strategies
   - What infrastructure services are most critical to achieving the enterprise's strategic objectives?
   - What infrastructure services should be implemented enterprise-wide and what are the service-level requirements of those services?
   - How should infrastructure services be priced?

- What is the plan for keeping underlying technologies up-to-date?
- What infrastructure services should be outsourced?

4. Business Application Needs
   - What are the market and business process opportunities for new business applications?
   - How are strategic experiments designed to assess success?
   - How can business needs be addressed within architectural standards? When does a business need justify an exception to a standard?
   - Who will own the outcomes of each project and institute organizational changes to ensure the value?
5. IT Investment and Prioritization
   - What process changes or enhancements are strategically most important to the enterprise?
   - What is the distribution in the current IT portfolio? Is this portfolio consistent with the enterprise's strategic objectives?
   - What is the relative importance of enterprise-wide vs. business unit investments? Do actual investment practices reflect their relative importance?
   - How is the business value of IT projects determined following their implementation?

IT governance effectiveness can be defined as the effectiveness of making decisions in these five decision areas.

Hypothesis 2: Knowledge sharing is positively related to governance effectiveness.

IT Governance Efficiency

Gottschalk and Solli-Sæther (2006) developed a model for IT governance. It was illustrated in Figure 8.5. The model consists of five elements (contracts, principles, resources, activities and managers), two main links (terms-exchanges link between contracts and resources, and norms-relationships link between principles and activities) and four local links (roles between contracts and principles, capabilities between principles and resources, efficiencies between resources and activities and outcomes between activities and contracts).

IT governance efficiency can be defined as the ability to coordinate through the four local links of roles, capabilities, efficiencies and outcomes.

Hypothesis 3: Knowledge sharing is positively related to governance efficiency.

Strategic IT Resources

Strategic resources are valuable, rare, nonimitable, nontransferable, nonsubstitutable, combinable and exploitable. If a resource is not valuable, that resource will not enable a firm to choose or implement strategies that exploit environmental opportunities or neutralize environmental threats. If a resource is valuable, but not rare, exploiting this resource in conceiving and implementing strategies will generate competitive parity and normal economic performance. Exploiting these valuable-but-not-rare resources will generally not create above-normal economic performance (Barney, 2002).

IT governance capability is the capability to integrate IS/IT effort with business purpose and activity. When this capability improves, we suggest that mobilization of strategic resources will improve in the company.

Hypothesis 4: Governance capability is positively related to the availability of strategic IT resources.

IT governance effectiveness was defined as the effectiveness of making decisions in five decision areas. When decision-making improves, we suggest that mobilization of strategic resources will improve in the company.

Hypothesis 5: Governance effectiveness is positively related to the availability of strategic IT resources.

IT governance efficiency was defined as the ability to coordinate through the four local links of roles, capabilities, efficiencies and outcomes. When coordination improves, we suggest that mobilization of strategic resources will improve in the company.

Hypothesis 6: Governance efficiency is positively related to the availability of strategic IT resources.

Leadership Roles

The resource allocator role is the most decision-oriented leadership role for chief information officers (Karlsen & Gottschalk, 2002). In this role, the manager makes allocation decisions concerning human, financial, technical, geographical and information issues. Since IT governance efficiency is concerned with coordination activities in governance decision-making, we expect the resource allocator role to be influenced by the extent of governance efficiency in the organization.

Hypothesis 7: IT governance efficiency is positively related to the importance of the resource allocator role.

The resource allocator role is concerned with the allocation of resources to achieve business goals using IT. We expect this role to influence the availability of resources, as increased focus on this role will imply greater emphasis on resource issues in the organization.

Hypothesis 8: The importance of the resource allocator role is positively related to the availability of strategic resources.

Figure 8.9. Stages of growth in IT outsourcing

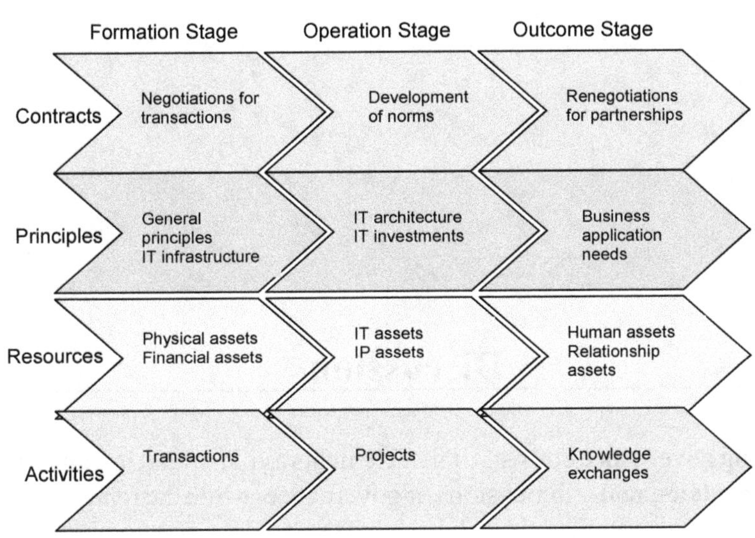

Figure 8.10. Managing successful IT outsourcing relationships through the governance model based on IT outsourcing theories

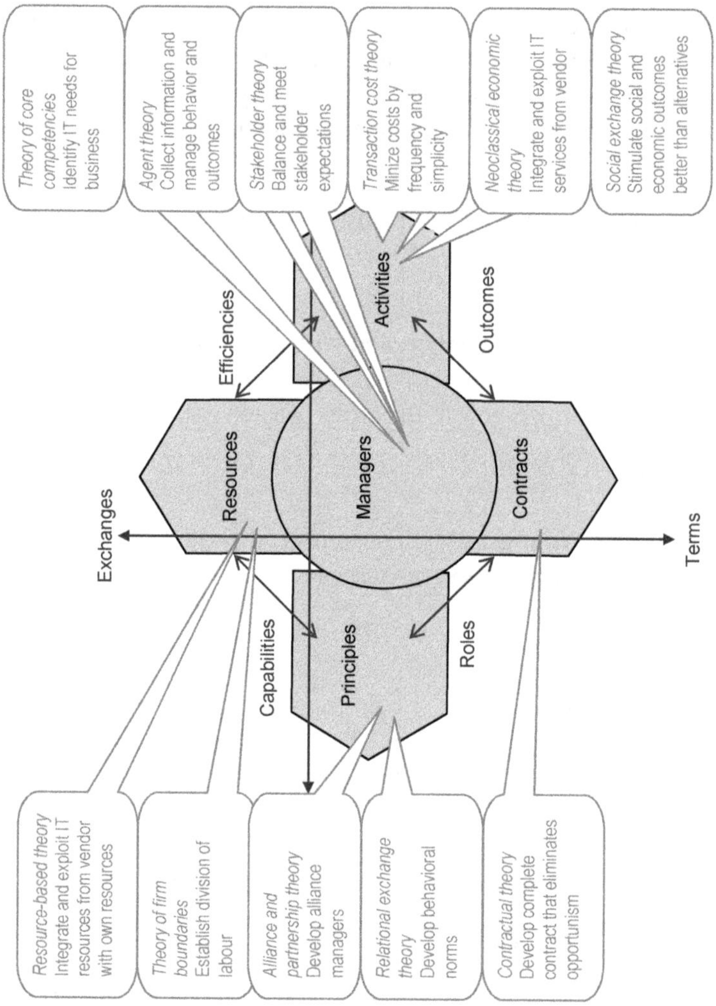

Discussion

IT outsourcing governance consists of five elements as illustrated in Figure 8.5. Four of these elements are really dimensions of governance, while the remaining element is management, which integrates the four dimensions of governance. In Figure 8.9, the four dimensions of governance are illustrated along the time dimension, defined as the formation stage (vision, evaluation and negotiation), the operation stage (transition and improvement) and the outcome stage (performance, results, goals and objectives).

In the formation stage, contracts are concerned with transactions in the outsourcing arrangement. Later, as relationships and norms develop between vendor and client, contracts will be renegotiated, shifting focus from transactions to relationships and partnerships. While the first contracts will be transactional contracts, later contracts will be relational contracts. Contract work is characterized by progressive contractual work, where focus slowly shifts from transactions to relationships as contract outcomes start to materialize.

It is important to design effective IT outsourcing governance. We defined governance as specifying the decision rights and accountability framework to encourage desirable behavior in an IT outsourcing relationship. Governance performance must then be how well the governance arrangements encourage desirable behaviors and ultimately how well both firms achieve their desired performance goals as vendor and client.

Early on in this book we presented several IT outsourcing theories. Each theory implies suggestions for managing successful IT outsourcing relationships. As a total set of suggestions and ideas from all theories, these guidelines represent critical success factors after outsourcing. The guidelines can be implemented in the governance model as illustrated in Figure 8.10. We see that resource-based theory and the theory of firm boundaries both provide guidelines for resource management. Alliance and partnership theory and relational exchange theory both provide guidelines for principles management. Transaction cost theory, neoclassical economic theory and social exchange theory all provide guidelines for activity management, while contractual theory provide guidelines for contract management. Theory of core competencies, agency theory and stakeholder theory provide guidelines directly to managers in charge of the outsourcing arrangement.

Conclusion

Knowledge management is a critical success factor in IT governance. In the causal loop diagram, improved knowledge management in the organization influences IT governance capability, IT governance effectiveness and IT governance efficiency. Strategic resource mobilization is influenced by allocation of decision rights and strategic alignment, in addition to IT governance capability, IT governance effectiveness and IT governance efficiency.

Figure 8.11. Causal loop diagram linking knowledge management to governance

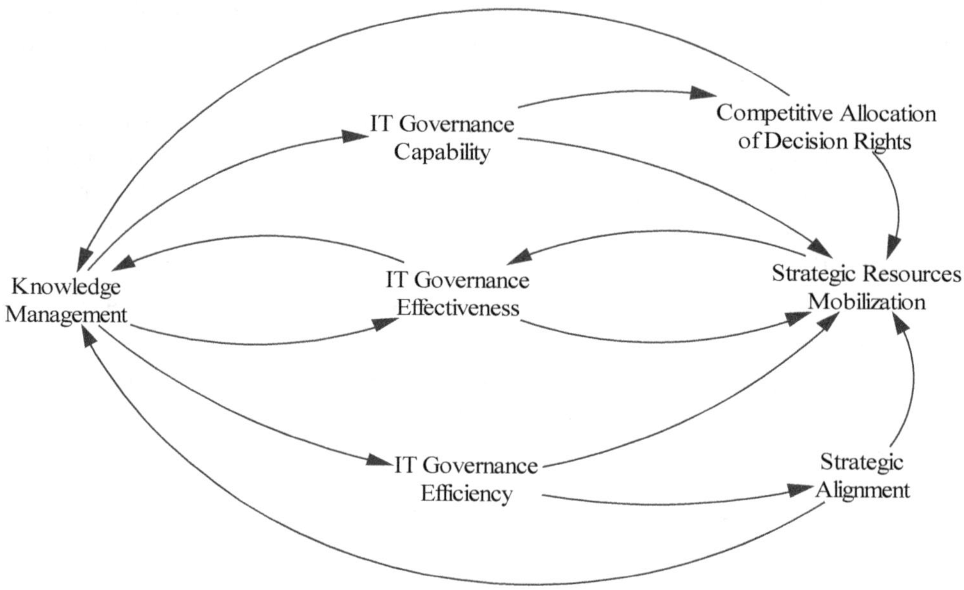

Figure 8.12. Positive feedback loop in the causal loop diagram

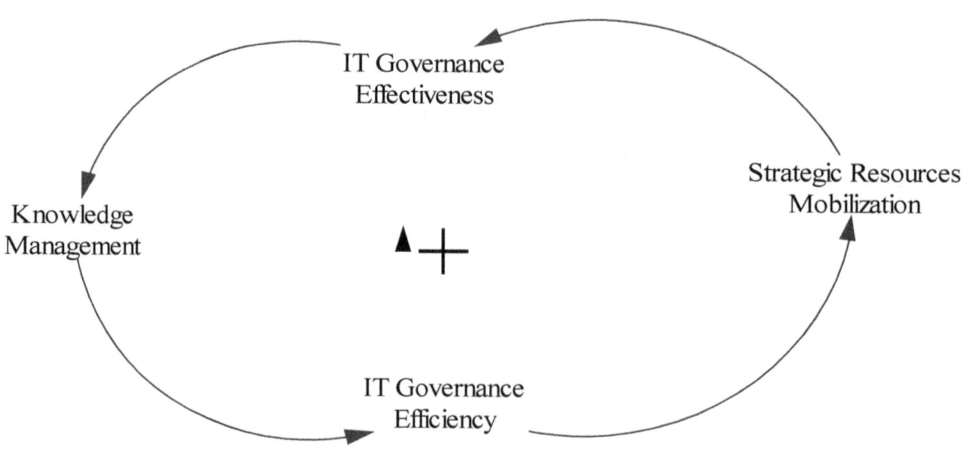

A positive feedback loop is illustrated in Figure 8.12. When knowledge management improves, IT governance efficiency improves, leading to mobilization of more strategic resources. More strategic IT resources lead to higher IT governance effectiveness, causing more improvement in knowledge management in the organization.

Questions for Discussion

1. Discuss strategic knowledge resources and strategic IT resources for the outsourcing cases of RR-EDS, ABB-IBM and SAS-CSC.
2. Who should decide on the principles in an outsourcing relationship?
3. How can IT governance be described as a value shop?

List of References

Barney, J. B. (2001). Is the resource-based 'view' a useful perspective for strategic management research? Yes. *Academy of Management Review, 26*(1), 41-56.

Barney, J. B. (2002). *Gaining and sustaining competitive advantage*. Upper Saddle River, NJ: Prentice Hall.

Callahan, J., Bastos, C., & Keyes, D. (2004). The evolution of IT governance at NB Power. In W. V. Grembergen (Ed.), *Strategies for information technology governance* (pp. 343-356). Hershey, PA: Idea Group Publishing.

Chin, P. O., Brown, G. A., & Qing, H. (2004). The impact of mergers & acquisitions on IT governance structures: A case study. *Journal of Global Information Management, 12*(4), 50-74.

Damianides, M. (2005, Winter). Sarbanse-Oxley and IT governance: New guidance on IT control and compliance. *Information Systems Management, 22*(1), 77-85.

Fairchild, A. (2004). A view on knowledge management: Utilizing a balanced scorecard methodology for analyzing knowledge metrics. In W. V. Grembergen (Ed.), *Strategies for information technology governance* (pp. 169-186). Hershey, PA: Idea Group Publishing.

Gottschalk, P., & Solli-Sæther, H. (2006). *Managing successful IT outsourcing relationships*. Hershey, PA: Idea Group Publishing.

Grembergen, W. V., & Haes, S. D. (2004a). IT governance and its mechanisms. *Information Systems Control Journal, 1,* 1-10.

Grembergen, W. V., & Haes, S. D. (2004b). *Mesuring and improving information technology governance through the balanced scorecard*. Research report no. 2, ITAG Research Institute, The Netherlands.

Grembergen, W. V., Haes, S. D., & Guldentops, E. (2004). Structures, processes and relational mechanisms for IT governance. In W. V. Grembergen (Ed.), *Strategies for Information Technology Governance* (pp. 1-36). Hershey, PA: Idea Group Publishing.

Grover, V., Jeong, S. R., Kettinger, W. J., & Lee, C. C. (1993). The chief information officer: A study of managerial roles. *Journal of Management Information Systems, 10*(2), 107-130.

Haanaes, K. B. (1997). *Managing resource mobilization: Case studies of Dynal, Fiat Auto Poland and Alcatel Tecom Norway.* PhD series 9.97, Copenhagen Business School, Copenhagen, Denmark.

Heijden, H. V. D. (2001). Measuring IT core capabilities for electronic commerce. *Journal of Information Technology, 16,* 13-22.

Johnson, G., & Scholes, K. (2002). *Exploring corporate strategy.* Harlow, Essex, UK: Pearson Education, Prentice Hall.

Karlsen, J. T., & Gottschalk, P. (2002). External or internal focus? A comparison of IT executive and IT project manager roles. *Engineering Management Journal, 14*(2), 5-11.

McManus, J. (2004, August). Working towards an information governance strategy. *Management Services, 48*(8), 8-13.

Meyer, N. D. (2004, Fall). Systemic IS governance: An introduction. *Information Systems Management, 21*(4), 23-34.

Mintzberg, H. (1994). Rounding out the manager's Job. *Sloan Management Review, 36*(1), 11-26.

O'Donnel, E. (2004). Discussion of director responsibility for IT governance: A perspective on strategy. *International Journal of Accounting Information Systems, 5,* 101-104.

Peterson, R. R. (2004a). Integration strategies and tactics for information technology governance. In W. V. Grembergen (ed.), *Strategies for Information Technology Governance* (pp. 37-80). Hershey, PA: Idea Group Publishing.

Peterson, R. R. (2004b, Fall). Crafting information technology governance. *Information Systems Management, 21*(4), 7-22.

Pettus, M. L. (2001). The resourced-based view as a development growth process: Evidence from the deregulated trucking industry. *Academy of Management Journal, 44*(4), 878-896.

Priem, R. L., & Butler, J. E. (2001). Is the resourced-based view a useful perspective for strategic management research? *Academy of Management Review, 26*(1), 22-40.

Rau, K. G. (2004, Fall). Effective governance of IT: Design objectives, roles, and relationships. *Information Systems Management, 21*(4), 35-42.

Read, T. J. (2004). Discussion of director responsibility for IT governance. *International Journal of Accounting Information Systems, 5,* 105-107.

Robbins, S. (2004, Fall). IS governance. *Information Systems Management, 21*(4), 81-82.

Trites, G. (2004). Director responsibility for IT governance. *International Journal of Accounting Information Systems, 5*(2), 89-99.

Wade, M., & Hulland, J. (2004). The resource-based view and information systems research: Review, extension, and suggestions for future research. *MIS Quarterly, 28*(1), 107-142.

Ward, J., & Griffiths, P. (1996). *Strategic planning for information systems.* Wiley Series in Information Systems. London, UK: Wiley & Sons.

Wasko, M. M., & Faraj, S. (2005). Why should I share? Examining social capital and knowledge contribution in electronic networks of practice. *MIS Quarterly, 29*(1), 35-57.

Weill, P. (2004). *Don't just lead, govern: How top-performing firms govern IT.* Center for Information Systems Research, CISR WP No. 341, Sloan School of Management, Massachusetts Institute of Technology (MIT).

Weill, P., & Ross, J. W. (2004). *IT governance.* Boston, MA: Harvard Business School Press.

Weill, P., & Ross, J. W. (2005, Winter). A matrixed approach to designing IT governance. *MIT Sloan Management Review*, 26-34.

Section III: Knowledge-Intensive Value Shop Organizations

In the knowledge economy, we see more knowledge firms emerging. Also, we see existing knowledge firms redefining themselves to exploit and explore their knowledge resources. Two examples are presented in this last part of the book. One example is drawn from the public sector in terms of law enforcement. The second example is drawn from the private sector concerning of legal work. While law enforcement is carried out in police organizations, legal work is carried out in law firms.

Like police organizations, law firms carry out a variety of tasks in legal cases. In the first example, we focus on police investigations in law enforcement. Police investigations are carried out by detectives who try to determine what happened so that criminals can be brought to justice. Police investigations can be understood in terms of knowledge work in the value shop. From initial crime scene assessment, via investigation alternatives and choice of investigation procedure, the investigation is carried out and evaluated. Often, the cyclical and iterative features of the value shop occur in police investigations. Examples are homicide and money laundering.

Similarly, law firm work takes place in the context of a value shop. Lawyers try to understand the client's problem in terms of legal consequences. Next, lawyers come up with alternative approaches to help the client. When lawyer and client agree, the optimal approach is carried out. Again, examples are homicide and money laundering.

Chapter IX

Police Investigation Knowledge

Introduction

Governments have become increasingly focused upon the setting of targets in efforts to improve the efficacy of police performance. However, performance assessments for police work are lacking clarity. In this chapter, we suggest the value shop for performance assessment. Based on a literature review, we suggest potential determinants of police performance in the value shop. Based on identified value configuration and determinants, this chapter develops research propositions linking police performance to team climate, knowledge sharing, leadership roles and stages of information technology. Future research should both consider revisions of propositions and also conduct an empirical study based on hypotheses derived from propositions. The police investigation leader will find guidance in leadership roles, knowledge-sharing initiatives, IT possibilities as well as team climate actions. Professional management thinking is introduced to police leadership by applying concepts from the business management research literature.

Police investigation units represent a knowledge-intensive and time-critical environment (Chen et al., 2002). The primary mission of any police force in the world is to protect life and property, preserve law and order and prevent and detect crime (Luen & Al-Hawamdeh, 2001).

In response to the September 11th terrorist attacks, major government efforts to modernize federal law enforcement authorities' intelligence collection and processing capabilities have been initiated worldwide. At the state and local levels in many countries, crime and police report data have rapidly migrated from paper to automated records management systems in recent years, making them increasingly accessible (Chen et al., 2003).

Police investigations are often dependent upon information from abroad. For example, the intelligence communities of different countries cooperate and share their information and knowledge, such as the Mossad with the CIA (Kahana, 2001). According to Lahneman (2004), knowledge sharing in the intelligence communities after 9/11 has increased rapidly.

According to Ashby and Longley (2005), there is a lack of clarity and clear methodology in assessing the performance of policing. We argue that police investigation units have the value configuration of a value shop. Furthermore, we argue that police investigation success can be defined as the extent to which each primary activity in the value shop is successfully conducted in police investigations.

Knowledge in Police Work

The public sector is turning to knowledge management, having recognized that they too face competition in funding and from alternative services. Increasingly, customers of the public sector are demanding higher service quality, particularly in the area of e-government. Services, particularly e-services, are expected to be available all the time with immediate response, simplified and with one-stop processing. According to Luen and Al-Hawamdeh (2001), knowledge management is thus a natural solution to improve operations and enhance customer service. Large organizations around the world are implementing knowledge management.

The activities and work carried out by police forces are primarily in the areas of crime prevention, incident management, investigation and community policing. Crime prevention implies the detection, and hence prevention, of crime. These activities can be carried out through both reactive and proactive means. Reactive measures such as roadblocks, spot-checks and showing police presence are routinely carried out by police officers as part of their investigation duties. Proactive measures include public education to help prevent crime. Police forces routinely use mass media as a means to convey crime prevention advice relating to current crime trends. In Singapore, police officers also reach out to the community via grassroots and community agencies to educate the public on the latest crime trends and threats. Police officers performing both reactive and proactive measures effectively, will need to know the latest legal and policy directions regarding these functions as well the latest information on crime trends and the corresponding knowledge about the detection and prevention of crime.

Luen and Al-Hawamdeh (2001) find that the amount of information that police officers come into contact with in the course of their work is astounding. This and the vast knowledge that police officers need in order to perform their normal duties suggest the need for police officers to be proficient knowledge workers, being able to access, assimilate and use knowledge effectively to discharge their duties.

Presently, such information and knowledge are captured within police organizations in various forms, ranging from computer records, to documented institutional orders, to the personal experiences of its officers. The crux of the issue is, then, how to surface such knowledge and bring it to bear on the problems faced by police officers in a timely and effective manner.

This is where knowledge management principles and practices can help. With the increased adoption of information technology within police organizations, and the increasing overall quality and IT competence of police officers, police organizations are well positioned to leverage knowledge management principles and practices. This, complemented by the enhanced skills, equipment and empowerment given to the officers, will enable them to perform their duties at an optimal level.

In discussing the scope of knowledge management in police work, Luen and Al-Hawamdeh (2001) take into consideration the two definitions of knowledge within the context of knowledge management. These two definitions of knowledge — explicit and tacit knowledge — give rise to different implementation approaches, which are complementary rather than exclusive. Both of these implementation approaches are necessary if the organization is to reap full benefits of knowledge management.

Explicit knowledge is used as guidance for police actions and decision-making. Explicit knowledge is captured in the form of documents (e.g., doctrines, police general orders and standard operating procedures) that have been verified and ascertained to be of value to police officers. Examples of these documents include procedures of arrest, handling a fire scene and illegal parking.

The second type of knowledge is implicit, or tacit, knowledge. This includes the competence, experience and skill of police officers. Tacit knowledge is usually dynamic and fast changing as compared with documented knowledge. Documented, or explicit, knowledge is normally kept as routine records in official police documents. Examples of such documented information include crime threats, crime trends and statistics, criminal records and situational information pertaining to the incident or crisis at hand.

Regarding tacit knowledge, the scope of knowledge management in police work is primarily in the areas of creating and sharing knowledge and information. The two main issues to be addressed here are the willingness and the ability of police officers to create and share knowledge. According to Luen and Al-Hawamdeh (2001), the more difficult issue to tackle is that of the willingness of police officers to create and share knowledge. There is a need for a culture characterized by openness, collaboration and sharing among police officers. This will require that police officers recognize the importance of collaboration and sharing knowledge with others.

The responsibility to surface knowledge lies with everyone in the police force, as knowledge is generated in all phases of work. In analyzing the content of the knowledge surfaced, it is necessary to check the subject matter of the knowledge as to what issues it addresses in relation to existing policies and procedures and whether such knowledge adds value for police officers. In assessing the complexity of the knowledge surfaced, it is necessary to check whether the knowledge is mostly explicit or tacit in nature. Explicit knowledge can be documented in writing with little loss in interpretation and understanding, while tacit knowledge tends to be difficult to document comprehensively due to its scope and nature (Luen & Al-Hawamdeh, 2001).

In police investigations, experienced officers not only check for a more complex and integrated set of traits, but they emphasize stable, generalized clues and actually look for fewer clues than recruits, according to Fielding (1984). Experienced officers have a more established idea of the important clues, which are then linked to lower-order clues. It has also been found that, compared to appearance, behavior is much more likely to be the basis of a classification of suspiciousness.

Analysis of police competence must acknowledge that police work aggravates several factors known to limit accurate judgment, for example, sources of information vary in credibility, and the police are particularly reliant on negative information (Fielding, 1984).An interesting example of knowledge acquisition in police investigations is interrogation. Interrogation is concerned with the questioning of person(s) suspected of a crime by police. Interrogation is to ask questions of a person, especially closely, thoroughly and formally. In most criminal justice systems there is a frequent reliance on confession evidence, and in some cases it may be the only evidence.

To understand interrogation in terms of investigative interviewing, Crawshaw et al. (1998) find it necessary to place the interviewing of victims, witnesses or suspects in the context of the investigation. In some cases the investigator may find that the victim is dead, there are no witnesses to the offence, the witnesses are too afraid to give evidence or information or there may be no forensic evidence. In such cases the investigator has to rely on obtaining a confession from a suspect, and this is acceptable in those jurisdictions where a person may be found guilty by a court on the basis of an uncorroborated confession.

Since most interviews take place in private where the suspect is alone with the interviewers and there is no independent record of what happened, there is a temptation for law enforcement officials to resort to physical and psychological abuse of the detainee in many countries. Sometimes the reasons for this can be understood, but such action is never justifiable (Crawshaw et al., 1998).

In most investigations it is normally the case that there are victims and witnesses from whom information can be obtained. Rather than over-relying on confessional evidence, steps can be taken to identify witnesses who may be able to provide such relevant information. Sometimes enquiries for this purpose have to be made a considerable time after the event, and a number of methods have been found to be successful in tracing witnesses. For example, "house to house enquiries," the methodological visiting of all premises in the vicinity of a crime in order to establish whether occupants are able to provide relevant information, appeals for witnesses through the news media, the distribution of leaflets giving details of a crime and appealing for information, and dramatized reconstructions of a crime on television programs (Crawshaw et al., 1998).

Forensic science can contribute greatly to investigations. In some countries techniques may be basic but nevertheless sound. For example, the physical (as opposed to technological) comparison of fingerprints found at the scene of a crime with those in a collection of previously convicted criminals. Other forensic science techniques, such as DNA profiling, are sophisticated and expensive and previously only available in well-resourced police agencies. Regardless of the degree of sophistication of techniques or facilities available, it is essential that police officials should be aware of them and maximize their use in order that they may be able to conduct an investigation which does not rely solely on confessional evidence.

A fundamental flaw is created in many investigations when the investigator secures a confession from a suspect at an early stage, and then attempts to establish a case against the suspect by selectively building up supporting evidence around the confession. The key word here is "selectively,"' for it means that the investigator is prepared to ignore, and even conceal, evidence which does not support the case against the accused. This can be fatal to the proper conclusion of any investigation, but especially so if the suspect has falsely confessed to a crime which he or she has not committed. If a person is convicted of a crime on the basis of evidence produced by such an "investigation," a double miscarriage of justice occurs — the wrongful conviction of any innocent person, and the avoidance of justice by the real author of the crime. It is more professional and more ethical to approach the case scientifically and with an open mind, to gather information systematically. In order for an investigation conducted on this basis to be successful, it is essential that each step of the investigation be documented (Crawshaw et al., 1998).

Police Leadership

In February 1994, William Bratton was appointed police commissioner of New York City. The odds were against him. The New York Police Department, with a $2 billion budget and a workforce of 35,000 police officers, was notoriously difficult to manage. Yet in less than two years, and without an increase in his budget, Bill Bratton turned New York into the safest large city of the nation.

Research conducted by Kim and Mauborgne (2003) led them to conclude that Bratton's turnaround was an example of tipping point leadership. The theory of tipping point, which has its roots in epiemiology, hinges on the insight that in any organization, once the beliefs and energies of a critical mass of people are engaged, conversion to a new idea will spread like an epidemic, bringing about fundamental change very quickly. The theory suggests that such a movement can be unleashed only by agents who make unforgettable and unarguable calls for change, who concentrate their resources on what really matters, who mobilize the commitment of the organization's key players and who succeed in silencing the most vocal naysayers. Bratton did all of these things.

Kim and Maugorgne (2003) find that in many turnarounds, the hardest battle is simply getting people to agree on the causes of current problems and the need for change. Most CEOs try to make the case for change simply by pointing to the numbers and insisting that the company achieve better ones. But messages communicated through numbers seldom stick.

Tipping point leaders do not rely on numbers to break through the organization's cognitive hurdles. Instead, they put their key managers face-to-face with the operational problems so that the managers cannot evade reality. Poor performance becomes something they witness rather than hear about. Communicating in this way means that the message — performance is poor and needs to be fixed — sticks with people, which is essential if they are to be convinced not only that a turnaround is necessary but that it is something they can achieve.

Leaders like Bratton use a four-step process to bring about rapid, dramatic and lasting change with limited resources. Tipping all four hurdles leads to rapid strategy reorientation and execution:

- **Cognitive hurdle:** Put managers face-to-face with problems and customers. Find new ways to communicate.
- **Resource hurdle:** Focus on the hot spots and bargain with partner organizations.
- **Motivational hurdle:** Put the stage lights on and frame the challenge to match the organization's various levels.
- **Political hurdle:** Identify and silence internal opponents; isolate external ones.

By addressing these hurdles to tipping point change, leaders will stand a chance of achieving the same kind of results as Bratton delivered to the citizens of New York. Between 1994 and 1996, felony crime fell 39%, murders 50% and theft 35%. Gallup polls reported that public confidence in the NYPD jumped from 37% to 73% (Kim & Mauborgne, 2003).

Police Intelligence

A special branch of police work, which seems extremely knowledge-intensive, is police intelligence. Lahneman (2004) suggests that intelligence agencies were the world's first knowledge companies. Managing knowledge has always been the primary mission of the intelligence community's leadership. Accordingly, the intelligence community can benefit substantially from knowledge management approaches.

According to Lahneman (2004), the intelligence community is now understood to have possessed several pieces of intelligence information that, in retrospect, might have warned of the September 11, 2001 terrorist attacks on Washington, DC and New York City. But, while U.S. intelligence agencies individually had collected considerable data on the strikes, they failed to interpret and share the information in a timely manner. In the wake of 9/11, the intelligence community clearly recognized that it needed to improve knowledge sharing among its component agencies, as well as with the new Department of Homeland Security and state and local organizations involved in the war against terrorism.

Experience so far with knowledge management indicates that two necessary conditions must prevail for improving knowledge sharing. First, given the volume of information that the intelligence community must possess, the use of large-scale IT systems is essential. Second, successful knowledge management depends on developing an organizational culture that facilitates and rewards knowledge sharing. In the absence of either of these components, knowledge management initiatives will fail.

The intelligence community has taken a number of steps in both areas to improve knowledge sharing. Several agencies have embarked on innovative, large-scale projects to upgrade their IT capabilities.

The intelligence community has also experienced several high-level organizational changes and proposals for organizational change. In Norway, the Police Security Service replaced the Police Surveillance Service. In the U.S., a clearinghouse for foreign and domestic terrorism analysis — the Terrorist Threat Integration Center (TTIC) — was located at the CIA compound at Langley, Virginia, reporting directly to the Director of Central Intelligence. The center will fuse all appropriate information and send summary reports to the Department of Homeland Security.

Knowledge collection activities require coordination to make sure that collected information gets to the right persons at the right time. They also need oversight to ensure that each agency's collection assets are so employed that the collection of potentially useful information is optimized. Optimizing knowledge sharing where intelligence analysis is concerned can be more difficult, because, unlike collection efforts, coordination is increasingly interagency in nature. Analysis related to terrorism and, in particular, terrorism against the U.S. homeland, is particularly dependent on fusing information from disparate sources — including the tacit knowledge of both government and nongovernment experts — into an appropriate product at the correct time (Lahneman, 2004).

Intelligence communities of different nations share information and knowledge. Intelligence activities usually remain secret, especially when the communities of different countries are involved. One known example is the cooperation between the CIA and the Mossad, where the U.S. and Israeli intelligence communities exchange information, when it served the interests of the side providing information to the other. Therefore, providing information may at times be one-sided. According to Kahana (2001), there has been an obvious interest not to provide information, and even to block it, in several cases. For example, the United States was reluctant to provide the Mossad with satellite photographs about what was happening in peripheral Arab countries. Israel, for its part, tried to stop surveillance by the U.S.S. Liberty.

Agency Theory of Police Work

Agency theory has broadened the risk-sharing literature to include the agency problem that occurs when cooperating parties have different goals and divisions of labor. The cooperating parties are engaged in an agency relationship defined as a contract under which one or more persons (the principal(s)) engage another person (agent) to perform some service on their behalf, which involves delegating some decision-making authority to the agent). Agency theory describes the relationship between the two parties using the metaphor of a contract.

According to Eisenhardt (1985), agency theory is concerned with resolving two problems that occur in agency relationships. The first is the agency problem that arises when the desires or goals of the principal and agent conflict, and it is difficult or expensive for the principal to verify what the agent is actually doing. The second is the problem of risk sharing that arises when the principal and agent have different risk preferences. The common element to principal-agent models is that principals are unable to monitor agents' actions or information; the heart of these models involves setting a wage for an agent without fully knowing the agent's effort (moral hazard) or ability (adverse selection).

Brehm and Gates (1993) applied agency theory to police work. They examined police supervision through an empirical analysis of the behavior of police officers with respect to their supervisor's orders. Their goal was to specify a statistical model that is appropriate for evaluation of compliance behavior in general, as long as the measure of compliance is a scale from 0 to 100% compliance. They found that some principal-agency models lead to strong predictions about the possible distribution shape of compliance by police subordinates.

Police Performance

Police performance is a complicated construct. The police reform in the UK has developed some performance indicators for policing within an assessment framework. The policing performance assessment framework is an initiative led by the Home Office (2005), with the support of the Association of Chief Police Officers and the Association of Police Authorities. Here are some examples of performance indicators for 2005/2006:

- Satisfaction of victims of domestic burglary, violent crime, vehicle crime and road traffic collisions
- Using the British Crime Survey, the percentage of people who think their local police do a good job
- Satisfaction of victims of racist incidents with respect to the overall service provided
- Using the British Crime Survey, the risk of personal crime
- Domestic burglaries per 1,000 households
- Number of offences brought to justice
- Percentage of notifiable offences resulting in a sanction detection
- Percentage of domestic violence incidents with a power of arrest
- Number of people killed
- Using the British Crime Survey, fear of crime
- Percentage of police officer time spent on frontline duties
- Delivery of cashable and noncashable efficiency target
- Average number of working hours lost per annum due to sickness per police officer

The guidance on statutory performance indicators for policing includes user satisfaction measures, confidence measures, fairness, equality and diversity measures, measures of crime level, offences brought to justice measures, sanction detection measures, domestic violence measures, traffic measures, quality of life measures, frontline policing measures and resource use measures.

One of the resource use measures is delivery of cashable and noncashable efficiency targets. A cashable gain is where a particular level of output of a particular quality is achieved for less cost. A noncashable gain is where more output and/or output of better quality is achieved for the same cost.

In 1993, there was a debate in the UK whether to allow and stimulate direct entry into police management. According to Leishman and Savage (1993), it was a fundamental fact of the British police service that everyone had to start at the bottom, at the "lowest" rank of constable, in which office all entrants must serve a minimum period of two years. On the surface, then, the police service may appear to occupy a unique position among public sector organizations, as an apparently egalitarian meritocracy in which all confirmed constables could be said to have the opportunity to aspire to senior management positions.

At that time, chief constables were the first generation of completely self-made chiefs, lacking even the middle-class socialization of university, although most went to grammar schools. Leishman and Savage (1993) argue that there are two important reasons in favor of direct entry. First, direct entry offers potential for the active furtherance of equal opportunities in the British police service. Whereas in Britain, target attainment would depend on the numbers of officers remaining in the service beyond their two-year probationary period, and then progressing through the rank of sergeant, this was not the case in Holland. Its system of direct entry, coupled with an explicit policy of positive action, allowed the recruitment and training of sufficient numbers of women and ethnic minority candidates directly into the rank of inspector, to achieve minimum targets within the time-scale agreed.

A second argument in favor of direct entry followed, in a sense, part of the rationale for "civilianization" within the service. While much of this process had been driven by the pursuit of economies, behind it also was the question of competencies and specialist skills. For example, staff with backgrounds in personnel management have been appointed to head the personnel department in place of police officers (Leishman & Savage, 1993).

According to Jackson and Wade (2005), the understanding of police behavior, especially proactive behavior, has been pursued throughout policing history. Researchers have examined the impact of environmental factors (i.e., weapons, crime, etc.), individual factors (i.e., attitude, personality, etc.), police subculture and organizational and departmental management on police behavior. Despite all of these research efforts, most, if not all, of the authors contributing to this line of research have concluded that the categorization, understanding and predicting of police behavior is arduous (if not impossible), or that the relationship between police attitudes and their behavior is weak at best.

Researchers have examined empirically and conceptually the impact of social capital and police sense of responsibility on police behavior. For example, community social capital has been identified in the literature as having a significant impact on police behavior mainly because social capital serves as a measure of the community's ability to solve its own problems. In communities with low social capital, police may perceive themselves as the only form of social order and may therefore develop a higher sense of responsibility towards protecting citizens, themselves and preventing crime.

Jackson and Wade (2005) suggest that the examination of the police sense of responsibility towards the community may be important in understanding police behavior. This assertion implies that a police sense of responsibility may serve as an influential variable in explaining why police may demonstrate higher levels of proactive policing in communities with low social capital in comparison to those with high social capital. A police sense of responsibility toward the community seems important for understanding how police function in areas under their command. In communities where crime is commonplace, police can become overwhelmed and may therefore focus on more serious crimes that pose a greater threat to police and citizen safety and ignore the lower level crimes that do not.

Given these arguments, the major purpose of the study conducted by Jackson and Wade (2005) was to examine the relationship between police perception of their community's social capital and their sense of responsibility toward the provision of public safety, and in turn to assess empirically the impact of sense of responsibility on their propensity to engage in proactive policing.

By studying police perceptions of social capital and their sense of responsibility, it was possible to not only understand why community policing is or is not successful but more importantly it was possible to understand police behavior in environments that by their structural and demographic make-up, complicate the task of effective policing.

Jackson and Wade's (2005) findings support the hypothesis that police who indicate a more negative perception of community social capital are more likely to indicate a higher sense of responsibility towards the community. This finding suggests that as the police perception of community social capital becomes negative, they are more likely to rely upon their own resources to solve community problems. Generally, the only real resources that police possess in low social capital communities are their law enforcement powers.

Another finding was that police who express a more negative perception of community social capital were more likely to indicate higher levels of proactive behavior. This finding suggests that in communities with low social capital, police may utilize their law enforcement powers more in comparison to communities that posses higher levels of social capital.

The data gathered through a questionnaire distributed among the Kansas City Police Department in the U.S. suggested that the amount of crime occurring within the community is the most important variable for the explanation of police proactive behavior. Police proactive behavior includes new patrol techniques, increased utilization of technology, the organization of specialized units and the use of criminal profiling. By being more proactive, police are conducting more stop-and-frisk contacts, requesting proof of identification more frequently, conducting more drug sweeps and dispersing citizens who gather to protest public policies of various kinds (Jackson & Wade, 2005).

Proactive policing might perpetuate and exacerbate the social distance rift between the police and their community, and it also increases the likelihood that an officer may abuse his or her authority. In a time period of three years, Prince George's County in the U.S. paid out eight million dollars in jury awards and settlements in lawsuits that involved police misconduct and excessive force. The increasing costs resulting from payouts in police litigation cases and liability claims, coupled with increased pressure from public insurance pools to cut losses, are a few of the reasons that some U.S. law enforcement agencies are beginning to implement risk management programs (Archbold, 2005).

Risk management is a process used to identify and control exposure to potential risks and liabilities in both private and public organizations. Almost all of the basic duties of police work expose police officers to liability incidents on a daily basis. One aspect of police work that makes it unique to all other professions is the ability of police officers to use lethal and nonlethal force. This unique aspect of police work also contributes to police officer exposure to high levels of risk, which could lead to litigation, liability claims or citizen complaints (Archbold, 2005).

Police personnel face some of society's most serious problems, often work in dangerous settings, are typically expected to react quickly and at the same time correctly. They must adapt to an occupation in which one moment may bring the threat of death, while other extended periods bring routine and boredom. They are expected to maintain control in chaotic situations involving injustice, public apathy, conflicting roles, injuries and fatalities. Yet they are expected by both the public and their peers to approach these situations in an objective and professional manner, to be effective decision-makers and independent problem solvers while working in a system that encourages dependency by its quasi-military structure (Kelley, 2005).

The nature of work in police professions requires optimal mental health. When their mental functioning is compromised, police professionals can lose touch with the common sense and resilience they need to minimize stress, enjoy their work and operate at peak performance. Over time, Kelley (2005) finds that poor mental health can dramatically increase police officers proneness to physical illness, emotional disorders, accidents, marital and family problems, excessive drinking and drug use, suicide and litigation ranging from excessive force and false arrest to failure to provide appropriate protection and services.

Knowledge Management Technology

Two examples of information technology in police work will be presented in the following. Our first example is COPLINK described by Chen et al. (2002, 2003), and the second is geocomputation described by Ashby and Longley (2005).

COPLINK Connect is an application for information and knowledge sharing in law enforcement. The system uses a three-tiered architecture. The user accesses the system through a Web browser. The middle tier connects the user interface and the backend databases and implements the work logic.

COPLINK Detect is targeted for detectives and crime analysts. The system shares the same incident record information as the Connect module and utilizes the database indexes it generates. However, the Detect system has a completely redesigned user interface, and employs a new set of intelligence analysis tools to meet its user needs.

Much of crime analysis is concerned with creating associations or linkages among various aspects of a crime. COPLINK Detect uses a technique called concept space to identify such associations from existing crime data automatically. In general, a concept space is a network of terms and weighted associations within an underlying information space. COPLINK Detect uses statistical techniques such as co-occurrence analysis and clustering functions to weight relationships between all possible pairs of concepts.

In COPLINK Detect, detailed criminal case reports are the underlying information space, and concepts are meaningful terms occurring in each case. These case reports contain both structured (for example, database fields for incidents containing the case number, names of people involved, address and date) and unstructured data (narratives written by officers commenting on an incident, for example, witness A said he saw suspect A run away in a white truck).

Several field user studies have been conducted to evaluate the COPLINK system. For example, a group of 52 law enforcement personnel from the Tucson Police Department representing a number of different job classifications and backgrounds were recruited to participate in a study to evaluate COPLINK Connect. Both interview-data and survey-data analyses support a conclusion that use of the application provided performance superior to using the legacy police records management system. In addition to the statistical data, these findings were supported by qualitative data collected from participant interviews (Chen et al., 2003).

The other application to be presented here is concerned with geocomputation for geodemographics. Geodemographic profiles of the characteristics of individuals and small areas potentially offer significant breakthroughs in clarifying local policing needs in the same way they have become an integral part of many commercial and marketing ventures. Geodemographic systems were one of the first emergent applications areas of what is now known as geocomputation.

Ashby and Longley (2005) conducted a case study of the Devon and Cornwall Constabulary. They found that geodemographic analyses of local policing environments, crime profiles and police performance provided a significantly increased level of community intelligence for police use. This was further enhanced by the use of penetration ranking reports where neighborhood types were ranked by standardized crime rates, and cumulative percentage of the crime was compared with the corresponding population at risk.

Police Investigations

Police investigations are a complex undertaking that have both reactive and proactive dimensions to them. The knowledge required to effectively carry out an investigation is built upon "three pillars," a term employed by the Singapore Police Force. These pillars are forensics, intelligence and interviews.

A well-grounded forensic understanding of a crime scene is the foundation of any investigation. Intelligence gathering is a crucial activity for an investigation, particularly so for proactive investigations into organized crime and/or terrorist related-operations. As regards interviews, the ability to derive relevant information from people through effective interviewing is seen by police as an essential activity in any investigation. Hence, as Chen et al. (2002) point out, police investigation units represent a knowledge-intensive and time-critical environment. The primary mission of any police force in the world is to protect life and property, preserve law and order and prevent and detect crime (Luen & Al-Hawamdeh, 2001).

We treat police investigation as value shop activities. As can be seen on Figure 5.14, these five activities are interlocking, and while they follow a logical sequence, much like the management of any project, the difference from a knowledge management perspective is the way in which knowledge is used as a resource to create "value" for the organization. Hence, the logic of the five interlocking "value shop" activities in this example is of a police organization and how it engages in its core business of conducting reactive and proactive investigations.

Also, noted on Figure 5.14 is how in practice these five sequential activities tend to overlap and link back to earlier activities, especially in relation to activity 5 (control and evaluation) in police organizations when the need for control and command structures are a daily necessity because of the legal obligations that police authority entails. Hence, the diagram on Figure 9.1 is meant to illustrate the reiterative and cyclical nature of these five primary activities for managing the knowledge collected during and applied to a specific police investigation in a "value shop" manner.

Figure 9.1. Knowledge-managed police investigations

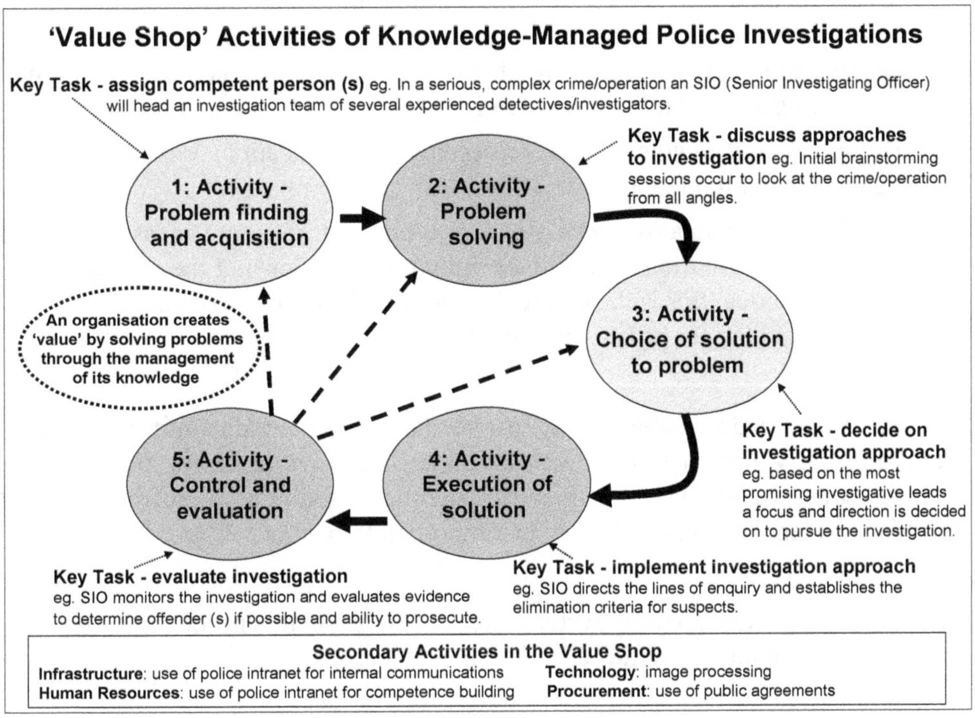

Moreover, the basic requirements needed to develop a Knowledge Management System with the appropriate level of IT support are shown in the box at the bottom of Figure 9.1. In this regard it is worth noting that research by Adhami and Browne (1996) into the possibility of developing a knowledge based system for sexually oriented child homicides in England found that the infrastructure of the HOLMES (Home Office Large Major Enquiry System) database could be used to structure and store such crime-specific information which would greatly assist detectives in investigating this type of crime.

Briefly, these five activities in relation to a police investigation unit can be outlined as:

1. Problem finding and acquisition involves working with parties to determine the exact nature of the crime. It involves deciding on the overall approach to police work for the case.
2. Problem solving is the actual generation of ideas and action plans for the investigation.

3. Choice represents the decision of choosing between alternatives. While the least important primary activity of the value shop in terms of time and effort, it is also the most important in terms of customer value. In this case, trying to ensure as far as is possible that what is decided on to do is the best option to follow to get an effective investigative result.
4. Execution, as the name implies, represents communication, organizing, investigating and implementing decisions.
5. Control and evaluation activities involve monitoring and measurement of how well the solution solved the original problem or met the original need. As noted above, this is the where the command and control chain of authority comes into play for police organizations.

The use of knowledge management systems has the potential of improving all of the five primary activities. However, based on the previous discussion of police investigations, we argue that the greatest potential is found in the second phase of problem solving. Hence, our first research proposition:

P1: Knowledge management systems are more important in problem solving than in other primary activities of police investigations.

Nested within this first proposition that police research efforts should be focused on developing knowledge management systems that concentrate on enhancing the activity of how "problem solving" takes place within investigations, is a second proposition based on the empirical research by Dean (2000) which identified four qualitatively different thinking styles (method-challenge-skill-risk) that investigators rely upon to guide them in solving crimes. The proposition is:

P2: Knowledge management systems are more important in the thinking styles of method and skill than in the thinking styles of challenge and risk.

As Dean (2005) notes in police investigations, the experience of investigation begins for detectives when they are given a crime to solve. When handed a case, detectives apply methods they were trained in. Often, they follow a set of five basic procedural steps: collecting, checking, considering, connecting, and constructing.

As detectives conduct a series and/or complex investigation, they become driven by the intensity of the challenge, which motivates them to do the best job they can for the victim(s) by catching the criminal(s) and solving the crime through the application of their investigative method.

In meeting this investigative challenge detectives require skill to relate and communicate effectively to a variety of people to obtain information so as to establish a workable investigative focus. Such skill also requires detectives to be flexible in the how they approach people and the case, while maintaining an appropriate level of emotional involvement towards victims, witnesses, informants and suspects.

When exercising their investigative skill, detectives seek to maximize the possibilities of a good result by taking legally sanctioned and logically justifiable risks across a wide latitude of influence. Such justifiable risk-taking requires detectives to be proactive in applying creativity to how they seek to discover new information and, if necessary, how they develop such information into evidence.

Many detectives are only trained in one way of investigative thinking — the method style. This style of investigative thinking is all about following the basic police procedural steps when doing investigation, which are the five Cs above. However, there are three other levels, or preferred ways, of thinking about the investigative process that experienced detectives use with serious and complex crimes. The three other levels are the challenge style, the skill style and the risk style of investigative thinking.

The challenge level is all about what motivates detectives. At this level detectives think about the job, the victim, the crime and the criminal. These four elements (job-victim-crime-criminal) are the key sources of intensity that drive detectives to do the best they can in a particular investigation.

At the skill level of investigative thinking, detectives are concerned with how they relate to people. Detectives must think about how they are going to relate to the victim, witnesses, possible suspects, the local community and the wider general public in order to get the information they need to make the case.

The risk style revolves around how detectives think through being proactively creative enough to discover new information and, if necessary, develop it into evidence that will stand up to testing in a court of law.

Although experienced detectives and investigators intuitively use these four levels of thinking in an investigation, it is rare that any one detective will give equal weight to all four styles of investigative thinking in a particular case because detectives, like everyone else, have a preference for maybe one or two particular styles or ways of thinking.

Dean (2005) calls this phenomenon *the cognitive psychology of police investigators*. It is about how police investigators (detectives) think when conducting a criminal investigation. The nature of the subject matter falls within the realm of the cognitive sciences, especially in relation to two branches of psychology. That is, cognitive psychology with its focus on the mental processes and complex behaviors involved in problem solving and decision-making, and the domain of investigative psychology as a more generic term that subsumes many of the more specific areas associated with police psychology and field of criminal or offender profiling.

Dean (2005) argues that essentially investigation is a mind game. When it comes to solving a crime, a detective's ability to think as an investigator is everything. Four distinctively different ways of thinking are investigation as method, investigation as challenge, investigation as skill and investigation as risk. All four ways of describing a criminal investigation can be seen as more or less partial understandings of the whole phenomenon of investigation.

Dean (1995, 2000, 2005) conducts empirical research in the overlapping domains of cognitive/investigative psychology in relation to a specific focus on investigative thinking. An example of one of the cases from this research is presented to illustrate the process of investigative thinking and the way in which various thinking styles come into play at critical points in the progress of this specific investigation to achieve a successful outcome.

The case involved a 73-year-old man who was found bound with duct tape and murdered in his flat in a Northern district of Singapore on August 21, 2002. A selection of mobile phones, jewelry, watches and cash were stolen from the safe in his house. The informant was a 56-year-old female Chinese national who worked as a part-time cleaner for the deceased. There were no witnesses to the crime and neighbors heard nothing unusual.

A state-action investigative chart was developed by Dean (2005) to assess the various states that a specific investigation goes through for a particular crime and the actions that investigators take as a result. In this murder case in Singapore, the topics on the state-action chart included: interview friends, forensic evidence, public pressure, investigator motivation, interview cleaner, locate cleaner's son, etc. In this case, the state-action chart clearly represented how the method style of investigative thinking was carried out through the collection of forensic evidence at the scene and gathered information from informal interviews with friends of the deceased that the cleaner's son was most likely involved in some capacity. This speculation by the deceased's friends was as indicated on the chart based on the fact that the cleaner's son stayed over some nights in the deceased's house.

The investigation stalled when all leads appeared to reach a dead end. Even the stolen mobile phones had not been used to make calls so the service provider was not able to pinpoint their exact location.

However, the determination of the investigator exemplified the challenging style of investigative thinking as he was being driven by the intensity of the job, the crime and the victim to such an extent that he engaged in some proactive creative thinking, (an example of the risk style) that kicked off the investigation again in an eventual positive direction.

The investigator approached the service provider to check if any of the previous phone calls could reveal anything of use for the investigation. The service provider was able to give an estimated location of the missing mobile phones based on the signal picked up by their station. The investigator then made extensive enquiries

Figure 9.2. Ways of thinking about the investigation process

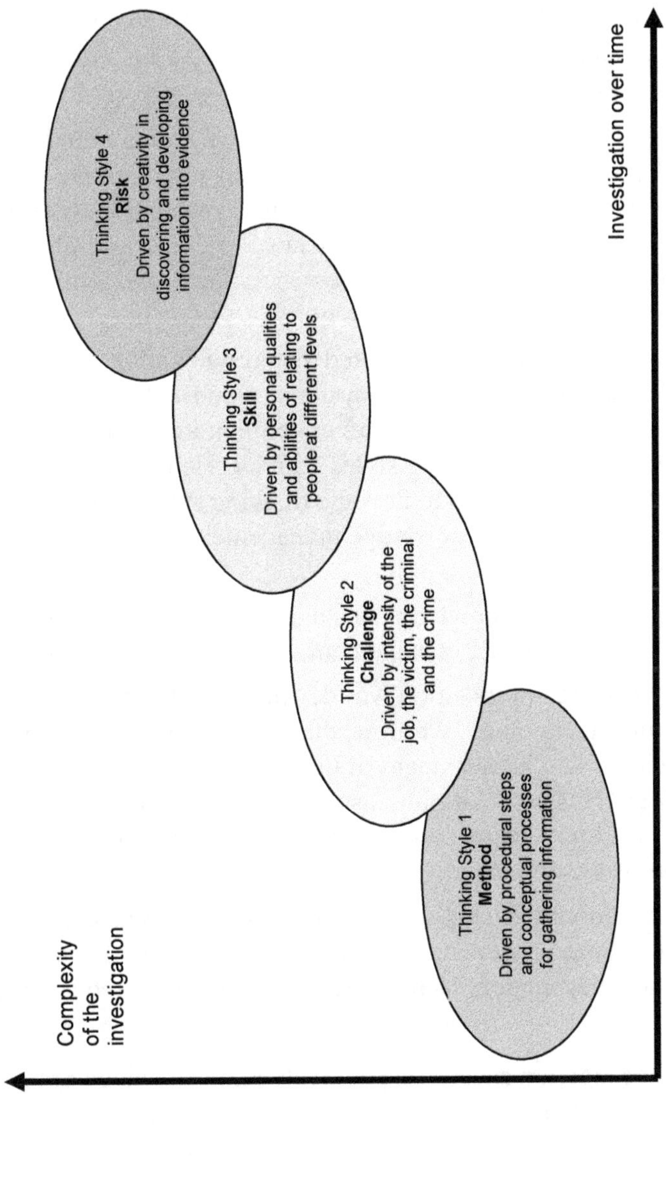

at the local mobile phone shops in the estimated area and eventually located the second-hand dealer's shop where the suspect sold the mobile for ready cash. Such an attempt was unprecedented in any other homicide cases in Singapore.

As the case example illustrates, a number of changes in thinking style took place throughout this investigation. The investigation started as all investigations do with the application of the "method" style of investigative thinking, then moved to investigation as "challenge," which helped spark off the next change from investigation as challenge to investigation as "skill" and finally the use of the "risk" style of investigative thinking was applied to the analysis of phone call details.

Dean's (2005) four distinctively different ways of thinking (styles) about the investigation process by detectives is illustrated in Figure 9.2.

As can be seen on Figure 9.2, there is a hierarchical structure to how investigators think. Not all cases will require the use of all four investigative thinking styles to solve them. However, as time marches on in an investigative without a result, then other styles of investigative thinking will need to come into play to increase the likelihood of a successful outcome. In essence, the more complex the crime the higher the investigative thinking style required to solve it.

These four ways of thinking can be related to the codification vs. the personalization strategy for knowledge management systems suggested by Hansen et al. (1999). Thinking styles 1 and 3 are based more on explicit knowledge and are more suitable for codification than thinking styles 2 and 4. Hence, the focus of our second research proposition in relation to how the thinking styles of method and skill may be more important to apply knowledge management systems to than the thinking styles of challenge and risk.

The ambition level using knowledge management systems can again be defined in terms of stages of knowledge management technology as illustrated in Figure 9.3.

The following research proposition was developed in light of the stages of knowledge management technology. We argue that a police investigation will find greater support in their work at higher stages of the growth model for knowledge management technology. This proposition is also congruent with the first proposition about the importance of knowledge management systems for police investigations being focused on problem solving activity.

Clearly, problem solving is a higher order thinking skill and therefore as Figure 5.15 indicates, a matching up of a stage 4 "how-they-think" KM system is required at this level in the investigation. Hence, the proposition is stated as follows:

P3: Police investigation success is positively related to stage of knowledge management technology.

With regard to the focus of this chapter on police investigations, knowledge is the most important strategic resource that police as a "firm" use to solve their particular crime problems. If police fail to fully utilize this resource then their return-on-the-investigative investment will be lower. Therefore, the proposition is:

Figure 9.3. Stages of growth model for police knowledge work

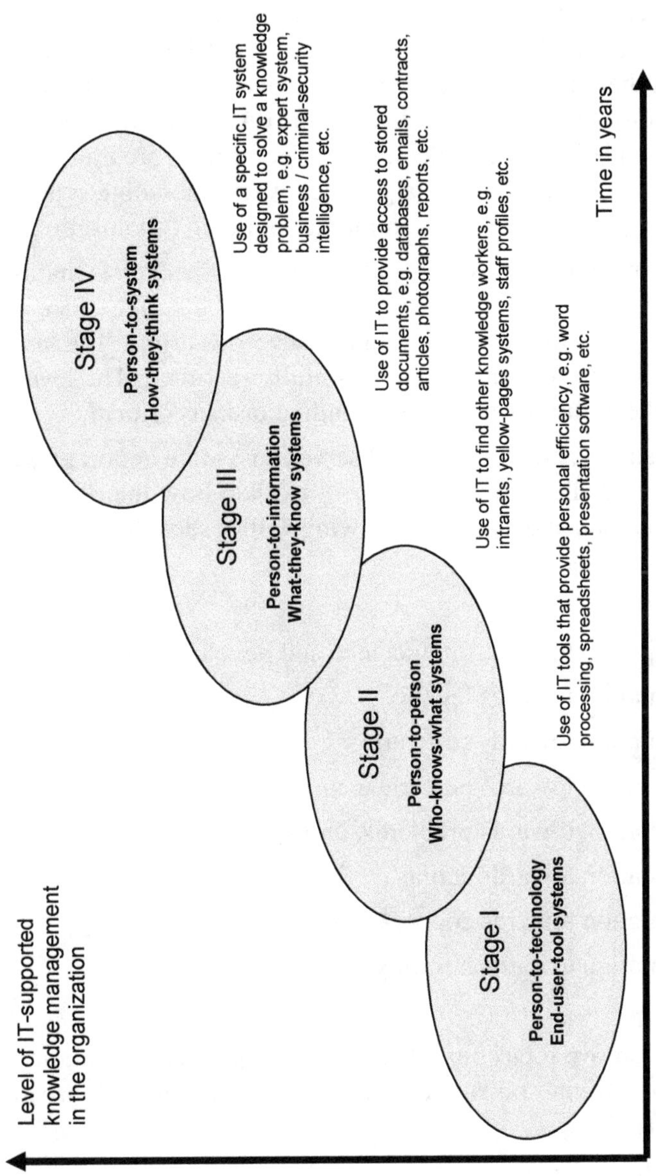

P4: Police investigation success is positively related to the extent of access to strategic knowledge resources.

The Case of Anti-Terror Police

Norway has one police service which is based on the principle of coherence, meaning that all functions are in one organization. There are 27 local police districts, each under the command of a Chief of Police. The Chiefs of Police head all kinds of policing in their districts. Each police district has its own headquarters and several police stations. The districts are divided into rural police districts, under the command of a Police Chief Superintendent. All police officers are trained as generalists, able to fulfill every aspect of ordinary police work, including criminal investigations, maintaining public order and community policing (Glomseth, 2004).

The anti-terror police in Norway are a group of specialists that is very well skilled and very well trained for extreme situations. The police officers are educated and trained to fight extremely serious and dangerous crime. The tasks are challenging and difficult. The officers are very carefully recruited. The level of competence is high, and the ability to execute demanding tasks is critical.

Through a survey, interviews and observations, some important occupational values were identified. These values can help explain how the officers in the anti-terror police think, plan and act. The following values seem to be strongly shared among the officers:

- Orientation towards competence and development
- Orientation towards legality
- Orientation towards structure
- Orientation towards performance
- Orientation towards problems, cases and tasks
- Orientation towards acting
- Orientation towards cooperation
- Orientation towards humility

In this section, we focus our attention on cooperative orientation in the anti-terror police by identifying potential predictors of such orientation.

Research Model

The dependent variable in the research model is cooperative orientation in terms of involvement, as illustrated in Figure 9.4. Cooperative orientation is concerned with the extent of task vs. relationship orientation, closed vs. open information sharing, competition vs. cooperation among police officers and single work vs. balanced life orientation. The dependent variable measures the extent of participation and involvement (Zamanou & Glaser, 1994). Three potential predictors of cooperative orientation have been identified, as illustrated in the figure. The potential predictors are labeled time perspective, power structure and leadership style.

First, we suggest that time perspective influences the extent of cooperative orientation (Fielding, 1984; Kiely & Peek, 2002). If the police officer perceives work to be short term, then the person will tend to be less cooperative oriented. If the police officer perceives work to be long term, then the person will tend to have a greater extent of cooperative orientation.

Hypothesis 1: A longer time perspective perceived by the police officer is positively related to the police officer's degree of cooperative orientation.

Next, we believe that hierarchy influences the extent of cooperative orientation. If the police officer perceives the organization to be hierarchical in terms of distance to the top of the anti-terror organization, then the person will tend to be less co-operative oriented (Christensen & Crank, 2001). If the police officer perceives the organization to be nonhierarchical by having easy access to decision-makers, then the person will tend to have a greater extent of cooperative orientation. Similarly, if the police officer perceives more equality in the organization, then the person will tend to be more cooperative oriented.

Hypothesis 2: More hierarchy and less equality perceived by the police officer are negatively related to the police officer's degree of cooperative orientation.

Figure 9.4. Research model to study predictors of cooperative orientation

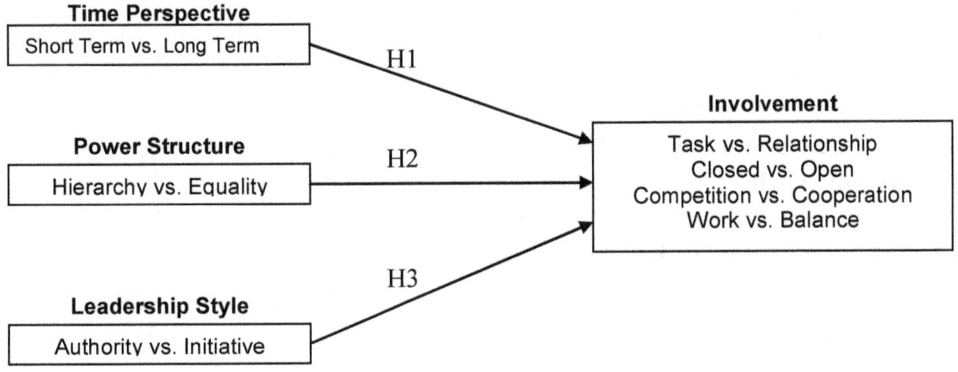

Finally, anti-terror work needs cooperative initiative in critical situations. Therefore, an authoritarian leadership style might damage cooperative orientation (Brehm & Gates, 1993). On the other hand, a leadership style characterized by managed initiative and creativity might strengthen cooperative orientation (Ashby & Longley, 2005; Luen & Al-Hawamdeh, 2001). We suggest that if the police officer perceives authoritarian leadership style, then the person will tend to be less cooperative oriented.

Hypothesis 3: Stronger authoritarian leadership style perceived by the police officer is negatively related to the police officer's degree of cooperative orientation.

The Case of Police Culture

There seems to be no such thing as one single police culture. Depending on organization, structure and task, culture in the police varies. In this research, anti-terror police and criminal investigation police in Norway are compared. Although Norway has one police service which is based on the principle of coherence, meaning that all functions are in one organization, significant occupational differences were found. The most significant difference in occupational culture is found on the scale from time firm vs. time floats. Police officers in the anti-terror police find that time schedules, deadlines and speed are important in their job. On the other hand, police officers in the criminal investigation police find sufficient time and not being run by the clock are important in their job. The second most significant difference in occupational culture is found on the scale from legality vs. effective. Police officers in the anti-terror police find it more important to follow laws and instructions.

There seems to be no such thing as one single police culture. Depending on organization, structure and task, culture in the police varies. For example, Christensen and Crank (2001) found cultural differences between police officers in urban and nonurban areas, while Reuss-Ianni (1993) made a distinction between street cops and management cops.

In this research, we study anti-terror police and criminal investigation police in Norway. We have formulated the following research question: *How does police culture differ in anti-terror vs. criminal investigation police?*

This research is important, as leadership approaches in police management are dependent on insights into the occupational culture of police officers. If, for example, the culture is focused on time constraints rather than work quality, then leadership might be effective if work performance is monitored by the time factor.

In this section, we compare the occupational culture of the anti-terror police with the occupational culture of the criminal investigation service in Norway. We conducted surveys in both organizations. The questionnaire had eighteen scales to measure occupational culture.

Survey results are listed in Figure 9.5. Each scale had two extremes, at 1 and 7, respectively. For example, one scale said that time is firm or time floats. Police officers in the anti-terror organization finds that time is firm (1,83), while police officers in the criminal investigation service finds that time floats (5,06).

The most significant difference in occupational culture is found on the scale from time firm vs. time floats, as illustrated in Figure 9.5. Police officers in the anti-terror police find that time schedules, deadlines and speed are important in their job. On the other hand, police officers in the criminal investigation police find sufficient time and not being run by the clock are important in their job.

The second most significant difference in occupational culture is found on the scale from legality vs. effective. Police officers in the anti-terror police find it very important to follow laws, regulations, guidelines and instructions in doing the job. On the other hand, police officers in the criminal investigation police find it just as important to be effective and efficient, by demonstrating a willingness to fight serious crimes, without necessarily following exactly laws and instructions.

Figure 9.5. Statistics for the comparison of occupational culture between anti-terror police and criminal investigation police in Norway (Likert scale 1 to 7)

#	Item	Anti-Terror	Criminal	Significance
1	Time firm vs. time floats	1,83	5,06	123,633***
2	Legality vs. effective	1,71	3,13	26,701***
3	Direct vs. indirect	2,54	4,06	22,366***
4	Open vs. closed	2,52	4,06	20,924***
5	Informal vs. formal	2,33	3,63	15,256***
6	Equality vs. hierarchy	2,38	3,75	14,296***
7	Safe vs. challenge	2,40	3,53	13,361**
8	Change vs. tradition	3,33	4,56	11,925***
9	Applied vs. theoretical	2,14	3,06	10,430**
10	Liberty vs. control	3,19	4,25	9,502**
11	Individualism vs. cooperation	5,44	4,56	7,042**
12	Privacy vs. openness	5,31	4,69	4,283*
13	Competition vs. cooperation	4,81	5,25	1,814
14	Task vs. relationship	3,31	3,63	1,087
15	Firm leader vs. individual	3,73	4,06	,799
16	Work vs. balance	4,35	4,00	,692
17	Short term vs. long term	4,38	4,56	,175
18	Act vs. plan	3,85	4,00	,169

*Note: The statistical significance of the t-values is ***for p<.001, ** for p<.01, and * for p<.05*

Differences in occupational culture can be explained by organization, structure and task. While the anti-terror unit has to react quickly and precisely in an emergency situation, criminal investigators have to spend time to organize and carry out the investigation. The timeframe for an anti-terror police officer to act can be extremely short, while criminal investigation can go on for quite some time. Therefore, it comes as no surprise that the scale time firm vs. time floats receives very different scores in the two organizations.

The second most significant difference in occupational culture is a little surprising. It might seem that criminal investigators can ignore the law as long as they are effective and efficient in their investigations. However, we have to remind ourselves of the scale here, running from 1 to 7. An average score of 3,13 is slightly closer to following the letter of the law than to following free initiatives.

We find many similar culture dimensions. For example, both prefer to work long term rather than short term. A long time perspective implies a thorough decision-making process and an ability to sustain relationships over long periods of time.

Overall, the anti-terror police officers have the highest average score on the scale from individualism to cooperation, where the average score is 5,44. This implies that the group's needs are put first, and that each officer takes responsibility for the group's actions.

Similarly, the criminal investigators have the highest average score on the scale from competition to cooperation, where the average score is 5,25. This implies that the internal cooperation in the organization has priority.

This section documents both similarities and differences in the Norwegian police. Both anti-terror police and criminal investigators find cooperation important. The anti-terror police officers are concerned with fixed time limits, while criminal investigators consider time to be flexible. This section illustrates the importance of understanding both similarities and differences for leadership in large organizations such as the police.

The Case of Police Value Shop

Based on a literature review, this section suggests potential determinants of police performance in the value shop. Determinants include occupational culture, knowledge sharing, leadership roles and stages of information technology. Because the pilot study of police investigation officers had a limited sample, hypotheses could not be tested. However, statistical results from the study provide interesting insights into both the dependent variable (value shop) and the independent variables (occupational culture, knowledge sharing, leadership roles and knowledge management technology).

At a seminar for criminal investigators, a questionnaire was handed out to measure the extent to which the participants found that they were performing the tasks in each primary activity. Results are listed in Figure 9.6.

The self reporting suggests good performance with slight variation, as illustrated in Figure 5.9 with average responses at or above 5.0 on a scale from 1 to 7. Figure 9.7 investigates whether there are significant differences in performance between primary activities.

Figure 9.7 shows significantly lower performance for the final primary activity. Evaluation of the implementation and learning received a significantly lower score. This might imply that police officers find that evaluation activities have the greatest potential for improvement.

Discussion

It is an investigative truism that "information is the lifeblood of an investigation." Yet in many investigations police and security personnel fail to fully utilize the diverse

Figure 9.6. Performance in primary activities of the value shop (1=little extent,

#	Primary activities in the value shop	Scale items	Scale reliability	Scale average
1	Problem understanding and diagnosis	7 (none deleted to improve reliability)	.70	5.5
2	Alternative solutions to the problem solutions	6 (none deleted to improve reliability)	.72	5.4
3	Choice of best solution to the problem	9 (none deleted to improve reliability)	.79	5.4
4	Implementation of best solution to the problem	8 (two deleted to improve reliability)	.71	5.9
5	Evaluation of the implementation and learning	9 (none deleted to improve reliability)	.84	5.0

Figure 9.7. Statistical test for significant performance differences

#	Primary activities in the value shop	1	2	3	4	5
1	Problem understanding and diagnosis		.406	.482	-1.594	4.383**
2	Alternative solutions to the problem solutions			.541	-2.336*	3.890**
3	Choice of best solution to the problem				-2.907*	2.435*
4	Implementation of best solution to the problem					4.163**
5	Evaluation of the implementation and learning					

range of different types of information readily available to them, which can add significant value to an investigation. In effect, potentially useful information simply falls between the cracks in an investigation. In serious, complex and/or high profile crimes and security type terrorism threats, the risks of missing such informational gaps and cracks poses a very real and present danger.

To address this "falling between the cracks" informational phenomenon, Dean (2005) devised and developed a deliberate low-tech "Cross+Check" system that the average investigator can be trained in to use on a daily basis without the need for expensive or sophisticated equipment. The C+C system teaches an investigator to think in a logically grounded and creatively systematic manner using different types of information about a crime or security problem.

The core of the C+C system is its ability to bring together and focus on the interrelationships between four qualitatively different levels of information. The goal of the C+C system is to generate and then prioritize the investigative leads that logically flow out of systematically "cross+checking" informational interrelationships in order to not only plan and manage an overall investigative strategy but also to develop leads into evidence.

The "Cross+Check" system originated out of attempts at playing around on paper with the idea of trying to make sense out of the bewildering array of often competing profiling approaches available in the criminal justice market place. Students were beset with claims and counter-claims of which approach is best.

What students and practitioners alike needed was a framework or "map" that charted where each criminal profiling approach and/or model fitted in relation to other approaches and which also provided a holistic way to understand and comprehend the various contributions of each approach.

Apart from the practical advantage of using one working folder with all the relevant investigative information itemized in it, the core operational advantage of the C+C system lies in its ability to bring together and visually analyze the interrelationships between four qualitatively different sources of information — that of *police/security* information, *descriptive* information, *diagnostic* information and *research* information.

The C+C system utilizes these four types of qualitatively different information to develop inferences and then test the veracity of such inferences by checking them against each of these four levels of information in the system. This systematic process of analysis also allows an investigator to place a relative weighting on developed inferences and hence to prioritize investigative leads.

Knowledge management as a field of study is concerned with simplifying and improving the process of sharing, distributing, creating, capturing and understanding knowledge. Hence, knowledge management has direct relevance to policing. So much so that Europol has a "Knowledge Management Centre" (KMC) at The Hague in the Netherlands. Europol regularly updates its database at KMC to ensure it keeps abreast of new developments in technology, science or other specialized fields in order to provide optimal law enforcement.

Conclusion

This chapter proposed that police investigation success is positively related to team climate, knowledge sharing perceptions and stage of knowledge management technology. Furthermore, we propose that police investigation success is more positively related to the spokesman role than to other leadership roles for the team manager. These four research propositions for determinants of police investigation success should be empirically explored in future research.

Some of the important causal influences between knowledge management and IT outsourcing relationships are mapped in the causal loop diagram in Figure 9.8. Causal loop diagramming is described by Sterman (2000) and presented as a tool by www.vensim.com.

As illustrated in Figure 9.8, police investigation success is dependent on knowledge sharing, leadership roles and organizational culture, in addition to crime complexity. When crime complexity increases, resource mobilization increases, leading to more knowledge management technology, which improves knowledge sharing, leading to a higher level of investigation success.

Figure 9.8. Causal loop diagram for knowledge management in police investigations

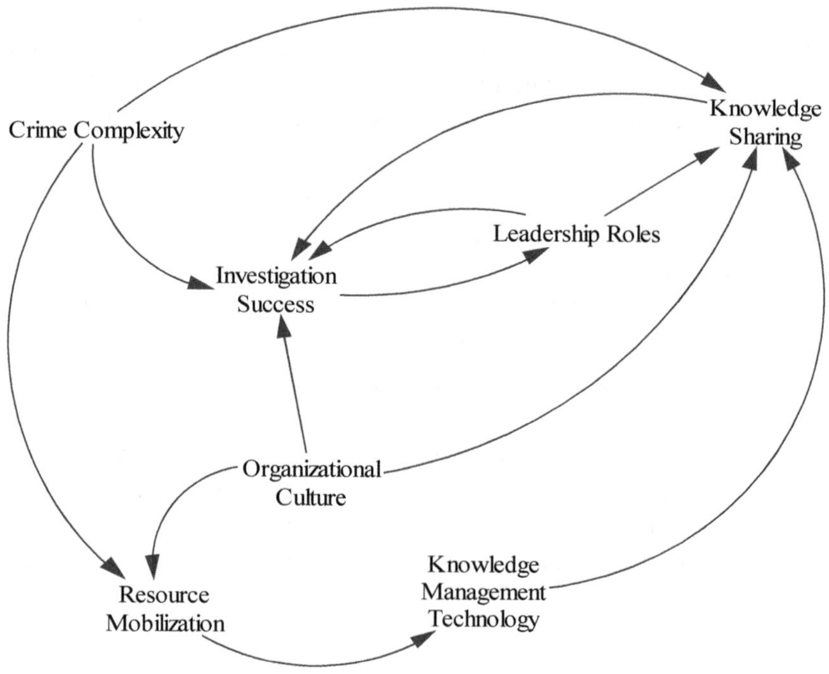

Figure 9.9. Positive feedback loop in the causal loop diagram

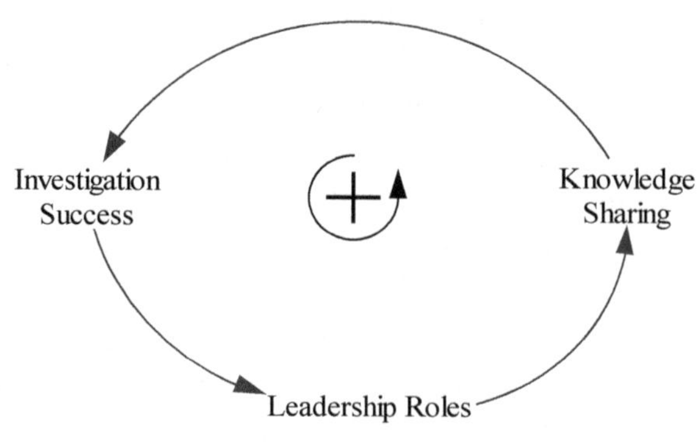

One positive feedback loop in Figure 9.8 is illustrated in Figure 9.9. When knowledge sharing increases, investigation success rises. As a consequence, management takes on leadership roles that further encourage knowledge sharing.

Questions for Discussion

1. How can technology at each stage support each investigative thinking style?
2. How can knowledge management systems support police investigation units as value shops?
3. How would you organize knowledge sharing among detectives who are working on the same criminal case?

List of References

Adhami, E., & Browne, D. (1996). *Major crime enquiries: Improving expert support for detectives*. Special Interest Series, Paper 9, London: Home Office Police Research Group.

Archbold, C. A. (2005). Managing the bottom line: Risk management in policing. *Policing: An International Journal of Police Strategies & Management, 28*(1), 30-48.

Ashby, D. I., & Longley, P. A. (2005). Geocomputation, geodemographics and resource allocation for local policing. *Transactions in GIS, 9*(1), 53-72.

Brehm, J., & Gates, S. (1993). Donut shops and speed traps: Evaluating models of supervision on police behavior. *American Journal of Political Science, 37*(2), 555-581.

Chen, H., Schroeder, J., Hauck, R. V., Ridgeway, L., Atabakhsh, H., Gupta, H., Boarman, C., et al. (2002). COPLINK Connect: Information and knowledge management for law enforcement. *Decision Support Systems*, 34, 271-285.

Chen, H., Zheng, D., Atabakhsh, H., Wyzga, W., & Schroeder, J. (2003). COPLINK — Managing law enforcement data and knowledge. *Communications of the ACM, 46*(1), 28-34.

Christensen, W., & Crank, J. P. (2001). Police work and culture in a nonurban setting: An ethnographical analysis. *Police Quarterly, 4*(1), 69-98.

Crawshaw, R., Devlin, B., & Williamson, T. (1998). *Human rights and policing.* The Netherlands: Kluwer Law International.

Dean, G. (1995). Police reform: Rethinking operational policing. *American Journal of Criminal Justice, 23*(4), 337-347.

Dean, G. (2000). *The experience of investigation for detectives*. Unpublished PhD thesis, Brisbane, Australia: Queensland University of Technology.

Dean, G. (2005). *The cognitive psychology of police investigators*. Conference paper, School of Justice Studies, Faculty of Law, Queensland University of Technology, Brisbane, Australia.

Eisenhardt, K. M. (1985). Control: Organizational and economic approaches. *Management Science, 31*(2), 134-149.

Fielding, N. (1984). Police socialization and police competence. *The British Journal of Sociology, 35*(4), 568-590.

Glomseth, R. (2004). *Norway, World Police Encyclopedia.*

Hansen, M. T., Nohria, N., & Tierney, T. (1999, March-April). What's your strategy for managing knowledge? *Harvard Business Review*, 106-116.

Home Office (2005). *Guidance on statutory performance indicators for policing 205/2006.* Police Standards Unit, Home Office of the UK Government, www.policereform.gov.uk.

Jackson, A. L., & Wade, J. E. (2005). Police perceptions of social capital and sense of responsibility. *Policing: An International Journal of Police Strategies & Management, 28*(1), 49-68.

Kahana, E. (2001). Mossad-CIA cooperation. *International Journal of Intelligence and CounterIntelligence, 14,* 409-420.

Kelley, T. M. (2005). Mental health and prospective police professionals. *Policing: An International Journal of Police Strategies & Management, 28*(1), 6-29.

Kiely, J. A., & Peek, G. S. (2002). The culture of the British police: Views of police officers. *The Service Industries Journal, 22*(1), 167-183.

Kim, C. W., & Mauborgne, R. (2003, April). Tipping point leadership. *Harvard Business Review*, 61-69.

Lahneman, W. J. (2004). Knowledge-sharing in the intelligence community after 9/11. *International Journal of Intelligence and Counterintelligence, 1,* 614-633.

Leishman, F., & Savage, S. P. (1993). Officers or managers? Direct entry into British police management. *International Journal of Public Sector Management, 6*(5), 4-11.

Luen, T. W., & Al-Hawamdeh, S. (2001). Knowledge management in the public sector: Principles and practices in police work. *Journal of Information Science, 27*(5), 311-318.

Reuss-Ianni, E. (1993). *Two cultures of policing: Street cops and management cops*. New Brunswick, NJ: Transaction Publishers.

Sterman, J. D. (2000). *Business dynamics: Systems thinking and modeling for a complex world*. Boston: McGraw-Hill.

Zamanou, S., & Glaser, S. R. (1994). Moving toward participation and involvement. *Group & Organization Management, 19*(4), 475-502.

Chapter X

Law Firm Knowledge

Introduction

A law firm can be understood as a social community specializing in the speed and efficiency of the creation and transfer of legal knowledge (Nahapiet & Ghoshal, 1998). Many law firms represent large corporate enterprises, organizations or entrepreneurs with a need for continuous and specialized legal services that can only be supplied by a team of lawyers. The client is a customer of the firm, rather than a particular lawyer. According to Galanter and Palay (1991, p. 5), relationships with clients tend to be enduring:

Firms represent large corporate enterprises, organizations, or entrepreneurs with a need for continuous (or recurrent) and specialized legal services that could be supplied only by a team of lawyers. The client 'belongs to' the firm, not to a particular lawyer. Relations with clients tend to be enduring. Such repeat clients are able to reap benefits from the continuity and economies of scale and scope enjoyed by the firm.

Lawyers as Knowledge Workers

Lawyers can be defined as knowledge workers. They are professionals who have gained knowledge through formal education (explicit) and through learning on the job (tacit). Often, there is some variation in the quality of their education and learning. The value of professionals' education tends to hold throughout their careers. For example, lawyers in Norway are asked whether they got the good grade of "laud," even thirty years after graduation. Professionals' prestige (which is based partly on the institutions from which they obtained their education) is a valuable organizational resource because of the elite social networks that provide access to valuable external resources for the firm (Hitt et al., 2001).

After completing their advanced educational requirements, most professionals enter their careers as associates in law. In this role, they continue to learn and, thus, they gain significant tacit knowledge through "learning by doing." Therefore, they largely bring explicit knowledge derived from formal education into their firms and build tacit knowledge through experience.

Most professional service firms use a partnership form of organization. In such a framework, those who are highly effective in using and applying knowledge are eventually rewarded with partner status, and thus own stakes in a firm. On their road to partnership, these professionals acquire considerable knowledge, much of which is tacit. Thus, by the time professionals achieve partnership, they have built human capital in the form of individual skills (Hitt et al., 2001).

Because law is precedent-driven, its practitioners are heavily invested in knowing how things have been done before. Jones (2000) found that many attorneys, therefore, are already oriented toward the basic premises of knowledge management, though they have been practicing it on a more individualized basis and without the help of technology and virtual collaboration. As such, a knowledge management initiative could find the areas where lawyers are already sharing information and then introduce modern technology to support this information sharing to make it more effective.

Lawyers work in law firms, and law firms belong to the legal industry. According to Becker et al. (2001), the legal industry will change rapidly because of three important trends. First, global companies increasingly seek out law firms that can provide consistent support at all business locations and integrated cross-border assistance for significant mergers and acquisitions as well as capital-market transactions. Second, client loyalty is decreasing as companies increasingly base purchases of legal services on a more objective assessment of their value, defined as benefits net of price. Finally, new competitors have entered the market, such as accounting and Internet-based legal services firms.

In this book, the notion *lawyer* is used most of the time. Other notions, such as *attorney* and *solicitor* are sometimes used as synonyms. In reality, these words can have different meanings, together with notions such as *barrister*, *counselor* and *advocate*. In Norwegian, a distinction is made between a lawyer (*jurist*) and a solicitor (*advokat*). There is no need to make such distinctions in this book.

Lawyers are knowledge workers. To understand the organizational form of lawyers as knowledge workers employed in companies such as law firms, there is a need to recognize the dual dependent relationship between knowledge workers and the organization. On the one hand, for the purpose of channeling the motivation and effort of employees to serve the interests of the firm, management will seek to exploit knowledge workers' need to rely on the organization for resources (i.e., advanced computer software and hardware, which are available at a high cost) to accomplish their work tasks. On the other hand, management depends on knowledge workers for their esoteric and advanced knowledge and their ability to synthesize theoretical and contextual knowledge. Management, therefore, needs to meet these employees' aspirations and expectations. As for knowledge workers, they need to depend on the organization as the locale to develop contextual knowledge and to create new knowledge. However, their ability to apply theoretical knowledge in other contexts, that is, in other organizations, means that to a certain extent, they are also able to pursue a limited form of marketization. This enables them to reap market-level rewards for their expertise (May et al., 2002).

Knowledge Categories

To get started on this job, legal industry knowledge has to be understood. Edwards and Mahling (1997) have suggested that law firms have four categories of knowledge: administrative, declarative, procedural and analytical, as defined earlier in this book. These knowledge categories are all important to the law firm. While any law firm needs to maintain efficient administrative records, there does not appear to be any significant possibility for gaining strategic advantage in the firm's core competency of providing sound legal advice to its clients by using these records. The detailed administrative knowledge they contain is essential to the operation of the law firm, but does not contribute to the substantive content. Declarative, procedural and analytical knowledge offer greater possibilities for creating strategic value to the firm.

Edwards and Mahling (1997) present a case drawn from the collection of one of the authors to illustrate the differences in strategic value among procedural, declarative and analytical knowledge. In the early 1990s, one of the authors, at the time engaged in the practice of law, represented a corporate client as seller in several sales of corporate businesses and real estate. At the time, buyers of businesses and real estate had become concerned about their possible liability for pollution existing on property when they purchased it. The U.S. federal laws governing the legal responsibility of landowners for environmental contamination on their property had been adopted a few years earlier and their full impact on sale of businesses was just beginning to be understood.

The relevant declarative knowledge was an understanding of several related state and federal laws and agency regulations governing liability for environmental contamination. The relevant procedural knowledge, in part, was to know how to transfer the environmental licenses and permits used by a given business to a new owner and how to transfer the real estate as an asset. The relevant analytical knowledge was to understand what risks the buyer of a contaminated property faced (legal and financial) and what contractual protections the seller could reasonably give to the buyer.

Law firms are interesting in themselves from both a knowledge and a management perspective. From a management perspective, law firm partners own a typical law firm. Among themselves, the partners appoint a board and a managing partner. In addition, they hire a chief executive officer (CEO) to run all support functions in the firm, such as financial management (CFO), knowledge management (CKO) and information technology management (CIO).

Jones (2000) found that top-down directives are complicated in the legal industry. In large U.S. and UK law firms. The power can be spread among as many as 150 partners, who generally have different specialty areas, different work and management styles and vastly different groups under their control. Earning a consensus is not an easy proposition — especially when the funding for new initiatives such as knowledge management is coming directly out of the partners' yearly income. At the same time, partners are the ones who have the most to gain if their firm is able to manage knowledge effectively to keep lucrative clients on board and attract new ones through new services.

The human capital embodied in the partners is a professional service firm's most important resource. Their experience, particularly as partners, builds valuable industry-specific and firm-specific knowledge, which is often tacit. Such knowledge is the least imitable form of knowledge. An important responsibility of partners is obtaining and maintaining clients. Partners build relationships with current and potential clients and, over time, develop social capital through their client networks. Therefore, the experience a professional gains as a partner contributes to competitive advantage (Hitt et al., 2001).

Partners with education from the best institutions and with the most experience as partners in particular legal areas represent substantial human capital to the firm. As partners, they continue to acquire knowledge, largely tacit and firm-specific, and build social capital. This human capital should produce the highest-quality services to clients and thereby contribute significantly to firm performance. The job of partner differs from that of associate, and new skills must be developed. Partners must build the skills needed to develop and maintain effective relationships with clients. Importantly, partners in law firms serve as project and team leaders on specific cases and thus must develop managerial skills.

Partners own the most human capital in a firm and have the largest stakes using the firm's resources to the greatest advantage. One of the responsibilities of partners is to help develop the knowledge of other employees of the firm, particularly its associates. Associates at law firms need to learn internal routines, the situation of important clients and nuances in the application of law (Hitt et al., 2001).

Information technology support for knowledge management in law firms has to consider the very special knowledge situation in each law firm. Edwards and Mahling (1997, p. 162) argue that knowledge is dispersed among many different members of the firm, and others outside the firm may contribute to knowledge. Law firm knowledge has a wide variety of sources, both inside and outside the firm. Much administrative knowledge is generated by the members of the firm as billing records for their services. The firm's administrative staff creates other administrative information. Attorneys are the major source of analytical, declarative and procedural knowledge. Legal assistants also have some declarative knowledge based on their experience. Declarative knowledge can also be found in publicly available sources intended for research purposes, primarily books, online subscription research sources and CD-ROM resources. The quantity of publicly available research material for any given topic depends significantly on the size of the market for the information. The more specialized the legal area, the smaller the potential market for material and the less that is usually widely available. Experienced legal assistants are usually an invaluable source of procedural knowledge, since much procedural work is delegated to them. Legal assistants are common in countries such as the U.S. and UK, but they are seldom found in law firms in countries such as Norway and Sweden.

Experienced legal secretaries may have a significant amount of procedural knowledge for transactions they handle often. Law firms in Norway employ many secretaries. It is common to find more than one secretary for every three lawyers in a law firm.

The role of others outside the law firm in generating analytical and procedural knowledge needs to be noted. While much of the useful procedural and analytical knowledge resides in firm employees, it is likely that there are sources outside the firm as well. One belief frequently expressed in the knowledge management literature is the view that learning is social: People learn in groups. These groups are known in the literature as communities of practice.

Communities of practice have been defined as groups of people who are informally bound to one another by exposure to a common class of problem. It is quite likely that the communities of practice for the lawyers in the firm include other members of professional associations such as bar associations. These groups usually have a number of committees devoted to practice areas, such as environmental law. In Norway, Den Norske Advokatforening (Norwegian Lawyers Association) has such committees.

Generally, the idea of communities of practice developed in the organizational learning movement. The idea posits that knowledge flows best through networks of people who may not be in the same part of the organization, or in the same organization but have the same work interests. Some firms have attempted to formalize these communities, even though theorists argue that they should emerge in self-organizing fashion without any relationship to formal organizational structures (Grover & Davenport, 2001).

A few more technologically advanced lawyers may use the Internet or such subscription services such as Counsel Connect in the U.S. on the World Wide Web as a sounding board for analytical and procedural issues in a community of legal practice. These external sources can provide knowledge in the form of informal conversations, written newsletters and updates, briefs filed in relevant litigation and other forms.

An obvious problem in law firms is that knowledge is not consistently documented, and documented knowledge is not always explicit. Much administrative information is captured in electronic form as part of the firm's billing records. Other administrative data resides in the firm's payroll and benefits records and file and records management systems. Much of the firm's declarative knowledge resides in the memories of the firm's attorneys and in their work product. As noted above, the firm has access to publicly available declarative knowledge in the form of published reference works, and declarative knowledge is typically the best-documented type of knowledge.

Much procedural knowledge is documented throughout the firm's files in the form of completed records of transactions, which provide guidance about what legal documents were necessary to complete a certain type of transaction. The knowledge of procedure reflected in these documents is often implicit rather than explicit. Explicit procedural knowledge is contained in a collection of written practice guides for popular areas like real estate transactions. These guides include standard checklists of items necessary to complete a particular transaction for the kinds of transactions that occur frequently.

Analytical knowledge resides primarily in attorneys' heads. Analytical knowledge is occasionally documented in client files through the notes of an attorney's thought processes. More often it is reflected in the completed contract documents or other transaction documents by the inclusion of specific clauses dealing with a particular topic. The analytical knowledge reflected in completed documents is very often not explicit, in the sense that it is often not clear from the face of the document what analytical issues are dealt with in the document.

Another law firm problem is that knowledge is often shared on an informal basis. Certain methods of sharing knowledge, at least within the firm, have traditionally been part of large law firm culture. One of the most important ways of sharing knowledge has been through the process of partners training associates to perform tasks. In larger firms, the practice of hiring young, bright law school graduates who were trained, supervised and rewarded by a partner has been followed throughout most of this century. The method focuses on transmitting knowledge from more experienced attorneys to less experienced ones, as distinguished from transmitting it to other partners in the firm or to legal assistants and other support staff.

This attorney training customarily has relied on informal methods of transmitting knowledge, such as rotating young attorneys through a series of practice groups within the firm. Much of this informal training takes place via collaborative work on documents such as contracts and pleadings. Some of it occurs through informal consultation between a senior attorney and a junior attorney about the best way to handle a specific task. These consultations may be carried out by face-to-face discussions, e-mail or telephone conversations. No attempt is usually made to capture the substance of the training through these informal methods, even where a form of communication, such as e-mail, may often be used that could produce documentation. It is important to note that this training often takes place under intense time pressure. Further, in an hourly billing system there is often little or no financial incentive to produce documentation, which cannot be billed directly to a client.

In addition to problems of knowledge dispersion, inconsistent documentation and informal knowledge sharing, Edwards and Mahling (1997, p. 164) argue that if knowledge has been documented, it is contained in a mixture of paper and electronic formats and located in dispersed physical locations. Administrative information typically exists in a combination of print and electronic formats. A large firm would customarily maintain computerized databases for key matters such as tracking lawyers' hourly billings, client contact data and staff assignments to projects but would usually generate paper invoices to clients. The data physically resides in the firm's computer network and in paper files.

Declarative, procedural and analytical knowledge is often documented in attorney work products such as briefs, memoranda and actual legal documents, such as contracts, wills and instruments of transfer. Work product documents typically are created in electronic form but are customarily stored in print format client files. The electronic format materials are stored in standalone personal computers or on the network. Paper materials are located throughout the firm's offices.

Where knowledge has been documented in a law firm, often only a few simple tools exist to facilitate the retrieval of this knowledge by topic. Attorney work files are usually indexed by client name and matter name but their contents are seldom indexed for subject matter in more than the most general way. An attorney creating a particular item of work product may place it in a firm's standards database maintained in electronic format. These standard documents can then be used by other lawyers as examples or models. In a typical installation, the standard forms library is stored on the network and is physically available to those who have network access. The standard forms library allows access to individual documents by name but subject matter classification is often limited to what can be included in a descriptive DOS format file name. Retrieving material from the forms library thus usually requires tedious sequential search and review of the contents of the library.

Access to the procedural and analytical knowledge embodied in client files is difficult at best for those not familiar with the files. The client files are often not indexed by subject matter, making it difficult to locate procedural or analytical knowledge on a particular topic if the contents of the file are not already familiar. Document management systems do support network-wide searches for documents in electronic form by selected attributes such as document author name or keywords appearing in the document. In the absence of a consistent system of classifying the document's contents by subject or topic, however, keyword searches by topic produce incomplete retrieval of all relevant documents.

Even if knowledge is documented by work product, such as a memorandum to file, access to the implicit procedural and analytical knowledge embodied in the firm's files is often difficult at best. Client files that are indexed according to a subject-based system may offer some help in searching for analytical knowledge. A large transaction, however, may include dozens of analytical issues and it is unlikely that all of them would be indexed. Procedural knowledge is unlikely to be indexed at all. This means that the user must often rely on the ability to search by keywords for relevant fact patterns to retrieve relevant procedural or analytical knowledge.

Some knowledge in a law firm raises issues of security and confidentiality. There are few confidentiality concerns with declarative knowledge. This type of knowledge is meant to be public and readily accessible to all. Analytical and procedural knowledge within the firm can, however, raise issues of security and client confidentiality. Attorneys in the firm have professional ethical obligations to their clients to maintain the confidentiality of information furnished by the client. While these ethical obligations are customarily interpreted to permit sharing the information among the firm's members and staff, appropriate precautions still must be taken to avoid disclosures outside the firm.

Implications for Systems Design

Edwards and Mahling (1997) find that their observations have implications for system design. They believe that their observations about the characteristics of knowledge within large law firms have implications for the design of knowledge management tools for these firms. There is not a one-to-one correspondence between their observations and the implications for design, as some observations have a number of ramifications for the design tools. The following discussion of the implications for system specifications is important. A number of specification issues concern the roles of different end users of a knowledge management system in a large law firm. Gatekeepers, knowledge librarians and other specialists should be named:

- A gatekeeper capable of evaluating materials for inclusion must be named;
- To assure accuracy, knowledge should be edited before being made accessible; and
- To assure currency, the knowledge should be reviewed periodically after it has been placed in the knowledge base.

Another set of specifications deals with the strategy and trail of knowledge items, thus putting isolated knowledge pieces into organizational context:

- To maximize the strategic value created by a knowledge base, it must focus on the type of knowledge that has been identified as having the best potential strategic value. A selection process must be established for inclusion in the knowledge base. There should be agreement about the types of knowledge that are to be captured in the knowledge base as having strategic value to the firm.
- Users must have access to the name the knowledge source. It must be easy to identify the creator of a particular item of knowledge.
- It must be easy to learn the history of a particular item in the knowledge base: the date it was added, the date of any revisions and the frequency with which it has been used.
- The tools must be able to extract the useful knowledge while preserving the confidentiality of client information. Some portions of the knowledge base must support restricted access.

The collaborative aspects of knowledge are related to specifications that border on the areas of organizational memory and collective intelligence:

- Because many firm members can create knowledge, all firm members should be able to share knowledge. All knowledge management tools should be in an electronic form and available on a network accessible by all firm members. Portions of the tools should be accessible by external users with appropriate security mechanisms.
- The system must facilitate the informal sharing of knowledge. Users should be able to identify creators of knowledge on a particular topic. The system should facilitate contact with the creator of knowledge by e-mail, telephone or online conference. Users should also be able to transmit items readily by e-mail or other electronic communications.

- To encourage users to document their knowledge, it should be easy to add material to the knowledge base. As far as possible, the system should capture information without requiring much additional effort from the creator.

Knowledge acquisition and the elicitation of knowledge are crucial factors on the input side. Technical and organizational factors are concerned:

- User tools should be suitable for use by users with a wide variety of both substantive legal knowledge and technological sophistication.
- There should be incentives to document knowledge. When items are added to the system, the source must be identifiable. It should be possible to measure the use of an item once it is placed in the system.

An electronic format of structured and unstructured knowledge objects is a rather basic specification for knowledge management tools. Closely connected to this aspect is the retrieval and presentation of knowledge:

- The tools must be able to capture and manipulate knowledge in a variety of formats, both electronic (word processing, e-mail and electronic database search results) and paper.
- Users should be able to retrieve knowledge in a format that can readily be exported to a word processor for inclusion in a work product.
- The tools must permit at least rudimentary subject matter indexing. Users must be able to search, sort and retrieve knowledge in the system by subject.
- The system must facilitate the retrieval of implicit procedural and analytical knowledge. Users must be able to conduct keyword searches for relevant fact attributes that are not indexed. The use of other tools, such as intelligent agents and collaborative filtering programs, which could facilitate the retrieval of implicit knowledge, should be explored.

IT support for knowledge management is only at the beginning. But some law firms are making progress, and these firms may be ready for the next technology wave. According to Jones (2000), for the firms that have already embraced knowledge management, the next wave will likely include a stronger focus on client-facing extranets and the development of expert systems. Extranets are essential for ensuring lasting relationships with clients, not only because they increase a client's access to their counsel, but because the firm gets linked tightly with the client so that the client will remain with the firm. Expert systems are showing huge potential efficiency returns and hold promise for much of the transactional work-tax matters, real estate closings and financial closings that make up the bulk of legal services. Capturing the knowledge upon which the systems are based is a more complicated process than setting up collaborative systems among practice groups.

Edwards and Mahling (1997) summarize the situation for IT support for knowledge management in law firms by stating that they believe a significant opportunity exists in large law firms for the successful use of knowledge management tools. These firms are currently performing some knowledge management tasks with tools which offer only rudimentary knowledge management capability and which are not fully integrated with the firms' existing technology. None of the currently available tools satisfies all of the user requirements they have identified. The tools that are currently available do not adequately support the informal knowledge sharing which is a key element of knowledge management in these firms. Tools must be configured to support and encourage informal collaboration and a stronger information-sharing culture. In these organizations, where performance is measured by the number of billable hours, knowledge management tools must minimize the amount of effort required of the user. They must become as invisible as possible.

Many authors are concerned with firm culture as a determining factor for knowledge management. O'Connor (2000) suggests that compensation, individuality, billing and tradition are some of the most important barriers to knowledge management initiatives in today's firm:

- **Compensation:** Compensation models are one of the toughest hurdles. Although some firms have lock-step compensation models, where attorneys are not as adversely impacted for spending time on knowledge sharing activities, most don't. In those firms that do typically place a premium on billable hours, lawyers not hitting billable targets feel the sting. The practical impact: It's a challenge to convince lawyers to contribute content into knowledge management systems.
- **Individuality:** Lawyers are lone wolves; moving to team collaboration can be a tough transition. Law is intensely competitive, from getting in to the right school, to making the school's law review, to clerking for the right justice, to getting a job at the right firm. Competitiveness is ingrained in the legal psyche. Most lawyers remain intensely competitive, even in their own firms. How do you reconcile this mindset with demands to share knowledge with your coworkers? Lawyers must transition from believing that by transferring knowledge they somehow become less important, to believing the old adage that "All boats rise with the tide."

- **Billing:** Most firms still bill principally on a time and materials basis. Although clients are demanding fixed price bids and not-to-exceed estimates; competition (beauty contests) are thriving and many firms have not fully embraced new billing models. Old school lawyers believe efficiency results in lower revenues. In their view, why spend lots of money to get more efficient, when it adversely impacts the business?
- **Tradition:** Attorneys are often skeptical about new ways of doing things. Tradition reigns, it can be difficult to accept radically different approaches.

So, how can a firm address these challenges? O'Connor (2000) suggests that first and foremost, management must be committed to the knowledge management program and provide tangible support:

- Executive managers must understand why the firm is investing in KM, commit the necessary funds and throw their weight behind the team doing the work. Ideally, firm leaders should prepare a *one-minute-speech* so that they can quickly and easily articulate the firm's KM strategy. Furthermore, second-tier management must be involved, that is, practice and department heads are also informed, and they must be active supporters. Discuss KM plans at partnership meetings and retreats — spread the message about why it is important.
- The first step is to conduct a *knowledge audit*. This involves spending time with the right people in the practice areas, and identifying how knowledge is created and transferred, with an eye for areas for improvement. Focus on the practice and spend time with lawyers in the practice areas; understand what they do, and ascertain how we can improve the practice. Consider a broad-based knowledge management team, comprised of attorneys and staff, representative of the firm's practice areas and locations. For example, Shearman & Sterling, a law firm in the U.S., has created a Knowledge Advisory Board composed of just such a collection of lawyers and staff. They meet regularly to direct the strategy and overall plan for the firm's knowledge management initiative, with a real focus on best practices.
- The next step is to develop a *plan* to address the needs, which have been distilled from this effort. It should focus on how the firm can capture and reuse important knowledge assets. Content is king. If we don't have a method and process for easily capturing and accessing helpful information, then we will not be successful.
- One of the key elements of the plan must be how we will create *processes that facilitate knowledge sharing*. The processes must be unobtrusive or they will not be followed, the content will provide marginal value and the utility and

benefits of the system will suffer. This may be the most important consideration of all. Sherman & Sterling created a role of Knowledge Coordinator in each practice group. These people not only help to determine what processes make sense, they are also directly responsible for ensuring that their respective practice areas participate.

- Try a little *marketing* and shameless self-promotion. How we pitch KM in the firm may be a great determinant of its success. When considering KM, it all sounds too dramatic and complicated for lawyers to really embrace. Bonnie Speer-McGrath, of Speer Software Training, suggests that the same tactics used to sell new technology innovations to lawyers as part of the training process can also be used to get lawyers excited about KM. Finding ways to tangibly demonstrate how lawyers perform tasks today, coupled with how they could accomplish the same tasks faster and with better results, is key. Given the structural impediments to implementing KM in law firms, firms must embrace a broad strategy for introducing it to their firms. Promotion and education can take many forms, from formal briefings, to hands-on training, to the use of success stories, where specific examples of the effective use of such tools and processes are highlighted. Lawyers want to know, "What's in it for me?"
- Focus on the *needs* of firm lawyers. Create a team to lead the effort that includes them. Spend time with them; ascertain needs, and focus efforts on building processes that will facilitate the incorporation of new content. If we've done a good job of understanding their needs and in providing useful content for them, then we can be sure that "If you build it, they will come."

Knowledge Management Matrix

To identify knowledge management applications, we can combine knowledge levels with knowledge categories. Core knowledge, advanced knowledge and innovative

Figure 10.1. Knowledge management matrix

Levels/ Categories	**Core Knowledge**	**Advanced Knowledge**	**Innovative Knowledge**
Administrative Knowledge			
Declarative Knowledge			
Procedural Knowledge			
Analytical Knowledge			

Figure 10.2. Knowledge management matrix for the current IS/IT situation

Levels/ Categories	**Core Knowledge**	**Advanced Knowledge**	**Innovative Knowledge**
Administrative Knowledge	Accounting system Hours billing Clients database E-mail Word processing Spreadsheet Salary system	Competence database Client firm information Internet	
Declarative Knowledge	Library system Electronic lawbook Electronic legal sources	Law database	
Procedural Knowledge	Case collection Document standards Procedural standards Document examples	Internal databases Intranet Public databases	
Analytical Knowledge	Law interpretations	Groupware	

knowledge are combined with administrative knowledge, declarative knowledge, procedural knowledge and analytical knowledge in Figure 10.1. We have created a knowledge management matrix with twelve cells for IS/IT applications.

The knowledge management matrix can first be used to identify the current IS/IT that support knowledge management in the firm as illustrated in Figure 10.2.

Now the knowledge management matrix can be applied to identify future IS/IT as illustrated in Figure 10.3. The systems only serve as examples, they illustrate that it is possible to find systems than can support all combinations of knowledge categories and knowledge levels.

Software and systems suitable for knowledge management in a law firm can now be identified using the knowledge management matrix. In Figure 10.4, examples of software to support systems in Figure 10.3 are listed.

Let us look at one example in Figure 10.4. *Knowledger* is listed as potential software in the innovative-analytical knowledge location. This is an ambitious location of a software product that has yet to demonstrate its real capabilities in knowledge firms. According to the vendor, Knowledge Associates (www.knowledgeassociates.com), Knowledger 3.0 is complete knowledge management software that can be integrated with other systems in the firm. Knowledger is Web-based and supports the

Figure 10.3. Knowledge management matrix for desired IS / IT situation

Levels/ Categories	Core Knowledge	Advanced Knowledge	Innovative Knowledge
Administrative Knowledge	Accounting system Hours billing Clients database E-mail Word processing Spreadsheet Salary system Electronic diary Electronic reception Office automation Message system	Competence database Client firm information Internet Videophone Video conference Quality system Financial services Intranet Net agent Electronic meetings	Client statistics Lawyer statistics Recruiting system Scanning Quality assurance Benchmarking Customer relationships Net-based services Electronic diary Mobile office Executive information
Declarative Knowledge	Library system Electronic lawbook Electronic legal sources Document management Legal databases Commercial databases	Law database Electronic library Electronic lawbook Extranet International legal sources	Law change base Precedence base Conference system Intelligent agents Artificial intelligence Portals Workflow systems
Procedural Knowledge	Case collection Document standards Procedural standards Document examples Planning system Standards archive Publishing system	Internal databases Intranet Public databases Experience database Image processing Document generation International law base Public Web access	Video registration Case system Online services
Analytical Knowledge	Law interpretations Voice recognition Case interpretations	Groupware Intelligent agents Client monitoring Extranet Discussion groups Video conference	Expert register Expert system Research reports Subject database Data warehouse

firm in categorizing internal and external information, as well as linking incoming information to existing information.

Let us look at one more application in the most demanding location of innovative-analytical knowledge. There we find something called Summation. *Summation* is a system for document handling for use in large court cases (www.summation.com). In the large court case of Balder in Norway, the law firm Thommessen Krefting Greve Lund (TKGL) used Summation in 2001. The Balder case is a dispute between Exxon and Smedvig about the rebuilding of an offshore vessel costing 3 billion Norwegian crones. TKGL had more than 2,500 binders when the court case started in the city of Stavanger. All these documents were scanned into a database for use

Figure 10.4. Knowledge management matrix for software supporting desired IS / IT situation

Levels/ Categories	**Core Knowledge**	**Advanced Knowledge**	**Innovative Knowledge**
Administrative Knowledge	Microsoft Word Microsoft Excel Microsoft Outlook SuperOffice Timex Concorde XAL DBMS SuperOffice Microsoft Office Oracle Agresso Powermarkt Uni økonomi Datalex Justice Data Systems GroupWise Alta Law Office ESI Law	Microsoft Access Lotus Approach Corel Paradox Infotorg IFS Rubicon Concorde K-link Akelius dokument Windows NT Explorer CheckPoint Firewall RealMedia Advisor klient Completo Advokat Visma Business Advokat	Intranet Internet Extranet WAP PDA/Palm KnowledgeShare IFS Business performance Mikromarc 2 statistic IFS Front Office Psion Nomade Netscape Netcaster
Declarative Knowledge	NorLex CarNov RightOn Lovdata NORSOK	Lovdata Celex BibJure Shyster Finder Prjus BookWhere	Hieros Gamos Eudor Abacus Law Lawgic Netmeeting Lov chat LegalSeeker KG Agent Lotus K-station Domino Workflow
Procedural Knowledge	Jasper Karnov Mikas Aladdin ePaper Action Request System DocuShare CyberWorks Training Learning Space	Lotus Domino Domino.Doc DOCS Open HotDocs Adobe photoshop EUR-Lex ODIN eCabinet	Justice Autonomy LegalSeeker Expert Legal Systems Hieros Gamos Real Media Amicus Attorney
Analytical Knowledge	PDA/Palm Lotus LearningSpace Lotus Quickplace Lotus Sametime IBM Content Manager IBM Enterprise Portal Voice Express Collaborative Virtual Work Search Sugar Vchip	Lotus Notes iNotes Lotus K-Station Jasper Novell GroupWise Microsoft Exchange Netscape Communicator JSF Litigator's Notebook Empolis K42 Legal Files	Summation Knowledger Lotus Raven Shyster XpertRule Miner Expert Choice Dragon Dictate

by Summation. When lawyers from TKGL present material in court, they submit it from their laptops. When new information emerges in court, then it is registered in Summation. When TKGL lawyers are to trace technical and financial developments for Balder, they make a search in the Summation database.

Another law firm is also using Summation. The law firm Bugge Arentz-Hansen Rasmussen (BA-HR) has the task of finding money after the late ship-owner Jahre. The money is expected to be found in banks in countries where there are no taxes. The hunt for Jahre funds has been going on for almost a decade, and BA-HR has developed a large Summation database enabling BA-HR lawyers to present important information in the court in the city of Drammen.

According to Susskind (2000, p. 163), six kinds of expert systems can play an important role in law firms in the future:

- **Diagnostic systems:** Those systems offer specific solutions to problems presented to them. From the facts of any particular case, as elicited by such a system, the system will analyze the details and draw conclusions, usually after some kind of interactive consultation. These systems are analogous to the medical diagnostic systems that make diagnoses on the basis of symptoms presented to them. An example of a diagnostic system in law would be a taxation system that could pinpoint the extent to which and why a person is liable to pay tax, doing so on the basis of a mass of details provided to it.
- **Planning systems:** In a sense, planning systems reason in reverse. These systems are instructed as to a desired solution or outcome and their purpose is to identify scenarios, involving both factual and legal premises, which justify the preferred conclusion. In tax law, a planning system could recommend how best a taxpayer should arrange his affairs so as to minimize his exposure to liability. The knowledge held within planning systems can be similar to that held within diagnostic systems; what is quite different is the way that knowledge is applied.
- **Procedural guides:** Many complex tasks facing legal professionals require extensive expertise and knowledge that is in fact procedural in nature. Expert systems as procedural guides take their users through such complex and extended procedures, ensuring that all matters are attended to and done within any prescribed time periods. An example of such a system would be one that managed the flow of a complex tax evasion case, providing detailed guidance and support from inception through to final disposal.
- **The intelligent checklist:** This category of system has most often been used to assist in auditing or reviewing compliance with legal regulations. Compliance reviews must be undertaken with relentless attention to detail and extensive reference to large bodies of regulations. Intelligent checklists provide a tech-

nique for performing such reviews. They formalize the process. In taxation, an intelligent checklist approach could be used to assist in the review of a company's compliance with corporation tax.

- **Document modeling systems:** These systems — also referred to as document assembly systems — store templates set up by legal experts. These templates contain fixed portions of text together with precise indications as to the conditions under which given extracts should be used. In operation, such a system will elicit from its user all the details relevant to a proposed document. This is done by the user answering questions, responding to prompts and providing information. On the basis of the user's input, the system will automatically generate a customized and polished document on the basis of its knowledge of how its text should be used.
- **Arguments generation systems:** It is envisaged that these systems are able to generate sets of competing legal arguments in situations when legal resources do not provide definitive guidance. Rather than seeking to provide legal solutions (as diagnostic systems strive to do), argument generation systems will present sound lines of reasoning, backed both by legal authority and by propositions of principle and policy. These lines of reasoning will lead to a range of legal conclusions. Such systems would help users identify promising lines of reasoning in support of desired outcomes, while at the same time advancing other arguments which may need to be refuted.

Figure 10.5. Research model for determinants of knowledge sharing intentions

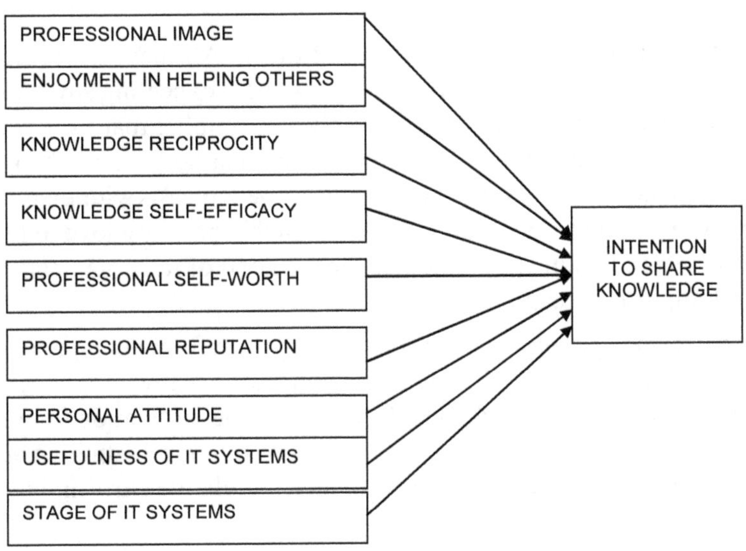

Law Firm Value Shop

The objective of this section is to deepen our understanding of the factors that increase or lessen employees' tendencies to engage in knowledge-sharing behaviors. Figure 10.5 depicts our research model. Intention to share knowledge is the dependent variable in the model.

Professional Image

In most organizations today, the importance of image is increasing as traditional contracts between organizations and employees based on length of service erode. In such working environments, knowledge contributors can benefit from showing others that they possess valuable expertise. This earns them respect and a better image. Therefore, knowledge sharers can benefit from improved self-concept when they share their knowledge. According to Kankanhalli et al. (2005), employees have been found to share their best practice due to a desire to be recognized by their peers as experts. People who provided high-quality knowledge have been found to enjoy better prestige in the workplace. Hence, this discussion suggests a positive relationship between image and intention to share knowledge.

P1: The more a lawyer's image is improved by knowledge sharing, the greater the intention to share knowledge will be.

Enjoyment in Helping Others

This benefit is derived from the concept of altruism. Altruism exists when people derive intrinsic enjoyment from helping others without expecting anything in return. According to Davenport and Prusak (1998), altruism implies that a knowledge seller may be so passionate about his or her knowledge that he or she is happy to share it whenever he/she gets a chance. This seems to be the case with many university professors. Many knowledge sharers are motivated in part by a love of their subject and to some degree by altruism, whether for the good of the organization or based on a natural impulse to help others.

Altruism exists when people derive intrinsic enjoyment from helping others without expecting anything in return. Although there may be very few instances of absolute altruism (involving absolute lack of self-concern in the motivation for an act), relative altruism (where self-concern plays a minor role in motivating an act) is more prevalent. Knowledge sharers may be motivated by relative altruism based on their desire to help others. According to Kanhanhalli et al. (2005), prior research shows that knowledge contributors gain satisfaction by demonstrating their altruistic behavior. Such satisfaction stems from their intrinsic enjoyment in helping others. Knowledge sharers who derive enjoyment in helping others may be more inclined to share knowledge.

P2: The greater enjoyment a lawyer finds in helping others, the greater the intention to share knowledge will be.

Knowledge Reciprocity

Reciprocity has been highlighted as a benefit for individuals to engage in social exchange. According to Davenport and Prusak (1998), reciprocity implies payment in terms of knowledge. A knowledge seller will spend the time and effort needed to share knowledge effectively if the person expects the buyer to be a willing seller when he or she is in the market for knowledge. Reciprocity may be achieved less directly than by getting knowledge back from the same person. In firms structured as partnerships, such as law firms, knowledge sharing that improves profitability will return a benefit to the sharer, now and in the future. Whether or not a knowledge seller expects to be paid with equally valuable knowledge from the buyer, the knowledge seller may believe that being known for sharing knowledge readily will make others in the company more willing to share with him or her. That is a rational assumption, since his or her reputation as a seller of valuable knowledge will make others confident of his/her willingness to reciprocate when he/she is the buyer, and they have knowledge to sell: The knowledge seller's knowledge credit is good.

Reciprocity has been highlighted as a benefit for individuals to engage in social exchange. It can serve as a motivational mechanism for people to contribute to discretionary databases. Reciprocity can act as a benefit for knowledge contributors because they expect future help from others in lieu of their contributions. According to Kankanhalli et al. (2005), prior research suggests that people who share knowledge in online communities believe in reciprocity. Further, researchers have observed that people who regularly helped others in virtual communities seemed to receive help more quickly when they asked for it. Furthermore, Kankanhalli et al. (2005) found a significant, positive relationship between reciprocity and usage of electronic knowledge repositories by knowledge contributors. These arguments suggest a positive relationship between reciprocity and intention to share knowledge.

P3: The more a lawyer expects knowledge reciprocity, the greater the intention to share knowledge will be.

Knowledge Self-Efficacy

Self-efficacy relates to the perception of people about what they can do with the skills they possess. When people share expertise useful in the organization, they gain confidence in terms of what they can do and this brings the benefit of increased self-efficacy. This belief can serve as a self-motivational force for knowledge contributors to share knowledge. Knowledge self-efficacy is typically manifested in the form of people believing that their knowledge can help solve job-related problems, improve work efficiency or make a difference to their organization.

Conversely, if people feel that they lack knowledge that is useful to the organization, they may decline from sharing knowledge because they believe that their contribution cannot make a positive impact for the organization. These arguments suggest a positive relationship between knowledge self-efficacy and sharing by knowledge contributors, which was found to be significant in the study by Kanhanhalli et al. (2005).

P4: The higher knowledge self-efficacy perceived by a lawyer, the greater the intention to share knowledge will be.

Professional Self-Worth

In an ongoing interaction setting, such as knowledge sharing in an organization, appropriate feedback is very critical. When others respond in the way that we have anticipated, we conclude that our line of thinking and behavior are correct; at the same time, role taking improves as the exchange continues according to role theory, which is the cornerstone of the symbolic interactionist perspective on self-concept formation. According to Bock et al. (2005), this process of reflected appraisal contributes to the formation of self-worth, which is strongly affected by sense of competence and closely tied to effective performance.

Therefore, Bock et al. (2005) found that employees who are able to get feedback on past instances of knowledge sharing are more likely to understand how such actions have contributed to the work of others and/or to improvements in organizational performance. The understanding would allow them to increase their sense of self-worth accordingly. That, in turn, would render these employees more likely to develop favorable attitudes toward knowledge sharing than employees who are unable to see such linkages. Defining this cognition as an individual's sense of self-worth from their knowledge-sharing behavior leads to the fifth hypothesis.

P5: The greater the sense of self-worth through knowledge sharing behavior is, the greater the intention to share knowledge will be.

Professional Reputation

In order to share knowledge, individuals must think that their contribution to others will be worth the effort and that some new value will be created, with expectations of receiving some of that value for themselves. These personal benefits or private rewards are more likely to accrue to individuals who actively participate and help others. Thus, the expectation of personal benefits can motivate individuals to contribute knowledge to others in the absence of personal acquaintance, similarity or the likelihood of direct reciprocity (Wasko & Faraj, 2005).

According to Wasko and Faraj (2005), social exchange theory posits that individuals engage in social interaction based on an expectation that it will lead in some way to social rewards such as approval, status and respect. This suggests that one potential way an individual can benefit from active participation is the perception that participation enhances his or her personal reputation in the firm. Reputation is an important asset that an individual can leverage to achieve and maintain status within a collective. Results from prior research on electronic networks of practice are consistent with social exchange theory and provide evidence that building reputation is a strong motivator for active participation. Wasko and Faraj (2005) came to the same conclusion in their empirical study of knowledge contributions in electronic networks of practice.

P6: The more a lawyer can improve his or her reputation by sharing knowledge, the greater the intention to share knowledge will be.

Personal Attitude

Intention to engage in a behavior is determined by an individual's attitude toward that behavior. Here, attitude toward knowledge sharing is defined as the degree of one's positive feelings about sharing one's knowledge (Bock et al., 2005). This leads to the seventh hypothesis.

P7: The more favorable a lawyer's attitude toward knowledge sharing is, the greater the intention to share knowledge will be.

Usefulness of IT Systems

Information technology can play an important role in successful knowledge management initiatives (Kankanhalli et al., 2005; Wasko & Faraj, 2005). However, the concept of coding and transmitting knowledge is not new: Training and employee

Figure 10.6. Law firm as value shop with activity examples

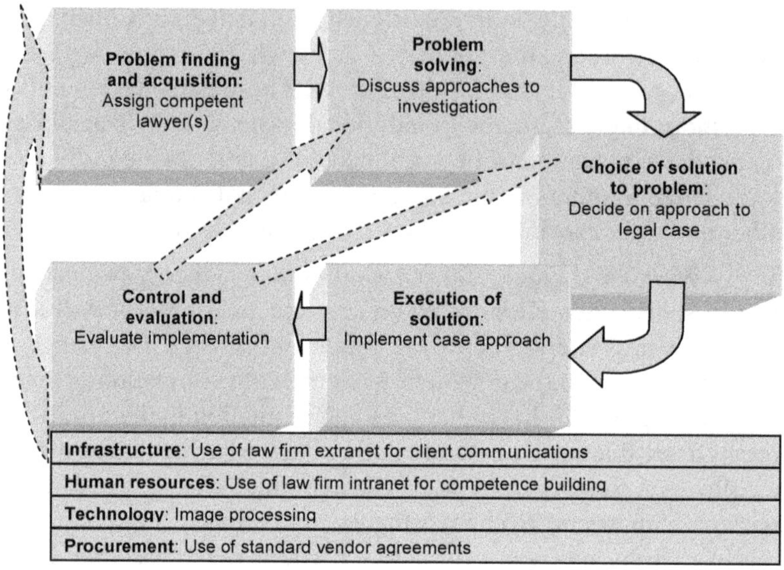

development programs, organizational policies, routines, procedures, reports and manuals have served this function for many years. What is new and exciting in the knowledge management area is the potential for using modern information technology (e.g., extranets, intelligent agents and expert systems) to support knowledge creation, sharing and exchange in an organization and between organizations. Modern information technology can collect, systematize, structure, store, combine, distribute and present information of value to knowledge workers.

The value of information presented to knowledge workers can be studied in terms of the organization's value configuration. A law firm has the value configuration of a value shop (Gottschalk, 2005). In the value shop, lawyers need information to access client problems, find alternative solutions to problems, select an optimal solution, implement the solution and evaluate the implementation. In this value creation, IT systems can help gain access to new cases, help find relevant court rulings, retrieve relevant documents, collect views from opposing sides and support quality assurance of the work.

A law firm as a value shop is an organization that creates value by solving unique problems. Knowledge is the most important resource. A value shop is characterized by five primary activities: problem finding and acquisition, problem solving, choice, execution and control and evaluation, as illustrated in Figure 10.6.

P8: The more a lawyer finds useful information in IT systems, the greater the intention to share knowledge will be.

Stage of IT Systems

The ambition level using knowledge management systems can be defined in terms of stages of knowledge management technology as illustrated in Chapter 1. When a firm reaches higher stages in the model, knowledge workers contribute information to the systems. At stage III, document systems and other information repositories are based on knowledge workers' contributions in electronic form. In our final hypothesis, we suggest that knowledge workers that are used to share information in IT systems will be more inclined to share their knowledge.

P9: The more higher stage IT systems are available to a lawyer, the greater the intention to share knowledge will be.

The Case of DLA Nordic

Fiskum and Sværen (2005) conducted research on job-related, psychological effects of knowledge database use and the impact on work outcomes. The research was conducted in DLA Nordic. DLA Nordic is the largest Pan-Scandinavian full service law firm, with offices in Copenhagen, Oslo, Stockholm and Bergen, and ranks among the leading law firms in Denmark, Norway and Sweden. There are 330 staff members, including 210 lawyers, across the three countries. The law firm was established in 2000 by three law firms (Lindh Stabell Horten) based in Stockholm, Oslo and Copenhagen in response to a demand for cross-border services. The firm provides a full range of services, including specialist lawyers in IT, intellectual property, tax, mergers and acquisitions, litigation, property and employment. Its unique cross-border approach has made it one of Scandinavia's most successful law firms and attracted an increasing number of international companies in a variety of sectors.

Fiskum and Sværen's (2005) research was conducted in the two Norwegian offices — Oslo and Bergen. They found that increased knowledge database use led to increased creativity. When lawyers used the firm's knowledge database more extensively, they produced more novel and useful ideas and fostered an environment that was conductive to the firm's ability to produce novel and useful ideas.

Furthermore, Fiskum and Sværen (2005) found that increased knowledge database use lead to increased sharing of tacit knowledge. Tacit knowledge sharing occurred

Figure 10.7. Empirical relationships between knowledge database use, effects and work satisfaction

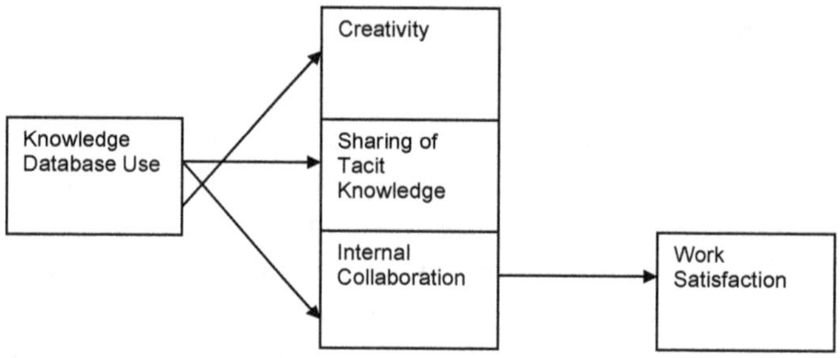

by gathering information from cases, sharing experience with co-workers, engaging in dialogue with competitors, finding new strategies and market opportunities by socializing inside the firm and creating a work environment that allows co-workers to understand the craftsmanship and expertise.

Increased knowledge database use also led to increased internal collaboration. This means that the more lawyers use the database, the more they feel they collaborate with co-workers. These findings are illustrated in Figure 10.7.

As illustrated in Figure 10.7, Fiskum and Sværen (2005) found that increased internal collaboration leads to increased job satisfaction. Internal collaboration is an important aspect to enhance when dealing with lawyers. They seem to be individualistic and competitive in nature, and the degree of collaboration tends to be low. The research suggests that when increasing the collaborative efforts, work satisfaction will increase. Lawyers are more satisfied with their work when the degree of collaboration is high. This is an important finding, since collaboration and support are principal criteria for many employees when assessing their work environment.

Discussion

Mountain (2001) has posed the question: Could new technologies cause great law firms to fail? In her article, she addresses the question of why law firms ought to invest in online legal services when studies to date show that there is no correlation between law firm technology capabilities and profitability. She divides online legal services into two types: digital delivery and legal Web advisors. The framework set out by Clayton Christensen in his book, *The Innovator's Dilemma* is used to explain how legal Web advisors is a disruptive technology that law firm competitors (i.e., accounting firms, dot-coms and corporate clients) are beginning to harness to erode law firm margins. Unless law firms reinvent themselves as technology organizations, they could find themselves increasingly marginalized. Large law firms need to develop legal Web advisors and should consider spinning off technology subsidiaries to do so. Small law firms need to link up with online advisory services on an application service provider basis.

Mountain (2001) finds that fifteen years ago, artificial intelligence (AI) was set to radically change the face of the legal profession, as we know it. As it turned out, neither expert systems nor any other kinds of AI lived up to their potential at that time. They required huge investments and provided marginal perceived payoffs. Eventually, both fell under the weight of their own start-up requirements. Today, AI has been reincarnated in the form of legal Web advisors. Legal Web advisors offer interactive legal advice delivered via extranets without human intervention, using questions to collect facts and then using decision tree analysis to produce answers. Some of the world's largest law firms in London, England are pushing ahead with developing legal Web advisors despite the absence of a link between law firm profitability and use of technology. Why would the London firms, who bill out their services at the highest hourly rates in the world, involve themselves in such risky, low margin endeavors? The answers lie in the disruptive power of these new technologies.

According to Mountain (2001), legal Web advisors were pioneered in London in 1994 when the law firm Linklaters introduced a browser-based product called Blue Flag. Blue Flag is now a suite of products covering regulatory compliance, derivatives documentation, employee share plans, funds, share disclosure and transaction management. Within months, another London law firm, Clifford Chance, followed with NextLaw, a Web-accessible online service that helps assess the legal and regulatory risks of e-commerce and reportedly required an investment of more than one million pounds sterling. Today, there are approximately a dozen online legal services in the UK and Australia and the pace of their introduction is accelerating. The revenue model to date has been to charge these services out by subscription and then to have lawyers leverage from these online services to attract value added legal work.

Blue Flag is an interesting example. Blue Flag is a legal risk management service designed to provide packaged legal advice on European financial and banking regulatory issues (hence the name Blue Flag). This service is designed to appeal to those concerned with legal compliance working in fund management, securities houses, investment and commercial banks and provides step-by-step legal advice on tap to subscribers for a fixed annual fee. Not surprisingly, having established the service, Linklaters have now extended it to cover other (non-European) jurisdictions where they have expertise.

Online legal services can be placed in two different categories: digital delivery services and legal Web advisors. Digital delivery services deliver human legal product by digital means: The simplest example is the use of e-mail to distribute legal documents. Both law firms and application service providers (ASPs) offer digital delivery. ASPs are companies that deliver software across the Internet by subscription instead of a packaged product. Many large London firms have opted for in-house capability instead and host their own transactions through branded extranets (Web sites that provide a private body of information to a limited number of external organizations). Examples are Clifford Chance's Fruit Net, Allen & Overy's Newchange Dealroom and Andersen Legal's Dealsight. Like e-mail, extranets will eventually become an invisible part of the technology infrastructure and will not form a basis of competitive advantage.

Legal Web advisors, on the other hand, offer interactive legal advice delivered via extranets using artificial intelligence. Legal Web advisors use AI in a more cost-effective and pragmatic fashion than did the systems of fifteen years ago. For example, they do not attempt to work independently of lawyer input. Lawyers and knowledge engineers work together to describe the order in which information is obtained and used to determine a solution. The software leads the client from one question to another using a decision tree system. This type of system uses a sequence of decisions based on user input to classify the problem before moving through nodes and sub-nodes to the problem solution. Once the client has completed the path and has answered all the relevant questions, the software produces output. This output is not in the form of a legal opinion; instead, it is in the form of "You need to do A, B, C, D and E." It is more similar to the advice a lawyer gives to a friend at a party than to traditional legal advice. It provides 90% of the answer in situations where the client doesn't care about the other 10% and is not willing to pay for it. The distinction between digital delivery and legal Web advisors may blur in the future as online legal services become increasingly sophisticated.

In our perspective of knowledge management ambition, legal Web advisors represent knowledge management level IV. Expert systems are applied to give clients direct access to an information system that can develop and recommend a solution to the client's problem. The system is based on a thorough process where lawyers and knowledge engineers worked together to describe the order in which information is obtained and used to determine a solution.

Conclusion

Knowledge management is a critical success factor in law firms. Firm cultures are slowly changing to online, electronic cultures; people are learning how to work and

Figure 10.8. Causal loop diagram illustrating dynamics of knowledge sharing in a law firm

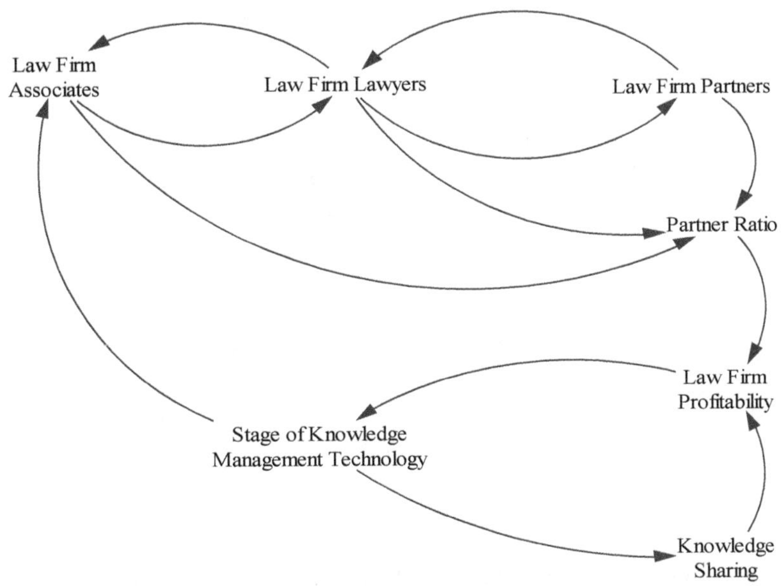

share in the virtual world. Geography is increasingly rendered irrelevant as people develop online relationships and personalities. If members of the law firm doubt this proposition, they should reflect on how the use of e-mail has evolved within organizations. In the process of creating electronic workspaces, the capture and sharing of the knowledge exchanged becomes increasingly easy. As the electronic firm culture develops, implementing new online-only systems becomes not only accepted but the norm. This creates a foundation from which true process evolution can occur. To understand how all of this relates to an Internet strategy, one must consider key tenets that drive Internet innovation.

Law firm knowledge management is the behaviors and processes by which a group of lawyers increases and maintains their personal, and collective, actionable knowledge to compete, to increase performance and to decrease risk. By extension, a knowledge strategy is the intended action, plan, or roadmap for those behaviors and processes (Parsons, 2004).

Figure 10.8 illustrates some of the links between knowledge sharing and law firm performance. When law firms hire new employees, they are typically law school graduates with little work experience, qualifying for the position of law firm as-

Figure 10.9. Positive feedback loop in the causal loop diagram

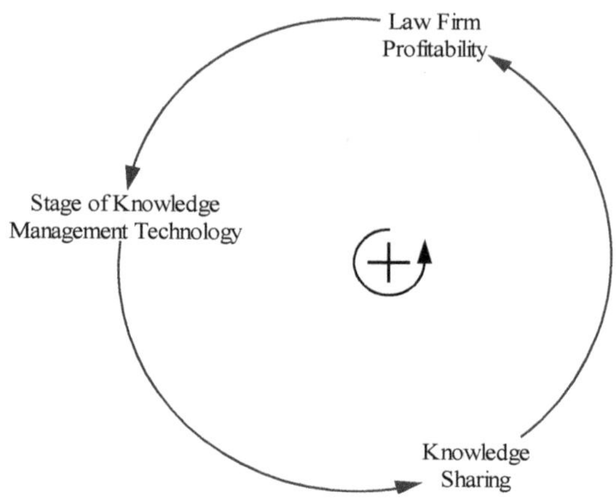

sociate. After some years, they become lawyers. Some of the lawyers qualify and join the partnership as law firm partners. This flow of legal employees is important in understanding law firm business, as the partner ratio influences law firm profitability.

One of the positive feedback loops in Figure 10.8 is illustrated in Figure 10.9. Typically, a law firm does not invest in knowledge management technology because of problems. Rather, they invest out of opportunity in terms of profits that they can spend on technology. A higher stage of knowledge management technology leads to more extensive knowledge sharing, which further improves law firm profitability.

Questions for Discussion

1. How would you describe a law firm as a value shop?
2. How would you organize a law firm's knowledge sharing with its clients?
3. What are differences between the police investigation value shop and the law firm value shop?

List of References

Becker, W. M., Herman, M. F., Samuelson, P. A., & Webb, A. P. (2001). Lawyers get down to business. *The McKinsey Quarterly*, (2), 45-55.

Bock, G. W., Zmud, R. W., & Kim, Y. G. (2005). Behavioral intention formation in knowledge sharing: Examining the roles of extrinsic motivators, social-psychological forces, and organizational climate. *MIS Quarterly, 29*(1), 87-111.

Davenport, T. H., & L. Prusak (1998). *Working knowledge*. Boston: Harvard Business School Press.

Edwards, D. L., & Mahling, D. E. (1997). Toward knowledge management systems in the legal domain. *Proceedings of the International ACM SIGGROUP Conference on Supporting Group Work Group '97*, The Association of Computing Machinery ACM, (pp. 158-166).

Fiskum, H. M., & Sværen, A. L. (2005). *Job-related, psychological effects of knowledge database use & the impact on work outcomes*. Master of science thesis, Norwegian School of Management, Oslo, Norway.

Galanter, M., & Palay, T. (1991). *Tournament of lawyers, the transformation of the big law firms*. Chicago: The University of Chicago Press.

Gottschalk, P. (2005). *Strategic knowledge management technology*. Hershey, PA: Idea Group Publishing.

Grover, V., & Davenport, T. H. (2001). General perspectives on knowledge management: Fostering a research agenda. *Journal of Management Information Systems, 18*(1), 5-21.

Hitt, M. A., Bierman, L., Shumizu, K., & Kochhar, R. (2001). Direct and moderating effects of human capital on strategy and performance in professional service firms: A resourced-based perspective. *Academy of Management Journal, 44*(1), 13-28.

Jones, E. (2000). Remaking the firm: How KM is changing legal practice. *Knowledge Management Magazine*. Retrieved from http://www.kmmag.com

Kankanhalli, A., Tan, B. C. Y., & Wei, K. K. (2005). Contributing knowledge to electronic knowledge repositories: An empirical investigation. *MIS Quarterly, 29*(1), 113-143.

May, T. Y., Korczynski, M., & Frenkel, S. J. (2002). Organizational and occupational commitment: Knowledge workers in large corporations. *Journal of Management Studies, 39*(6), 775-801.

Mountain, D. (2001). Could new technologies cause great law firms to fail? *Journal of Information, Law and Technology*, (1). Retrieved from http://elj.warwick.ac.uk/jilt/

Nahapiet, J., & Ghoshal, S. (1998). Social capital, intellectual capital, and the organizational advantage. *Academy of Management Review, 23*(2), 242-266.

O'Connor, K. (2000, May). How to overcome the cultural barriers that can blockade knowledge management. *Law Technology News*. Retrieved from http://www.lawtechnews.com

Parsons, M. (2004). *Effective knowledge management for law firms*. UK: Oxford University Press.

Susskind, R. (2000). *Transforming the law*. UK: Oxford University Press.

Wasko, M. M., & Faraj, S. (2005). Why should I share? Examining social capital and knowledge contribution in electronic networks of practice. *MIS Quarterly, 29*(1), 35-57.

About the Author

Petter Gottschalk is a professor of information and knowledge management at the Norwegian School of Management in Oslo. He teaches at the Arab Academy in Alexandria, Fudan University in Shanghai and Nanyang University in Singapore. Gottschalk has written several books published by Idea Group Inc., including *Strategic Knowledge Management Technology*, *Managing Successful IT Outsourcing Relationships* with Hans Solli-Sæther, *E-Business Strategy, Sourcing and Governance*, *Knowledge Management Systems in Law Enforcement: Technologies and Techniques*, *CIO and Corporate Strategic Management: Changing Role of CIO to CEO* and *Knowledge Management Systems: Value Shop Creation*. Gottschalk earned his MBA at the Technical University of Berlin, Germany, his MSc at Thayer School of Engineering, Dartmouth College and Sloan School of Management, Massachusetts Institute of Technology, USA and his DBA at Henley Management College, Brunel University, UK. For more than 15 years, Gottschalk was an executive in business organizations. He was the CIO of ABB Norway, the CEO of ABB Datacables and the CEO of the Norwegian Computing Center.

Index

Q

R

S

T

V

W

www.ingramcontent.com/pod-product-compliance
Lightning Source LLC
LaVergne TN
LVHW062114200926
848484LV00007B/1669